THE UNITED KINGDOM CONSTITUTION

An Introduction

CLARENDON LAW SERIES

Introduction to Company Law
(3rd edition)
PAUL DAVIES QC

The Conflict of Laws (4th edition)
ADRIAN BRIGGS

Bentham and the Common Law Tradition
(2nd edition)
GERALD J. POSTEMA

Law and Values in the European Union
STEPHEN WEATHERILL

Personal Property Law (4th edition)
MICHAEL BRIDGE

The Idea of Arbitration
JAN PAULSSON

The Anthropology of Law
FERNANDA PIRIE

Law and Gender
JOANNE CONAGHAN

The Concept of Law (3rd edition)
H. L. A. HART
With a Postscript edited by
PENELOPE A. BULLOCH
AND JOSEPH RAZ

With an Introduction and Notes by
LESLIE GREEN

Land Law (3rd edition)
ELIZABETH COOKE

Administrative Law (5th edition)
PETER CANE

Discrimination Law (2nd edition)
SANDRA FREDMAN

An Introduction to the Law of Trusts
(3rd edition)
SIMON GARDNER

Natural Law and Natural Rights
(2nd edition)
JOHN FINNIS

Employment Law (2nd edition)
HUGH COLLINS

International Law
VAUGHAN LOWE

Civil Liberties
CONOR GEARTY

Intellectual Property
MICHAEL SPENCE

Policies and Perceptions of Insurance Law
in the Twenty-First Century (2nd edition)
MALCOLM CLARKE

Philosophy of Private Law
WILLIAM LUCY

Law in Modern Society
DENIS GALLIGAN

An Introduction to Tort Law
(2nd edition)
TONY WEIR

Equity (2nd edition)
SARAH WORTHINGTON

Atiyah's Introduction to the Law of
Contract (6th edition)
STEPHEN A. SMITH AND
P. S. ATIYAH

Unjust Enrichment (2nd edition)
PETER BIRKS

An Introduction to Family Law
(2nd edition)
GILLIAN DOUGLAS

Criminal Justice
LUCIA ZEDNER

Contract Theory
STEPHEN A. SMITH

Public Law
ADAM TOMKINS

Personal Property Law (3rd edition)
MICHAEL BRIDGE

THE UNITED KINGDOM CONSTITUTION

An Introduction

N. W. BARBER

Professor of Constitutional Law and Theory,
Oxford University

OXFORD
UNIVERSITY PRESS

OXFORD
UNIVERSITY PRESS

Great Clarendon Street, Oxford, OX2 6DP,
United Kingdom

Oxford University Press is a department of the University of Oxford.
It furthers the University's objective of excellence in research, scholarship,
and education by publishing worldwide. Oxford is a registered trade mark of
Oxford University Press in the UK and in certain other countries

First Edition published in 2021

Impression: 1

Published in the United States of America by Oxford University Press
198 Madison Avenue, New York, NY 10016, United States of America

British Library Cataloguing in Publication Data
Data available

Library of Congress Control Number: 2021940641

ISBN 978–0–19–885231–5 (hbk.)
ISBN 978–0–19–885232–2 (pbk.)

DOI: 10.1093/oso/9780198852315.001.0001

Printed and bound in the UK by
TJ Books Limited

This book is dedicated to the memory of
J. W. Davies, Fellow of Brasenose.

PREFACE

This is a monograph on the United Kingdom's constitution. It is intended to be read as an introduction to that system, one which will give the reader a sense of its scope, complexities, and problems. Whilst the book can be read by itself, it builds upon my earlier work on constitutions and constitutionalism and explores some of the ideas found there in the context of the United Kingdom (UK) constitution. Those who want to know more about principles such as sovereignty, separation of powers, rule of law, democracy, or subsidiarity will find a discussion of them in *The Principles of Constitutionalism*, whilst the nature of constitutions, states, and constitutional rules are examined in *The Constitutional State*.[1] I have avoided citing these books in the chapters that follow, but many of the questions left open here are answered in these earlier works.

None of the chapters in this book has been previously published elsewhere, but a few paragraphs from the following papers are scattered around the text: 'The Afterlife of Parliamentary Sovereignty' (2011) 9 International Journal of Constitutional Law 144; 'Must Legalistic Conceptions of the Rule of Law Have a Social Dimension?' (2004) 17 Ratio Juris 474; 'Prelude to the Separation of Powers' (2001) 60 Cambridge Law Journal 59.

A book of this type covers a great deal of ground, and I have incurred many debts whilst writing it. With apologies to those I have missed, thanks are owed to: Tom Adams, Adam, James, and Edward Carrick, Martin Chamberlain, Cora Chan, Cathryn Costello, Anne Davies, Graham Gee, Jeff Goldsworthy, Tom Hickman, Hayley Hooper, Jeff King, Maris Köpcke, Chris McCrudden, Jen McKenzie, Colin Murray, Adam Perry, Aileen McHarg, Luke Rostill, Ewan Smith, and Leah Trueblood. Particular thanks are owed to Kacper Majewski, Oskar Sherry, and Nathan van Wees, who provided editorial assistance and saved me from errors of style and substance, and Jackie Fernholz,

[1] NW Barber, *The Constitutional State* (Oxford University Press 2010); NW Barber, *The Principles of Constitutionalism* (Oxford University Press 2018).

who, once again, with great patience and tolerance, read and commented on the manuscript.

Nick Barber
Oxford, March 2021

Note: In chapter 17, I describe the English Votes for English Laws (EVEL) system as 'constitutionally fragile'. It was even more fragile than I had supposed. In July 2021, far too late to be incorporated in the main text of this book, the House of Commons abandoned the system. It is unclear what, if anything, will take its place as an answer to the West Lothian Question.

CONTENTS

TABLE OF CASES

UNITED KINGDOM

EUROPEAN COURT OF HUMAN RIGHTS

EUROPEAN COURT OF JUSTICE

HONG KONG

UNITED STATES

TABLE OF LEGISLATION

TABLE OF STATUTORY INSTRUMENTS

OTHER LEGISLATION

Canada

China

Ireland

1
INTRODUCTION

Whilst all constitutions are constantly changing, the changes seen by the constitution of the United Kingdom (UK) over the last thirty or forty years have been especially profound. As Vernon Bogdanor argues, the importance of these developments permits us to talk of a shift between constitutional models, a move from the Old Constitution, that existed up to the late 1980s, to the New Constitution.[1] Up until the 1980s, a student wanting to learn about the UK constitution could have done far worse than rely on Albert Venn Dicey's classic, *An Introduction to the Law of the Constitution*.[2] First published in 1885, Dicey's *Introduction* is the embodiment of Bogdanor's Old Constitution. At the core of the Diceyean constitution lay parliamentary sovereignty: the unlimited legal capacity of Parliament to pass any law it chose. Parliamentary sovereignty was a deceptively simple legal rule: no area of law was outside of Parliament's legislative competence; no constitutional institution had the capacity to invalidate or set aside Parliament's statutes. Other institutions within the constitution were understood through their relationships with this rule; their powers and liberties were either a consequence of an exercise of Parliament's sovereignty or a consequence of its self-restraint. In terms of the territorial distribution of constitutional power, parliamentary sovereignty required that the UK be a unitary state. Because of the unqualified law-making power of Parliament, the powers possessed by regional institutions were dependent on Parliament's restraint: there were, and could be, no legal limits on Parliament's capacity to alter or override their jurisdictions. Federal settlements, of the sort seen in America, where a constitution divided power between the centre and the regions, could not operate in a system characterised by

[1] Vernon Bogdanor, *The New British Constitution* (Hart Publishing 2009) ch 1.

[2] Albert Venn Dicey, *Introduction to the Study of the Law of the Constitution* (John Allison (ed), Oxford University Press 2013).

The United Kingdom Constitution. N. W. Barber, Oxford University Press. © Nick Barber 2021.
DOI: 10.1093/oso/9780198852315.003.0001

parliamentary sovereignty. Similarly, the constitutional principle of the separation of powers appeared alien to the UK constitutional order; this was a system that rested, as Walter Bagehot claimed, on fusion rather than separation.[3] Whereas other constitutions set a constitutional division between the executive and legislative branches, with each limited to its own area of power, and the courts ready to apply these limits, in the UK constitution Parliament exercised control over the executive. Finally, the notion of a bill of rights, a set of legal limits that citizens could plead against the institutions of the state, appeared incompatible with the UK constitutional order: under parliamentary sovereignty, Parliament could, after all, always override these supposed rights. In the Old Constitution, the best that people could enjoy were liberties; the freedoms left over once the law had set limits on their conduct.

Whereas the Old Constitution was characterised by the centralisation of power, Bogdanor's New Constitution is characterised by its diffusion. The decision of the UK to join what was then the European Economic Community (EEC) in the early 1970s might be taken as the starting point for this transformation. The legal implications of the decision to join the EEC amounted to an unprecedented acceptance by Parliament of the law-making authority of another constitutional entity: the EEC did not just bind the UK in international law, requiring Parliament to change domestic laws that were in conflict with European obligations, it changed domestic law directly, sometimes requiring UK judges to apply European law in preference to domestic law. Although proving a causal connection is probably impossible, it could be that the experience of applying European law shifted the way judges understood their constitutional role and expanded the constitutional imagination of politicians. In joining the EEC Parliament had managed to place constraints on its law-making capacity; suddenly, the types of limits characteristic of federal settlements and bills of rights thought impossible under the Old Constitution were no longer inconceivable. At the end of the century, amid a range of constitutional changes, Tony Blair's Labour Government enacted a set of statutes establishing the devolution

[3] Walter Bagehot, *The English Constitution* (Watts & Co 1964) 65.

settlement which created law-making assemblies and executives in Scotland, Wales, and Northern Ireland, and passed the Human Rights Act 1998, giving citizens positive rights they could assert against state institutions. Alongside these changes, Blair's government created a new court, the Supreme Court, to sit at the apex of the UK's legal orders. Under the Old Constitution the highest court in the system sat in the House of Lords and was, in form, a committee of the legislature, although in practice, by the twentieth century it had established an autonomous constitutional identity. Whilst the new Supreme Court possessed no additional powers to those exercised by the old House of Lords, the shift, combined with Labour's other reforms, marked, and perhaps encouraged, an increasingly important role played by judges in the New Constitution.

Of course, not all features of the Old Constitution disappeared; many important elements live on. For instance, Dicey was amongst the first scholars to emphasise the particular importance of non-legal rules, known as conventions, within the constitution. All constitutions include a mix of legal and non-legal rules, but in the UK an unusually high proportion of important constitutional rules are found in the political realm, unenforced by judges and without a legal formulation of their content. Although the legal side of the constitution has expanded in recent years, it remains the case many of the UK's most important constitutional institutions are, to a significant extent, shaped by conventions. Conventions play a central role in determining the constitutional obligations of the monarch, the office of the prime minister, the relationship of the executive to Parliament, and the constitutional position of the devolved assemblies. The second feature of Dicey's work that remains relevant today is his account of the rule of law, a principle that shapes the operation of the UK constitution and, indeed, other constitutions too. The rule of law requires that law makes the differences it purports to make; that it is effective as an instrument of government. Where the rule of law is absent, constitutions are meaningless. Without the rule of law, constitutional institutions cannot be formed, laws cannot be produced or applied; in short, the state is unable to act, or even to constitute itself. The Old Constitution, like the New, contained structures that ensured the realisation of this constitutional principle.

It will be argued later in this book that parliamentary sovereignty, the claimed heart of the Old Constitution, is not a characteristic of the New Constitution. The impact of European law, an impact that will shape the constitution even after Brexit, ended parliamentary sovereignty and a new set of legal relationships has arisen in its place. But even those still wedded to this element of the Old Constitution would have to concede it no longer plays the role it did when Dicey was alive. A range of statutes, decisions made by Parliament itself, have placed legal and political constraints on what Parliament can accomplish, and have shifted power within the constitution.

This book is divided into four parts. Part I examines the constitution itself; the rules that construct the state. The chapters examine the variety of rules that form parts of the UK constitution, and examine the ways in which these rules are combined into a unified expression of state sovereignty. Part II looks at the separation of powers within the UK, the operation of the legislatures, executives, and courts. It argues that, whilst the separation of powers takes different forms in parliamentary and presidential systems, the UK's constitution is characterised by the principle and, moreover, this characterisation is more pronounced in the New Constitution than in the Old. Part III considers the regionalisation of power within the UK, in particular the role of the UK's constituent territories: England, Wales, Scotland, and Northern Ireland. Whilst the devolution settlement has accorded them renewed importance in the constitution, they have always been constitutionally significant, with the UK presenting itself, more or less plausibly, as grounded in the consensual coming together of these entities. The implications of the principle of subsidiarity are considered in this part, and it is argued that subsidiarity provides an explanation of, and a guide to, the modern devolution settlement. Part IV turns on the relationship between the individual and the state, examining the principle of the rule of law and the protection of liberties, the rise of rights in the New Constitution, and, finally, the emergence of citizenship as a constitutional office within the UK. The book charts the emergence of the New Constitution, tracing its diffusion of constitutional power, the rise of constitutional principles as structural and as legal features of the constitution, and, most generally of all, the move from a state with subjects, the passive recipients of the commands of a sovereign, to one containing citizens, who share in its governance.

I

SOVEREIGNTY

2

INTRODUCTION TO CONSTITUTIONS

One of the first things anyone learns about the UK constitution is that it is unwritten, in apparently sharp contrast to most other countries that possess a written constitutional text. Although the unwritten nature of the UK constitution is an issue that preoccupies constitutional scholars, it is not always clear what it means to say the UK constitution is 'unwritten' or, more importantly, why we should care. This chapter examines the divide between written and unwritten constitutions within the broader context of the point of a constitution and asks whether the lack of a written constitution for the UK matters.

2.1 WRITTEN AND UNWRITTEN CONSTITUTIONS

We can distinguish between Constitutions, with a capital 'c', and constitutions, with a small 'c'.[1] A capital 'c' Constitution is a single document, or a set of documents, that presents itself as the foundational law of the state. Allied to this, there are a number of secondary features that are commonly, but not invariably, possessed by a capital 'c' Constitution. The document normally establishes and empowers the principal institutions of the state and, in a federal system, delineates the broad competences of the national-level institutions and their regional counterparts. It is normally judicially enforceable, in whole or in part, with the courts making use of the document to determine institutions' constitutional powers. As part of this process, the courts often possess the power of strong-form judicial review; that is, the judges have the capacity to strike down statutes that violate the Constitution; the Constitution stands above the legislature, and the legislature,

[1] The distinction is explored in Joseph Raz, 'On the Authority and Interpretation of Constitutions: Some Preliminaries' in Joseph Raz, *Between Authority and Interpretation* (Oxford University Press 2009).

The United Kingdom Constitution. N. W. Barber, Oxford University Press. © Nick Barber 2021.
DOI: 10.1093/oso/9780198852315.003.0002

like all other constitutional institutions, is constrained by its rules. Furthermore, because of its special status, the Constitution is harder to change than ordinary legislation; some or all of its provisions are entrenched. Finally, the Constitution is normally the product of some special law-making process: it has been authored by a body that is established to create the Constitution, and which disappears once that Constitution is created.

A small 'c' constitution, in contrast, consists of those rules that constitute the state. All states must possess a small 'c' constitution, but not all need possess a capital 'c' Constitution. The small 'c' constitution includes both legal and non-legal rules. These rules come from a variety of sources and have a range of different legal statuses. Some of the rules have a canonical statement; a written statement of the rule that is treated as authoritative by state institutions. Other rules lack a formal articulation and are deduced from the past practices or decisions of institutions. Capital 'c' constitutions may be quite short, but small 'c' constitutions will always be extensive. After all, in a broad sense, it could be argued that all state law is constitutional law: all law, ultimately, requires that someone acts or does not act in a certain way, and all state law is validated by the state. Every piece of state law is, then, an attempt to shape a relationship between the state and those subject to its authority, either directly, by seeking to determine the actions of individuals, or indirectly, by seeking to determine the actions of institutions of which individuals are a part. Sometimes, treating criminal or private law as constitutional law can be revealing, and can illuminate the ideologies and assumptions of the state. For example, the fact that a state adopts property laws that enable the rich to avoid paying their share of tax could be as constitutionally interesting as a bill of rights; it tells us something about the relationship between individuals and the state, the type of relationship which the state aspires to create between its members, and the values that the state seeks to pursue. But for the purposes of this book, a narrower account will be adopted: constitutional law is that law which relates specifically to state institutions, which includes the institution of citizenship. On this understanding, rules that apply to people in their interactions outside state institutions are not considered constitutional. The boundaries of this narrower understanding are vague, but it excludes most of criminal and private law. However, it should be remembered that this is not presented as a categorical divide, but one of convenience. When it is useful and interesting to do so, constitutional lawyers should be happy to venture beyond the traditional boundaries of their discipline.

In states that possess a written Constitution, there is an unavoidable gap between the Constitution and the constitution; the written Constitution is never identical with its small 'c' counterpart. Sometimes, this is because the Constitution only includes a subset of the rules of the state. The United States of America, for example, probably possesses the most famous example of a written Constitution, but that document only includes a small number of the rules that constitute American institutions. In part, this is because the text of the Constitution has been interpreted, and its full legal import can now only be established by looking both at the articulation of the rules found in the document and at the interpretations of those rules developed by the courts and other institutions. So, for example, the 14th Amendment to the American Constitution has been interpreted as protecting access to abortion and enshrining the right of same-sex couples to marry, even though neither of these is explicitly set out in the Constitution.[2] But, in addition, there are many small 'c' constitutional rules in the American system that are outside of the Constitution. These range from the grand, such as the constitutions of the states, to the modest, such as the administrative rules governing the discretion of civil servants. In other countries, the gap between the Constitution and the constitution is even more profound. A person who read the Chinese Constitution hoping to learn how power is exercised in that state would be disappointed: the rules found in the Chinese Constitution are radically different from the actual constitutional rules that regulate power within China.

The UK's lack of a Constitution has led some to describe it as 'unwritten', and it certainly has no document that can parallel America's Constitution. But, as with all small 'c' constitutions, large parts of the UK constitution take written form. Many constitutional rules are found in statutes. Some, such as the Human

[2] *Roe v Wade* 410 US 113 (1973); *Obergefell v Hodges* 576 US 644 (2015).

Rights Act 1998 and the devolution statutes, play a crucial role in structuring the state. Other statutes are less obviously constitutional but still contain provisions that empower and constrain institutions. Moving beyond statutes, other elements of the UK constitution also have written sources. The common law, for example, consists of the decisions of judges, most of which are reported and, in recent times, are available online. Extracting a rule from this mass of material can be tricky, but it is a written source, none the less. Perhaps the most obvious example of a non-written set of rules are constitutional conventions, discussed in chapter six. These are non-legal rules, grounded in the practices and beliefs of those who work within and around constitutional institutions. But even here, some of these conventions are written. As we will see, parts of the convention of ministerial responsibility and the conventions that structure the devolution settlements possess an authoritative, written, statement.

The upshot of this discussion is that we should take care not to overestimate the differences between written and unwritten constitutions: large parts of the UK constitution are written, whilst large parts of the constitutions of states with a capital 'c' Constitution lie outside of that document.

2.2 WHAT DO CONSTITUTIONS DO?

There is a temptation to think of the constitution as something imposed on the state, as an external set of limits placed on its institutions. As Martin Loughlin has argued, this is a mistake.[3] The constitution constitutes the state, it establishes, empowers, and, in establishing and empowering, limits, state institutions. Consequently, the purpose of a constitution is largely determined by the purpose of the state. It might be possible to talk, at a general level, of purposes that all states possess, and so all constitutions, pursue—perhaps all states exist for the benefit of their people, for example—but once we move beyond the very abstract, the purposes of any given constitution will depend on the

[3] Martin Loughlin, 'What is Constitutionalisation?' in Petra Dobner and Martin Loughlin (eds), *The Twilight of Constitutionalism?* (Oxford University Press 2010).

ideologies and decisions of the particular state. So, for example, amongst many other features, the UK aspires to be a democratic state and is committed to providing a level of social support to its citizens; these objectives can also be said to be objectives of its constitution. Is there anything further that can be said about the purposes of constitutions with a small 'c', are there any distinctive roles played by the constitution within the state? There may be a number, but two are worth highlighting here: the integrative role of constitutions and their unifying function.

Dieter Grimm has written about the integrative role of constitutions.[4] One of the things that constitutions attempt to do, and must succeed in doing to an extent, is to contain disagreement. For the state to function, conflict within its community must generally occur within and through constitutional structures. People may disagree passionately about their rights and duties, or about the best course of action for the state, but, by and large, they accept that the decisions made by state institutions bind. States achieve this acceptance partly through compulsion but also by persuading their people of the legitimacy of the state's constitutional processes. People might not like the decision that the judge reaches in their case or the outcome of a vote in Parliament, but they accept these as embodying legitimate processes through which decisions can be reached and then acted upon. Where the constitution fails to play this integrative role, where its structures are not broadly accepted, disagreement will arise over the institutions of the state themselves with people declining to accept their decisions. This impairs the capacity of the state to act and, more worryingly still, people might resort to violence to achieve their public goals, rather than arguing their case through the structures of the state. For a constitution to succeed in playing this integrative role, people must be prepared, on the whole, to submit to its rules and structures. Perhaps one of the reasons the debate over Brexit proved so divisive was that it became not just a dispute over a particular policy, the UK's membership of the European Union, but a debate over the constitutionally appropriate way to make decisions over that policy. A tension emerged between

[4] Dieter Grimm, 'Integration by Constitution' (2005) 3 International Journal of Constitutional Law 193, 194.

some supporters of Brexit who believed that the referendum, an exercise in direct democracy, had decided the issue, and others who believed that the decision should be made by Parliament, an institution that embodies representative democratic values. For those focused on the constitution, rather than the substance of Brexit, a fear is that this disagreement weakens the capacity of the constitution effectively to resolve the dispute, with each side appealing to different types of constitutional legitimacy.

The second distinctive thing that constitutions attempt to do—and, again, to an extent must succeed in doing—is to unify the state, combining its various elements into a single system. It is the constitution that enables the state to articulate a claim of sovereignty, a necessary feature of statehood. States consist of a people, a territory, and a set of institutions. Each of these elements is constituted by rules, rules that identify state-members, determine territory, and construct institutions. But, in addition, these elements are bound together by constitutional rules, rules which operate to bind them into elements of a single state. In some constitutional orders, the unifying role of the constitution is obvious and express: the written Constitution empowers and establishes the primary institutions of the state and these institutions, in turn, create more rules and institutions. But in the UK things are less clear. As we will see, some of the trickiest questions about the UK constitution relate to its unity. Why, for example, can we confidently claim that the English and Scottish legal systems are two legal systems within a single state? Why are we so sure that common law and statutes are part of the same legal order? How can we distinguish between those non-legal rules that are parts of the constitution, such as ministerial responsibility, and those non-legal rules that fall outside of the constitution, such as the rules of social etiquette? These are questions that will be answered over the coming chapters.

2.3 SHOULD THE UK HAVE A WRITTEN CONSTITUTION?

For most states, the adoption of a written Constitution is a practical necessity. States born in the modern era, whether emerging from war or gaining independence from a colonial power, have adopted Constitutions to mark the creation of the new polity and to indicate a breach from whatever political structures preceded them. The debate over whether the UK should adopt a written constitution, a capital 'c' Constitution, is unusual in that even its staunchest advocates accept that the UK is able to function reasonably effectively without such a document. Consequently, the UK has an option which most other states lack: it can choose whether or not it wants to adopt a written Constitution, and advocates of a written Constitution must find positive arguments for its creation. Moreover, these must be arguments for the adoption of a single, written text, and not simply wider arguments for constitutional reform; it might, for example, be desirable to give the judges the power to strike down statutes that infringe human rights, to turn the UK into a federation, or to abolish the House of Lords, but none of these changes requires the adoption of a written Constitution.

A focused argument for the adoption of a written Constitution has been provided by Vernon Bogdanor.[5] A written constitution, he contends, enables people to know the rules of the club, and benefits both existing members and incomers. For members, the written Constitution plays an educative role, providing a clear statement of the fundamental rules of the state and an outline of its key institutions. Every American student knows the outline of the American Constitution. The document also amounts to an offer made to incomers, to those who want to join the state. Individuals who wish to become citizens are presented with something akin to a contract: if you want to join our club, here are the rules you must accept. By including values in the Constitution, specifying, for example, respect for democracy and human rights, we can then legitimately require those who join the state to accept these values, or, at least, accept that any changes to them must be undertaken through the processes of constitutional change.

Jeff King has provided a further pair of arguments that advocate for the creation of a written Constitution. First, he conceptualises

[5] Vernon Bogdanor, *The New British Constitution* (Hart Publishing 2009) 216. For a suggested draft see Vernon Bogdanor, Tarunabh Khaitan, and Stefan Vogenauer, 'Should Britain Have a Written Constitution?' (2007) 78 Political Quarterly 499.

written constitutions as 'mission-statements', documents that play a role in structuring the state but which, in addition, amount to visions of what the state aspires to become; the objectives towards which constitutional development and political action are oriented.[6] Secondly, and allied to this, he argues that democracy requires that a community author its own constitutional order; making its own decisions about the functioning and ends of the state.[7] For King, states should rewrite their Constitutions on a regular basis, each generation should recraft the Constitution. Resting content with a Constitution inherited from past generations or, worse still, maintaining a Constitution handed down from another state, amounts to a failure to exercise democratic control over the rules that govern a people. The very act of writing a Constitution is, for King, of value; by requiring the people to rewrite the Constitution every twenty years or so, we ensure that the Constitution is a truly democratic document, and that the people truly govern themselves.

Bogdanor's and King's arguments for a written constitution are powerful and attractive. But there are also disadvantages in the UK adopting a written Constitution, and these disadvantages are the flipside of the arguments invoked by its advocates.

Bogdanor's argument for a written Constitution turned on the virtues of clarity: people know where they stand when the fundamental rules of the state have been written down. But recall the split between the Constitution, with a capital 'c' and the constitution with a small 'c'. Merely producing a Constitution does not, necessarily, mean that these are, in reality, the rules that constitute the state: the Chinese Constitution is a document more celebrated than used; reading this document will prove of only limited help to those members of the Chinese state who want to understand the rules of the club to which they belong. North Korea's Constitution is even further removed from the

[6] Jeff King, 'Constitutions as Mission Statements' in Denis J Galligan and Mila Versteeg (eds), *Social and Political Foundations of Constitutions* (Cambridge University Press 2013).

[7] Jeff King, 'The Democratic Case for a Written Constitution' (2019) Current Legal Problems 1. See also Bruce Ackerman, 'Why Britain Needs a Written Constitution: And Can't Wait for Parliament to Write One' (2018) 89 Political Quarterly 584.

true constitution of that state and is little more than a work of fiction. A written Constitution has the potential to mislead as much as to inform.[8] Furthermore, those writing a Constitution face a choice: whether the document should be short or long. A short Constitution, like that of the United States, can be taught in schools and will be widely read. But short Constitutions can only contain a small subset of the rules that constitute the state. Whilst the American Constitution is not a 'sham' Constitution like North Korea's, a student who only knew the content of that Constitution would have a very odd view of the American state. In contrast, a long Constitution, like that of Germany, is more comprehensive. Studying this document would give the reader a far better sense of how the German state operates, but its length makes it less accessible. This presents a challenge for those who see a written Constitution as an educative instrument: make it too short, and it risks misleading the reader, but make it too long, and it risks being left unread.

There is a further set of issues that arises from the supposed virtue of clarity. Producing a written constitution, particularly the type of rational, coherent, document called for by King, brings risks. As Grimm contends, constitutions need to keep political disagreements within the institutions of the state; people may disagree passionately over some issue or other, but they accept state decisions as the basis for collective action, even if they continue to believe those decisions are mistaken. Perhaps surprisingly, a lack of clarity may sometimes help constitutions succeed in this function.

Inconsistency and vagueness in constitutions may allow rival visions of the future of the state to co-exist within a single constitutional order.[9] This may be because different visions of the state exist in different parts of the constitutional order or because, more radically still, conflicting rules exist within the constitutional order giving, for example, precedence to rival constitutional bodies. This sort of ambiguity would be anathema to King's rationalist model of constitutions, in which the people are

[8] David S Law and Mila Versteeg, 'Sham Constitutions' (2013) 101 California Law Review 863.

[9] Gary Jacobsohn, *Constitutional Identity* (Harvard University Press 2010) 4.

expected, even required, to specify the end goals of the state and craft a constitution well-suited to achieving those goals. But ambiguity has served the United Kingdom well. As Walter Bagehot wrote many years ago, the UK is a republic in the guise of a monarchy.[10] For republicans, the UK is characterised by democracy, egalitarianism, and a belief that people who hold positions of public power do so through merit; but for those attracted by the pageant of monarchy, we have a queen and an established church. More recently, Sir Stephen Sedley has argued that the UK has shifted from being a unitary state to what is, in effect, a federation.[11] On a unitary conception of the UK, the UK Parliament in Westminster retains its supremacy, able to override the decisions of devolved assemblies or remove the devolution settlement altogether, but for those attracted by the federalist model, the devolution settlement is politically irrevocable, and may be legally entrenched against change. Once more, these rival visions of the UK can both be found in its rules and structures. By allowing these different visions to co-exist, different parts of the UK's community are given bits of the constitution with which they can identify.

If retaining inconsistency within a constitution may broaden the constituency that will support that structure, seeking to eradicate these inconsistencies may force the community to resolve disagreements that do not yet need to be resolved. Could the UK produce a written Constitution without choosing between a monarchy and a republic? Could it avoid addressing the question of federalism and, if so, would it be required to answer the difficult question of a parliament for England? These are important questions, but they are questions that we may not yet need to answer. Forcing them to a resolution risks causing unnecessary political disagreement and conflict, producing winners and losers. Worse still, if King's advice of a regular constitutional convention were followed, these tough constitutional questions

[10] Walter Bagehot, *The English Constitution* (Watts & Co 1964) 94.

[11] Stephen Sedley, *Ashes and Sparks: Essays on Law and Justice* (Cambridge University Press 2011) 388; see also Andrew Gamble, 'The Constitutional Revolution in the United Kingdom' (2006) 36 Publius 19.

would be reopened every twenty years or so, unsettling the structure of the constitution.

2.4 CONCLUSION

In countries with a written Constitution, constitutional scholarship often focuses on that document, examining the ideologies that underpin it and the ways in which it should be developed and interpreted. Perhaps because the UK lacks such a document, its constitutional scholars have tended to examine a wider range of issues; some questions that might seem simple to a German or American scholar appear more complex in the context of the UK. The next few chapters will examine the ways in which the UK constitution forms and unifies the constitutional order, enabling the UK to exist and to act as a single entity, whilst also being characterised by deep pluralities. There are at least three challenges to the unity of the UK constitution that need to be answered. First, there are multiple legal orders within the UK; English law and Scots law are distinct legal systems. Secondly, there is a multiplicity of legal sources within the constitutional order. Different institutions in the UK are able to draw on different legal sources to produce laws. Thirdly, there are multiple types of rule: the UK is constituted by a mix of legal rules and non-legal rules ('conventions'). Everyone agrees that these multiple legal sources, multiple legal orders, and multiple types of rule, are parts of a single constitutional order, but what draws them together? How can it be that they are parts of a unified entity, yet remain distinct? Scholars in countries with a written Constitution might ignore these questions because the written Constitution is seen as providing a simple and comprehensive answer to them: the Constitution is the unifier of the sources, systems, and rules of the state. But this may be too quick. As we have seen, in such states there is a gap between the capital 'c' Constitution and the small 'c' constitution that establishes the state. The existence of this gap entails that the questions that preoccupy UK scholarship about the unifying function of constitutions are often relevant to these states, too, and the greater the gap, the more pressing these questions become.

3

THE LEGAL CONSTITUTION: LEGAL ORDERS

Most books on constitutional law largely ignore the diversity of legal orders within the United Kingdom (UK) and focus on English law. But if there are multiple legal orders within the UK constitution, there must also be multiple sets of constitutional laws. These rules may be identical in wording but if they are parts of different legal orders they are legally distinct: they are members of different sets of rules and have a different territorial reach. More interestingly still, this diversity allows for the possibility for division: perhaps the constitutional laws found within these legal orders differ, perhaps the different legal orders of the UK have different understandings of the powers of Parliament or the Crown. It is surprisingly difficult to determine how many distinct legal orders the UK possesses. We can start by excluding the legal orders of Jersey, Guernsey, and the Isle of Man: these territories are Crown Dependencies, not parts of the UK, so fall outside of the scope of this book. But when we turn to the UK itself, England, Northern Ireland, Scotland, and Wales, it still proves difficult to distinguish the number of discrete legal orders. This is partly because the criteria we use to distinguish legal orders is disputable and, even when not disputed, are vague; often the difference between two possible legal orders is one of degree rather than a clear categorical divide. But it is also because the relationship between the sets of laws and institutions within the UK is unsettled; in some important respects the connections are ambiguous, and, indeed, this ambiguity may sometimes be deliberate.

3.1 THE NATURE OF A LEGAL ORDER

What is a legal order? When Herbert Hart, in his classic book *The Concept of Law*, sought to provide an answer to the question of the nature of law, he did so in terms of rules. For Hart,

The United Kingdom Constitution. N. W. Barber, Oxford University Press. © Nick Barber 2021.
DOI: 10.1093/oso/9780198852315.003.0003

legal systems were composites of primary and secondary rules. Although his account of these rules varied over the course of the book, in essence primary rules are those that impose legal obligations on people to behave in a certain way, whilst secondary rules are those that relate to the operation of primary rules, enabling their identification, change, and application.[1] Consequently, the statutory rule against theft, found in the Theft Act 1968, is a primary rule, whilst the rule telling the judges that the Theft Act 1968 is valid law and the rule empowering them to provide authoritative interpretations of that Act, are each secondary rules. The most fundamental secondary rule, for Hart, was the rule of recognition.[2] This rule identifies the sources of law, telling the judges, and others, which rules are legally binding, and, in so doing, serves to weave these sources into a single legal system. The legal system, created by the interaction of these rules, presents itself as autonomous and comprehensive. We can delineate the boundaries of a legal system, distinguishing one legal system from another, because legal systems do not ground their legal legitimacy in another legal system and, instead, contain rules that distinguish and regulate their relationship with other legal systems they encounter.[3] Scholars writing after Hart added to and modified his account of a legal system. Although an enormous amount has been written on the subject, for our purposes perhaps the most important qualification has been the emphasis placed by later scholars on the role of institutions. Law cannot simply be understood as a set of rules. It is a set of rules created and applied by an institutional structure, a legal order: law-making, law-interpreting, and law-applying institutions are also necessary for the operation of law.[4]

Turning to the UK, there are five possible territories that might possess discrete legal orders: England, Scotland, Northern Ireland, Wales, and the UK, taken as a whole. In what follows it will be argued that there are only two legal orders: with England,

[1] HLA Hart, *The Concept of Law* (3rd edn, Clarendon Press 2012) ch 5.

[2] ibid ch 6.

[3] Joseph Raz, 'The Institutional Nature of Law' in Joseph Raz (ed), *The Authority of Law* (2nd edn, Oxford University Press 2009) 115–20.

[4] Joseph Raz, *Practical Reason and Norms* (Princeton University Press 1990) ch 4.

Wales, and Northern Ireland forming one legal order, and Scotland forming a second. But this is contestable: it is arguable that Northern Ireland should be regarded as possessing its own legal order and, to a lesser extent arguable, that Wales should also be regarded as distinct. It could be that as the centrifugal forces of devolution accelerate, the distinctiveness of these legal regions will become more pronounced.

3.2 ENGLISH AND SCOTS LAW

English and Scots law are probably the two best known legal orders operating within the UK. Each has a long history that predates the creation of the UK; these were the functioning legal orders of distinct states. When Britain was formed, Scots law was given explicit protection in the Acts of Union of 1707. The Acts of Union consist of two statutes, one passed by the Scottish Parliament and the second passed by the English Parliament, that gave legal effect to the Articles of Union that Commissioners representing the two countries had negotiated.[5] The Acts of Union purport to protect both the institutional structure of the Scottish legal system and the substance of that legal order.[6] Article XIX requires that the Scottish Court of Session and Court of Justiciary should enjoy 'in all time coming' the same rights and privileges that they possessed before the Union, and, furthermore, that litigation in Scotland should not be brought within the jurisdiction of the English courts. Article XVIII empowers the new, British, Parliament to alter Scots law to bring unity across Britain in the areas of public policy and civil government, but only to alter private rights where such alterations are for the 'evident utility of the subjects within Scotland'. As J. D. B. Mitchell notes, these Articles had the effect of protecting Scots law as a distinct legal system whilst enabling the British Parliament to pass statutes that would be effective in that system.[7] Curiously, perhaps, the Acts

[5] Union with England Act 1707 (Scottish Parliament) and Union with Scotland Act 1707 (English Parliament).

[6] Colin Kidd, *Unions and Unionisms: Political Thought in Scotland 1500–2000* (Cambridge University Press 2008) ch 3; JBD Mitchell, *Constitutional Law* (2nd edn, W Green & Son 1968) ch 5.

[7] Mitchell (n 6) 95–96.

of Union do not include parallel protections for English courts or for the continuing operation of English law; the Parliaments appear to have assumed that such protection was not necessary, and there was no need to make explicit provision for the continuing validity of English law.[8]

Whilst the Acts of Union provided protection for much of the existing Scottish court system, they did not resolve the question of the highest appeal court, the body or bodies that would have the final say over Scottish litigation. This omission was not accidental, and reflected a lack of agreement both between the English and Scottish commissioners and, indeed, within the Scottish negotiating team.[9] The strategy of deliberate omission is a common one in negotiations of this type; where the parties are unable to agree, the decision is postponed, ideally to a time when its resolution becomes easier or, if not easier, unavoidable. In the event, the question was rapidly answered when, in *Rosebery v Inglis*, the House of Lords made its first decision in the area of Scots law.[10] But the jurisdiction of the House of Lords over Scots law was not unlimited. In *Bywater v Lord Advocate*, Lord Mansfield determined that Scottish criminal cases could not be appealed to the House of Lords because no right of appeal to the Scottish Parliament had existed before 1707 in this area of law.[11] Consequently, for appeals over the substance of criminal law or sentencing, the High Court of Justiciary, a Scottish court, is the highest court in the system.[12]

It might be thought that the jurisdiction of the House of Lords over Scottish cases (including the implicit claim of the House of

[8] JD Ford, 'The Legal Provisions in the Acts of Union' (2007) 66 Cambridge Law Journal 106, 116–17.

[9] Ford (n 8) 122–26. See also Neil Walker, *The Final Appellate Jurisdiction in the Scottish Legal System* (The Scottish Government 2010) Appendix I.

[10] House of Lords Journal, xviii, 464 (16 February 1708) http://www.british-history.ac.uk/lords-jrnl/vol18/pp463-464 (accessed 10 April 2019); Walker (n 9) Appendix I, 14–15. See also Exchequer Court (Scotland) Act 1707.

[11] (1781) 2 Paton 563 (HL) 564–71; DL Jones, 'The Judicial Role of the House of Lords Before 1870' in Louis Blom-Cooper, Brice Dickson, and Gavin Drewry (eds), *The Judicial Role of the House of Lords 1876-2009* (Oxford University Press 2009) 8.

[12] Unless, as we shall see, the appeal relates to the devolution settlement or the application of the Human Rights Act 1998.

Lords in *Bywater* to be empowered to determine the limits of its jurisdiction) entails that English law and Scots law were combined into a single legal order, with the House of Lords as its highest court. But this would be to overlook the chameleon-like capacity of the Lords to sit as the highest court of whatever legal order it was exercising jurisdiction within: in English cases it sat as an English court, whilst in Scottish cases it sat as a Scottish court.[13] The House of Lords lost its judicial function as a result of the Constitutional Reform Act 2005, which established the Supreme Court.[14] Section 41(2) of that Act states that: 'A decision of the Supreme Court on appeal from a court of any part of the United Kingdom, other than a decision on a devolution matter, is to be regarded as the decision of a court of that part of the United Kingdom.'

And so maintains the capacity of this court to shift its constitutional identity depending on the source of appeal it is hearing. Consequently, when hearing appeals from Scottish courts, the Supreme Court sits as a court of that system. Unless the Supreme Court makes it clear its decisions about the English common law are also correct statements of Scots law, it is only cases decided by the Supreme Court in its capacity as a Scottish court that are binding within the Scottish system.[15] The tricky question of whether a decision of the Supreme Court in an English case on the interpretation of a statute that applies to both England and Scotland binds Scottish courts remains open.[16]

3.3 IRISH AND WELSH LAW

Whereas Scots law was given protection by the Acts of Union, Irish law and Welsh law have a less happy history. In each instance, the native law of those territories was extinguished as parts of the process of English colonisation. Welsh law was the first to go; in a series of English statutes, culminating in Acts of 1535 and

[13] Walker (n 9) 23–25 charts some of the uncertainty around this dual identity of the House of Lords.

[14] Constitutional Reform Act 2005, s 23.

[15] See the discussion in *Willers v Joyce* [2016] UKSC 44 [22].

[16] Compare *Dalgleish v Glasgow Corporation* 1976 SC 32, 52 and *McDonald v Secretary of State for Scotland* 1994 SC 234, 240.

1543, English law was expanded to Wales, excluding Welsh law from the court system.[17] This was part of a gradual process, spanning more than two centuries, during which the constitutional autonomy of the Welsh rulers was gradually limited.[18] In Ireland, *The Case of Tanistry* has been taken to mark the point at which the courts declined to accept the operation of Irish (Brehon) law.[19] In this case it seems that the Irish Court of the King's Bench accepted the defendant's claim that only English law, and not Brehon law, should be applied by the courts.[20] Following the Scottish model, Ireland and Britain became a single state with a pair of statutes passed by the British and Irish Parliaments in 1800 which brought the United Kingdom Parliament into existence the following year.[21] As with the Acts of Union of 1707, these statutes provided for the continuity of the laws currently operating in Ireland but, unlike the 1707 Union, they provided little protection for the law of that territory.

Whilst the English common law has long been applied in Ireland, it has largely been applied by Irish courts. Indeed, for a period just prior to Union, the Irish court system was completely distinct from the English[22] and, although the UK House of Lords swiftly regained its position as the final appellate court for Ireland after 1801, the Irish court system retained significant autonomy.[23] This autonomy was accentuated after 1920 when a new regional

[17] Laws in Wales Act 1535 and Laws in Wales Act 1543. These are the short titles given to these statutes by the Statute Law Revision Act 1948. The original, and more evocative, title of the 1535 Act was 'An Acte for Lawes & Justice to be ministered in Wales in like fourme as it is in this Realm', which is discussed further in ch 14.

[18] Glanmor Williams, *Renewal and Reformation: Wales c.1415–1642* (Oxford University Press 1993) ch 11.

[19] *The Case of Tanistry* (1608) Davis 28, 80 ER 516, which is discussed further in ch 16.

[20] The decision and effect of *The Case of Tanistry* may be more equivocal than is often thought. For a careful reassessment see Shaunnagh Dorsett, 'Since Time Immemorial: A Story of Common Law Jurisdiction, Native Title and *The Case of Tanistry*' (2002) 26 Melbourne University Law Review 32, 44–50.

[21] An Act for the Union of Great Britain and Ireland 1800 (Irish Parliament); Act of Union (Ireland) 1800 (British Parliament).

[22] See ch 16.

[23] Jones (n 11) 8–9; Brice Dickson, *Law in Northern Ireland* (3rd edn, Hart Publishing 2018) 4.1–4.8.

legislature, the Northern Ireland Parliament, was established in Northern Ireland, lasting until its abolition by the UK Parliament in 1972.[24] Perhaps partly because there was a great deal of law specific to Northern Ireland, enacted by its devolved institution, the courts in Northern Ireland still enjoy a significant amount of autonomy from parallel English institutions. Mirroring England, Northern Ireland has its own set of High Courts and its own Court of Appeal. Below the Supreme Court, Northern Ireland's courts are not bound to follow decisions of English courts: the Northern Ireland High Court is bound by the Northern Ireland Court of Appeal, whilst decisions of the English Court of Appeal are accorded only persuasive value.[25] Consequently, the common law in Northern Ireland is, in some areas, different from that in England; although the two regions' laws were born from the same source, they have grown apart. Once we get to the level of the Supreme Court, however, the two judicial systems are brought back together: all decisions of the Supreme Court bind in both England and Northern Ireland, irrespective of whether the case comes from an English or a Northern Irish court.[26]

The unifying role of the Supreme Court allows us to regard England and Northern Ireland as sharing a legal order, within which there is a significant devolution of legal competence at the level of the Courts of Appeal. Wales is also part of this legal order but, in contrast to Northern Ireland, Wales never possessed the autonomous court system that would have allowed it to develop its own legal jurisdiction within that legal order. Recently, perhaps in response to the legal autonomy enjoyed by Northern Ireland and Scotland, Wales has sought to establish a greater degree of autonomy.[27] In 2017, the Government of Wales Act 2006 was

[24] Dickson (n 23) 1.9–1.15. The NI Parliament was established by the Government of Ireland Act 1920, suspended by the Northern Ireland (Temporary Provisions) Act 1972, and abolished by the Northern Ireland Constitution Act 1973, s 31.

[25] Dickson (n 23) 4.42.

[26] ibid. The point is not entirely beyond dispute: FH Newark, 'Law and Precedent in Northern Ireland' (1972) 23 Northern Ireland Legal Quarterly 100. See also I Walsh, 'Precedent in Former Irish Superior Courts' (2005) 40 Irish Jurist (NS) 160, 176–78.

[27] The Laws in Wales Act 1535 and the Laws in Wales Act 1543 were repealed by the Welsh Language Act 1993.

amended to include a section recognising a body of Welsh law.[28] At present, it seems that Welsh law implies little more than that there is a body of law that applies specifically to Wales, but this, in itself, is unremarkable. After all, there are many laws that only apply to regions of the UK, such as laws that apply to London or Manchester, and we would not normally talk of these cities having their own legal orders. It remains to be seen if the Senedd, the Welsh Parliament, is able to build on the statutory recognition of Welsh law to create the sort of autonomy for Welsh courts enjoyed by the courts of Northern Ireland.[29]

3.4 UK LAW

Finally, it could be argued that the UK possesses its own legal order. Those who are unconvinced by the claims that English law and Scots law are distinct legal orders could argue that these are subsets of a wider UK system, unified, perhaps, by their joint acceptance of the supremacy of Parliament. But, as we shall see, Scots law has long been equivocal about the position of Parliament within the Scots system.[30] The distinction between the contents of English and Scots law, and the distinction between the institutions that apply and create that law, are sufficient for us present them as separate systems. Until recently, there was no law that could be said to be part of a UK legal system; it was either part of the English or Scottish systems. But the Constitutional Reform Act 2005 appears to have changed this. Looking back at section 41(2), quoted above, when the Supreme Court decides a devolution issue it does not do so as a Scottish or English court. We could, perhaps, take this section as creating a new, if limited, legal order: the Supreme Court sits as a UK court, making decisions of UK law. Perhaps there is a small category of 'UK law' in the area of devolution. However, the Constitutional Reform Act 2005 is legally valid because it is recognised as a statute by *both* the English and Scottish legal orders, and decisions made under

[28] Government of Wales Act 2006, s A2 (as amended by the Wales Act 2017, s 1).

[29] See Report of the Commission on Justice in Wales (Cardiff 2019), discussed further in ch 14.

[30] See ch 5.

section 41(2) depend, for their legality, on their reception by these legal orders: there is not a distinct set of rules establishing UK courts. Consequently, the better interpretation of this section is that, in devolution issues, the Supreme Court sits as an English and Scottish court, and the law of devolution should be seen as a subset of the law of these legal orders, although a subset that, unlike other areas of the law, is always identical in content.[31]

[31] There could still be disagreement between the lower courts over a devolution issue, but the Constitutional Reform Act 2005 makes it plain that all these courts are bound by decisions of the Supreme Court.

4

THE LEGAL CONSTITUTION: COMMON LAW, PREROGATIVE, AND PRIVILEGE

This chapter and the following chapter examine the legal sources of the UK constitution, looking at the ways they empower institutions to make law, and the ways in which the courts regulate the process of law-making. The focus of these chapters will be on the non-derived sources of law, the foundations of the legal side of the UK constitution. This chapter will consider the place of common law, prerogative, and privilege in the constitution, whilst the next chapter will examine statute law. In that chapter, it will be argued that statute law should be understood as falling within the broader context of non-derived legal sources; the analytical structures developed in this chapter will be relied upon to clarify the position of statute law and to tackle one of the most controversial topics in UK constitutional scholarship, that of parliamentary sovereignty.

4.1 THE LEGAL SOURCES OF THE UK CONSTITUTION

A source of law is a set of rules with a shared point of origin that are recognised as law by the legal order because of this shared characteristic. Their recognition as law turns on their mode of creation; the legal order recognises these rules as law because they were produced in a certain way. So, for example, statutory law is a source of law, consisting of a set of rules (found in the statutes) that have a common point of origin recognised by the legal order as triggering legal validity (they were enacted by Parliament).[1] That common origin will be, in some form or other, a law-making institution: a body recognised by the legal order as having the capacity to generate

[1] For a discussion of the nature of legal validity see Maris Köpcke, *Legal Validity: The Fabric of Justice* (Oxford University Press 2019).

The United Kingdom Constitution. N. W. Barber, Oxford University Press. © Nick Barber 2021.
DOI: 10.1093/oso/9780198852315.003.0004

law.[2] Consequently, a legal source is both a set of rules produced by an institution, and, additionally, a capacity that has been exercised by that institution. The legal sources of the UK constitution can be placed into two groups: non-derived and derived legal sources. Non-derived legal sources are those which do not require some further empowering rule for their legal force; they stand alone, recognised, but not validated, by the courts and other legal officials. Derived legal sources, in contrast, depend on an instrument drawn from some other legal source for their validity. For example, Parliament's statutes are a non-derivative source of law; they do not depend on any other source for their legal authority. In contrast, statutory instruments, delegated legislation, drawn up by government departments, are also a source of law, but are a derived source of law: their legal validity rests on the authority of an empowering statute. The legal authority of a derived source of law can always be traced back to an instrument located within a non-derived source. Where a state possesses a written Constitution, it is possible for that document to be the only instrument validated by and found within a non-derived source of law, with the rest of the legal sources within the state being derived, taking their legal validity from that instrument.[3] The UK lacks such a foundational constitutional point and, consequently, contains a number of non-derived legal sources. Each of the historic branches of the UK constitution can draw on its own, non-derived, legal source to produce legal instruments: the executive has the prerogative, each chamber of Parliament can utilise parliamentary privilege, the courts have the common law, and Parliament, as a whole, has statute law.

4.2 THE COMMON LAW

The roots of the common law are found in the local laws and customs of the people, stretching back before the Norman Conquest

[2] In the case of customary law, the institution is the community whose customs provide the basis for the law.

[3] For an exploration of this idea see John Gardner, 'Can There Be a Written Constitution?' in John Gardner (ed), *Law as a Leap of Faith* (Oxford University Press 2012).

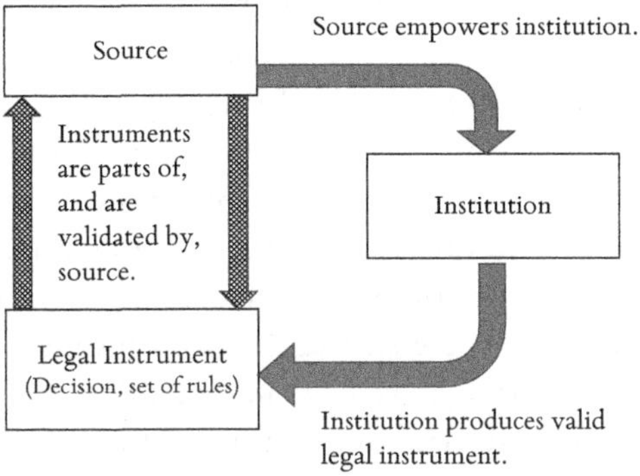

Figure 4.1 The relationship of sources, institutions, and instruments

in 1066.[4] Over the course of the following two centuries, there was a gradual movement towards the standardisation of these laws, as 'common' law replaced diversity. This process of standardisation was undertaken by the judiciary: judges were sent by the king on tours of the country and, over time, came to apply a consistent set of rules in the various locations in which they heard cases. Whilst local variations persisted for many centuries, it was gradually recognised that a single set of rules applied throughout the realm.[5]

The king created the courts that applied the common law, but was not the originator or legitimator of the common law.[6] The origins of the common law, as grounded in customs applied by the judges, may continue to shape the way in which modern judges present the law in their decisions and reach conclusions about the content of the law. As a matter of presentation, when

[4] Sir John Baker, *An Introduction to English Legal History* (5th edn, Oxford University Press 2019) ch 1. Scottish common law also has its origins in custom, although it also drew from Roman law: Robin White, Ian Willock, and Hector MacQueen, *The Scottish Legal System* (5th edn, Bloomsbury 2013) ch 2.

[5] Baker (n 4) ch 2.

[6] William Blackstone, *Commentaries on the Laws of England* (David Lemmings (ed), 1st edn, Oxford University Press 2016) bk 1 ch 7 para 3. On the constitutional status of the common law see Jeffrey Goldsworthy, *Parliamentary Sovereignty: Contemporary Debates* (Cambridge University Press 2010) ch 2.

a judge hands down a decision in a case she writes as if she were declaring what the law *is*, not what she thinks it should become; judicial decisions are presented as if the judges had no role in the making of the law. This rhetorical style reflects the notion that the rules of the common law are external to the court; judges are identifying rules that already bind the parties before them. Few believe this fiction: the content of the common law today is radically different from its content in the twelfth century, and these differences were not achieved by judges diligently unearthing buried rules. But the declaratory rhetoric of the common law may have conditioned the way in which this process of law-creation has been undertaken: the common law judge must provide arguments supporting her decision that tie it back to previous cases; she cannot simply state what she would like the law to be. The creation of law under the common law is grounded in the incremental development of rules through successive cases; new common law rules rest upon past decisions.

The requirement to make new decisions square with past cases even applies to the system's highest court, the Supreme Court. To give a recent example, in *Patel v Mirza* the Supreme Court considered a case in which Patel had transferred money to Mirza in the hope of making money from insider trading.[7] Patel believed that Mirza would be able to discover the contents of an important government statement about a company listed on the stock exchange before that statement was made public. Mirza would then make a bet using this insider knowledge, and scoop up the profits after the announcement. This conduct amounted to a criminal offence, as using confidential information to make money on the movement of shares is illegal, and the agreement was therefore unlawful. In the event, the announcement was not made and no bet was placed, but when Patel asked for his money back, Mirza refused. Before the case was decided by the Supreme Court, the law was unclear. On the one hand, in some previous cases the judges had refused to help those whose claims were founded on an unlawful act: Patel had tried to commit a crime, and the court would not protect him by requiring his money to be returned. On the other hand, in other cases the judges had required those

[7] [2016] UKSC 42, [2017] AC 467.

who had been unjustly enriched to repay their enrichment; Mirza had Patel's money and could provide no good explanation to the Court as to why he should keep it. In the end, the Supreme Court found for Patel, and the money had to be returned. *Patel* was a case in which the law was unsettled, and the Court had discretion about how it should develop, but this discretion was not unconstrained. The Supreme Court could not, for example, have decided that both of the parties were rogues and the money should go to a charity. However sensible this outcome might have appeared, it could not be tied back to previous common law decisions.

When developing the law, judges distinguish between *binding* and *persuasive* elements in previous cases. A past case binds when a judge is legally obliged to apply the rule in that case to the litigation before her. A past case is persuasive when, even if not binding, the reasoning is relevant to the decision before the judge. These two features of the common law method, the capacity of past cases to bind and their capacity to persuade, require further examination.

Identification of the *binding* aspects of a previous case requires an assessment of two factors: first, the rule that was applied by the judge in the case needs to be identified; second, the status of the court that made the decision needs to be assessed. Classically, lawyers distinguish between the *ratio* of a case and the *dicta* surrounding it.[8] The *ratio* is the reason for the decision: the rule that was applied to resolve the dispute. The *dicta* are the arguments made by the judge to justify the formulation of that rule. The *ratio* may be binding, the *dicta* are persuasive. In practice, it can be hard to pin down the *ratio* for a decision. Courts are not required to provide a crisp encapsulation of the rule they purport to apply in their judgments, and later courts, looking back at the case, may struggle to extract a sharp, clear, *ratio* from the reasoning given by the judge. In *Patel*, the majority of the judges declined to adopt a clear rule requiring the restoration of money paid for an unlawful act, and instead decided that the question of whether such money

[8] Rupert Cross and JW Harris, *Precedent in English Law* (4th edn, Oxford University Press 1991) ch 2.

could be recovered would depend on a range of policy considerations, leaving future judges a broad area of discretion.[9] More troublesome still, judges in the higher courts sit in panels and there are often multiple speeches delivered in a single case. It is possible that, in such cases, there is no single *ratio* for the outcome, merely a series of judicial *ratios* which converge on an agreed outcome: the plaintiff wins, but with different judges giving different grounds for her victory. Furthermore, even once a *ratio* has been identified it only binds future cases that possess the same set of legally significant facts as the earlier case. If a judge who would otherwise be bound can find some material difference in the case before her, she can 'distinguish' the earlier case, and avoid applying the *ratio*.

Once the *ratio* has been identified, its reach will depend on the court that articulated it.[10] The Supreme Court's decisions bind all other courts that are faced with a legally identical issue. Before the decision in *Patel*, the Court of Appeal, the High Court, and the lower courts could have reached a range of different views about the recovery of money paid under an unlawful agreement. After *Patel*, they are constrained to follow the approach set out by the Supreme Court. In the English legal system, decisions of the Court of Appeal bind lower courts and, in addition, are binding on future Court of Appeal decisions, but do not bind the Supreme Court.[11] Until 1966, the House of Lords (the precursor to the modern Supreme Court) also regarded itself as bound by its own past decisions.[12] However, in 1966 the House of Lords issued a Practice Statement declaring that it was no longer so fettered; the House could now depart from its past decisions.[13] The apparent paradox of a court first declaring itself bound by its past decisions and then, in violation of this supposedly unchangeable decision, declaring that it is not, has prompted a great deal of

[9] *Patel* (n 7) [107]–[121] (Lord Toulson).

[10] There are a number of exceptions to the simplified picture of judicial hierarchy presented in this paragraph: see Cross and Harris (n 8) ch 3.

[11] *Young v Bristol Aeroplane Co Ltd* [1944] KB 718. Of course, these decisions do not bind Scottish courts: see ch 3.

[12] *London Tramways Co Ltd v London County Council* [1898] AC 375 (HL).

[13] Practice Statement (Judicial Precedent) [1966] 1 WLR 1234 (HL).

scholarship.[14] But the 1966 declaration has proved effective, and has been relied upon by the highest court in the UK system from time to time.[15] Most of the rules that govern the relationships between courts, determining when a decision binds and when it does not, are found in the common law; to a significant extent, the common law regulates its own operation.

Past decisions may be *persuasive* even if they are not formally binding. When the judges are not bound by the *ratio* of a case decided by a higher court, they have space to develop the law, but their law-making role is still conditioned by what has gone before. The common law judge does this by showing that her decision is in line with the *ratios* of related cases which, even if distinguishable from the case before her, possess points of similarity with the current case, and by examining the *dicta* of judges, seeking to identify reasoning in previous cases that is applicable to the dispute before her. This past reasoning is persuasive rather than binding, and its persuasive force will depend on a host of factors including the level of the court in which the reasoning was articulated, the reputation of the judge who articulated the reasons, and, most importantly of all, the cogency of the reasoning. When these elements are especially strong, when a respected judge in a senior court has articulated a powerful argument that is relevant to the case, the persuasive force of the reasoning may be such that it is effectively binding, and the lower court judge may be all but compelled to apply it in the case before her. As well as past cases, the judge may make use of other types of arguments. Changes in the law outside of the common law may be relevant; the judge might look to the principles animating statutes for inspiration.[16] Other legal jurisdictions may also provide material for

[14] Cross and Harris (n 8); Neil Duxbury, *The Nature and Authority of Precedent* (Cambridge University Press 2008) ch 4.

[15] When the Judicial Committee of the House of Lords transmuted into the modern Supreme Court, it was not felt necessary to reissue the 1966 statement: Supreme Court of the United Kingdom, 'Practice Direction 3' para 3.1.3; *Austin v Southwark London Borough Council* [2010] UKSC 28, [2011] 1 AC 355 [24], [25].

[16] As with the introduction of the Human Rights Act 1998, which appears to have shifted the courts' understanding of the role of rights in the common law; see ch 21.

the judge; the judges in *Patel*, for instance, considered Australian and American decisions. Coming from outside of the judge's legal order, these decisions cannot bind but they can persuade; a UK judge might draw on foreign materials to justify a decision, using them to illustrate an argument or develop a principle that she wishes to apply in the case. Finally, and most generally, the judge may identify and articulate arguments relevant to the decision that are not drawn from other legal materials. If the judge believes that deciding a case in a particular way will produce an immoral or foolish outcome, she can say so, and reject this potential modification of the law.

The common law grows through the interaction of these two types of decision-making: developing through the obligation to apply the decisions of higher courts, coupled with the persuasive force of argument. The common law provides an example of an organic model of constitutional change: the judges change the law, but they do so gradually, over a long period of time. The very nature of the court system requires this: there are a great many judges, even in the higher courts, and the capacity of any single judge to bring about a change in the law is limited. It is impossible for one judge, even a senior one, to monopolise all of the cases in an area of law, and, to be effective, the judge must persuade her fellow judges of the correctness of her views. The success of a proposition of law advanced by a single judge will therefore depend on the response of her colleagues: the more widely her understanding of the law is accepted, the more it becomes embodied in other judicial decisions, and the more established this legal position becomes. And, in the course of this process, it is likely that the original proposition will develop. Even those judges who are attracted to the original articulation of the law will re-frame that proposition in their own words, giving it a slightly different meaning, and other judges will suggest qualifications or modifications. This process has an evolutionary aspect, as the judges seek to identify the most attractive form of the legal proposition in previous cases, and, having attempted to select the best version of the proposition, then, deliberately or unintentionally, articulate it in such a way as to create a new variation of that position.

4.3 THE ROYAL PREROGATIVE

The royal prerogative consists of those special legal powers possessed by the Crown.[17] Although the significance of the prerogative has narrowed over the centuries as various areas of executive action have been brought under statutory control, it remains an important source of law. To give a few examples, domestically, the prerogative can be relied upon to stop prosecutions, to pardon offenders, to appoint ministers, and to issue passports. In foreign affairs, it is the prerogative that is relied upon when the military is deployed, when foreigners are granted entry to the country, and in the making of treaties.[18] Legal actions undertaken within the prerogative may take the form of a decision, a discrete and focused action directed towards a particular individual, or may take the form of legislation, a set of rules that guide a range of conduct and which may establish new institutional structures which, in their turn, may be empowered to take legally effective decisions.[19] In sharp distinction to law created through the common law, there is no obligation for exercises of the prerogative to be consistent with past prerogative acts.

It is telling that when William Blackstone wrote about the prerogative in 1789, he wrote of powers exercised by the monarch, whereas when Albert Venn Dicey wrote on the prerogative in 1885, he referred to powers exercised by the Crown.[20] Whilst the prerogative was originally exercised by the monarch, by the time Dicey was writing these powers were effectively exercised by the monarch's ministers; the monarch's personal role in deciding how those powers should be exercised was slight. This remains the

[17] Blackstone (n 6) bk 1 ch 7 para 3. Dicey drew the boundaries of the prerogative more broadly, including all those legal powers held by the Crown that were not conferred by statute: AV Dicey, *Introduction to the Study of the Law of the Constitution* (10th edn, Macmillan & Co 1959) 424–25. The distinction is discussed further in ch 11.

[18] Although Parliament now has a significant role in the ratification of treaties: Constitutional Reform and Governance Act 2010.

[19] For example, the BBC is established under the prerogative: see Department for Culture, Media and Sport, 'Copy of Royal Charter for the Continuance of the British Broadcasting Corporation' (Cm 9365, 2016).

[20] Blackstone (n 6); Dicey (n 17).

position: although as a matter of law the prerogative is still exercised by the Queen, in almost all cases the prerogative is exercised by her ministers, who are accountable to Parliament for their decisions. Here, a set of conventions, the non-legal rules of the constitution, have the effect of transferring a legal power from the monarch to her ministers. The conventions that regulate the exercise of the prerogative will be discussed further in Chapter 6.

Scholars and judges sometimes present the prerogative as a part of the common law.[21] If this were correct, the prerogative would be a subset of the source discussed in the previous section, and not a distinct source of law at all. There are a number of reasons for rejecting this way of understanding the prerogative. First, it is ahistorical: the medieval monarchs, exercising their prerogatives, would not have conceived of themselves as reliant on a common law power; this was an independent set of legal rights, vested in the Crown.[22] Second, whilst the content of the common law is deduced from the decisions of the courts, the content of the prerogative does not turn on past cases or on prior judicial recognition. An exercise of the prerogative does not have to wait for judicial approval before it is legally valid: the minister does not have to check with the court (or, indeed, with Parliament) before the decision becomes effective. Because the validity of an exercise of the prerogative does not require judicial approval, it is possible that there are areas of the prerogative that have never been brought before a court and there may be aspects of the prerogative that have been exercised by ministers, or which could be so exercised, that judges have never commented on.[23] So, whilst looking at past case law on the existence of the prerogative is a good place to start when testing a claim that a prerogative power exists, and most areas of the prerogative will have received judicial recognition at one time or another, it is not definitive. Finally, collapsing the distinction between the common law and the prerogative obscures the interaction between these two sources: as

[21] See eg *Council of Civil Service Unions v Minister for the Civil Service (CCSU)* [1985] AC 374, 407 (HL); *R v Criminal Injuries Compensation Board, ex p Lain* [1967] 2 QB 864, 874.

[22] Goldsworthy (n 6) ch 2.

[23] *R v Secretary of State for the Home Department, ex p Northumbria Police Authority* [1989] QB 26, 56–58.

we will see, there is an interesting story to tell about the ways in which the common law has come to regulate the prerogative over the course of centuries. This story, of the steadily increasing control exercised over the prerogative by the judges, will form the final parts of this section. As Colin Munro puts it, '[s]trictly speaking, the prerogatives are recognised, rather than created, by the common law, for their source is in custom'.[24]

The earliest type of control exercised over the prerogative by the courts was the judges' insistence on their right to determine whether a purported exercise of the prerogative was actually validated by it, a form of review we might style *jurisdictional review*. That the courts would possess such a power seems obvious to us now, but it could have been otherwise: the institution that produced the instrument (the Crown, in this instance) could have taken it upon itself to decide the validity of that instrument, and the courts could have then accepted that decision as definitive. Looking back at Figure 4.1, the institution empowered by the prerogative would then have been the institution that was competent to decide whether its instruments fell within its reach. Such constitutional self-policing is not unprecedented; it is, after all, the common law courts that decide if their own actions fall within the scope of the common law. In the area of the prerogative, however, the institution that produces a legal instrument purportedly empowered by the prerogative is distinct from the institution that tests whether that instrument is validated by that source.

The entitlement of the court to undertake this form of supervision is commonly tied to a pair of seventeenth century cases decided by Sir Edward Coke. In *Prohibitions del Roy*, Coke asserted that the king was not competent to decide disputes over law; law was a form of artificial reasoning and legal questions were ones which required the skills of a judge to answer.[25] Whilst in *The Case of Proclamations*, Coke held that the king only possessed the authority given to him by the law; the prerogative was a source of law, but a bounded source.[26] Taken together, these cases amounted

[24] Colin Munro, *Studies in Constitutional Law* (2nd edn, Butterworths 1999) 257.

[25] (1607) 12 Co Rep 64, 77 ER 1342.

[26] (1610) 12 Co Rep 74, 77 ER 1352.

to an assertion by the courts that it was for the judges, not the king, to determine the scope of the prerogative.[27]

The Case of Proclamations also held that the king could not use his prerogative power to alter common law or statute law.[28] The scope of the prerogative was limited by the rules produced by these other sources of law. Consequently, where there is a conflict between a legal rule drawn from the prerogative and a legal rule drawn from statutory law or common law, the purported exercise of the prerogative is invalid: once statute or common law has occupied an area of law, the prerogative must give way. So, when in *Attorney-General v De Keyser's Royal Hotel Ltd* the government sought to rely on the prerogative to avoid paying the compensation required by the Defence Act 1842 for property confiscated during wartime, the House of Lords held that the prerogative had been curtailed by the statute.[29] Before 1842, the state could have confiscated the hotel and determined the level of compensation due, but after the statute was passed the scope of the prerogative was limited, and could no longer be relied upon to validate this action. Relatedly, in *R (Miller) v Secretary of State for Exiting the European Union*, the Supreme Court held that the government could not rely on the prerogative to initiate the process of withdrawal from the European Union.[30] Whilst the initiation of withdrawal was a matter of foreign affairs, the enactment of the European Communities Act 1972 had limited the prerogative: the prerogative could not be used in a manner that would have effectively removed the rights granted by the 1972 Act and, more generally, could not be used in a way that would undermine the purpose of that statute.[31]

[27] Adam Tomkins provides a healthily sceptical view of Coke's motivation and the significance of these cases: Adam Tomkins, *Public Law* (Oxford University Press 2003) 54–58.

[28] Or, Coke added, the customs of the realm: (1610) 12 Co Rep 74, 75; 77 ER 1352, 1353.

[29] [1920] AC 508 (HL).

[30] [2017] UKSC 5, [2018] AC 61; Paul Craig, 'Miller, Structural Constitutional Review, and the Limits of Prerogative Power' [2017] Public Law 48.

[31] *Miller* (n 30) [60]–[68], [83]. This reasoning is more clearly articulated in the Divisional Court decision: [2016] EWHC 2768 (Admin).

The invocation of common law rights as a ground for restricting the prerogative is far rarer. This may be because of the rhetoric of the two sources: both common law and the prerogative are normally presented as having existed since time immemorial, so the notion of there being an undiscovered conflict between the two is harder to entertain. Rather than expressing the relationship as one of conflict, the courts tend to present the identification of the extent of the prerogative as being conditioned by the presence of the common law. In *Burmah Oil Co Ltd v Lord Advocate*, the common law was taken to require the UK government to pay compensation for oil facilities destroyed by British troops acting under the prerogative during the Second World War.[32] Whilst a similar decision was reached in *De Keyser* by holding that a statute requiring compensation displaced the prerogative, in *Burmah Oil* the common law right to compensation was presented as complementing the prerogative, shaping its operation.[33] But once we move beyond the rhetoric and recognise that common law (and, indeed, prerogative) can develop over time, it is possible that the two might come into conflict and the hierarchy rule articulated in *The Case of Proclamations* might need to be deployed. In *Cherry v Advocate General for Scotland*, the Supreme Court relied upon the emerging doctrine of common law constitutional principles to shape the prerogative power to prorogue Parliament.[34] Parliament is often prorogued (suspended) for a few days before a new parliamentary session commences. The power to prorogue is part of the prerogative, and the monarch exercises this power on the advice of her prime minister. However, when the prime minister, Boris Johnson, attempted to suspend Parliament for an unusually long period of time, the Supreme Court found this to be unlawful: the prerogative did not grant the prime minister this power. The common law principles of parliamentary sovereignty

[32] [1965] AC 75 (HL).

[33] The decision in *Burmah Oil* was reversed by statute: see War Damage Act 1965.

[34] [2019] UKSC 41, [2020] AC 373. This case was heard alongside and is sometimes referred to as *R (Miller) v Prime Minister*. On this case see Stefan Theil, 'Unconstitutional Prorogation of Parliament' [2020] Public Law 529 and Paul Craig, 'The Supreme Court, Prorogation, and Constitutional Principle' [2020] Public Law 248.

(which the court seems to have understood as Parliament's broad capacity to make law) and parliamentary accountability shaped the prerogative power to prorogue. Allowing Johnson to suspend Parliament for a prolonged period of time would prevent that institution from undertaking its constitutional roles, as identified by the common law. It seems, then, that the prerogative gives way to common law, just as it gives way to statute.

The type of judicial regulation of the prerogative discussed in previous paragraphs is quite constrained: the court is merely seeking to determine if a given instrument did, indeed, fall within the reach of the source that purportedly validated it. A further form of judicial regulation focuses on the instrument itself: the instrument may fall within the validating source, but it might yet be subject to challenge because of its contents or the manner in which it was produced. We might style this *substantive review*. In *Council of Civil Service Unions v Minister for the Civil Service* (*CCSU*), the House of Lords concluded that the exercise of a prerogative power can be reviewed on much the same terms as the exercise of a statutory power.[35] This enabled the judges to review the process by which the decision to exercise the prerogative was made, testing whether that decision had been reached in a procedurally fair manner, and to review the contents of the decision, checking that it was not an unreasonable exercise of that power.[36] In the *CCSU* case, the House of Lords divided the prerogative into those areas that were justiciable, that would be subject to review, and those that were non-justiciable, that the court could not review. But since the decision in *CCSU*, the non-reviewable part of the prerogative has shrunk, with the courts willing to test the reasonableness of formerly non-justiciable matters such as the decision not to renew a passport[37] and the decision not to grant a

[35] [1985] AC 374 (HL). There were traces of a willingness to review the exercise of the prerogative in earlier cases. See eg *Re Petition of Right* [1915] 3 KB 649; *The Zamora* [1916] 2 AC 77; *Ex p Lain* (n 21).

[36] That what is being reviewed is a prerogative power rather than a statutory power may affect how the court tests the reasonableness of the decision: *R (Sandiford) v Secretary of State for Foreign and Commonwealth Affairs* [2014] UKSC 44, [2014] WLR 2967 [60]–[66]. See also *CCSU* (n 21) 418 (Lord Diplock).

[37] *R v Secretary of State for Foreign and Commonwealth Affairs, ex p Everett* [1989] QB 811.

pardon.[38] With some exceptions in the area of foreign affairs, it seems that most legal acts undertaken under the prerogative can now be reviewed.[39]

There is one final form of regulation that the courts have exercised over the prerogative, and it is, perhaps, the most controversial. In a few cases, the courts have taken it upon themselves to decide what the scope of that legal source *ought* to be and to reshape it to match this ideal, rather than confining themselves to determining what the scope of that source *is*. We might style this *scope review*. The line between jurisdictional review and scope review is a fine one, but important. In cases such as *Proclamations* and *De Keyser*, the court did not assert the right to determine whether or not the existence of the prerogative was desirable; instead, the judges sought to identify its pre-existing boundaries and determine if the legal instrument produced was within the scope of that source. In contrast, when the court seeks to determine the powers it would be desirable for the prerogative to confer, it asserts the right to tailor the legal sources of the constitution, determining the powers it would be good for the executive to possess. The judicial tailoring of the prerogative could either expand its scope, giving additional powers to the executive, or reduce its reach, removing from the executive powers it would have otherwise enjoyed.

It might be thought unlikely that the courts would be willing to expand the prerogative. For many years, the prerogative was regarded as something of an historical anachronism. Dicey's description of it as the 'residue of discretionary or arbitrary authority' left in the hands of the Crown, gives the impression that the prerogative is a steadily diminishing legal source.[40] As Tom Poole argues, Dicey's language suggests he was less than comfortable with the continued existence of the prerogative; seeing it as an anachronism, rather than as a part of a modern, democratic,

[38] *R v Secretary of State for the Home Department, ex p Bentley* [1994] QB 349.

[39] In *Cherry* (n 34), the justiciability question was dodged, with the Supreme Court conflating the question of the reasonableness of the exercise of the prerogative with the question of its scope. On the expansion of review of the prerogative in foreign affairs see Ewan Smith, 'Is Foreign Policy Special?' (2021) Oxford Journal of Legal Studies (forthcoming).

[40] Dicey (n 17) 242.

constitution.[41] Allied with this view, in *BBC v Johns (Inspector of Taxes)*, Lord Justice Diplock, as he then was, confidently asserted that it was '350 years and a civil war too late for the Queen's courts to broaden the prerogative'.[42] But in *R v Secretary of State for the Home Department, ex p Northumbria Police Authority*, the Court of Appeal appeared to do exactly that.[43] The *Northumbria* case turned on the question of who could supply plastic bullets and CS gas for policing purposes. The Police Act 1964 empowered local police authorities to provide the vehicles, apparatus, and so forth required to undertake policing in their regions. The Home Secretary argued that he, too, could supply items to the local police force, whether or not the police authority wanted them supplied; so, even though the Northumbria Police Authority did not want plastic bullets and CS gas used in their region, the Home Secretary, using the prerogative, could set aside their concerns and provide these items. The Court of Appeal held that the supply of these materials fell within the prerogative power to keep the peace, and, moreover, this prerogative power had not been displaced by the statute. The Police Act 1964 had created a second, lawful, means by which these items could be supplied, leaving the pre-existing prerogative power untouched. *Northumbria* seems different in tone from earlier cases on the prerogative.[44] The court had at least two opportunities to take a restrictive view of the prerogative.[45] It could have concluded that the principle in *De Keyser* applied, and that once Parliament had created a statutory way of doing a thing, the prerogative power could no longer be relied upon. Or, more robustly still, it could have decided that the prerogative power to keep the peace did not extend to plastic bullets and CS gas; after all, the supply of those items could certainly not

[41] Thomas Poole, 'The Strange Death of Prerogative in England' (2018) 43(2) University of Western Australia Law Review 42, 47.

[42] [1965] Ch 32, 79. Whilst in *Burmah Oil* (n 32) 101, the prerogative was described as a 'relic of a past age'.

[43] [1989] QB 26.

[44] Possibly because of *CCSU* (n 21). As Poole puts it, that case served to 'normalise' the prerogative, subjecting it to similar forms of legal scrutiny as statutory powers: Poole (n 41) 58.

[45] See the powerful critique of the case by AW Bradley, 'Police Powers and the Prerogative' [1988] Public Law 298.

have been undertaken by a mediaeval monarch. In *Northumbria*, the Court effectively decided that it was desirable that the Home Secretary possess the power to circumvent local police authorities and then adapted its understanding of the scope of the prerogative to fit this conclusion. Given that prerogative powers are often expressed in very broad terms (such as the power to keep the peace, conduct foreign affairs, and to act as the 'fount of justice'), if the court decides to take an expansive view of the prerogative it will often be possible to do so by interpreting these old, broad, prerogative powers as encompassing the new activity.

Courts can also narrow the prerogative. Until recently it would have been hard to point to a case in which a court has explicitly decided that an old prerogative power has become unsuitable and has declined to allow the Crown to rely upon it, but the case of *Miller*, discussed earlier in this section, might provide such an example. One line of reasoning in the majority judgment was orthodox, turning on the relationship between prerogative and statute. But a second line of reasoning was more surprising. The majority contended that major changes to the UK constitution required parliamentary legislation.[46] Whilst the judges presented this proposition as 'the ordinary application of basic concepts of constitutional law', this was a novel argument: never before had a court held that the prerogative could not be used to bring about a major constitutional change. Before *Miller*, the constitutional implications of the exercise of the prerogative were beyond the province of the courts. If the Crown possessed a prerogative power, if it had not been abrogated by statute or, perhaps, the development of the common law, and if its exercise conformed to the principles of judicial review, the courts were required to accept the act as a valid exercise of that power. But *Miller* reduced the scope of the prerogative: in future, the Crown will not be able to rely on the prerogative if its exercise would have significant constitutional implications.

[46] *Miller* (n 30) [82].

4.4 THE PRIVILEGES OF PARLIAMENT

Each House of Parliament possesses its own set of rights, powers, and immunities. These constitute the *lex parliamentaria* and are to be found in the customs and resolutions of the Houses, and the rulings of the Speakers.[47] In modern times, *lex parliamentaria* is more commonly labelled the 'privileges' of the Commons and Lords. The classic statement of privilege is found in Article 9 of the Bill of Rights 1689: 'That the freedom of speech and debates or proceedings in Parliament ought not to be impeached or questioned in any court or place out of Parliament.'

Article 9 encapsulates two of the most important aspects of privilege: the freedom of speech for statements made in the course of parliamentary proceedings and the protection of the processes of the chambers of Parliament from review by the courts. The first of these, the right to freedom of speech, serves to protect members of the Commons and Lords from litigation based on speeches undertaken in the course of parliamentary proceedings. Perhaps the most important aspect of this is that legislators cannot be sued for defamation based on speeches made in Parliament,[48] but privilege also extends to other aspects of legal regulation of speech, protecting parliamentarians from prosecution for contempt of court[49] and, probably, from speech-related offences such as incitement to racial hatred. The second element of Article 9 extends to the running of Parliament, which encompasses both the treatment of parliamentarians and the production of legislation. The courts cannot review the regulation or disciplining of legislators by the House authorities. So, when the Speaker refused to allow a member of Sinn Fein access to parliamentary expenses and other facilities on the basis that the MP had declined to take

[47] On whether these rules should be considered law see David Howarth, 'Is the *Lex Parliamentaria* Really Law? The House of Commons as a Legal System' in Paul Evans (ed), *Essays on the History of Parliamentary Procedure: In Honour of Thomas Erskine May* (Hart Publishing 2017).

[48] *Church of Scientology of California v Johnson-Smith* [1972] 1 QB 522, 529–30.

[49] Joint Committee on Parliamentary Privilege, *Parliamentary Privilege: Report of Session 2013–14* (2013–14, HL 30, HC 100) paras 158–60.

up his seat, the court was not able to review this decision.[50] And if the Commons or Lords expel one of their number, applying the most severe sanction available to the chambers in the modern constitution, the excluded parliamentarian could not challenge the decision in the courts.[51] Privilege also extends to the manner in which legislation is produced; the internal workings of the chambers are determined by the Commons and Lords themselves. When, in *British Railways Board v Pickin*, a litigant sought to argue that a statute should be disregarded because it was obtained by fraud, his action was dismissed for this reason: because of privilege, the court could not examine the processes leading to the enactment of the statute.[52]

The significance of Article 9 of the Bill of Rights to the law of privilege raises a doubt about privilege as a non-derived legal source. After all, the Bill of Rights is a statute, and if privilege really is a non-derived source, it cannot be grounded in statute. The question of whether Article 9 of the Bill of Rights supplanted privilege or merely provides a statutory articulation of privilege is contested. In *Re Parliamentary Privilege Act 1770*, the Privy Council presented the Bill of Rights as a 'reassertion' of privilege,[53] but in his dissenting judgment, published many years later, Lord Denning contended that the Bill of Rights had placed this aspect of privilege on a separate statutory footing.[54] In practical terms, the characterisation of the Bill of Rights has little real significance; whether it restates or establishes the protections accorded to Parliament is largely irrelevant to the question of how those protections should be interpreted. But if Denning is

[50] *Re McGuiness's Application* [1997] NIQB 2. Sinn Fein MPs refuse to take seats in the Commons because to do so they are required to swear allegiance to the Crown. The House of Commons subsequently decided that non-sitting MPs could access many of the facilities of the Commons, but could not draw a salary: House of Commons, Journals of the House of Commons (vol 258, 2001–02) 274. See further House of Commons Library, *The Parliamentary Oath* Briefing Paper No CBP7515 (26 February 2016).

[51] Josh Chafetz, *Democracy's Privileged Few: Legislative Privilege and Democratic Norms in the British and American Constitutions* (Yale University Press 2007) 155–58.

[52] [1974] AC 765 (HL).

[53] [1958] AC 331. See also Blackstone (n 6) bk 1 ch 2 para 5.

[54] Lord Denning, 'The *Strauss* Case' [1985] Public Law 80.

correct, the reach of privilege as a legal source is far narrower than is often assumed; most of the case law that presents itself as interpreting and delineating privilege is, instead, an exercise in statutory interpretation.

Even so, Article 9 does not cover the whole of privilege, and elements of the non-derived source persist.[55] For instance, Article 9 does not purport to empower the Commons and Lords to produce the rules that regulate their processes and the regulation of their members; the standing orders of the Houses and the Speakers' rulings do not derive their authority from the Bill of Rights. Similarly, the capacity of the Commons and Lords to hold individuals in breach of privilege remains an exercise of an inherent power.[56] And finally, the courts have recognised that there may be areas beyond Article 9 over which the Commons and Lords enjoy exclusive competence under privilege, because of the inappropriateness of judicial intervention.[57]

Like the prerogative, privilege is distinct from common law, yet operates in a complicated, and sometimes tense, relationship with it.[58] Whereas the entitlement of the courts to determine the boundaries of the prerogative was settled relatively early on, their entitlement to determine the boundaries of privilege remained a matter of dispute until very recently. The classic case on the relationship between the courts and the Commons over the boundaries of privilege is *Stockdale v Hansard*.[59] In that case, a committee of the Commons had ordered the publication of a report by the Inspector of Prisons, in which the Inspector had described a book published by Stockdale as 'obscene'. Had this accusation been made in the course of a debate in the Commons, it would have unarguably been privileged, but, Stockdale argued, the publication of the report did not constitute part of a 'proceeding in Parliament' in the words of Article 9, and so fell outside of

[55] Thomas Erskine May, *Erskine May's Treatise on the Law, Privileges, Proceedings and Usage of Parliament* (David Natzler and others (eds), 25th edn, LexisNexis 2019) para 12.1 https://erskinemay.parliament.uk/.

[56] Joint Committee on Parliamentary Privilege (n 49) ch 3.

[57] *Prebble v Television New Zealand Ltd* [1995] 1 AC 321 (PC) 332; *Re McGuiness's Application* (n 50); *R v Chaytor* [2010] UKSC 52, [2011] 1 AC 684.

[58] Chafetz (n 51) ch 1; Goldsworthy (n 6) 26, 32-35.

[59] (1839) 9 Ad & Ell 96, 112 ER 1112.

its protection. Stockdale sued Hansard, the publisher, for libel. Rather than defend the case on the merits, on which he might well have won, Hansard was ordered by the Commons to claim privilege: this was argued to be a matter that fell within the jurisdiction of the Commons, on which the court should not adjudicate.[60] The Court of the Queen's Bench disagreed, finding that the issue fell outside privilege and, as the substance of the litigation was not contested, found for Stockdale.[61] The Commons then imprisoned the two officials of the court who had been tasked with enforcing the judgment, on the basis that they were guilty of breach of privilege.[62] Having promised not to enforce the court orders against Hansard, the luckless officials were released, but then imprisoned by the court for refusing to carry out the court's instructions.[63] The dispute was ended by the enactment of the Parliamentary Papers Act 1840, which enabled the speakers and clerks of the Houses to stop any legal action relating to documents published by order of the Commons or Lords. Whilst the courts rejected the assessment of the boundaries of privilege advanced by the Commons, they did not question Parliament's capacity to restrict the reach of libel through a statute.

Stockdale provides a colourful example of the consequences of two constitutional institutions asserting jurisdiction over a single question.[64] Both the Commons and the courts asserted the right to determine the scope of privilege and, as a corollary of that right, each asserted that the other was under a legal duty to accept that determination. During the immediate period surrounding *Stockdale*, up to the 1840 Act, this was destabilising.

[60] House of Commons, *Journals of the House of Commons* (vol 92, 1837) 418.

[61] *Stockdale* (n 59).

[62] In the *Case of the Sheriff of Middlesex* (1840) 11 Ad & El 273, 113 ER 419, the court declined to uphold a petition for *habeas corpus* on the basis it could not review the Commons' decisions on breaches of privilege.

[63] Munro (n 24) 236–37.

[64] If this is a matter of statutory interpretation, the question remains, although reconfigured: does the court or the Commons have jurisdiction to interpret Article 9? See *Bradlaugh v Gossett* (1884) 12 QBD 271, in which the court accepted that interpretation of the Parliamentary Oaths Act 1866 fell within the jurisdiction of the Commons. If the Commons possesses the jurisdiction to authoritatively interpret statutes, this jurisdiction must be located within *lex parliamentaria*. See Howarth (n 47) 315.

The disagreement between the Commons and the courts produced a constitutional crisis that could not be resolved through the adjudicative processes of the constitution because it was the constitution's adjudicative processes that were in dispute; it could only be answered by legislation. After *Stockdale*, the wider disagreement between the courts and the Commons was left unresolved for many years. Rather than seeking to clarify the relationship between the courts and Commons, the issue was put to one side: each institution maintained its position, but each avoided pushing the matter to a conclusion. Although this lack of clarity may be regretted by some scholars, as a practical matter it allowed a potentially costly dispute to be shelved, and may have encouraged each side of the dispute to treat the other with cautious respect, aware of the risks of any attempt to win the battle.

Sometimes, delaying the resolution of a constitutional dispute can make its eventual resolution easier. By the time the court heard *R v Chaytor*, the attitude of the Commons had shifted.[65] *Chaytor* was a case that arose out of the 2009 expenses scandal, when a large amount of confidential information relating to MPs' expenses claims was made public. Much of this was embarrassing, but in a few cases criminal conduct was exposed: Chaytor had been claiming expenses for paying a mortgage that had already been paid and, unsurprisingly, quickly found himself charged with false accounting under the Theft Act 1968. In an effort to avoid prosecution, Chaytor argued that the matter fell within privilege: the conduct of the expenses scheme by the Commons fell within Article 9 and, if this was not accepted, the question of the scope of privilege nevertheless fell within the exclusive jurisdiction of the Commons. The Supreme Court declined to accept that submitting dishonest expenses claims fell within the reach of privilege; the expenses system was not part of the 'proceedings in Parliament'. Furthermore, the exclusive competence of the Commons did not extend to criminal behaviour beyond that covered by Article 9; ordinary criminality within Parliament was a matter for the police, courts, and, as Chaytor later discovered,

[65] *Chaytor* (n 57); Eve Samson, 'Privilege: The Unfolding Debate with the Courts' in Paul Evans (ed), *Essays on the History of Parliamentary Procedure: In Honour of Thomas Erskine May* (Hart Publishing 2017) 300–302.

the prisons. In *Chaytor* there was no attempt by the Commons, as there had been in *Stockdale*, to assert the right to determine the boundaries of privilege. Indeed, the Clerk of Parliaments, with the approval of the Committee for Privileges, wrote to one of the defendants in *Chaytor* stating the opposite: decisions about what constituted 'proceedings in Parliament' was a matter for the courts, not the Commons or the Lords.[66] That the Commons and the Lords were content to leave the issue to the courts suggests that, some 160 years after *Stockdale*, the controversy in that case may have come to a close.

Whilst the courts have consistently asserted the right to determine the scope of privilege, it is harder to see occasions in which judges have sought to review the substance of an exercise of privilege, and, indeed, there have been many occasions in which judges have explicitly rejected such jurisdiction. There is no equivalent to the *CCSU* case to be found in the law on privilege. However, there are instances where the court has reviewed the process by which statutes have been produced, placing weight on the thoroughness or accessibility of the debates when deciding how to respond to those statutes. This can be seen as a form of review of decisions made by the Commons and Lords about the process of legislation, matters that would normally be thought to fall within privilege. So, for example, in *R (Animal Defenders International) v Secretary of State for Culture, Media and Sport*, the House of Lords was asked to consider whether the restrictions placed on political advertising by the Communications Act 2003 could be reconciled with the right to freedom of expression contained within the Human Rights Act 1998.[67] If the two statutes were in conflict, the House of Lords could have issued a declaration of incompatibility under section 4 of the Human Rights Act. This would not have affected the validity of the Communications Act—it would still have been legally valid—but when courts have issued

[66] *Chaytor* (n 57) [15]; Joint Committee on Parliamentary Privilege (n 49) para 31.

[67] [2008] UKHL 15, [2008] AC 1312. See also *R (Williamson) v Secretary of State for Education and Employment* [2005] UKHL 15, [2005] 2 AC 246 [51]; *R (HS2 Action Alliance Ltd) v Secretary of State for Transport* [2014] UKSC 3, [2014] 1 WLR 324; Aileen Kavanagh, 'Proportionality and Parliamentary Debates: Exploring Some Forbidden Territory' (2014) 34 Oxford Journal of Legal Studies 443.

section 4 declarations in other cases; the relevant legislation has always been modified by Parliament to make it compliant with the Human Rights Act. The House of Lords concluded that the Communications Act was compatible, and so no declaration was issued, but part of their decision involved scrutinising the manner in which the Communications Act had been enacted. Lord Bingham, delivering the leading judgment, noted the attention paid by Parliament to the jurisprudence of the European Court of Human Rights, and the close scrutiny of the bill undertaken by various committees of the Houses, in particular by the Joint Committee on Human Rights, which had concluded that the decision to introduce the restrictions in the Communication Act did not show a lack of concern for human rights and was, in the circumstances, legitimate.[68] Partly because of the strength of the legislative process adopted by Parliament, Lord Bingham concluded that weight must be given to Parliament's decision to enact the Communications Act; Parliament was aware of the implications that the Communications Act had for the rights found in the Human Rights Act, but had concluded that the integrity of democracy required these constraints.[69] This examination of Parliament's law-making processes caused little controversy at the time as, after all, this worked to the benefit of Parliament, enabling the judges to avoid calling for a change to the statute, but there is an uncomfortable implication to be drawn from *Animal Defenders International*. As Aileen Kavanagh argues, if the strength of Parliament's legislative processes can be invoked to defend a statute, where those processes are weak this argument cannot be made, and, worse still, this could be debated in court: the claim that Parliament has fully engaged with the human rights implications of a bill could be disputed.[70] This case, along with others that have applied similar scrutiny to the internal workings of

[68] *Animal Defenders International* (n 67) [20] (Lord Bingham), citing Joint Committee on Human Rights, *Fourth Report of Session 2002–03* (10 February 2003, HL 50, HC 397) para 41.

[69] *Animal Defenders International* (n 67) [33] (Lord Bingham).

[70] Kavanagh (n 67) 466. The hazard is noted in *Office of Government Commerce v Information Commissioner* [2008] EWHC 737 (Admin) [58]–[59]. See also *Huang v Secretary of State for the Home Department* [2007] UKHL 11, [2007] 2 AC 167 [17].

Parliament, stands in stark contrast with *Pickin*, and indicates a shift in the judges' attitudes towards privilege over the last forty years.

Finally, do the courts ever take it upon themselves to decide what the scope of privilege ought to be, rather than confining themselves to identifying the existing boundaries of that source of law? Once again, in contrast to the treatment of the prerogative in *Miller*, it is hard to point to clear instances in which the courts have undertaken this role, but in cases in which the limits of privilege are in dispute, such as *Chaytor*, the court frequently considers the purpose of privilege, and seeks to draw the boundaries in a way that enables privilege to serve its role as a protector of Parliament's operation whilst limiting other legal rights as little as possible. Similarly, in *Cherry* the Supreme Court was quick to dismiss the prime minister's argument that the effect of the decision to prorogue Parliament was a proceeding in Parliament and so beyond the jurisdiction of the court: the judges concluded that, as prorogation brought the functioning of Parliament to an end, it should not be considered to fall within privilege. Here, the judges' understanding of the point of privilege (which is to enable Parliament to undertake its constitutional role) was relied upon to delineate the scope of privilege.

4.5 CONCLUSION

As we have seen, when approaching a non-derivative source of law there are at least three forms of review the judges might assert over the source and the legal instruments it validates. First, there is *jurisdictional review*. The courts claim to determine whether a given legal act falls within the reach of a legal source and, as a corollary of this, a party before the court may assert that an instrument is legally invalid because it falls outside the jurisdiction conferred by the source. Secondly, there is *substantive review*. The court might review the process by which the instrument was produced and the reasonableness (or some similar standard) of its contents. In those cases, the instrument falls within the jurisdiction conferred by the source, but it is still subject to challenge. Finally, there is *scope review*. The court might assert the right to determine where the boundaries of the legal source *should* lie, the judges taking it upon themselves to decide where it would be useful for the boundaries of these sources to be drawn. In practice, it will be hard to distinguish the first and the third of these activities.

Looking back over this chapter, we can see that the court exercised jurisdictional review in *The Case of Proclamations* for prerogative and in *Stockdale* for privilege. Substantive review was clearly established for the prerogative in *CCSU*, and traces of this type of review can be detected in the context of privilege, most arguably in the *Animal Defenders International* case. However, substantive review in the context of privilege has been, so far, only indirect. The courts have reviewed the merits of the legislative processes adopted by the Commons and Lords, but only in the context of assessing the merits of another legal instrument: statute. Scope review in the context of the prerogative was explicit in *Miller* and was arguably applied to privilege in *Chaytor* and *Cherry*.

Returning to Figure 4.1, we can supplement it as follows:

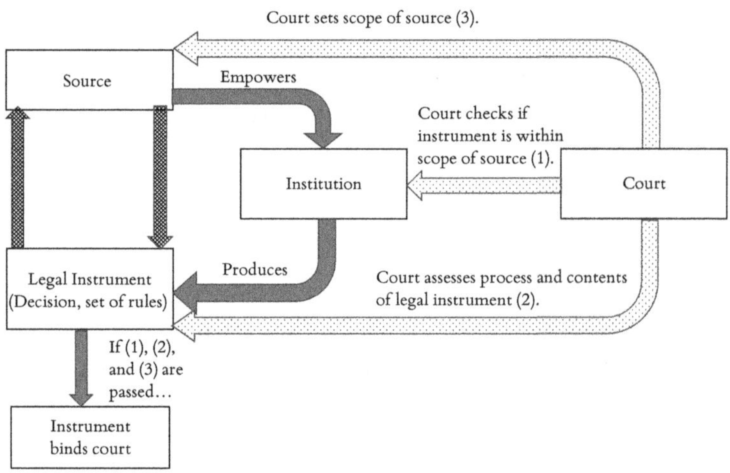

Figure 4.2 Sources, Institutions, Instruments, and Courts

The rules that govern the relationship of the courts to these sources are found in the common law. Whilst statutes can override or curtail common law, prerogative, or privilege, there are no statutory rules that instruct the courts how to identify or interpret prerogative or privilege, or which tell the courts how to resolve conflicts between the sources. When the courts apply a legal instrument created under the prerogative or privilege, they are applying a rule from that legal source; the common law does not purport to validate this legal act. But the rules surrounding that instrument are almost entirely found in the common law.[71] The common law acts as a web around these sources, drawing them into a single legal order.

[71] The exception is where the instrument produced under the prerogative or privilege includes rules that specify the instrument's own interpretation or place in the legal hierarchy. But even then, these rules depend on the common law identifying them as within the scope of the empowering source.

5

THE LEGAL CONSTITUTION: STATUTES

In the last two chapters we examined the ways in which the courts engage with the different legal sources of the UK constitution and the different legal orders through which those sources are identified and rendered effective. As we have seen, the executive, the courts, the Commons, and the Lords (as distinct constitutional institutions) possess their own autonomous power to create law. Parliament also possesses such a law-making power through the production of statutes. This capacity is often presented as established by parliamentary sovereignty: one of the most discussed, and perhaps most opaque, rules of the UK constitution. This chapter will provide a sceptical account of that rule. Whilst sovereignty may have been a defining, even *the* defining, feature of Dicey's constitution, the Old Constitution, it is no longer a feature of the New Constitution. The first part of this chapter will examine the nature of sovereignty within the Old Constitution, locating this rule within a broader account of the sources and orders of the UK constitution. The second part of the chapter documents the death of sovereignty in the *Factortame* case. Finally, this chapter assesses the consequent reconfiguration of the relationship between the courts and Parliament, a reconfiguration that has yet to reach a settled position. It will be argued that, just like prerogative and parliamentary privilege, the courts have gradually expanded their control over statutes; moving from a limited claim to identify the existence of statutes, jurisdictional review, through to a more radical claim to set the boundaries of the power to create statutes, scope review, and to review their contents, substantive review.

The United Kingdom Constitution. N. W. Barber, Oxford University Press. © Nick Barber 2021.
DOI: 10.1093/oso/9780198852315.003.0005

5.1 PARLIAMENTARY SOVEREIGNTY IN THE OLD CONSTITUTION

Much has been written about parliamentary sovereignty and much about parliamentary sovereignty is open to debate. Despite this, before 1991 there was broad agreement about its content. Parliamentary sovereignty was a legal rule that specified the legal force of statutes and, as a result of this, the capacity of Parliament to make law. The rule could be expressed in deceptively simple terms:

Whatever the Queen-in-Parliament enacts as a statute is law.[1]

When the two houses of Parliament, the Commons and Lords, approved a bill, and it had received royal assent, it became law. A number of inferences about the legal status of statutes could be drawn from this rule.

First, no institution within the constitution had the capacity to declare a statute beyond the power of Parliament. Once the court, or anyone else operating within the legal order, had concluded that a document was a statute, it was obliged to treat that document as legally binding, unless it had been repealed by a later Act. The good sense of the statute or the manner in which it had been produced was irrelevant.[2]

Secondly, when there was a conflict between an older and a newer statute, the newer statute took precedence: conflicting rules of the earlier statute were impliedly repealed.[3] Implied

[1] See eg AV Dicey, *An Introduction to the Law of the Constitution* (10th edn, Macmillan 1959) 39–40; Jeffrey Goldsworthy, *The Sovereignty of Parliament: History and Philosophy* (Oxford University Press 1999) ch 2; Peter Oliver, *The Constitution of Independence: The Development of Constitutional Theory in Australia, Canada, and New Zealand* (Oxford University Press 2005) chs 2–4.

[2] See eg *Edinburgh and Dalkeith Railway v Wauchope* (1842) 8 Cl & Fin 710 (HL); *Pickin v British Railways Board* [1974] AC 765, 789 (HL); *Duport Steels Ltd v Sirs* [1980] 1 WLR 142 (HL).

[3] See eg *Ellen Street Estates Ltd v Minister of Health* [1934] 1 KB 590 (KB). For discussion see Alison L Young, *Parliamentary Sovereignty and the Human Rights Act* (Hart Publishing 2009) ch 2. Goldsworthy challenges the view that implied repeal is an aspect of sovereignty: Jeffrey Goldsworthy, *The Sovereignty of Parliament: History and Philosophy* (Oxford University Press 2001) 14–15; Jeffrey Goldsworthy, *Parliamentary Sovereignty: Contemporary Debates* (Cambridge University Press 2010) 179–82.

repeal was an important aspect of sovereignty: when Parliament legislated, its statute was always valid law; no legal challenges could be made at the point of enactment, even if these challenges were grounded in other statutes.

A third inference could also be drawn: the court's inability to rule that a statute was beyond the power of Parliament, coupled with the rule of implied repeal, entailed that Parliament could not effectively impose substantive limits on itself.[4] A statute that purported to deny Parliament the power to legislate in a specified area would be impliedly repealed (or could be expressly repealed) by any later statute on the same subject matter.[5]

A number of debates swirled around this simple rule. Perhaps the most important of these was between the 'orthodox' view of sovereignty, advanced by a group led by Sir William Wade, and the 'manner and form' view of sovereignty, advanced by R. F. V. Heuston.[6] Both Wade and Heuston would have agreed with the account of parliamentary sovereignty advanced in the preceding paragraphs. They disagreed, however, over the capacity of the legislature effectively to limit its future incarnations by redefining the entity that courts should treat as constituting Parliament. Heuston contended that Parliament could specify what would, in future, count as 'Parliament'.[7] It could introduce 'manner and form' restrictions, requiring that, perhaps, a future measure would require the support of two-thirds of the Commons before becoming law, or the support of a majority of the population in a referendum. It remained the case that whatever Parliament enacted was law, but now 'Parliament' was defined as something more than just a simple majority vote in the Commons and Lords (coupled with the assent of the monarch). For Heuston, whilst Parliament could not place substantive limits

[4] *Godden v Hales* (1686) 11 St Tr 1165 (KB). [5] Dicey (n 1) 67–68.

[6] RFV Heuston, *Essays in Constitutional Law* (2nd edn, Stevens 1964) ch 1. Similar arguments have been advanced by other scholars: Ivor Jennings, *The Law and the Constitution* (5th edn, University of London Press 1959) ch 4; Geoffrey Marshall, *Constitutional Theory* (Clarendon Press 1971) 41–43; RTE Latham, 'What is an Act of Parliament?' [1939] King's Counsel 152.

[7] Heuston (n 6) 9–16. Challenging the equation of procedural regulation and the definition of Parliament see Goldsworthy, *Contemporary Debates* (n 3) 160–66, 198–99.

on its future selves, it could determine the process by which these parliaments could change the law. And, of course, if sufficiently exacting, these procedural requirements would be practically equivalent to a substantive limit. Heuston, who came from an Irish Protestant background, was particularly concerned that Northern Ireland might be united with the Republic of Ireland without the consent of the Northern Ireland Parliament, a statutory requirement found in the (now repealed) section 1(2) of the Ireland Act 1949.[8] The manner and form account of sovereignty made it arguable that in the 1949 Act Parliament had redefined itself to include the Northern Ireland Parliament in decisions about unification. Wade, in contrast, argued that the rules by which statutes are identified are beyond the reach of Parliament. Although the 'manner and form' model could exist within a legal order, it was not, said Wade, found within the legal orders of the United Kingdom (UK).[9] If Parliament sought to redefine itself, this purported redefinition would be impliedly repealed the next time legislation was passed in the area. The courts, following the common law rules of identification, would see through the earlier statute that purported to redefine the legislature. Legal force would then be accorded to the enactments of Parliament as defined by the common law, and the supposed 'manner and form' restriction of the earlier act would be impliedly repealed.

The debate between the 'orthodox' and the 'manner and form' schools of sovereignty had a number of dimensions, but the key area of dispute was the status of the Parliament Acts 1911 and 1949. The Parliament Act 1911 created a mechanism whereby statutes could be passed without the consent of the House of Lords. The Lords could delay bills for two years, spread over three sessions, but if the Commons persevered, the bill would become a law. In 1947, the Commons sought to limit further the power of the Lords by reducing its capacity to delay bills: the limit was reduced from two years to one year, spread over two sessions rather than three. The House of Lords refused to give consent to this measure

[8] Heuston (n 6) 29; 'RVF Heuston', *Oxford Dictionary of National Biography* (Oxford University Press 2004). See now Northern Ireland Act 1998, s 1.

[9] William Wade, 'The Basis of Legal Sovereignty' [1955] Cambridge Law Journal 172, 175–76.

and, in the end, the 1911 Act was invoked to enable the enactment of the Parliament Act 1949.

The 'orthodox' and 'manner and form' schools offered different interpretations of the Parliament Acts. Supporters of the 'manner and form' model of sovereignty argued that this was a clear instance of Parliament altering the rules under which the courts identified legislation; the Queen-in-Parliament was still sovereign, but now, sometimes, the Commons and the Queen, without the Lords, constituted 'Parliament' for the purposes of the rule. Wade, in contrast, argued that the Parliament Act 1911 created a mechanism through which delegated legislation could be produced.[10] On this account, Parliament, through the 1911 Act, had granted the Commons and the Queen a limited power to create law. Unusually, there was a pay-off to this debate. If the legislation produced under the 1911 Act was delegated legislation, if the 'orthodox' school was correct, the courts could check that these enactments fell within the scope of the power granted by the 1911 Act. Furthermore, it was argued that the legislative power conferred by the 1911 Act did not include the power to alter that same statute; more precisely, that the delegated law-making power found in the 1911 Act could not be used to expand the scope of the power delegated. If all of these arguments held, the Parliament Act 1949 went beyond the scope of legislative power conferred by the 1911 Act on the Commons and the Queen, and the 1949 Act, and all the statutes passed under it, were invalid.[11]

In *R (Jackson) v Attorney General* supporters of foxhunting sought to challenge the restrictions placed on that activity by the Hunting Act 2004, a statute which was passed under the Parliament Act 1949.[12] The fox hunters ran the now fifty-year old argument over the validity of the 1949 Act: they argued that as the 1949 Act was outside the powers conferred by the 1911 Act,

[10] Wade (n 9) 193–94; see also Peter Jackson and Patricia Leopold, *O Hood Phillips and Jackson: Constitutional and Administrative Law* (8th edn, Sweet & Maxwell 2001) 79–81.

[11] O Hood Phillips, *Reform of the Constitution* (Chatto & Windus 1970) 18–19, 91–93; Graham Zellick, 'Is the Parliament Act *Ultra Vires*?' (1969) 119 New Law Journal 716.

[12] *R (Jackson) v Attorney General* [2005] UKHL 56, [2006] 1 AC 262.

the Hunting Act 2004, which relied on the 1949 Act, had not been validly enacted, and, as a result they were permitted to continue chasing foxes with dogs. Pragmatically, the chance of the fox hunters winning their case was slim. The political and legal consequences of declaring the 1949 Act invalid would have been profound. It was not only the Hunting Act 2004 that would have been affected: other statutes would also have been caught. In particular, a victory by the fox hunters would have invalidated the statute that lowered the homosexual age of consent from eighteen to sixteen and which also created a new sexual offence of abuse of position of trust.[13] Consequently, deciding that the 1949 Act was invalid would have had widespread implications for people's present and past criminal liabilities. In addition, the judges would have been aware that the Hunting Act had been foreshadowed in Labour's 1997 manifesto, which promised a free vote on the issue, and that it had been extensively debated both within and outside Parliament. In the UK, the outcome of court cases is rarely determined by raw political calculation, but the likely political implications of a case can shape the way the judges approach their task. In *Jackson*, the judges would have known that supporting the fox hunters' submissions would have run against the democratic processes of the constitution, overturning a decision made by the elected part of Parliament after extensive debate and consideration.[14] To win, the fox hunters would have had to persuade the judges that the law left the court little or no discretion in the matter; their case would have had to be overwhelming.

In the event, the fox hunters' case fell far short of this. None of the members of the House of Lords endorsed Wade's view that the statutes passed under the Parliament Acts were forms of delegated legislation, and, although the judges provided a number of different explanations for their decisions,[15] the 'manner and form' view that Parliament can redefine what counts as primary

[13] Sexual Offences (Amendment) Act 2000. The War Crimes Act 1991 and the European Parliamentary Elections Act 1999 would also have been affected.

[14] Although it may have been closer than it seemed: Lord Hope, *Lord Hope's Diaries: 1996–2009* (Avizandum Publishing 2018) 250–51.

[15] See the careful discussion of the case in Alison L Young 'Hunting Sovereignty: *Jackson v Attorney General*' [2006] Public Law 187.

legislation lies at the core of the judgment.[16] Legislation passed under the 1911 Act was not passed by a subordinate legislature; it was enacted by Parliament. As such, the legislative process established under the 1911 Act could be used to modify the process by which statutes were made. The 1949 Act was valid, the Hunting Act 2004 was valid, and the capacity of the hunters to chase foxes was legitimately restricted.

Even though it was decided in 2005, *Jackson* is a case rooted in the Old Constitution, directly concerned with the nature and content of parliamentary sovereignty. We can draw a number of important lessons about sovereignty from the decision.

First, it demonstrates that the courts possess the capacity to identify the existence of a statute: recalling Figure 4.2, the courts asserted jurisdictional control over statutes in *Jackson*. The question of whether a purported statute was indeed a statute fell to the courts. Whilst Parliament could legislate to create structures through which legislation was produced, the courts made the final determination whether an instrument before them was a statute.

Secondly, and relatedly, *Jackson* reveals the underlying nature of sovereignty. There is some dispute over the species of rule of which sovereignty is a member, with some arguing sovereignty is a special, even unique, type of rule.[17] But in *Jackson* the judges treated sovereignty as they would any other rule of the common law: faced with a dispute over its implications, they interpreted the rule, drawing on previous case law. It is occasionally argued that sovereignty cannot be a common law rule because the courts are not, legally, permitted to alter it; it imposes a duty on the courts, not a discretion. But a comparison can be drawn with the jurisdictional rules identifying the prerogative and privilege, discussed in Chapter 4. In *The Case of Proclamations* and *Stockdale v Hansard*, the courts developed common law rules to *identify* the existence of an exercise of the prerogative and to determine whether an action fell within privilege. They did not, at first, claim to be entitled to *shape* these sources or review the way in which institutions exercised their law-making powers. Sovereignty can be both a rule of

[16] For a different view see Richard Ekins, 'Acts of Parliament and the Parliament Acts' (2007) 123 Law Quarterly Review 91.

[17] Wade (n 9) 188.

the common law, developed and authoritatively clarified by the court where ambiguous, and yet also remain a rule that imposes a duty on the judge, a rule which she is not legally empowered to alter.[18]

Thirdly, *Jackson* demonstrates that, even under the Old Constitution, some forms of entrenchment were possible. A legal rule is entrenched when it is rendered legally more difficult to change than other rules generated from the same legal source. So, for example, if Parliament wanted to enact a bill of rights and protect it from change by future legislatures, it might specify that a two-thirds vote of the Commons is required before the bill of rights can be repealed. If Wade's understanding of sovereignty had been correct, such entrenchment would be futile; a future Parliament could repeal the bill of rights by simple majority, either expressly or by implication. After *Jackson*'s embrace of manner and form, the success of the entrenching statute would depend on the interpretation given to it by the courts. If the courts treated the entrenchment clause in the bill of rights as a form of substantive entrenchment, the clause, under the manner and form conception of sovereignty, would be ineffective: a future Parliament could, by ordinary legislation, expressly or impliedly repeal the clause. But if the courts treated the entrenching clause as redefining what constituted Parliament for the purposes of legislation in this area, the clause would be effective: a purported statute that sought to repeal the bill of rights would not, as a result of the entrenchment clause, be treated by the courts as a valid statute. As Alison Young argues, the manner and form conception of sovereignty effectively makes Parliament's capacity to bind itself dependent on the joint action of Parliament and the courts: Parliament can attempt to entrench, but the success of entrenchment will depend on the court's willingness to interpret the rule as redefining Parliament within a given area of law.[19] And there is the potential for surprises: the court could decide that some statutes redefine Parliament even if the enacting Parliament had not foreseen the possibility of entrenchment. Section 63A(3) of the Scotland Act 1998 states that it 'is declared that the Scottish

[18] Goldsworthy, *Contemporary Debates* (n 3) ch 2.

[19] Young (n 3) ch 7.

Parliament and the Scottish Government are not to be abolished except on the basis of a decision of the people of Scotland voting in a referendum'.[20] It is doubtful that Parliament intended this to be legally binding, but it is not impossible that a future Supreme Court, applying *Jackson*, might conclude it has this effect: for the abolition of the Scottish Parliament, the electorate of Scotland may have become part of the legislative process, and it is only once the Commons, Lords, Queen, *and* a referendum have supported its abolition that a statute will have been passed.[21]

5.1.1 Was Parliamentary Sovereignty Only Ever a Rule of English Law?

In Chapter 3, we examined the multiplicity of legal orders within the UK constitution. At the very least, Scots law and English law are distinct and, as a consequence, each must have their own rules identifying and regulating sources of law in the constitution. Whilst the two systems each have their own set of rules relating to privilege and the prerogative, the content of these rules is probably the same, and that they have a distinct identity in law is of limited interest.[22] The situation is different in respect of statutes, though, where there may be a significant difference between the two systems, which this section will consider. As we saw in Chapter 3, the Acts of Union between England and Scotland include provisions that purport to constrain the UK Parliament; in particular, the Acts explicitly protect the autonomy of the Scottish legal order. It is arguable that, as regards Scots law, the UK Parliament is a limited, non-sovereign, institution, constrained by

[20] The section was inserted by the Scotland Act 2016, partly in response to the Scottish independence referendum of 2014. A parallel provision can be found in the Government of Wales Act 2006, s A1. A similar requirement is found in the Northern Ireland Act 1998, s 1. See further ch 18.

[21] For a related argument see Harry Calvert, *Constitutional Law in Northern Ireland* (Stevens & Sons 1968) 29–33. In *Re McCord's Application for Judicial Review* [2016] NIQB 85, Maguire J left open the possibility that a special procedure would be required to amend s 1 of the Northern Ireland Act 1998.

[22] But see JDB Mitchell, *Constitutional Law* (2nd edn, W Green & Son 1968) 23–25; JDB Mitchell, 'The Royal Prerogative in Modern Scots Law' [1957] Public Law 304; Adam Tomkins, 'The Crown in Scots Law' in Aileen McHarg and Tom Mullen (eds), *Public Law in Scotland* (Avizandum Publishing 2006).

elements of the treaty and statutes that led to its creation.[23] This argument formed the core of the applicant's submission in the case of *MacCormick v Lord Advocate*.[24] John MacCormick argued that whilst Queen Elizabeth was Queen Elizabeth II of England, she was the first Queen Elizabeth of the UK as a whole, and so to style her Queen Elizabeth II was contrary to the Acts of Union. To succeed in his case, MacCormick would have had to persuade the court to invalidate or set aside a statute, the Royal Titles Act 1953, that gave assent to the Queen's choice of title.[25] Unsurprisingly, MacCormick's claim failed, not least because he struggled to demonstrate why the Acts of Union, even if binding on Parliament, should be interpreted as stopping the Queen choosing her own title. But in the course of his decision Lord Cooper, the Lord President, said:

> The principle of the unlimited sovereignty of Parliament is a distinctively English principle which has no counterpart in Scottish constitutional law. It derives its origin from Coke and Blackstone, and was widely popularised during the nineteenth century by Bagehot and Dicey, the latter having stated the doctrine in its classic form in his Law of the Constitution. Considering that the Union legislation extinguished the Parliaments of Scotland and England and replaced them by a new Parliament, I have difficulty in seeing why it should have been supposed that the new Parliament of Great Britain must inherit all the peculiar characteristics of the English Parliament but none of the Scottish Parliament, as if all that happened in 1707 was that Scottish

[23] In discussion of this area, the potential limits on the UK Parliament are sometimes presented as flowing from a treaty (the Treaty of Union 1706) or from the statutes passed by the English and Scottish Parliaments incorporating that treaty (the Union with Scotland Act 1707 and the Union with England Act 1707 respectively). There is not space to explore this distinction here, but given current judicial discussion of constitutional statutes, it is most likely a contemporary court would treat the incorporating statutes as the source of constraint, rather than the treaty.

[24] *MacCormick v Lord Advocate* 1953 SC 396. See also *Gibson v Lord Advocate* 1975 SC 136 and *Pringle, Petitioner* 1991 SLT 330; Chris Himsworth and Christine O'Neill, *Scotland's Constitution: Law and Practice* (Bloomsbury 2015) 135–38.

[25] For the context of the case see Colin Kidd, *Unions and Unionism* (Cambridge University Press 2008) ch 3. For the application of a similar argument in the context of Northern Ireland see Calvert (n 21) ch 1.

representatives were admitted to the Parliament of England. That is not what was done.[26]

There are a number of ways of interpreting the significance of *MacCormick*. First, we could take it at face value: perhaps Lord Cooper was right, and there are different rules relating to statutes in England and Scotland. If this were the case, the UK constitution would be characterised by a form of legal pluralism: a statute might be valid as a matter of English law, but invalid as a matter of Scots law. Given the question of validity would likely be decided by the Supreme Court, a tricky question of jurisdiction arises. If that court were to accept Cooper's argument, it would have to decide in which capacity it was hearing the case. Would the Supreme Court hear the case as an English, Scottish, or a UK court, or some combination of these, handing down a bifurcated judgment?[27] The tempting answer, that it would sit as a UK court, is problematic: the Supreme Court sits as a UK court when considering devolution issues, but this question, about the significance of the Acts of Union from 1707, is not a question about the devolution framework established in 1998. If Cooper is right, perhaps the Supreme Court would be compelled to hand down paired judgments, in both English and Scots law. Such a judgment would be a constitutional oddity in a number of respects. Perhaps most notably, the Scottish side of the judgment would be effective (that is the territory, after all, in which the statute violating the Acts of Union would have had the majority of its effects), whilst the English side of the judgment, declaring the statute valid in English law, would have only limited effect.

Secondly, in sharp contrast, the case might be of no real significance. This was the view of Neil MacCormick, John MacCormick's son and one of the leading scholars on the position of Scotland within the UK constitution. Neil MacCormick

[26] *MacCormick* (n 24) 411. Aileen McHarg argues that Lord Cooper may have been influenced by the Declaration of Arbroath (1320), which some have interpreted as embracing a doctrine of popular sovereignty, grounding sovereignty in the people rather than an institution: Aileen McHarg, 'The Declaration of Arbroath and Scots Law' in Klaus Muller (ed), *Scotland and Arbroath 1320–2020* (Peter Lang 2020).

[27] As was the case in *Cherry v Advocate General* [2019] UKSC 41, [2020] AC 373, in which the Supreme Court handed down two identical decisions.

argued that the UK constitution was an evolution of the old pre-1707 English constitution, and that the *obiter* in *MacCormick* was not an accurate statement of the constitutional position.[28] The old English doctrine of sovereignty survived the Acts of Union and, indeed, extended its reach to Scotland, supplanting Scottish constitutional traditions that favoured a limited legislature. It might be surprising that MacCormick, a staunch supporter of Scottish independence, would take such a cautious view of his father's case, but his interpretation might connect to his calls for greater constitutional autonomy for Scotland. By downplaying the present constitutional distinctiveness of Scotland, MacCormick may have hoped to buttress calls for more radical constitutional change.

Thirdly, *MacCormick* might provide material from which a new model of the constitution emerges, a model realised in both the English and Scottish legal orders. Later in this chapter the topic of constitutional statutes will be examined: under the New Constitution, in a radical departure from the old certainties of parliamentary sovereignty, the courts have accorded statutes different legal weight depending on their constitutional significance. Potentially, courts could treat the Acts of Union as constitutional statutes of fundamental significance, either limiting the UK Parliament in some respects or requiring that UK statutes which depart from the protections of the Acts of Union do so in the clearest possible terms. The New Constitution may draw from the old Scottish constitutional order as it moves away from parliamentary sovereignty.[29] Indeed, as we shall see, one of the key figures in the move away from sovereignty is Lord Hope, a Supreme Court justice who came from the Scottish system. His scepticism about sovereignty echoes, and may have been shaped by, the judgment in *MacCormick*.[30]

[28] Neil MacCormick, 'The United Kingdom: What State? What Constitution?' in Neil MacCormick (ed), *Questioning Sovereignty* (Oxford University Press 1999).

[29] Although Lord Cooper's claims about the constitutional position of the Scottish Parliament have been challenged by some historians: see Goldsworthy, *History and Philosophy* (n 3) 165–69, 270–72.

[30] See his comments on *MacCormick* in *Jackson* (n 12) [106]. Lord Hope was also the presiding judge in *Pringle* (n 24).

5.2 THE EUROPEAN UNION AND THE QUIET DEATH OF SOVEREIGNTY

When Britain was considering joining the European Community in the late 1960s and early 1970s, many politicians wondered if the limitations of membership were desirable.[31] Constitutional scholars, in contrast, wondered if these limits were possible. By 1972, it was clear that membership of the Community brought with it the requirement that domestic courts give European law priority over conflicting rules of national law. In the seminal case of *Van Gend en Loos* the European Court of Justice (ECJ) held that treaty Articles take precedence over conflicting rules of national law and, moreover, that it is the duty of national courts to apply these European rules in preference to their domestic law.[32] This obligation on domestic courts arose because their state had signed the treaties establishing the European Community, and not, in the view of the ECJ, because of any domestic legal obligation. This assertion of the supremacy of the content of European law was buttressed by two further supremacy claims: first, that it is for the ECJ to have the final say about the interpretation of European law;[33] secondly, that it is for the ECJ to have the final say about the scope of European law.[34] These three claims to supremacy make a powerful combination. Whilst European law does not claim jurisdiction over all areas of national law, it is for the ECJ to decide the extent of its coverage, and what the duties of national courts are in these cases. As far as the ECJ is concerned, when European law is directly effective it takes precedence over *any* conflicting rule of national law, even core constitutional principles.[35] In short,

[31] Danny Nicol, *EC Membership and the Judicialization of British Politics* (Oxford University Press 2001) ch 2.

[32] Case 26/62 *Van Gend en Loos v Netherlandse Administratie der Belastingen* [1963] ECR 1. Regulations also have direct effect: see Case 6/64 *Costa v ENEL* [1964] ECR 585.

[33] Consolidated Version of the Treaty on the Functioning of the European Union [2012] OJ C326/47 art 234 (formerly art 177).

[34] Case 314/85 *Foto-Frost v Hauptzollamt Lübeck-Ost* [1987] ECR 4199.

[35] Case 11/70 *Internationale Handelsgesellschaft mbH v Einfur- und Vorratsstelle für Getreide und Futtermittel* [1970] ECR 1125, para 3.

according to the ECJ, European law is the highest source of law within national legal orders, one to which all conflicting rules must give way.

The claimed supremacy of European law was an established aspect of the European legal order when the UK applied for membership. But this supremacy was clearly contrary to parliamentary sovereignty. Whilst it was simple enough to deal with statutes passed before the UK's accession, which, if in conflict with European law, could be taken to have been impliedly repealed by any statute incorporating European law into the UK systems, it was harder to see how conflicting statutes passed after this date could be reconciled with European law. In the event of a conflict, parliamentary sovereignty would require that the later statute impliedly repeal the earlier, incorporating, statute: whatever the Queen-in-Parliament enacts as statute is law. Rather than utilising some cunning constitutional device to circumvent this conundrum, Parliament chose to address the issue directly. Section 2(4) of the European Communities Act 1972 asserted that any statute 'passed or to be passed ... shall be construed and shall have effect subject to the foregoing provisions of this section'; that is, subject to the incorporation of European law into the UK legal systems. This was a blunt challenge to parliamentary sovereignty, an attempt to impose a substantive limit on the effective legislative capacity of subsequent parliaments.

During the period between 1972 and 1988 Parliament and the courts contrived to avoid a dispute in which the efficacy of the 1972 Act would be tested.[36] Parliament strove to avoid legislating in conflict with European law, whilst the judges zealously interpreted domestic legislation to avoid inconsistencies.[37] But in the Merchant Shipping Act 1988 these strategies ran out. The Merchant Shipping Act 1988 sought to restrict the ability of non-UK fishers to access UK waters, whilst the treaty Articles, in sharp contrast, protected the rights of European nationals to establish businesses in the UK and, more generally, prohibited

[36] Nicol (n 31) ch 7.

[37] See eg *Litster v Forth Dry Dock* [1990] 1 AC 546 (HL).

discrimination on grounds of nationality. The Merchant Shipping Act 1988 clearly violated both of these directly effective European law obligations. In the *Factortame* cases, a group of Spanish fishers brought an action in the English courts against the 1988 Act. The first set of *Factortame* cases turned on the question of whether an interim injunction could be secured; that is, an order suspending the operation of the Merchant Shipping Act prior to a full hearing of the legality of the statute. In the first *Factortame* case to reach the House of Lords, their Lordships held that interim relief could not be granted; the court lacked the power to order that the 1988 Act be disapplied in the case before them.[38] Nevertheless, the question was sent to the ECJ, which ruled that, under European law, a national court was obliged to set aside any national rule that restricted its capacity to grant interim relief.[39] When the case returned to the English court, the House of Lords interpreted this as requiring that the remedy could be provided and, further, decided that in this instance the statute's operation would be suspended.[40]

*Factortame*is not an isolated case. In a series of judgments, the courts have shown themselves willing to suspend the operation of statutes that run contrary to directly effective European law. For example, in *R v Secretary of State for Employment ex p Equal Opportunities Commission* the House of Lords disapplied provisions found in the Employment Protection (Consolidation) Act 1978 that indirectly discriminated against female workers, treating them less favourably than men doing similar jobs.[41] The domestic statutes that sought to prevent sex discrimination could not be invoked against the legislation, but Article 119 EEC (now Article 157 TFEU) could be relied upon by the litigants. Similarly, in *Benkharbouche v Foreign Secretary* a worker in the Sudanese embassy sought to bring actions against her employer for various breaches of employment law, including unfair dismissal and paying less

[38] *R v Secretary of State for Transport, ex p Factortame (No 1)* [1990] 2 AC 85 (HL).

[39] Case 213/89 *The Queen v Secretary of State for Transport, ex p Factortame Ltd* [1990] ECR I-2433.

[40] *R v Secretary of State for Transport, ex p Factortame (No 2)* [1991] 1 AC 603 (HL).

[41] *R v Secretary of State for Employment, ex p Equal Opportunities Commission* [1995] 1 AC 1 (HL).

than the minimum wage.[42] The Supreme Court concluded that provisions of the State Immunity Act 1978 that protected the embassy from litigation were incompatible with the EU Charter of Fundamental Rights and should be set aside. Once again, the comparable domestic statute, the Human Rights Act 1998, could not be invoked to disapply the legislation, but the European provisions did have this effect.

In all these cases, the courts did not declare the whole statute unconstitutional, nor did they strike down a section of the statute. Instead, the court concluded that it would not apply a statutory provision that, but for the intervention of European law, would have determined a person's legal rights. Looking back at the first part of this chapter, such reasoning is a form of implied repeal: so far as there was a conflict between directly effective European law and a UK statute, it seems that the UK statute (in most cases) was displaced by European law. But there is one radical difference: whereas under parliamentary sovereignty, the more recent statute took precedence over the earlier statute, in the context of European law it was the earlier statute, the European Communities Act 1972 (which incorporated European law), that took precedence over the later, conflicting, statute.

After *Factortame*, the old rule of parliamentary sovereignty ceased to be part of the UK constitution. Before *Factortame*, every statute was born wholly effective; the duty of the courts was to apply all of its provisions to the cases before them. After *Factortame*, some statutes were born with limited effect; a portion of their provisions are ineffective, in some or all of the cases in which they would otherwise apply.

Given the constitutional significance of *Factortame*, we might expect to find a carefully reasoned explanation of its constitutional implications in the speeches of the judges. In fact, the constitutional aspect of the decision is only briefly addressed, in Lord Bridge's judgment. Lord Bridge provided two defences of the Lords' willingness to suspend the operation of the statute. These were, first, that whatever limitation of sovereignty our membership of the Community had entailed, it was a limitation Parliament

[42] *Benkharbouche v Secretary of State for Foreign and Commonwealth Affairs* [2017] UKSC 62, [2019] AC 777.

had accepted by enacting the 1972 Act, an Act that made the duty of the courts clear; and, secondly, that since that date, Parliament had accepted the obligation to alter domestic law promptly when that law failed to track European law, making changes to statutes when necessary. A curiosity about these arguments is that they seem political rather than legal. Lord Bridge does not provide us with an earlier case where the courts had made an analogous decision or some principle of the common law that justifies the reasoning of the court. Instead, the reasons remind us that this is an outcome willed by Parliament and, moreover, has been accepted by successive parliaments of various political complexions. For the judges to have stuck with the old rule of parliamentary sovereignty would have frustrated a conscious and sustained choice made by the democratic side of the constitution: even if the law required the court to find the Merchant Shipping Act 1988 had impliedly repealed the European Communities Act 1972, politics required the judges to do the opposite. The law needed to change to facilitate this new political settlement.

That Lord Bridge's reasoning appears more political than legal came as no surprise to one of the foremost writers on parliamentary sovereignty, Sir William Wade. In his original article on sovereignty, back in 1955, Wade presented it as a legally unalterable feature of the constitution. The doctrine of implied repeal prevented Parliament from imposing effective limits on itself, whilst the duty that sovereignty imposed upon the judges permitted no exceptions. But at the time Wade was writing, the British Empire was midway through its protracted collapse; territories that had been governed by the UK were taking control of their own affairs. This process provided some clear examples of territories that were once subject to Westminster's parliamentary sovereignty freeing themselves of its bonds; even if legally unchangeable, change could happen. Amongst the first constitutional events in these newly independent territories was often the formal renunciation of the sovereignty of the UK Parliament by the courts of the newly liberated state.[43] Wade described these decisions as 'revolutions'; decisions made by the judges that lack a

[43] See, amongst other examples, *The State (Ryan) v Lennon* [1935] IR 170 in Ireland and *HKSAR v Ma Wai-Kwan* [1997] 2 HKC 315 in Hong Kong.

legal base, but which were effective, nonetheless. The term 'revolution' was not intended as pejorative: often, these courts were doing the right thing. Even if a sound legal justification could not be found for its decision, the decision of the court was politically (and, arguably, constitutionally) defensible. The judges were recognising a new constitutional reality, and the legitimacy for their decision was grounded in the legitimacy of that new constitutional order. According to Wade, whilst parliamentary sovereignty could not be legally changed, the judges could, nevertheless, discard it in a judicial 'revolution'. When *Factortame* was decided, Wade suggested that this, too, was a 'revolution'; a change made by the judges that lacked a legal justification, but which may, nonetheless, have been politically justifiable. To return to the *schema* set out in Chapter 4, *Factortame* amounted to a tailoring of the capacity of Parliament to produce legislation, a form of scope review. At the invitation of the legislature, the courts reshaped the boundaries of the source Parliament relied upon for its legal jurisdiction.

5.3 THE COURTS, PARLIAMENT, AND STATUTES IN THE NEW CONSTITUTION

The significance of the death of parliamentary sovereignty should not be overstated. It remains the case that, almost invariably, statutes enacted by Parliament are loyally applied by the courts, with the most recent statute taking precedence over earlier statutes. The cases after *Factortame* have produced two qualifications to this state of affairs. First, the courts no longer treat all statutes as of equal weight. A new (or rediscovered) legal category of 'constitutional statute' has emerged which builds on the decision in *Factortame* to give priority to an earlier statute, the European Communities Act 1972, over a later statute, the Merchant Shipping Act 1988.[44] Secondly, in a series of decisions a number

[44] Although the idea that some statutes might be legally harder to alter than others could not be squared with the Old Constitution's allegiance to parliamentary sovereignty, traces of the notion can be seen in earlier case law: *Attorney General v Wilts United Dairies* (1922) 38 TLR 781; *Re Parliamentary Privilege Act 1770* [1958] AC 331, 350–51 (PC).

of judges have suggested that the courts should be willing to review the contents of statutes; that potentially the courts could decide that a statute is, in some way, legally unacceptable, and refuse to apply it. As we shall see, the rise of constitutional statutes amounts to a rejection of parliamentary sovereignty but preserves parliamentary supremacy: Parliament can bring about any changes to the law it wishes, but, sometimes, it must explicitly repeal the 'constitutional statute' to achieve this end. In contrast, the second challenge is more profound. If the courts can review the contents of a statute Parliament is neither sovereign nor supreme: it is the judges who have the final say about the contents of the law.

5.3.1 Constitutional Statutes

Any account of constitutional statutes has two questions to answer: first, we need to identify which statutes are classified as constitutional; and, secondly, we need to know the legal implications of this classification. Ideally, the answers to these two questions would be connected: the reasons for classifying a statute as constitutional would also explain its special legal status.

The modern law on constitutional statutes starts with the case of *Thoburn v Sunderland District Council*—also known, with a touch of hyperbole, as the Metric Martyrs case.[45] This case turned on the scale of measurement used by a greengrocer to weigh his vegetables: Thoburn wanted to use imperial measurements but was told by a trading standards inspector that he was now obliged to use metric measurements. His refusal to change the labels on his scales led to a prosecution which Thoburn argued rested on a legal mistake, contending that the Weights and Measures Act 1985 did not require the use of metric measurement. Simplifying slightly, three domestic legislative instruments were relevant to the case.

First, section 2(2) of the European Communities Act 1972, read alongside section 2(4), empowered the executive to alter statutes to bring UK law into line with its Community obligations. This

[45] *Thoburn v Sunderland City Council* [2002] EWHC 195 (Admin), [2003] QB 151. See NW Barber and Alison L Young, 'The Rise of Prospective Henry VIII Clauses and their Implications for Sovereignty' [2003] Public Law 113.

was an example of a 'Henry VIII clause', a statutory provision that empowers an entity other than Parliament to make changes to statutes.

Secondly, section 1 of the Weights and Measures Act 1985 stated that yards and pounds, alongside metres and kilograms, were lawful units of measurement.

Thirdly, a piece of delegated legislation, the Units of Measurements Regulations 1994 (passed under the European Communities Act 1972), purported to amend the 1985 Act: from the year 2000, yards and pounds could not be used as primary units of measurement.

Resting his case on the rule of parliamentary sovereignty, Thoburn argued that the delegated legislation was ineffective. There was a conflict between two rules: the rule specifying imperial as acceptable units of measurement in the 1985 Act and the rule excluding their use as primary units of measurement in the 1994 delegated legislation. Thoburn argued that in the event of a conflict implied repeal required that the court give precedence to the more recent statutory rule. The 1994 delegated legislation depended, for its validity, on the 1972 Act. The European Communities Act predated the Weights and Measures Act, and so the executive's capacity to alter statutes conferred by the European Communities Act had been impliedly repealed by the Weights and Measures Act: an earlier statute could not be relied upon to alter a later statute.

In his judgment, Lord Justice Laws found against Thoburn on two grounds. The first was comparatively orthodox. Laws contended that Thoburn had misunderstood the operation of implied repeal: implied repeal applied when two statutes were on the same subject matter and not simply whenever statutes produced conflicting rules.[46] Given that the European Communities Act 1972 and the Weights and Measures Act 1985 could, when the latter Act was passed, co-exist without conflict, implied repeal did not apply and the law-changing power in the 1972 Act was not limited by the 1985 statute. Laws' second line of reasoning was more radical. Even if Thoburn was right about implied repeal in general, the rule did not apply to 'constitutional statutes' such as

[46] *Thoburn v Sunderland City Council* (n 45) [50]–[51].

the European Communities Act 1972. Grounding his decision on that of the House of Lords in *Factortame*, Laws argued that constitutional statutes could not be impliedly repealed; they could only be repealed expressly or by specific provision.[47] Although this was not made explicit in *Factortame*, Laws argued it must have been the basis for the decision.[48] After all, he could have added, the first line of argument used in *Thoburn*, over the nature of implied repeal, was not open to the judges in *Factortame*: the European Communities Act 1972 was in conflict with the Merchant Shipping Act 1988 from the moment that latter statute was enacted, and on either understanding of implied repeal the 1988 Act should have taken precedence. Laws' characterisation of the nature and implications of the European Communities Act 1972 was later explicitly supported by the majority of the Supreme Court in *R (Miller) v Secretary of State for Exiting the European Union*.[49] *Thoburn*, building on *Factortame*, was a further form of scope review: the court refined the scope of law-making power, allowing Parliament to place some constraints over its future incarnations when legislating certain types of statute.

After *Thoburn*, it was in the area of devolution that constitutional statutes were next invoked by the courts. Both the Government of Wales Act 2006 and the Scotland Act 1998 were identified as constitutional statutes, most notably by Lord Hope, in *H v Lord Advocate*, contending that the Scotland Act 1998 could not be altered other than by express enactment.[50] But the most important case on constitutional statutes came a dozen years after *Thoburn* and, once more, arose in the area of European law. In *R (HS2 Alliance) v Transport Secretary* a challenge was launched against the executive's decision to determine the route of the High Speed 2 rail link by statute, rather than through the ordinary planning

[47] ibid [60]. [48] ibid [61].

[49] *R (Miller) v Secretary of State for Exiting the European Union* [2017] UKSC 5, [2018] AC 61 [88].

[50] *H v Lord Advocate* [2012] UKSC 24, [2013] 1 AC 413. *R (Governors of Brynmawr Foundational School) v The Welsh Ministers* [2011] EWHC 519 (Admin) identified the Government of Wales Act 2006 as a constitutional statute with special hierarchal status. See also Farrah Ahmed and Adam Perry, 'The Quasi-Entrenchment of Constitutional Statutes' (2014) 73 Cambridge Law Journal 514.

process.[51] The statutory process proposed by the executive allowed the protestors some opportunity to participate in the decision, but the opportunities were less extensive than would have been the case in a planning inquiry. The HS2 Action Alliance argued, amongst other things, that this process went against an EU directive which required that the approval of projects such as HS2 include an environmental impact assessment, an assessment that included opportunities for the public to participate in this aspect of the decision-making process.[52] The protesters contended that the proposed legislative process did not meet the standards of the directive, and sought judicial review of the executive's decision to use legislation to set the route of the project.

The protesters' made their claim prior to the enactment of legislation and it was, effectively, a challenge to the propriety of using legislation in this area. Recalling Article 9 of the Bill of Rights 1689, discussed in Chapter 4, the resolution of the case might appear simple: the court is prevented from reviewing the ways in which statutes are produced. However, rather than declining to examine the process by which the decision was to be made, the Supreme Court contended that the legislative process satisfied the requirements of the directive. The protestors' claims that the existence of political parties and the whipping system rendered public participation ineffective were dismissed.[53] In so doing, and in sharp contrast with earlier cases on privilege, the court showed itself to be willing to assess the merits of the processes adopted by the Commons and Lords to make legislation.[54] To return to the categories set out in Chapter 4, it undertook a form of substantive review. However, in the course of their reasoning the judges also considered what would have been the position if the legislative process could not have been squared with

[51] *R (HS2 Alliance) v Secretary of State for Transport* [2014] UKSC 3, [2014] 1 WLR 324. See Paul Craig 'Constitutionalising Constitutional Law: HS2' [2014] Public Law 373.

[52] Parliament and Council Directive 2011/92/EU of 13 December 2011 on the assessment of the effects of certain public and private projects on the environment [2012] OJ L26/1.

[53] *HS2* (n 51) [108]–[109] (Lord Reed). The whipping system is discussed further in ch 10.

[54] Compare *Pickin v British Railways Board* [1974] AC 765 (HL).

the directive. Could European law override parliamentary privilege, as articulated in the Bill of Rights 1689, and require the judges to criticise the workings of Parliament? Lord Neuberger and Lord Mance delivered a joint speech, which was endorsed by the rest of the Supreme Court, in which they suggested (without deciding the point) that there were certain constitutional instruments and fundamental constitutional principles 'of which Parliament when it enacted the European Communities Act 1972 did not either contemplate or authorise the abrogation'.[55] The possibility was raised that there are some statutes, and principles, that are so fundamental they should be given even greater weight than the European Communities Act 1972.

As a consequence of Brexit, *HS2* probably marks the final stage in the adaptation of the UK's constitution in response to European law. Whilst *HS2* endorses the decision in *Factortame*, with the Supreme Court reminding us that European law can require the UK courts to treat statutes as invalid if they cannot be reconciled with European law, it also indicates limits to that duty.[56] In *Factortame*, the extent of the courts' acceptance of the supremacy claims articulated by the ECJ was left, possibly deliberately, unclear. Lord Bridge confined himself to declaring that rules of European law should be treated as supreme 'in those areas to which they apply'.[57] This formulation coyly left open the possibility that UK courts might one day decide that it was for them to determine the proper scope of European law and, furthermore, that they might conclude that this scope was limited by aspects of the UK constitution. The model of the UK's relationship with European law presented by *HS2* makes use of both of these ambiguities. Contrary to the ECJ's understanding of the relationship, *HS2* asserts that UK courts would not automatically accept the rulings of the Luxembourg court about the extent of European law nor would they necessarily accept rules of European law that run against some of the fundamental statutes and principles of the UK constitution. Following many other national courts, the UK's Supreme Court adopted a model of European law in which

[55] *HS2* (n 51) [207] (Lords Neuberger and Mance). See also [78] (Lord Reed).
[56] ibid [206] (Lords Neuberger and Mance).
[57] *Factortame (No 2)* (n 40) 659.

European law took effect through the national constitution, not directly as a result of the signing of the European treaties. This means that national courts have the final say about the laws within their territories and, moreover, can decide that some national constitutional principles take precedence over European law.[58] In this way, *HS2* does not just embrace the concept of constitutional statutes; it presents us with a hierarchy of constitutional statutes. Just as the Merchant Shipping Act 1988 failed impliedly to repeal the European Communities Act 1972, it seems that had the point required decision, the European Communities Act 1972 would have failed impliedly to repeal the Bill of Rights 1689. The old rule of parliamentary sovereignty had been turned on its head.[59]

There is a final set of questions raised by constitutional statutes: which statutes count as 'constitutional' and, after *HS2*, in what order of precedence should these statutes be placed?[60] There are at least three ways we could attempt to answer these questions. First, we could try to deduce a test from the concept of a 'constitution': perhaps if we could pin down what a constitution is, those statutes that fall within this category should be labelled 'constitutional statutes'. Secondly, we could attempt to use Parliament's intentions as a guide: perhaps we can deduce from the text and context of statutes those which Parliament intended as 'constitutional'. Finally, we could ask why we might want statutes to be given a special legal status, to be protected from implied repeal; if we can identify reasons for providing this protection to statutes, perhaps this will help us identify the statutes that ought to be protected.

The first answer, what we might call the formalist answer, was given by Laws in *Thoburn*. Laws defined a constitutional statute as one which either conditioned the legal relationship between the citizen and state in some general, overarching, manner, or which affected the scope of a fundamental constitutional right,

[58] See P Craig and G de Búrca, *EU Law: Text, Cases, and Materials* (7th edn, Oxford University Press 2020) ch 10.

[59] A further suggested legal implication of constitutional statutes was that they should be interpreted in a special manner: see ch 18.

[60] Rivka Weill, 'Exploring Constitutional Statutes in Common Law Systems' in Richard Albert and Joel Colón-Rios (eds), *Quasi-Constitutionality and Constitutional Statutes* (Routledge 2020).

drawing a line between statutory rules that are parts of the constitution and those that are parts of non-constitutional law.[61] There are a number of criticisms that could be made of Laws' test. We might, first of all, critique it in its own terms. As Farrah Ahmed and Adam Perry point out, the test appears too narrow, excluding aspects of important statutes that would commonly be thought to be constitutional. Depending on how the test was interpreted, elements of both the Parliament Acts and the devolution legislation would be excluded. In other respects, Laws' test appears overbroad: it could be argued that most of criminal law affects the scope of fundamental constitutional rights in some way. Indeed, it could be argued criminal law shapes the legal relationship between the citizen and the state.[62] We might add to this test a criterion of importance, perhaps only 'important' statutes count as constitutional, but now the test has become evaluative, rather than conceptual and we will need an explanation of the reasons why we should regard a statutory rule as being important enough to be included in the category.

A second strategy, grounded in the presumed intentions of Parliament, is found in the work of Ahmed and Perry. In a sophistication of Laws' test, they argue we should understand a constitutional statute to be one 'that is about state institutions and which substantially influences, directly or indirectly, what those institutions can and may do',[63] a definition that focuses on the role played by the statute in shaping state institutions. In their defence of this test they point to a presumption of consistency: Parliament can be 'presumed to favour stability over disruption, and continuity over change'.[64] When an earlier constitutional statute and a later ordinary statute are in conflict, giving the latter statute precedence would have a substantial impact on the operation of a constitutional institution, and the presumption speaks against Parliament having intended this outcome—inverting the ordinary rule of implied repeal. Ahmed and Perry's proposal has much to recommend it. In particular,

61 *Thoburn* (n 45) [62]; Weill (n 60) 79–82.

62 The difficulty of defining the 'constitution' is discussed further in ch 2.

63 Ahmed and Perry (n 50) 471; Goldsworthy, *Contemporary Debates* (n 3) 312–14.

64 Ahmed and Perry (n 50) 476.

it binds the definition of a constitutional statute to a reason for wanting to treat a statute as constitutional. And the test it advances, resting on the changes that would be brought about if implied repeal were to occur, is a matter of degree: there can be a greater or lesser impact, depending on the statute, and so the test allows us to rank constitutional statutes. But there are difficulties with the argument. Is it appropriate to use presumptions about Parliament's intentions to change the law relating to the hierarchy of statutes? Given that when the Merchant Shipping Act 1988 and the Weights and Measures Act 1985 were enacted, the old law did not give priority to the European Communities Act 1972, can it reasonably be said that Parliament intended a legal rule of priority that did not yet exist to be applied to their conflict? There is always a risk in making presumptions about Parliament's intentions. Beyond what is written in the statute and some implications that can be drawn from the act of legislating itself, it becomes increasingly difficult confidently to ascribe intentions to that institution. Often, judicial talk of presumed parliamentary intentions is best understood as a rhetorical device giving cover to the judges as they develop rules to shape the meaning of, and relationships between, statutes; whilst these rules are presented as resting on the intentions of Parliament, they are the creation of the courts and embody the choices made by the judges. This leads to a final concern about Ahmed and Perry's rationale for delineating constitutional statutes: why should we prioritise consistency over other possible constitutional goods?

The third option for the identification of constitutional statutes builds on these concerns. Perhaps we should accept that constitutional statutes are the creation of the judges, a product of scope review, and that the identification and ordering of these statutes depend on a range of values. When the courts identify a statute as a constitutional statute, they entrench it, making it more difficult to alter than other statutory rules within the system. The reasons for designating a statute constitutional should, ideally, link to our reasons for wanting to see it made more difficult to alter. Constitutional statutes require explicit repeal, with the latter statute either formally repealing the constitutional statute or, perhaps, if not formally repealing the statute, making Parliament's intention to repeal exceptionally clear. Why might judges want to give statutes this type of protection? One reason might be because judges want to force Parliament to admit that it is altering the constitutional statute, requiring this admission where the earlier statute establishes or protects something of value. So, if the earlier statute provides a protection for fundamental rights—such as the Bill of Rights 1689, Magna Carta or the Human Rights Act 1998—or establishes a new form of democratic decision-making—such as the devolution legislation or the European Communities Act 1972—the courts might conclude that any alterations Parliament wishes to make to these statutes should be made overtly. This third option is less elegant that Ahmed and Perry's proposal. It requires us to accept that there is a variety of possible values protected by constitutional statutes and, also, requires us to accept that these values are selected by the judges, not Parliament. But this pragmatic explanation may better explain how the judges are using and developing constitutional statutes.

5.3.2 Common Law Principles as Limits on Parliament

The emerging category of constitutional statutes has so far preserved the supremacy of Parliament: Parliament can change any statutes it wishes, save that, in some instances, it must make these changes expressly. Alongside this, a number of judges have suggested that there are more fundamental constraints on Parliament's law-making powers; perhaps there are some constitutional principles that are so deeply embedded in the constitution that even Parliament cannot change them. In a series of House of Lords and Supreme Court cases, a range of judges have indicated that they would be willing to disapply provisions of statutes if those statutes ran contrary to fundamental common law principles. So, for example, in *Jackson* Lord Steyn identified parliamentary sovereignty as a 'construct of the common law' which the judges could qualify if necessary. Steyn warned that in the event of legislation which attempted to abolish judicial review or the ordinary role of the courts, the judges might 'have to consider whether this is a constitutional fundamental which even a sovereign Parliament acting at the behest of a complaisant House of Commons cannot abolish'.[65] In the same case, Lord Hope, having discussed the legal implications of the Acts of Union, opined that 'the concept of a Parliament that is absolutely sovereign is not entirely in accord with the reality'.[66] Furthermore, in *Moohan v Lord Advocate* Lord Hodge, with the agreement of the majority of the Supreme Court, warned:

> I do not exclude the possibility that in the very unlikely event that a parliamentary majority abusively sought to entrench its power by a curtailment of the franchise or similar device, the common law, informed by principles of democracy and the rule of law and international norms, would be able to declare such legislation unlawful.[67]

If the long history of the common law is sifted carefully, many other comments made by judges questioning the orthodoxies of sovereignty can be found.[68] But, as Jeffrey Goldsworthy has shown in his magisterial study of the history of parliamentary sovereignty, there has never been a case in English constitutional history in which the courts relied upon common law principles to invalidate an act of Parliament.[69] Until very recently, the *dicta* in cases such as *Jackson* and *Moohan* were just that: *dicta*, comments that might suggest a path for the development of the law, but not a path that the courts would necessarily take. Arguably, this changed in the recent case of *R (Privacy International) v Investigatory Powers Tribunal*, a case that has come closer than any other to reviewing a statute on the basis of common law principles.[70]

[65] *Jackson* (n 12) [102].

[66] ibid [106]. See also Lord Hope's speech in *AXA General Insurance Ltd v Lord Advocate* [2011] UKSC 46, [2012] 1 AC 868 [51].

[67] *Moohan v Lord Advocate* [2014] UKSC 67, [2015] 1 AC 901 [35].

[68] See in particular *Dr Bonham's Case* (1608) 8 Co Rep 113b, 118a, although the case should be read with caution: Goldsworthy, *History and Philosophy* (n 3) 111–12, 122–23.

[69] Goldsworthy, *Contemporary Debates* (n 3) ch 2.

[70] *R (Privacy International) v Investigatory Powers Tribunal* [2019] UKSC 22, [2019] 2 WLR 1219. A similar analysis could be undertaken of some other recent cases: see *R (Cart) v Upper Tribunal* [2011] UKSC 28, [2012] 1 AC 663 and *R (Evans) v Attorney General* [2015] UKSC 21, [2015] 1 AC 1787. See further Hayley Hooper, 'Legality, Legitimacy, and Legislation: The Role of Exceptional Circumstances in Common Law Judicial Review' (2021) 41 Oxford Journal of Legal Studies 142.

Privacy International concerned an ouster clause, a statutory provision inserted by Parliament into the Regulation of Investigatory Powers Act 2000 to prevent the courts reviewing decisions of the Investigatory Powers Tribunal, a body with jurisdiction to examine the operation of the security services. Section 67(8) stated:

> Except to such extent as the Secretary of State may by order otherwise provide, determinations, awards, orders and other decisions of the Tribunal (including decisions as to whether they have jurisdiction) shall not be subject to appeal or be liable to be questioned in any court.

This section was similar to section 4(4) of the Foreign Compensation Act 1950, which was examined by the House of Lords in the case of *Anisminic Ltd v Foreign Compensation Commission*.[71] That section stated: 'The determination by the commission of any application made to them under this Act shall not be called in question in any court of law.'

Each statute sought to limit the capacity of the courts to review decisions made by an adjudicative body outside of the court system. In each case, at first glance, the ouster clause appeared to completely oust the court: it seemed that Parliament did not want the judges to second-guess decisions made by the Foreign Compensation Commission and the Investigatory Powers Tribunal. In the earlier case of *Anisminic*, the court read the section as applying only to errors made by the body within its jurisdiction. The judges argued that when the Foreign Compensation Commission made an error in its reasoning that took it outside of its jurisdiction, its supposed decision was a nullity: it had not made a decision, and so was not protected by the ouster clause. This neat piece of reasoning stripped the ouster clause in *Anisminic* of much of its effect: if the FCC misunderstood the law it was supposed to apply, the court could argue it had stepped outside of its jurisdiction, and review the decision. When section 67(8) of the Regulation of Investigatory Powers Act 2000 was being written, it is likely that *Anisminic* was at the forefront of the drafters' minds. The decision to include the words 'including decisions as to whether they have jurisdiction' in the section might

[71] *Anisminic Ltd v Foreign Compensation Commission* [1969] 2 AC 147 (HL).

have been taken as a conscious decision by Parliament to avoid that ouster clause being given the narrow effect accorded to its ancestor in *Anisminic*. Indeed, when *Privacy International* reached the Court of Appeal, Lord Justice Sales concluded that the language of the statute was so clear that the courts were compelled to accept that Parliament had chosen to oust their jurisdiction, and decisions of the tribunal could not be reviewed, including mistakes made by the tribunal over issues of law.[72] The Supreme Court, however, thought differently.

The decision of the Supreme Court in *Privacy International* is hard to interpret. Of the seven judges, four decided that section 67(8) provided only a very limited constraint on the capacity of the courts to judicially review decisions of the tribunal, two asserted that the provision managed to exclude a significant range of (but not all) possible challenges, and only one, Lord Wilson, gave the section its natural reading, contending with a note of asperity that the language of the section was 'totally clear in excluding judicial review'.[73] Of the four judges in the majority, Lord Carnwath delivered the leading judgment, with which Lady Hale and Lord Kerr agreed. Lord Lloyd-Jones delivered a separate judgment which allied with elements of Carnwath's reasoning. The common ground between these four judges, and so the formal *ratio* of the case, was that section 67(8) was insufficiently explicit to exclude judicial review.[74] Lloyd-Jones went so far as to say that Parliament's failure expressly to protect the tribunal's 'purported determinations' indicated that Parliament had not intended to exclude judicial review.[75] Carnwath also suggested that Parliament, if it had really wanted to exclude judicial review, would have used more explicit wording, but placed less weight on the supposed intentions of Parliament when construing the section.[76] When dealing with ouster clauses, Carnwath argued, the courts are not engaged in an ordinary exercise of statutory interpretation, seeking to give effect to the policies chosen by Parliament. Instead, the common law militates strongly against

[72] *R (Privacy International) v Secretary of State for Foreign and Commonwealth Affairs* [2017] EWCA Civ 1868, [2018] 1 WLR 2572 [26].

[73] *Privacy International* (n 70) [229].

[74] ibid [104]–[110].

[75] ibid [164].

[76] ibid [111].

readings of the statute that would exclude judicial review; the common law presumption against such exclusion can only be overcome with the clearest and most explicit words.[77]

Carnwath's second line of argument was more radical. With the agreement of Hale and Kerr, he argued that:

> [a]lthough it is not necessary to decide the point, I see a strong case for holding that, consistently with the rule of law, binding effect cannot be given to a clause which purports wholly to exclude the supervisory jurisdiction of the High Court to review a decision of an inferior court or tribunal, whether for excess or abuse of jurisdiction, or error of law. In all cases, regardless of the words used, it should remain ultimately a matter for the court to determine the extent to which such a clause should be upheld, having regard to its purpose and statutory context, and the nature and importance of the legal issue in question; and to determine the level of scrutiny required by the rule of law.[78]

This was not the ostensible basis for the decision in *Privacy International*, but it constitutes a further, radical challenge to the old rule of parliamentary sovereignty: if the path suggested by Carnwath was taken by a future court, that court would then explicitly assess the merits of a statutory provision and decide, based on that assessment, whether or not to give effect to the section.

As well as the problems raised by the multiplicity of judgments, *Privacy International* is a hard case because of the implausibility of the reasoning of the majority. Reading section 67(8) it is difficult to see how Parliament could have been much clearer or more explicit about its intentions; the interpretation given to the section by Lord Justice Sales in the Court of Appeal and Lord Wilson in the Supreme Court is hard to dispute. The majority's attempt to link their interpretation to Parliament's choice of words was half-hearted, at best. It is never the case that the meaning of a statute is entirely deduced from Parliament's intentions, as courts must fill gaps and resolve conflicts, but in *Privacy International* the court's decision runs against both the language of the statute and reasonable conclusions we can draw about Parliament's intentions from that language. In the majority judgments, the common law rule requiring ouster clauses to be read narrowly has changed into

[77] ibid [107], [111]. [78] ibid [144].

a rule empowering judges to assess the merits of ouster clauses and rewrite or remove them—a clear example of substantive review.[79] It is worth noting that all of the Supreme Court judges in *Privacy International* carefully examined the nature of the Investigatory Powers Tribunal when considering the legal implications of section 67(8). Even Lord Wilson, the strongest dissenter, emphasised the judicial qualifications of those sitting in the tribunal, its autonomy, and its similarity to a court.[80] It seems to have been universally accepted that the court should not focus narrowly on the text of the ouster but, instead, consider what the relationship between the tribunal and courts ought to be, with Parliament's opinion about that relationship, as expressed in the statute, playing only part of that assessment.

That the line of reasoning based in parliamentary intent is unconvincing does not necessarily mean that *Privacy International* was wrongly decided: the second line of reasoning provided by Carnwath gives a more credible, and perhaps more honest, justification. The claim is that the principle of the rule of law, a common law principle, mandates judges to review ouster clauses. The rule of law will be considered later in this book but, for now, there are two possible ways of understanding its application in *Privacy International*. First, given that the courts are necessary features of a legal order, there may be some legal questions surrounding ouster clauses that can never be removed from the jurisdiction of the courts. At the most basic level, the courts must be able to check whether a claimed ouster clause exists and whether the body claiming it is the body protected by the ouster clause. If the courts lacked either of these capacities, anyone could claim that the jurisdiction of the courts was ousted at any time by pretending to benefit from an ouster clause. Furthermore, if the decisions of a body protected by an ouster clause are to have legal effect, for example if they affect property rights, the court must have the capacity to identify whether the body has made a decision, and the contents of that decision. If the court were not able to do this, the legal system would produce irresolvable conflicts, with the body protected by the ouster clause making one set of

[79] The court undertook a similar exercise in *Cart* (n 70).

[80] *Privacy International* (n 70) [245]–[254].

decisions about people's legal positions, and the courts adopting a different view that ignored the decisions of that body.[81] So, the judges in *Privacy International* were correct to contend that there are some issues that the rule of law requires fall within the remit of the courts. But the invocation of the rule of law in *Privacy International* goes beyond this minimalist conception of the principle. The version of the rule of law invoked in this case is much broader and less clearly defined. Rather than being tied to some account of the necessary aspects of a legal order, it rests on the judges' understanding of the courts' position in the constitutional order and the legal structures required for the courts to acquit that role successfully. Ouster clauses that exclude the courts from scrutinising tribunal decisions inhibit the court from playing this role, but there might be other statutory interventions that would raise rule of law concerns by creating barriers of access to the courts.[82]

Privacy International did not rely on a common law principle to invalidate a statutory provision; the majority presented their decision to us as one of statutory interpretation. But the argument from statutory interpretation was radically unconvincing; indeed, it is hard to accept that even the judges themselves really believed it. On occasion, the common law has developed through the fashioning of legal fictions. Legal fictions sometimes emerge when a rule is stretched to cover a new problem that the judges believe needs legal regulation, but falls outside of the current law. So, for example, where one person mistakenly pays another money, rather than allowing the recipient to keep it the courts might claim that there is a contract, a legally enforceable agreement, which requires its return. At first, many judges and lawyers might believe in the fiction; they try hard to argue, perhaps, that, despite contrary appearances, there really was an intention to form a contract. At this stage the legal fiction, the pretended existence of a contract has emerged, but those applying it might not be aware they are relying on a fiction. Over time, as judges

[81] Considerations of this type may lie behind parts of Lord Sumption's decision: *Privacy International* (n 70) [210].

[82] *R (UNISON) v Lord Chancellor* [2017] UKSC 51, [2017] ICR 1037. See further ch 22.

and scholars reflect on the law, it becomes obvious that the rule requiring repayment of mistaken money rests on a different basis to the rule enforcing agreements. But the courts might still use the language and rationale of contract law to defend their decisions. Now we have a knowing legal fiction. All of those involved are now aware that the rule being applied is distinct from contract law, but continue to use the language of contract law, the fiction, as it provides a superficial legal legitimation of the rule; it appears to justify the court's demand that the mistaken money be repaid in pre-existing law. But this is now untrue: the rule has split from its supposed justification. It may yet be justified, but for other, unarticulated, reasons. At the third stage, the legal fiction withers; judges start to admit that the rule is distinct, and to explain the reasons behind it.

In the lifecycle of a legal fiction, *Privacy International* falls at the very end of the second stage. The fiction that the radical reading of section 67(8) is grounded in the words of the statute and compatible with the intentions of Parliament is weakly asserted. The true basis of the decision, both the rule and its reasoning, have been cautiously asserted in the leading judgment. In *Privacy International* the Supreme Court effectively decided that courts should review ouster clauses included in statutes by Parliament, testing the merits of the clause by examining their reach and the bodies they protect. The outcome of this review may require that the clause be given a radically different effect to that intended by Parliament or, in some cases, no effect at all, and effectively disapplied. The rational for this rule comes from a broad common law principle of the rule of law, a principle that, it seems, the judges have elevated above the rules requiring them to give effect to statutes.

5.4 CONCLUSION

As with the other non-derived legal sources of the constitution, the courts have gradually expanded their power to regulate statute. Whilst jurisdictional review has always been asserted by the judges—the courts have always claimed to be entitled to authoritatively determine the existence of statutes—over the last forty years the courts have expanded their role to include scope review (in cases such as *Factortame* and *HS2*) and are moving towards substantive review (in cases such as *Privacy International*). There are a number of possible explanations of these moves away from parliamentary sovereignty. The clear trigger for these developments, although they may have happened in any event, was the UK's decision to join the European Community, and the consequent need to adjust the UK constitution to accommodate the supremacy claims of European law. Prior to 1972, Parliament was the most significant democratic institution in the UK. But by joining the European project, Parliament committed itself to having some important decisions made elsewhere, by an alternative process that was still democratic, but democratic in a different way, with its legitimacy grounded in the agreement of Member States and the scrutiny of the European Parliament. Part of the justification for this new mechanism for decision-making was that, because of the scale of their effects, some decisions needed to be taken on a supra-state level and the European Union provided a democratic structure within which these decisions could be taken. Before 1972, the courts, by insisting on parliamentary sovereignty, effectively protected the UK's democratic processes, according each newly elected legislature unconstrained law-making power. But after 1972, adhering to parliamentary sovereignty would have unsettled a newly established democratic process and, as a result, the law had to change.

Brexit does not presage a return of parliamentary sovereignty. For one thing, sovereignty's old absolutism has been broken; Parliament did succeed in binding its future incarnations through the 1972 Act, and the courts have disapplied sections of statute. Having happened once, it could happen again. Furthermore, alongside the impact of European law there have been other legal developments that may have pushed, and may continue to push, judges away from sovereignty. First, in a mirror image of the European project, the devolution settlement has opened new modes of democratic decision-making within the state. These devolved institutions will be examined later in this book, but it is arguable that, in some areas, their democratic credentials are stronger than Parliament's. It would be unsurprising, then, if the current law on constitutional statutes continued to develop, offering more protection to the devolved assemblies. Secondly, since 1972, the emphasis on the role of the courts as protectors of human rights has increased, both through the UK's international obligations, such as the European Convention on Human Rights and the European Union's Charter of Fundamental Rights, and also through domestic developments, such as the enactment of the Human Rights Act 1998. Whilst many of the cases in which the rule of law and other common law principles have been mooted as constraints on Parliament have had nothing to do with European law, it may be that the judges' experience of European law has provided a spur for this development. After all, having allowed, in *Factortame*, the right to establish a company in the UK to trump a statute forbidding such access, it might seem odd, in a case like *Privacy International*, for the court not to invoke the right of access to a court, which might be thought to be an even more important right, against a statute that sought to remove that capacity.

Of course, just because the relationship between the courts and Parliament is shifting, it does not follow that this shift is desirable or inevitable. It could be that the old rule of parliamentary sovereignty is more attractive than our present situation. The move from the Old to the New Constitution has served to empower the judges. Outside of European law, where the European Communities Act 1972 sought to establish a new form of legal relationship, it is the courts that have determined the new rules on constitutional statutes and common law principles. Sceptics of the growth of judicial power, such as Richard Ekins, ask why an unelected branch of the constitution should take it upon itself to challenge the decisions made by the elected branch.[83] A significant amount of power has passed from Parliament to the courts and, moreover, this shift is being brought about by the judges themselves, using the gradual, incremental, method of the common law. Partly as a result of this incremental mode of constitutional

[83] Richard Ekins, 'Judicial Supremacy and the Rule of Law' (2003) 119 Law Quarterly Review 127, 144–47.

change, we are left with a considerable amount of vagueness around constitutional statutes and those common law principles that can be relied upon against statutes. This vagueness is, in itself, worrisome. We know that the judges might be prepared to review statutes, but on what grounds and in what ways this review will be undertaken remains unclear.

6

THE POLITICAL CONSTITUTION: CONSTITUTIONAL CONVENTIONS

When Blackstone wrote his *Commentaries on the Laws of England* in 1765, his account of the (then) British constitution concentrated on its legal rules. The result was a profoundly distorted picture of the state. As Albert Venn Dicey commented, Blackstone's account had the effect of 'ascribing ... to a modern monarch and constitutional King the whole, and perhaps more than the whole, of the powers actually possessed and exercised by William the Conqueror'.[1] One of the great advances of Victorian constitutional scholarship, an advance often attributed to Dicey but heralded by others, was the recognition of the role of conventions in the constitution.[2] Conventions are those non-legal rules which shape and direct the ways in which constitutional power is exercised within the state. All constitutions possess some conventions, but, perhaps partly because it lacks a written constitution, conventions play a particularly important role in the UK system. When Sir Ivor Jennings wrote that conventions were the 'flesh which clothes the dry bones of the law', he understated their importance.[3] It is conventions that limit the power of the monarch, define the office of the prime minister, determine the relationship between the executive and Parliament, and, more recently, have shaped the relationships between Westminster and the devolved institutions.[4] Often, it is conventions that provide the constitutional foundations on which laws rest.

[1] AV Dicey, *An Introduction to the Study of the Law of the Constitution* (10th edn, Macmillan 1959) 7–8.

[2] O Hood Phillips, 'Constitutional Conventions: Dicey's Predecessors' (1966) 29 Modern Law Review 137.

[3] Ivor Jennings, *The Law and the Constitution* (5th edn, University of London Press 1959) 81.

[4] Richard Rawlings, 'Concordats of the Constitution' (2000) 116 Law Quarterly Review 257.

The United Kingdom Constitution. N. W. Barber, Oxford University Press. © Nick Barber 2021.
DOI: 10.1093/oso/9780198852315.003.0006

6.1 THE NATURE OF CONVENTIONS

There are many different types of convention in the UK constitution. There are at least three distinctions that we can usefully draw: between those conventions that are parts of a system and those that stand alone; between bottom-up and top-down conventions; and between conventions that take the form of specific rules and those that take the form of broader principles. None of these categories form sharp divisions but stand as spectrums on which particular conventions can be placed. Once we have explored the variety of specific conventions in the constitution, the final part of this section will ask if there is anything that can be said about conventions in general.

6.1.1 Systemic and Non-Systemic Conventions

The classic model of a convention is a stand-alone rule.[5] For example, there is the convention of royal assent: by convention, the Queen signs all bills that have been passed by the Commons and the Lords. In law, she is entitled to refuse assent, but by convention she should not exercise this power. This convention is self-contained and can be expressed as an apparently simple rule. In contrast, many of the conventions governing the conduct of ministers have been gathered together in a single document: the Ministerial Code.[6] Before 1945, these conventions were unwritten and uncodified. The test for ministerial propriety depended on the expectations of the political community around Westminster. In 1945, Clement Attlee produced a document entitled 'Questions of Procedure for Ministers' designed to give new Labour cabinet ministers information about their role. An enlarged version of this document was published in 1992, and gained its present name, the Ministerial Code, in 1997. The most recent version of the Code was published in 2019 and runs to 36 pages. Amongst other things, the Code outlines ministers' duties towards Parliament, the extent to which they can receive gifts

[5] Colin R Munro, *Studies in Constitutional Law* (2nd edn, Butterworths 1999) 231–34.

[6] Cabinet Office, *Ministerial Code* (2019).

and payment from private bodies, and their relationship with the Civil Service.[7] The Ministerial Code also refers to, and reminds, ministers of their duty to abide by law.[8] The Code is written under the authority of the prime minister, and senior civil servants are sometimes asked to investigate potential breaches of the Code, although, as Boris Johnson recently demonstrated, the prime minister is not obliged to accept their findings.[9]

The Ministerial Code is a clear example of a systemic convention. The rules are presented as a set, there is a defined author who is empowered to produce an authoritative text, and there are also the beginnings of a structure to adjudicate breaches. As will be discussed later in this chapter, the Code is at the extreme end of systematisation, to the extent that it arguably tips into a form of law, a pocket legal order that has sprung up within the political side of the constitution. But, as Oren Tamir has shown, even discrete conventions, such as royal assent, still connect with, and rely upon, other conventions.[10] For example, the prime minister plays a special, if contested, role in this convention. By convention, the prime minister advises the Queen on the exercise of her legal powers. Consequently, the convention on royal assent sits within a mesh of other conventions, including the wider convention (the so-called 'Cardinal Convention') that the Queen exercise her legal powers on the advice of her ministers and, indeed, those conventions that establish the office of prime minister, which is an office almost entirely created by convention. Furthermore, a set of rules about the interpretation of conventions encompasses the convention on royal assent. For instance, it is accepted that when the convention requires interpretation, part of that interpretation involves looking back at past precedents; this is a rule, a convention, that helps regulate the interpretation of conventions.[11] The distinction between systemic and non-systemic conventions is one

[7] ibid ss 9, 7.20–24, and 5, respectively. [8] ibid s 1.3.

[9] Michael Gordon, 'Priti Patel, the Independent Adviser, and Ministerial Irresponsibility', UK Constitutional Law Blog (23 November 2020) https://ukconstitutionallaw.org/.

[10] Oren Tamir, 'Constitutional Norm Entrepreneuring' (2021) 80 Maryland Law Review (forthcoming).

[11] ibid.

of degree rather than a categorical divide; all conventions depend on and relate to other conventions in some way or other.

6.1.2 Top-Down and Bottom-Up Conventions

A further distinction, introduced by Adam Perry and Adam Tucker, can be drawn between top-down and bottom-up conventions.[12] Bottom-up conventions are the classic form of convention: a set of political practices that has gradually solidified into a rule. So, for example, the convention governing the monarch's selection of a prime minister includes the requirement that the prime minister sit in the Commons. Up until comparatively recently, prime ministers could sit in the Lords (the Marquess of Salisbury was the last, holding office until 1902), but in the modern constitution the prime minister must be able to defend her policies to the elected part of Parliament. Consequently, when Alec Douglas-Home, then the Earl of Home, became prime minister in 1963, he promptly renounced his peerage, and secured a seat in the Commons.[13] In the modern constitution this convention may have developed further; now it is hard to imagine a member of the House of Lords being appointed prime minister, even if she planned to stand for a seat in the Commons. There is no defined point at which we can say that the practice of requiring a prime minister to sit in the Commons evolved from being prudent political conduct to being constitutionally required; this convention emerged without a defined author, a set text, or a single moment of creation. It was, in Perry and Tucker's language, a convention that emerged from the bottom up. In contrast, some of the conventions surrounding the devolution settlement were drawn up by the executive and announced to Parliament.[14] The Sewel conventions limit the constitutional capacity of the Westminster Parliament to legislate on matters passed to the devolved institutions, stating that Parliament will not normally legislate on matters within the jurisdiction of the devolved assemblies without

[12] Adam Perry and Adam Tucker, 'Top-Down Constitutional Conventions' (2018) 81 Modern Law Review 765.

[13] Peter Hennessy, *The Prime Minister: The Office and its Holders Since 1945* (Allen Lane 2000) ch 11.

[14] HL Deb 21 July 1998, vol 592, col 791.

their consent. These conventions have a defined author, a set text to which political actors refer, and we can, probably, specify the date on which the conventions took effect.

There is some debate over whether or not these top-down conventions exist. Aileen McHarg has argued that when a putative convention is announced in this way, the convention does not become established until it shapes the practice of political actors.[15] Perry and Tucker, in contrast, argue that there can be conventions that identify actors as possessing authority to formulate conventions.[16] So, the Ministerial Code is written by the prime minister and, within some undefined boundaries, she is empowered to modify the rules it contains; there is no need to wait and see if these new rules will become parts of the constitution. It is likely that both McHarg, on the one hand, and Perry and Tucker, on the other, are correct. Some top-down conventions are immediately effective, as with the most recent edition of the Ministerial Code, but others, perhaps like the Sewel conventions, are of uncertain status until political actors comply with them. It is now clear the announcement of the Sewel conventions succeeded in shaping the conduct of Parliament, but it might have been that MPs declined to accept it as a constraint on their legislative conduct. We have, then, two forms of top-down convention: one group in which the announced convention is immediately effective because of a further convention empowering a person or institution to create it, and another group in which the announcement acts as a seed from which, it is hoped, a convention will grow.

The line between top-down and bottom-up conventions is blurred in at least two respects. First, as McHarg argues, some top-down conventions come into existence only once political actors have accepted that the convention should guide their conduct; although the impetus for the convention is top-down, its existence is determined bottom-up. Secondly, even where top-down conventions come into existence by virtue of a convention empowering the creation of the new convention, that empowering convention is, normally, bottom-up; it emerges

[15] Aileen McHarg, 'Reforming the United Kingdom Constitution: Law, Convention, Soft Law' (2008) 71 Modern Law Review 853, 861.

[16] Perry and Tucker (n 12) 773–74.

over time and lacks a single author. A consequence of this is that the empowering rule may be unclear: the prime minister's power to modify the rules in the Ministerial Code is limited, but the extent of these limits is uncertain.

6.1.3 Conventions as Specific Rules and Conventions as Broader Principles

Many conventions are as certain as a rule found in a statute: that the Queen should give her assent to bills that have been approved by the Commons and Lords is a rule as clear as any to be found in legislation. Other conventions, though, are far less clear. It is, for example, arguable that it is a convention of the constitution that Parliament not legislate contrary to some of the basic principles of constitutionalism, such as the rule of law; this is a principle that has been invoked in parliamentary debates as a reason to shape the contents of legislation.[17] There might be other principles of this type in the UK constitution: perhaps we could include representative government, constitutional monarchy, maybe even the separation of powers, in the list. Even if not legally enforceable (or enforceable only in part) these principles still shape the conduct of constitutional actors. They help form the constitutional ideology of the state: a set of broad commitments about the structure and functioning of the constitution.

This type of convention should be distinguished from direct assertions about the morally, or prudentially, correct course of action. So, when Geoffrey Marshall wrote that the most obvious and undisputed convention was that Parliament not use its 'power of legislation in an oppressive or tyrannical way', he might have been right about how Parliament should behave, but wrong to identify this as a convention.[18] As we will see, conventions mediate between the reasons on which they rest and the course of action they propose. The principle of the rule of law rests on a great many reasons connected to legal certainty, equality, and so on. When treated as a convention, it allows political actors to

[17] See eg HC Deb 23 May 2011, vol 528, col 638 (Dominic Grieve).

[18] Geoffrey Marshall, *Constitutional Conventions: The Rules and Forms of Political Accountability* (Clarendon Press 1984) 9.

present the principle in argument without having to return to the reasons on which the principle rests. In contrast, the claim that Parliament should not legislate tyrannically is a direct statement of a reason; there is no mediating role for a principle.

Once again, the divide between conventions that take the form of specific rules and those that present themselves as broader principles is a soft one.[19] In this context, principles should be understood as a vaguer type of rule; requiring those they address to behave in a certain way, but often leaving a wide discretion over their interpretation. Any given convention could travel along this spectrum over time, becoming more or less tightly defined.

6.1.4 Conventions: The General Part

Conventions are rules and, moreover, they are rules which operate within a community; these rules are not merely hypothetical, they have an effect. As functioning rules, there are at least three elements that require consideration:

Reason(s) for the Rule → Formulation of the Rule → Conduct affected by the Rule
Democratic government → Queen should assent to legislation → Queen gives her assent

Figure 6.1: Elements of Conventions.

Rules present themselves as authoritative, they tell people what to do. Conventions are no exception: the convention requiring the Queen to give assent to legislation purports to impose an obligation on the Queen; she should give assent *because* of the convention. Looking at Figure 6.1, there is a gap between the reasons for the rule and the rule itself. Whilst a convention should, and often does, rest on solid reasons, it stands separate from those reasons; if the convention is operative, when the Queen considers giving assent, she does not go back to consider the reasons on which the convention rests but relies on the convention itself as a reason for acting. In Joseph Raz's terminology, conventions are, in part, exclusionary reasons: they purport to exclude from

[19] HLA Hart, *The Concept of Law* (2nd edn, Clarendon Press 1994) 259–63 and Joseph Raz, 'Legal Principles and the Limits of the Law' (1972) 81 Yale Law Journal 823, responding to Ronald Dworkin, 'The Model of Rules 1' in Ronald Dworkin, *Taking Rights Seriously* (Duckworth 1977).

consideration some of the reasons that would otherwise apply to actors' deliberations.[20]

In the literature on conventions, the role of reasons is disputed. It is undeniably the case that conventions *should* be grounded in reasons, and, as they present themselves as authoritative, conventions implicitly *claim* that they exist for good reasons. But do conventions actually require the existence of a reason? Sir Ivor Jennings and Geoffrey Marshall both thought so. Jennings argued that when we are attempting to identify conventions, one of the features we should look for is the reason for the rule,[21] whereas Marshall wrote that 'conventions are the rules that the political actors *ought* to feel obligated by, if they have considered the precedents and reasons correctly'.[22] On Marshall's account, an apparent convention that lacked a basis in reason would not be a convention at all. But the gap between the reasons and the formulation of the rule permits the existence of a convention which lacks a grounding in a reason. Because actors do not keep returning to the reasons behind the convention when using the convention in their reasoning (this is, after all, part of the nature of reasoning with rules), it is possible that conventions exist without a grounding in reasons, or that the reasons on which they were at one time based have withered away. Marshall may be right that political actors should disregard conventions that lack reasons, but he is wrong to think that these reason-less conventions cannot exist. As Sir Kenneth Wheare wrote, it is enough that a convention is 'a rule of behaviour accepted as obligatory by those concerned in the working of the Constitution'.[23]

The requirement that it be 'accepted' takes us to the behavioural element of conventions. Conventions affect behaviour in two ways: they affect how actors deliberate and they affect actors' visible conduct. In terms of deliberation, for the convention to function, at least a portion of those whom the convention purports to bind must accept the rule. This need not mean they

[20] Joseph Raz, *The Morality of Freedom* (Oxford University Press 1986) 57–62. Jaconelli also notes this quality of conventions: see Joseph Jaconelli, 'The Nature of Constitutional Convention' (1999) 19 Legal Studies 24, 28.

[21] Jennings (n 3) 136. [22] Marshall (n 18) 12.

[23] Kenneth Wheare, *Modern Constitutions* (2nd edn, Oxford University Press 1966) 122.

endorse the rule: acceptance does not require that they believe it to be morally obligatory, it is enough that they will comply with the rule, that they accept it as governing their conduct. So, the Queen might believe the royal assent convention lacks a basis in reason, that it would be better if she could pick and choose the bills she approved, but she might still reluctantly accept the convention nevertheless. However, in addition to acceptance, for a convention to exist at least some of the community must regard it as genuinely authoritative, believing that it does rest on good reasons. If this were not the case, if no one believed the supposed convention ought to be followed, it would not be a convention at all; it would merely be an assertion of political pressure. If no one believed there were good reasons for the royal assent convention, yet were still pressuring the Queen to follow it, this would be a threat that governed her behaviour, not a rule.[24]

As we saw in our discussion of McHarg's work on conventions, it is sometimes argued that for a convention to exist there must be, as Jennings puts it, precedents; it is not enough that people accept the convention, the convention must be shown to have shaped their conduct.[25] The requirement that precedents be identified is prudent. A person wishing to establish the existence of a convention should check to see if it has been acted upon in the past, but it is not necessary, as the acceptance of the convention is itself an action establishing its existence. Once a significant portion of the political community accepts the convention as binding, the convention exists, even if it has yet to be acted upon: it has become a rule of the group.

And finally, as Joseph Jaconelli prudently reminds us, a convention is a *constitutional* convention when it is constitutional in nature. There are lots of social rules, some of which affect the operation of the state, but not all of which are constitutional conventions.[26] We would not, for example, think of rules of grammar or

[24] The position is slightly different in systemic conventions where, like law, a rule could exist that no one thought was backed by reason, but which was identified as a convention by other rules. But some, at least, of the rules of systemic conventions must be endorsed by some of the community.

[25] Jennings (n 3). [26] Jaconelli (n 20) 35–39.

basic social etiquette as constitutional conventions, even though they may be indispensable to the operation of the state.

6.2 WHY CONVENTIONS BIND

Lawyers very rarely wonder why law binds.[27] For legal reasoning to be useful, it is enough that, in general, law works, and the miracle on which this rests, people's willingness to accept laws as a guide to their conduct, can be set to one side.[28] Lawyers probably should worry more about the basis for this miracle—maintaining the effectiveness of law is something that should concern us, and is relevant to the principle of the rule of law, discussed in Chapter 20—but in the area of conventions, perhaps because of the lack of explicit sanctions backing the rules, the question is especially pressing. As with the binding nature of law, there are probably a number of reasons for the efficacy of conventions. The immediate basis for their effectiveness is commonly a fear of the criticism that will be generated if they are disobeyed: an essential characteristic of a social rule is that its breach triggers criticism; a portion, at least, of the community in which the rule operates regards it as a rule that merits obedience.[29] This criticism serves as a form of sanction: constitutional actors who breach conventions may see their political capital diminish. In extreme cases, this may require resignation; for example, when in 2018 Amber Rudd, then the Home Secretary, was found to have misled Parliament and breached the convention of ministerial responsibility, she lost her job as a result of the consequent political pressure.[30] But sanctions may also be less direct; a politician may find they miss out on promotion or just have less capacity to persuade others as a consequence of breaching convention.

Recognising the significance of social criticism and political capital in making conventions effective (or, at least, making them

[27] Although see Tom R Tyler, *Why People Obey the Law* (rev edn, Princeton University Press 2006).

[28] And there is something miraculous to this: states rarely, if ever, have the capacity to make law bind solely through the use of threats and bribes.

[29] Hart (n 19) 55–57.

[30] 'Amber Rudd Resigns as Home Secretary' *BBC News* (30 April 2018) https://www.bbc.co.uk/news/uk-politics-43944988.

costly to breach) only gets us part of the way to answering the question set at the start of this section. We still need to know *why* social criticism is generated when a convention is breached, why people within the political community regard it as a binding rule. In an important article, Joseph Jaconelli argues that the binding force of conventions is grounded in reciprocity: the party in power honours conventions because it knows that, one day, it will be out of power, and will then be the beneficiary of those conventions.[31] Similarly, in respect of some conventions that exist between institutions, such as the Sewel conventions, Jaconelli argues a *quid pro quo* can be identified: the Scottish Parliament acquiesces to its subordinate status, whilst the Westminster Parliament resists the temptation to legislate in devolved areas.[32] Many conventions may depend on the fear of tit-for-tat: political actors bear the burdens of the convention because of the benefits generated by the reciprocal conduct of other constitutional actors.

Jaconelli's work on the binding force of conventions is persuasive, but there are a few caveats that must be drawn. First, Jaconelli does not claim that his account of the binding force of conventions is a complete account; some conventions might not fit into the *quid pro quo* model, and, more generally, there may be other reasons why actors are constrained by ones that do. It could be, for example, that that some people obey conventions, and regard others as obliged to obey conventions, simply because they think it is the right thing to do. Or there might be some conventions that are effective because the people 'bound' by them want to be bound. One of possible reasons for the effectiveness of ministerial responsibility is that ministers *want* to be responsible for their departments; responsibility is the flipside of power. Secondly, Jaconelli's explanation of the effectiveness of conventions depends on the continuity of political actors over time; for the *quid pro quo* to work, the entity bearing the burden now must anticipate enjoying the benefit later on. It is unlikely that individuals could play this role: a politician holding a post in government today is unlikely to hold a post in opposition in five or so years'

[31] Joseph Jaconelli, 'Do Constitutional Conventions Bind?' (2005) 64 Cambridge Law Journal 149, 170.

[32] ibid 175.

time, and a minister might, rationally, conclude that the chances of their benefiting from a convention later on in their career are too slight to justify the burden. Jaconelli's argument is rendered plausible because of the role played by political parties in the constitution; it is parties that provide the necessary continuity.[33] So, whilst individual politicians come and go, the Labour Party, as an entity, can reasonably expect to be in and out of power over time. It may be that parties play a crucial role in the effectiveness of some conventions, and it is party members, with an awareness of long-term political practice, that constrain politicians to comply with conventions. This leaves us with a worry: if political parties do play a central role, a weakening of party structures, as has occurred during the Brexit debates, may lead to a weakening of the effectiveness of some conventions.

6.3 HOW SHOULD CONVENTIONS BE INTERPRETED?

All rules are unclear in some situations. Rules normally have a clear core, a range of situations in which anyone who understands the rule would agree it applies, but outside of this core the significance of the rule may be reasonably disputed. Conventions are not invariably less clear than statutory rules, but even if we take a very clear rule, such as royal assent, there will still be aspects of it that lack clarity. The convention of royal assent requires that the Queen give assent to all bills that have been approved by the Commons and the Lords. But what if the prime minister advised the Queen not to grant assent? Some constitutional lawyers argue that in this circumstance the Queen should regard herself as bound by this advice: the Cardinal Convention of the constitution, it is claimed, is that the Queen exercises her legal powers on the advice of her ministers.[34] Others doubt this is correct, and Anne Twomey, in the standard work on the powers of the monarch, leaves the question open.[35]

[33] ibid 171–72.

[34] Adam Tomkins, *Public Law* (Oxford University Press 2003) 63–64; Rodney Brazier, 'Royal Assent to Legislation' (2013) 129 Law Quarterly Review 184.

[35] Anne Twomey, *The Veiled Sceptre: Reserve Powers of Heads of State in Westminster Systems* (Cambridge University Press 2018) ch 9.

To decide which of these versions of the convention is correct, we need to interpret the convention. The starting point for any interpretation is the precedents: how the convention has operated in the past, looking at both what was done and considering the actors' views of the convention. The common law, discussed in Chapter 4, possesses rules that regulate the identification and use of precedents in developing the law; but in the context of conventions, whilst it is generally agreed that precedents are important, there are no, or few, parallel rules to guide interpretation. Consequently, the status and significance of these precedents is unclear, and, we might add, the reason we would want to look at the precedents is unclear, too. Although it is generally agreed that precedents are important, it can sometimes be difficult to know what the invocation of a precedent is supposed to prove. It could be that it is the precedent itself that shapes the convention: because constitutional actors behaved a certain way in the past, and did so believing themselves bound by convention, that precedent defines the contemporary rule. This would treat conventions as resembling a form of customary law, where past practice is taken as solidifying into a rule that binds the present. It would be surprising if conventions worked in this way: it would require the political community to have accepted this as a general rule regulating the development of conventions, and there seems little, if any, evidence of support for such a rule amongst political actors. An alternative explanation of the use of precedents is that they are not binding in themselves, but, instead, are relied upon to indicate the reasons for the convention, invoked as examples of where the convention achieved its purpose. The precedent will need to be interrogated, and its underlying reason identified. Sometimes, this may be simple and conclusive: the reason is obvious, and its implications for the contemporary crisis straightforward. But on other occasions the interrogation might reveal that the invocation of the convention in the past was mistaken, or relied upon an understanding of the constitution that has changed: the supposed precedent no longer acts as a signpost to the reason behind the contemporary convention, and can be set aside.

At the core of any interpretation of a convention, then, is its animating reason, if one can be identified. As Ronald Dworkin wrote of law, any interpretation of a convention should strive to show it in its best light.[36] Returning to the question of royal assent, those who argue that the Queen should accept the advice of her ministers do not explain why this interpretation of the convention is attractive, they merely classify the convention on royal assent together with the rest of the conventions surrounding prerogative powers. As we have seen, most of these powers are exercised on the advice of ministers, normally the prime minister, and the reason animating these conventions, removing the discretion of the Queen, is the value of democratic government: ministers are accountable to Parliament and, ultimately, to the electorate, for the ways they use these powers. But does this reason justify the inclusion of royal assent within the group of prerogative powers that are exercised on ministerial advice? It is hard to see that it does. The point of the convention on royal assent is to uphold the primacy of the democratic element of the constitution in the making of law. But just as it would be undemocratic to allow the monarch to veto legislation, so too it would be undemocratic to give this power to the prime minister. In short, when presented with a bill that has passed through Parliament in the proper manner, the duty of the monarch is to give assent irrespective of the advice of her ministers. On the best interpretation of the convention, if the monarch were to accept the advice of her prime minister to decline royal assent, she would be acting unconstitutionally.

6.4 CONVENTIONS AND LAWS

To most constitutional scholars who have written on conventions one thing is beyond dispute: conventions are, by definition, not laws. This confident statement requires two qualifications. First, even if conventions are not laws, they may still condition how the courts decide cases by shaping and informing legal rules. Secondly, conventions can change their nature and become laws, either through incorporation by a law-making institution or, more controversially, through a process of crystallisation. These two aspects of the relationship between conventions and laws will be considered in turn.

[36] Ronald Dworkin, *Law's Empire* (Hart Publishing 1998) ch 3, 90.

6.4.1 Courts and Conventions

Albert Venn Dicey boldly stated that constitutional conventions are neither 'enforced or recognised by courts'.[37] But Dicey was wrong. Courts can recognise anything they wish to recognise. Judges frequently make reference to dictionaries, encyclopaedias, and myriad other sources. It would be surprising if they never recognised constitutional conventions. The courts may recognise conventions in the course of interpreting legislation and may sometimes use conventions as proof of facts required in the course of proving a legal right. For example, in a number of cases the courts have relied upon a convention when interpreting a statute, having decided that the statute presupposes the existence of the convention.[38] Similarly, the courts have made reference to conventions when deciding whether a public body has acted reasonably in making its decision. In *Evans v Information Commissioner*, Evans, a journalist, sought the disclosure of memos written by Prince Charles to various government departments.[39] The departments declined to release the memos and Evans applied to the Upper Tribunal to review the decision to keep the memos confidential. The Upper Tribunal found for Evans, and in the course of this finding spent some time examining the conventions that touched on Prince Charles' communications with the government. In particular, the Information Commissioner argued that the 'Education Convention' required the creation of an environment in which the heir to the throne could learn about the operation of government. Such education, it was argued, could only occur in private; the convention required that the memos remain confidential. Having examined the Education Convention, and related conventions, in detail, the Upper Tribunal concluded that the scope of, and weight due to, the convention was not sufficient to justify the refusal to disclose the memos.[40]

[37] Dicey (n 1) 417.

[38] See eg *British Coal Corporation v R* [1935] AC 500 (PC).

[39] *Evans v Information Commissioner* [2012] UKUT 313 (AAC). The case eventually went to the Supreme Court on another issue: *R (Evans) v Attorney General* [2015] UKSC 51, [2015] 1 AC 1787.

[40] The discussion by the Upper Tribunal of the conventions is surprising, as the legal question before the Upper Tribunal turned on the public interest. The

Furthermore, it is possible for a convention to be enforced indirectly when its demands match those of a distinct legal right. In *Attorney General v Jonathan Cape*, the court relied upon the convention of collective responsibility when deciding a case about breach of confidence.[41] Richard Crossman was a former cabinet minister who wanted to publish his diaries written during his time in government. The Attorney General argued that the legal rule of confidence bound Crossman: information received in an atmosphere of confidence should not be divulged. The Attorney General invoked the convention of collective responsibility to show that this atmosphere of confidence existed; the convention required that ministers not disclose cabinet discussions. In the event, the court decided that the lapse of time between the cabinet meetings and the publication of the diaries was sufficiently long that the public interest allowed publication. Reflecting on the reason for the convention—that it permitted and encouraged uninhibited discussion—the court concluded that it was no longer necessary to enforce confidentiality. Had the court found for the Attorney General, it would have enforced the convention, but the convention would not have formed the basis of its decision: the basis of the decision would have been a legal right, the law of confidence. The convention stood as evidence of one element needed to establish that legal right.

Finally, in rare situations the court may make a declaration about the existence of a convention, even if the convention is not connected to a legal claim. In *Re Amendment of the Constitution of Canada*, the Supreme Court of Canada was asked by the governments of Manitoba, Newfoundland, and Quebec whether a convention existed that required the consent of the provinces before the Canadian government made a request to the UK Parliament to amend the Constitution of Canada.[42] The Canadian government wished to 'patriate' the Canadian Constitution, enacting a new Constitution grounded in the Canadian legal order, rather

discussion of conventions was probably a red herring: the Upper Tribunal should have focused on what the public interest required, and not on the conception of the public interest implicit in the conventions.

[41] *Attorney General v Jonathan Cape Ltd* [1976] QB 752.

[42] *Re Amendment of the Constitution of Canada* (1981) 125 DLR (3rd) 1.

than in an Act of the UK Parliament.[43] In a complicated set of judgments, majorities of the Supreme Court of Canada ruled that there was a convention requiring a substantial measure of provincial consent for the change, that such consent was lacking, but, in addition, that as this was a convention, not a law, the Canadian government could not be legally prohibited from making the application.[44] There is much of interest in this case, but for our purposes it is the process by which the court was able to rule on the existence of the convention and the significance of that ruling that are of importance.

Whilst many courts have recognised conventions in the course of an argument about a legal right, the Canadian case is unusual because the court was asked, directly, to adjudicate on the existence and content of a convention. The court could be asked this question because Canadian legislation empowered provincial governments to apply to courts for advisory opinions, and the courts were willing to accept that this referral power included questions about conventions. These Canadian statues may have been modelled on a UK statute, the Judicial Committee Act 1833,[45] which empowers the monarch to refer questions to the Judicial Committee of the Privy Council for advice, and is similarly broadly drawn: the monarch could refer any matters 'whatsoever as his Majesty shall think fit' to the Committee.[46] It is possible, then, that the monarch, either on the advice of her ministers or acting directly, could ask the Judicial Committee of the Privy Council for advice about conventions. If the monarch were advised by the prime minister to refuse royal assent she could utilise this power to secure the advice of her judges. However, the success of any such reference would depend on the willingness of the judges to engage with the question set, and when the Supreme Court was given an opportunity in *R (Miller) v Secretary of State for the European Union* to rule on the applicability of the Sewel conventions, the judges dodged the issue.[47]

[43] At this time the Canadian constitution was set out in a UK statute: the British North America Act 1867.

[44] Carissima Mathen, *Courts Without Cases: The Law and Politics of Advisory Opinions* (Hart Publishing 2019) ch 6.

[45] ibid ch 1.

[46] Judicial Committee Act 1833, s 4.

[47] [2017] UKSC 5, [2018] AC 61, [136]–[151].

When lawyers write about conventions, there is a temptation to focus tightly on the role played by courts; examining both the judges' tests to identify conventions and their interpretations of those conventions. This court-centred approach should be treated with caution. In contrast to pronouncements about the law, judges' pronouncements about the nature and content of conventions have no direct authority; they are not legally empowered to deliver binding rulings on these issues. So, when the Canadian Supreme Court adopted Sir Ivor Jennings' test of a convention, that adoption did not make Jennings' test authoritative for those of us studying the operation of the constitution. And when the court purports to identify the existence or content of a convention, the judges could just be wrong. However, judges' interpretation of conventions can shift the views of the community in which the convention operates, potentially both modifying the general view of the convention as well as making it harder to avoid complying with it. In the Canada case, the decision of the Supreme Court was broadly accepted; the judgment clarified the implications of the convention and, in response to the ruling, the national government went back to negotiate with the dissenting provinces to secure their assent for the proposed constitutional changes.[48]

6.4.2 Conventions That Become Laws

The simplest way a convention can become a law is through the action of a law-making institution transforming it into a law. Once the law moves into the space previously occupied by the convention, the convention is extinguished even if the substance of the constitutional rule remains. The clearest example of a convention being turned into a law is found in the Parliament Act 1911. By the first decade of the twentieth century, a set of conventions had emerged that gave the elected Commons precedence over the unelected Lords. When these conventions broke down following the Lords' rejection of the 1909 budget, Parliament

[48] In the end, Manitoba and Newfoundland agreed, but Quebec continued to dissent. The national government treated this as sufficient agreement to satisfy the convention and applied to the UK Parliament to change the law.

enacted the 1911 Act to put the rules on a statutory footing. The Lords lost their power to veto money bills and saw their broader power to refuse assent replaced by a power to delay, but not veto, legislation approved by the Commons. The conventions had been replaced by laws.

It is not only Parliament that can transform conventions into laws. In principle at least, any law-making institution in the constitution could bring about this transformation. As Mark Elliott notes, the *Factortame* litigation could be interpreted as an instance of the courts giving legal force to a convention that governed the relationship between English and European Law.[49] *Factortame* was discussed in Chapter 5, and was the case in which an English court gave precedence to directly effective European Law over a UK statute. Prior to *Factortame*, it was arguable that a convention had emerged that Parliament would not legislate in conflict with directly effective European law.[50] The decision in that case transformed this into a legal constraint.[51]

Finally, it is arguable that in some instances conventions crystallise into laws. This process of crystallisation is possible because the difference between laws and conventions is one of degree, rather than an absolute divide; conventions can accrete the features of a legal order. As we have seen, like laws, there can be systems of conventions, with rules emerging that enable their interpretation and the creation of new conventions. As these rules become formalised, systemic conventions start to look similar to a legal system. When these systems develop institutions, bodies empowered to create and adjudicate the conventions, and include rules that regulate their relationships with other sets of rules, such as domestic law, we have entities that resemble legal orders. The Ministerial Code, discussed above, possesses all of these attributes,

[49] *R v Secretary of State for Transport, ex p Factortame (No 2)* [1991] 1 AC 603 (HL); Mark Elliott, 'Parliamentary Sovereignty and the New Constitutional Order' (2002) 22 Legal Studies 340, 371.

[50] See Munro's account of the relationship prior to *Factortame*: Colin R Munro, *Studies in Constitutional Law* (Butterworths 1987) 132.

[51] It is also arguable that the Supreme Court in *Cherry v Advocate General for Scotland* [2019] UKSC 41, [2019] 3 WLR 589 transformed some of the conventional constraints on the power to prorogue Parliament into legal constraints.

and provides an example of a systemic convention that comes close to constituting a pocket legal order within the constitution.

6.5 CONCLUSION

Rather than approaching conventions from a legal perspective, this chapter has sought to address them on their own terms: as political rules with their own mode of creation, their own reasons for binding, and requiring a distinct method of interpretation. But the contrast between laws and conventions remains important, and is often connected to a broader question about conventions: that is, whether this type of rule is inferior to, and should be replaced by, law. Although the question is often posed, it is misdirected. First, it would be impossible to replace all conventions with laws. This is partly because all constitutions include conventions, and even if a diligent lawyer transposed all the existing conventions into a statute, new conventions would swiftly emerge. More worrying still for that diligent lawyer, many conventions cannot be transmuted into law because their purpose is to provide a political countermand to a legal power. So, the convention on royal assent effectively negates a legal right possessed by the Queen. It would be nonsensical to make this negation a legal rule: it would, of course, be possible to abolish the need for royal assent, but that would be an alteration of the law rather than a juridification of the convention. Furthermore, some conventions appear to play knowingly on their lack of legal enforceability. The Sewel conventions, for example, may have been given the quality of conventions rather than laws precisely to avoid their being legally enforced. As conventions, they can be overridden by political actors, if those actors are willing to pay the political cost, and so form a different type of constraint to laws. Turning them into laws would alter the substance of the rule, as well as the form that the rule took. Secondly, there may be some situations in which conventions are preferable to laws simply because it is difficult to see how a court could step in to enforce the rule. Ministerial responsibility is a complicated set of conventions that partly regulates the relationship between Parliament and the executive. But it is hard to see how a court could judge if a minister has fallen below the standards Parliament should expect her to meet, or decide if the answers given to a parliamentary question are insufficiently informative. Whilst there may be particular conventions that would benefit from being turned into laws, it would be a mistake to attempt to undertake this transformation on all conventions.

7

CONSTRUCTING STATE SOVEREIGNTY

Whilst United Kingdom (UK) constitutional lawyers have focused, sometimes to the point of obsession, on parliamentary sovereignty, there is a second sense of sovereignty that is of far greater constitutional importance: state sovereignty. State sovereignty is a necessary feature of states and, moreover, a feature of states that we have reason to value. It is state sovereignty that enables the state to regulate power exercised within its territory successfully and, when the state is functioning well, that enables democratic decision-making.

State sovereignty consists of two elements: a claim and the vindication of that claim. As to the claim, states present themselves as the supreme authority over their territory and their people. As such, the commands of the state may be, and often are, backed by a threat of force, but the state does not rest its claim on its capacity to wield power. Instead, its claim is to authority, an assertion of an entitlement to rule: the state claims that its people *ought* to obey it. The sovereign claim of the state points in two directions. Internally, it is a claim that people should obey the commands of the state. Externally, it is a claim that the state itself decides on the use of power within its territory, that its decisions are not determined by some other powerful body, such as a multinational corporation or a rival state. For state sovereignty to be present, this claim must, to some extent, be effective; the state must actually be able to exercise some control over its territory and people. There is an important distinction to be drawn between the claim of sovereignty and the realisation of the claim: the claim is absolute, amounting to an unqualified assertion that the state is entitled to determine the legitimate exercise of power within its territory, but, for sovereignty to be established, the claim needs only be partially effective. No state ever manages to control the exercise of power completely.

The United Kingdom Constitution. N. W. Barber, Oxford University Press. © Nick Barber 2021.
DOI: 10.1093/oso/9780198852315.003.0007

This chapter focuses on the articulation of the authority claim made by the UK, one half of the sovereignty equation. The ways in which this claim is rendered effective are addressed in the rest of the book; indeed, the whole institutional structure of the state could be seen as an answer to the question of effectiveness. State institutions articulate the claim of sovereignty whenever they require a person to act in a certain way; an assertion of sovereignty is implicit in every such command. The state institution must be obeyed, unless there is some other constitutional rule that permits disobedience or creates the possibility of appeal. But the previous chapters have revealed a problem for the articulation of state sovereignty in the context of the UK. There are three fundamental, interconnected, pluralities within the UK constitution: a plurality of constitutional sources, a plurality of legal systems, and a plurality of territories. In terms of constitutional sources, as we have seen the UK constitution is drawn from a number of non-derived legal sources—statute, common law, prerogative, and privilege—and it also includes non-legal rules, conventions, some of which are amongst the most important rules of the constitution. Allied to this, the UK constitution has at least two legal systems, English law and Scots law, that have their own, distinct, rules relating to these sources. To constitute a state, the UK must advance a claim to sovereignty over its people and territory, but these pluralities within the UK constitution make it hard to see how the state draws these elements together into a unified assertion of sovereignty. Or, to put it another way, why should we conceptualise the UK as a single state rather than a collection of institutions with separate constitutional identities, all making distinct assertions of sovereignty?

We are entitled to be reasonably sure that there is an answer to be found—the UK is clearly a state—but finding that answer is harder than might first be thought. As Janet McLean demonstrates in her important book, *Searching for the State in British Legal Thought*, UK constitutional scholars have, for generations, failed to engage with the question of the state, and, by failing to engage with it, have struggled to answer some fundamental constitutional questions.[1] These questions may seem abstract, but

[1] Janet McLean, *Searching for the State in British Legal Thought: Competing Conceptions of the Public Sphere* (Cambridge University Press 2012).

they have important constitutional consequences: it is through reflection on them that we can identify when the state has acted and, relatedly, the scope of the state's (and our) responsibilities. We need some explanation of why and how the disparate actions of, for example, the Scottish Parliament, the UK Supreme Court, and the Minister for Transport, are all actions of the UK state, and actions for which the state, and its citizens, bear responsibility.

UK constitutional lawyers have offered a range of answers to the unity question. These can be grouped into three broad categories: those that rely on an overarching institution as unifier, principally the Crown; those that rely on the identification of a fundamental constitutional rule as unifier, normally parliamentary sovereignty; and, finally, those that invoke a system of rules, in particular the common law, as the unifying structure of the UK constitution. None of these three is completely satisfactory, but each has something to teach us about the elements that draw the UK constitution together.

7.1 THE CROWN AS UNIFIER

At first glance, it is hard to see why the concept of the Crown might be thought to play a unifying role in the UK constitution; judicial deliberation over the nature of the Crown stretches back more than 500 years and has resulted in a legal concept of unparalleled obscurity. As we shall see, part of this obscurity is due to the Crown being employed as an answer to a number of different constitutional questions, including the unity question. However, even when the discussion focuses on a single question, the use of the Crown in legal reasoning is inconsistent. Cases on the nature of the Crown are infrequent and span a long historical period. Consequently, the legal and social assumptions on which these decisions rest have changed radically. This, in turn, has rendered it hard for judges and scholars to understand fully the pronouncements of their predecessors, or, indeed, to accept these pronouncements even if they understood them. It is impossible not to sympathise with Fredric Maitland, when that distinguished legal historian bluntly described many cases on the Crown as 'nonsense'.[2]

The core use of the Crown in constitutional law is to distinguish the office of the monarch from the individual who holds that office. Taken in this sense, the Crown is understood as a legal institution occupied by a single person, a 'corporation sole'. As a corporation sole, the Crown has a distinct legal identity: it is an artificial legal person that can undertake legal acts that natural persons, people, can accomplish. For example, the Crown can hold land and form contracts in its own right. The Queen, the natural legal person who occupies the office of the Crown, can also possess property and agree contracts in a personal capacity. In contrast to holders of the office, the Crown can never die; as an artificial legal person it has an indefinite lifespan, which allows for legal continuity despite the deaths of individual monarchs.[3] The common law used the concept of the Crown to explain how the rights, duties, and property of the monarch could transfer from one king to another without the intervention of some other constitutional institution.

This simple account of the nature of the Crown needs to be qualified. In the *Case of the Dutchy of Lancaster*, the judges opined that the king had a 'body natural and a body politic together indivisible'.[4] This mingling of the person and office is a recurrent feature of case law on the Crown; whilst the logic of the Crown as corporation sole requires a sharp divide between the person and the office, the common law has failed successfully to delineate the division between these two entities.[5] The person and the office were mixed, and in a number of areas statute has had to intervene to sort out the resulting mess.[6] Indeed, a countervailing scepticism of the separation of the person and office has pervaded a number

[2] FW Maitland, *The Constitutional History of England* (Cambridge University Press 1908) 35.

[3] Martin Loughlin, 'The State, the Crown and the Law' in Maurice Sunkin and Sebastian Payne (eds), *The Nature of the Crown: A Legal and Political Analysis* (Oxford University Press 1999) 53.

[4] (1561) 1 Plowd 212, 213; 75 ER 325, 327.

[5] HWR Wade and CF Forsyth, *Administrative Law* (11th edn, Oxford University Press 2014) 689–91; Loughlin (n 3) 57.

[6] McLean (n 1) 133–40.

of cases. For instance, in *Calvin's Case* an English court concluded that those born in Scotland after 1603 should be considered English subjects, entitled to the benefits of English law, because James I of England was also James VI of Scotland.[7] But England and Scotland were still separate states, and would not be united for another 100 years; if the person and office of the Crown were distinct, those born in Scotland should have been taken to owe allegiance to, and to be entitled to protection from, the Scottish Crown, not the English Crown, even if the same person sat on each throne. Similarly, in *Viscount Canterbury v Attorney General* the court found that Queen Victoria did not inherit the liabilities incurred by George IV.[8] As these liabilities related to activities undertaken by servants of the Crown acting in an official capacity, it might have been thought that liability fell on the office of the Crown, and the change in the identity of the officeholder should not affect that liability, but the court was unswayed. As Maitland wrote, English lawyers liked their persons to be real.[9]

As well as being ambiguous in its core usage, the scope of the concept of the Crown was also unclear and, as John Allison has shown, even in the late middle ages the Crown was defined 'in capacious terms'.[10] In *Calvin's Case* the court presented the Crown as signifying the doing of justice, distinguishing right from wrong, and tasked with maintaining the peace.[11] Here, the Crown is equated with the exercise of public power.[12] Whilst in the *Dutchy of Lancaster Case* the Crown extended to include the whole of government and the management 'of the public-weal'[13] and, in more recent times, Lord Diplock interpreted the Crown as embracing the government and Lord Simon argued that the Crown was a corporation aggregate, which included the departments of state.[14]

[7] (1608) 7 Co Rep 1a, 77 ER 377. See further ch 15.

[8] (1843) 1 Ph 306, 41 ER 648. See now the Crown Proceedings Act 1947, s 32.

[9] Maitland (n 2) 33.

[10] JWF Allison, *The English Historical Constitution* (Cambridge University Press 2007) 54–58.

[11] (1608) 7 Co Rep 2a, 11b; 77 ER 379, 390.

[12] See also *Willion v Berkley* (1561) Plowd 223; 75 ER 339.

[13] (1561) Plowd 212, 213; 75 ER 325, 326.

[14] *Town Investments Ltd v Department of the Environment* [1978] AC 359, 380–81 (Lord Diplock), 400 (Lord Simon). As Allison notes, the Crown achieved the

As Janet McLean argues, at several points in its history the Crown has come close to being treated as a synonym for the state as a whole.[15] In effect, the Crown became an attempted answer to the unity question: we know the disparate systems, sources, and institutions of the UK constitution are a single entity because they are all aspects of, or defined in relationship to, the Crown. This conclusion might be reinforced by the presence of the Crown in each of the three branches of state. When Parliament legislates, the Crown counts as one of the three parts of the constitution (the other two being the Lords and the Commons) that must give assent to legislation. In the courts, the Crown acts as the fount of justice; the judges administer the law in its name.[16] And finally, in the executive it is nominally the Crown who appoints ministers and the Crown to whom civil servants owe their loyalty.[17]

There are two problems with the equation of the Crown with the state. First, and most superficially, it avoids the unity question rather than answering it. If we decide to treat the Crown as the state, we are still left unsure how the state should be defined and identified; all we have really achieved is its relabelling. How the elements of the UK constitution are drawn together into a single entity would remain unresolved: as so often in its history, invocation of the Crown would have obscured rather than resolved a constitutional issue.[18] Secondly, it would be ahistorical. Aside from some rhetorical flourishes, the Crown has never been equated with the state in UK constitutional thought; it was never taken as the source of all public power or regarded as an amalgam of all public offices. As McLean notes, the common law never regarded all public bodies as emanations of the Crown.[19] So, for example, whilst the Crown might claim to be the source of judicial authority, it never claimed to be the source of the authority of the common law. As discussed in Chapter 4, the common law's authority was, and is, constitutionally grounded in the customs of the people, not the dictates of the monarch. Indeed, the Crown

bizarre distinction of being *both* a corporation sole and a corporation aggregate: Allison (n 10) 56.

[15] McLean (n 1) 131.

[16] Loughlin (n 3) 58.

[17] Cabinet Office, *Civil Service Management Code* (2016) s 4.1.1.

[18] Maitland (n 2) 418.

[19] McLean (n 1) 143–48.

does not even encompass the whole of the executive branch: local authorities and some statutory bodies are not regarded as included within its reach.[20]

7.2 PARLIAMENTARY SOVEREIGNTY AS A FOUNDATIONAL RULE

Chapter 5 argued that parliamentary sovereignty is no longer, if it ever was, a feature of the UK constitution. Setting that argument aside, one of the reasons parliamentary sovereignty may have had such a strong appeal to constitutional lawyers is that it appears to provide an answer to the unity question. Parliamentary sovereignty might be thought to be a foundational rule of the UK constitution, the UK constitution's ultimate rule of recognition. The idea of the rule of recognition was developed by Herbert Hart in his classic book, *The Concept of Law*.[21] In some of his formulations of that rule, Hart presented it as identifying, and in identifying, validating, the various rules of the legal system.[22] For Hart, the rule of recognition is an answer to the question of the unity and continuity of legal systems, seeking to explain how we can distinguish between separate legal systems and how legal systems can change over time whilst maintaining their identities.[23] We know that the various sources of law are parts of a single legal order because they are identified as such by the rule of recognition, and we know that a legal system retains its identity over time because the changes it undergoes are undertaken by virtue of rules of change identified by the rule of recognition. Hart presented parliamentary sovereignty as an instance of a rule of recognition,[24] and recent constitutional scholars, following his lead,

[20] *Mersey Docks and Harbour Trustees v Gibbs* (1866) LR 1 HL 93.

[21] HLA Hart, *The Concept of Law* (2nd edn, Oxford University Press 1994).

[22] ibid 109–17.

[23] The answer is not wholly successful: Joseph Raz, 'The Identity of Legal Systems' in *The Authority of Law: Essays on Law and Morality* (Oxford University Press 1979) esp 97–98; Joseph Raz, *The Concept of a Legal System: An Introduction to the Theory of a Legal System* (2nd edn, Oxford University Press 1980) ch 8; John Finnis, 'Revolutions and Continuity of Law' in AWB Simpson (ed), *Oxford Essays in Jurisprudence (Second Series)* (Oxford University Press 1973).

[24] Hart (n 21) 111, 295. John Allison documents private exchanges between Hart and Wade: Allison (n 10) 110–19.

have also made the equation.[25] Perhaps, then, it is parliamentary sovereignty that answers the unity question: we know that the various rules, sources, and systems of the UK constitution are parts of a single state because they are identified as such by parliamentary sovereignty.

Whilst it is tempting to clutch at parliamentary sovereignty as an answer to the unity question, doing so raises a number of problems. First, there is a set of problems around treating the rule of recognition as a constitution. The rule of recognition, even in its most ambitious forms, only ever purported to provide an answer to the question of the unity of the legal system, not the constitution. As a result, the rule of recognition is unable to explain the inclusion of constitutional conventions within the structures of the state. We could, following some legal positivists,[26] equate the state with the legal order but, as we have seen, this would produce a radically distorted picture of the UK. Secondly, from the other direction, treating parliamentary sovereignty as the fundamental rule of recognition is problematic.[27] As Michael Gordon notes, parliamentary sovereignty must be part of the rule of recognition, as parliamentary sovereignty is, after all, a rule that identifies other rules.[28] But it cannot play the role of a foundational rule as it does not purport to identify all of the legal rules in the UK constitution: as we have seen, the rules that identify the prerogative are found in the common law, not in statute, and the common law itself lacks a statutory basis. Indeed, as was argued in Chapter 5, parliamentary sovereignty is itself a common law rule, developed and interpreted by the judges. Finally, it is worth recalling once more the doubts about parliamentary sovereignty expressed earlier in this book: a strong case can be made that parliamentary sovereignty is no longer an element of the UK constitution.

[25] See the discussion in Alison L Young, *Parliamentary Sovereignty and the Human Rights Act* (Hart Publishing 2008).

[26] Hans Kelsen, *General Theory of Law and State* (Anders Weberg and Wolfgang Herbert Kraus (trs), Harvard University Press 1945) 181–201.

[27] Douglas Edlin, 'The Sovereignty of Positivism' (2021) Jurisprudence 1, 9–12.

[28] Michael Gordon, *Parliamentary Sovereignty in the UK Constitution: Process, Politics and Democracy* (Hart Publishing 2015) 81.

7.3 THE COMMON LAW AS CATALYST

These reflections on parliamentary sovereignty lead us to another candidate for the unifier of the UK constitution: the common law itself.[29] As we have seen in previous chapters, it is the common law, developed and applied by the courts, that identifies the disparate legal sources of the constitution. Although it does not purport to validate these sources, it delineates their scope and, frequently, reviews the exercises of legal powers conferred by these sources. Increasingly, judges present the common law as containing broad constitutional principles, as articulating a constitutional ideology for the state, and use these principles to shape the development of law and conduct of state agencies. The role of the common law in establishing the state has been stressed in the writings of judges, most notably Sir John Laws and Sir Stephen Sedley. Laws has argued that the common law provides the unifying principle of the UK's constitution,[30] whilst Sedley presents the common law as the 'crucible' of constitutional law.[31]

Once again, whilst the common law clearly plays a crucial role in drawing together the legal sources of the UK constitution, it cannot provide a complete answer to the unity question. First, and most obviously, this is because there is no single common law spanning the UK. As we have seen, Scots law and English law remain two distinct systems. The common law cannot, and does not purport, to unify these territories. Secondly, the common law has never purported to validate the various legal sources of the UK constitution. So, for example, an exercise of the prerogative is valid before it has been recognised by the courts and, indeed, it is possible that prerogative powers exist which have never been the subject of a case. Finally, the common law cannot unite the conventions of the constitution. Whilst conventions are recognised by the courts from time to time, the courts play a very limited role in this area.

[29] Loughlin (n 3) 64–66.

[30] John Laws, *The Common Law Constitution* (Cambridge University Press 2014) 4–6; John Laws, 'Law and Democracy' [1995] Public Law 72, 92.

[31] Stephen Sedley, 'The Sound of Silence' in Stephen Sedley, *Ashes and Sparks: Essays on Law and Justice* (Cambridge University Press 2007) 87.

7.4 CONCLUSION

This chapter started out with a challenge. States must, by their very nature, make an authority claim over their people and territory. Moreover, this authority claim is of a particular type: it is an assertion of supreme authority, that the state has the final say about the rights and duties of its people. The pluralities of the UK constitution seem to throw the capacity of the UK to make this claim into doubt: how can it be said that the UK makes this claim, when there are multiple sources, systems, and institutions within the UK that lack a shared legal root? Might the UK fragment under scrutiny, with rival sovereignty claims being asserted by different parts of the constitution, and, if this fragmentation does occur, is the UK really a state at all? Three possible responses to the risk of fragmentation have been examined, and each approached the question from a different angle. The Crown provided an answer in terms of a single institution, an overarching constitutional office that served to draw the UK constitution together. Parliamentary sovereignty provided an answer in terms of a fundamental rule, a rule that identified and validated the other legal rules within the system. And the common law provided an answer in terms of a mesh of interlocking rules that created and bound together the UK's systems and institutions. As we have seen, none of these answers is entirely successful, but neither are they complete failures. To appreciate the unity of the UK constitution we need to move away from looking for the one thing, the single golden thread, that unites the constitution, and instead recognise that the UK constitution is not united by a single element, but rather by a collection of interlocking features. Its unity is established through the interactions of institutions and the rules that constitute those institutions, through the mutual recognition of institutions that they are part of a single state, and, ultimately, in the broad recognition of the integrity of the UK by its citizens. These features allow us to identify the UK as a state, even if the elements within that state disagree, from time to time, about their relative constitutional position within that order.

First, there is a collection of interlocking constitutional relationships, in which each institution recognises the other as part of a larger constitutional unit. The simplest example of this is direct empowerment: when an institution is established through statute, the legal relationship between that body and Parliament is obvious. The unity of the territories of the UK is brought about through statutes, although precisely which statutes is open to dispute. But these relationships can also exist where there is no obvious hierarchy between the bodies. So, for example, when the courts adjudicate on the powers of the executive, implicit (or sometimes explicit) in that process of adjudication is the recognition that the executive is part of the same constitutional order as the courts. Consequently, the courts do not approach their task as they would if trying to interpret foreign law, where they treat the law as a matter of fact that needs to be identified; instead, they treat the question as one of right—what the institution is entitled to do, the legal powers it is entitled to exercise. But the flipside of this is the executive's recognition that the courts are entitled to make these determinations. The executive, and equally importantly, those active in the UK constitutional community more generally, ordinarily accept that the courts' determinations are conclusive of the legal powers of the executive, even if they disagree with the courts' decisions. These institutions recognise each other as institutions within a single constitutional order, parts of a larger constitutional entity. These interlocking relationships exist throughout the UK constitution and need not always rest on agreement between the institutions: two elements of the constitution may agree they are parts of a single entity, but disagree about their legal relationship. As these institutions are created and regulated by conventions as well as by laws, this mutual recognition allows us to identify those non-legal rules which form part of the constitution: they are those which speak to the powers and duties of constitutional institutions.

Secondly, and relatedly, some constitutional institutions play a broader role in binding the UK system together. They are recognised by, and in turn recognise, many different parts of the constitution, and this shared recognition helps tie the constitution together. Parliament and the Crown are the two most obvious institutions that play an overarching role of this type. The UK Parliament is recognised by both the English and Scottish legal systems as the highest legislative body within the constitution, and it, in turn, enacts legislation intended to take effect in those systems. Even if English law and Scots law lack a shared apex court, they each recognise a common institution as possessing legislative supremacy.[32] The vagueness of the Crown as a constitutional concept may be frustrating, but this vagueness allows many institutions to express their identification with the state by presenting themselves as tied to the Crown in some manner. In terms of fostering unity, the symbolic aspect of these relationships is as significant as any legal consequences they bring. That the courts present themselves as an emanation of royal power has limited direct legal consequences, but is symbolically powerful. It locates the courts within the state; even when the judges are reviewing the decisions of the executive, they undertake this review from within the constitutional order. Similarly, the civil service and the army also have symbolic links to the Crown. In all three cases, judges, civil servants, and army, their connection to the Crown facilitates a degree of independence from the government whilst maintaining a connection to the state.

Finally, and most fundamentally, the disparate elements of the constitution are tied together by the beliefs of the people of the UK in general, and, in particular, by those who hold offices within the constitutional order. There is a collective recognition that the plurality of elements of the UK constitution are elements of a coherent whole. If someone within the UK challenged this unity, they are likely to be corrected, and criticised if they persisted in their opinion. Perhaps this should be considered one of the most fundamental of all the conventions in the UK constitution: the convention that requires the acknowledgement that the systems, institutions, and territories of the UK are all aspects of a single state.

[32] See ch 4.

II

SEPARATION OF POWERS

8

INTRODUCTION TO THE SEPARATION OF POWERS

The separation of powers is a constitutional principle with a long history. Its longevity can be explained by its intuitive attractiveness: when public power is concentrated in the hands of a few, it will not be exercised effectively and will often be used oppressively. It seems obvious that for a state to function well a diverse range of institutions, skills, powers, and people need to be combined in the making and executing of state decisions. Contemporary accounts of the separation of powers normally trace the principle back to the work of Baron Montesquieu in the eighteenth century.[1] In *The Spirit of the Laws*, Montesquieu derived his account of the separation of powers from the British constitution, presenting a constitutional model in which state power was divided between three branches: judicial, executive, and legislative.[2] The extent to which Montesquieu's account of the British state was accurate is questionable, but his writings proved influential. In *The Federalist Papers*, a series of essays produced during the formation of the American Constitution, James Madison made use of Montesquieu's work, and it is arguable that elements of Montesquieu's conception of the separation of powers underlie the basic structure of the modern American state.[3] The principle fell out of fashion somewhat in the latter part of the twentieth century, but in the last couple of decades has experienced a resurgence of attention: constitutional scholarship

[1] Although its history can be traced back hundreds, and arguably thousands, of years before Montesquieu. See Maurice Vile, *Constitutionalism and the Separation of Powers* (2nd edn, Liberty Press 1998) ch 2.

[2] Baron de Montesquieu, *The Spirit of the Laws* (Anna Cohler, Basia Miller, and Harold Stone (trs), Cambridge University Press 1989) bk 11 ch 6.

[3] James Madison, 'The Particular Structure of the New Government and the Distribution of Power Among Its Different Parts' in James Madison, Alexander Hamilton, and John Jay, *The Federalist Papers* (Isaac Kramnick (ed), Penguin Books 1987) no 47.

The United Kingdom Constitution. N. W. Barber, Oxford University Press. © Nick Barber 2021.
DOI: 10.1093/oso/9780198852315.003.0008

has become increasingly concerned with institutions and institutional interaction, concerns that have reawakened interest in the issues addressed by Montesquieu, Madison, and others writing on the separation of powers.[4]

That the separation of powers is a characteristic of the American Constitution is widely accepted, but the applicability of the separation of powers to the UK constitution is open to dispute.[5] In presidential-style constitutions, like America's, the outline of the separation of powers is easy to see. The head of the executive branch is elected and has her own, independent, democratic mandate; the President consequently pursues her own policies, and picks her own executive team. Thus, in presidential systems, a sharp divide can be drawn between the legislative and executive branches. In contrast, in parliamentary systems such as the UK, the executive and legislative branches are closely linked; the prime minister's authority depends on the support of Parliament. It has been argued that whilst presidential systems are characterised by a separation of powers, parliamentary systems are characterised by their fusion.[6] The question of the applicability of the separation of powers to parliamentary systems will be explored over the following four chapters, and it will be argued that whilst the parliamentary form of the separation of powers differs from the presidential, it is, nevertheless, a working through of the demands of that principle.

8.1 THE BASIC STRUCTURE OF THE SEPARATION OF POWERS

In this section a highly simplified account of the separation of powers will be introduced, bringing forward some of the core elements that will be considered in more detail in later chapters. Most accounts of the separation of powers present the principle as requiring three types of division between three branches of state.[7]

[4] Roger Masterman and Se-shauna Wheatle, 'Unpacking the Separation of Powers: Judicial Independence, Sovereignty, and Conceptual Flexibility in the UK Constitution' [2017] Public Law 469.

[5] O Hood Phillips 'A Constitutional Myth: Separation of Powers' (1977) 93 Law Quarterly Review 11.

[6] Walter Bagehot, *The English Constitution* (Watts & Co 1964) ch 1.

[7] See generally Vile (n 1) ch 4; Montesquieu (n 2) bk 11 ch 6.

The three branches of state are the legislature, the courts, and the executive, whilst the three divisions are between institutions, powers, and officials in those institutions. These nine elements can be placed on a table.

Table 8.1 The Elements of the Separation of Powers

Institution	Legislature	Courts	Executive Office
Officials	Legislators	Judges	Executive Officials
Power	Legislative	Judicial	Executive Power

The first row distinguishes institutional form. The principle requires the state to possess three broad types of institution: the legislature, the court, and the executive office. These three institutional forms differ in some important respects. Legislatures consist of a large number of people gathered in a single institution, with internal structures and party groupings that enable the institution to produce decisions. Courts are smaller institutions, taking a triadic form, with the judge sitting at the head of the triangle, hearing arguments from the disputing litigants (who form the other two points). Whilst there are normally only a few legislatures in a state, there will be a great many courts, with a large number of first instance courts, fewer appellate courts, and a supreme court at the apex. Finally, the executive is divided into offices, teams of people focused on particular tasks. Like a series of Russian dolls, smaller offices exist within the larger offices of state, with the smallest of all operating at a local level, located in towns and villages around the country.

The second row distinguishes types of persons; people with differing types of skills and talents occupy these institutions. In the legislature, members are normally elected, and are not selected because of some particular ability or skill. In contrast, judges and those in the executive branch are commonly chosen because of their technical abilities: judges are appointed because of their knowledge of the law, and members of the executive are selected because of their ability to accomplish the particular goals of the offices they work within.

The third row distinguishes types of powers. The differing types of institution, occupied by people with differing skills, make use of differing tools. The legislature's characteristic means of action is through legislation, the production of statutes: broad, general, laws normally designed to be comprehensible to lay people as well as lawyers. The courts' characteristic means of action is through judgments: decisions about people's rights and liabilities in the case before the judge. The executive's characteristic means of action is through the issuance of commands, backed up by the threat of force.

The separation of powers is a principle that calls for creation, for division, and for unity. In terms of creation, the separation of powers requires states to create structures with the various elements found in Table 8.1. Although this is a point easy to overlook, the principle assumes that these features are features that states need. The divisions are found between the columns, and can be absolute or of degree. Where the division is absolute, the principle demands that there be no overlap at all. So, for example, it might be that people who are judges should never simultaneously hold an office in the legislature: the division of persons is, in this context, absolute and unqualified. More commonly, the division is a matter of degree: the legislature may, occasionally, act like a court when disciplining its members, or perhaps there will be some overlap of members of the executive and legislative branches. Sometimes an absolute divide may not be necessary, or even desirable. The requirement for unity relates to the columns, demanding that institutions, persons, and powers be grouped together. The separation of powers not only requires the creation of certain constitutional types, it also requires that certain types of institutional structure be staffed by certain types of people, and exercise certain types of power.

8.2 THE POINT OF THE SEPARATION OF POWERS

It might seem odd to discuss the purpose of the separation of powers after outlining its contents; after all, what the separation of powers requires will be determined by what it is seeking to achieve. But whilst there is broad agreement about the demands of the separation of powers, there is far less agreement about its objectives. Two broad groups of theories are on offer: those that tie the separation of powers to the protection of liberty, and those that tie the principle to effective state action.

Liberty-based accounts of the separation of powers focus on the role played by the principle in preventing state oppression. Eric Barendt has provided an account of a liberty-model of the separation of powers in the context of the UK. For Barendt, the separation of powers protects liberty by making tyrannical and arbitrary state action more difficult.[8] By dividing power between the various branches of the constitution, with each element checking the others, state action is made more difficult, requiring the cooperation of a range of persons and institutions. Separation of powers is presented as a principle that introduces friction into the constitution, slowing down rash action by the state.

There are a number of difficulties with simple liberty-based models of the separation of powers. First, they assume that strong states are invariably opposed to liberty. However, on occasion, it is the state that acts as the protector of liberty, protecting its people both from other states and from powerful private actors. Furthermore, whilst liberty, interpreted as mere freedom from interference, is valuable, there are positive things that we might want the state to undertake.[9] If states are to provide education, healthcare, and social support, amongst many other possible activities, states need to be able to act effectively; a recognition of the potential value of state action is, perhaps, at the core of the modern welfare state. As Jeremy Waldron notes, it would be democratically problematic if the constitution were structured in such a way as to prevent these policy goals being achieved.[10] Finally, whilst liberty-based models of the separation of powers may explain the divisions drawn between the rows in Table 8.1,

[8] Eric Barendt, 'Separation of Powers and Constitutional Government' [1995] Public Law 599.

[9] Some philosophers argue that seeing liberty as 'freedom from' is too narrow, and that liberty should be understood as 'freedom to'. See Isaiah Berlin, 'Two Concepts of Liberty' in Isaiah Berlin, *Four Essays on Liberty* (Oxford University Press 1969), discussed further in ch 19.

[10] See Jeremy Waldron, 'Constitutionalism: A Skeptical View' in Jeremy Waldron, *Political Political Theory* (Harvard University Press 2016).

they cannot explain the unity found in the columns. For instance, why should the legislature consist of elected representatives and act through statute? Indeed, if the liberty-based models of the separation of powers were correct, we might want to mix things up: if we had the legislature undertaking the tasks of the executive, or required bewigged judges to run government departments, state action would become exponentially harder.

A second set of models of the separation of powers takes efficiency as its animator.[11] On these accounts, the separation of powers requires the creation of a set of institutions that will enable the state to function well. As part of this, institutional form, persons, and powers should be combined in an effective manner. It is arguable that this formulation of the principle underpins many of its classic formulations. When James Madison invoked the separation of powers he was certainly aware of the dangers of tyrannical government, but he was also concerned to establish structures that would enable good government; it is sometimes forgotten that the aim of *The Federalist Papers* was to establish a stronger government for America, not to weaken it.[12] If efficiency is the purpose of the separation of powers, the principle will need to be located within a broader account of the point of the state: to say that a given institutional structure is efficient requires the identification of standards by which efficiency can be tested. So, the requirement that the separation of powers include an elected legislature presupposes that the state should be committed to democracy, and the demand that the executive include officials who are capable of accomplishing the policies of the state presupposes that we have reason to want the state to secure its policy goals. Lying behind any conception of the separation of powers, then, is a conception of the state, and any working through of the demands of the principle will require us, whether consciously or not, to take decisions about the point of having states in our community.

[11] Jeremy Waldron, 'Separation of Powers and the Rule of Law' in Jeremy Waldron, *Political Political Theory* (Harvard University Press 2016).

[12] Gordon Wood, *The Creation of the American Republic 1776–1787* (University of North Carolina Press 1969) chs 10 and 11; Isaac Kramnick, 'Introduction' in James Madison, Alexander Hamilton, and John Jay, *The Federalist Papers* (Isaac Kramnick (ed), Penguin Books 1987) 24–31.

8.3 CONCLUSION

This chapter has provided a brief outline of the separation of powers, presenting some of the relationships and distinctions that will be developed over the next four chapters. These chapters will examine the three branches of state found in the UK constitution, and ask whether Montesquieu was right—whether the separation of powers can be said to be a feature of the UK's constitutional order. The next three chapters consider the unity of the three elements of the separation of powers—the structures, people, and powers—within the three branches of state, whilst the fourth chapter, concluding this part of the book, considers the interactions of these branches. It will be argued that whilst the separation of powers is not a *legal* principle of the UK constitution, it is an implicit *feature* of the UK constitution, the structures of which track the demands of the principle.

9

COURTS

Courts resolve disputes, apply, and develop, the law. The first two of these tasks are complementary. In Chapter 2 we saw that one of the objectives of a constitution was to contain disagreement within society: people may not like the decisions reached by the state and may continue to think that the state got it wrong, but they accept these outcomes and do not attempt to unsettle the decisions through unlawful means. Courts play a crucial part in this process. Whilst legislatures seek to bring closure to disagreement at a broad societal level, the courts seek to bring closure to disagreement involving a limited number of parties, commonly just two. The parties bring their disagreement to the court and, rather than these disputes being ended through the exercise of private force, the court determines the legal entitlements of the litigants. These determinations are then backed by the threat of public force, but, outside of criminal law, such force rarely needs to be used to render the courts' decisions effective: the disappointed party normally complies with the ruling, accepting it even if they continue to disagree with the outcome. Implicit in the way courts present their decisions to litigants is an explanation of why the decision should be accepted by the party who has lost. The decision is presented as resting on the application of the law, not on the judge's personal feelings about the parties; it is a decision determined by legal rules that predate the dispute, and, moreover, rules that were chosen, in one way or another, by the community in which the dispute arose. There are, then, reasons why the disappointed party should accept the court's ruling, even if she dislikes the outcome.

The courts' law-applying function complements their dispute-resolving function, but their third task, the development of the law, can stand in tension with these other two. Whilst older accounts of the separation of powers present the judge in almost mechanical terms, confined to applying law to the disputes before

The United Kingdom Constitution. N. W. Barber, Oxford University Press. © Nick Barber 2021.
DOI: 10.1093/oso/9780198852315.003.0009

her, contemporary accounts of the principle recognise that judges also possess a law-making role, clarifying the law where it is vague or contradictory, filling in gaps, and, on occasion, altering rules when the court decides it has the capacity to improve the law.[1] The law-making role of the court will come as no surprise to those who study the UK constitution: English and Scottish common law, which are developed by the courts, are substantial components of the UK's legal orders. The law-making capacity of the judges brings strengths to the constitution; when exercised well, this capacity complements law-making undertaken by the other branches. But it presents a challenge: if the judge is making law, the decision could have gone the other way. The disappointed litigant has not lost out because a *pre-existing* rule has been applied to her case, but because the court has chosen to apply a *new* rule to her dispute—one which did not exist, in that form, when the dispute initially arose. Thus, a challenge for the courts is to find ways of developing the law that do not unsettle their capacity effectively and fairly to resolve disputes.

If judges are to resolve disputes effectively, if they are to persuade the parties to accept their decisions, they need to be independent: the decision of the court must turn on the contents of the dispute, and not be determined by extraneous factors, such as the judge's personal interactions with a litigant, or pressure brought by another constitutional institution. Maintaining independence from other constitutional bodies is especially tricky, given that the courts depend on these bodies for their efficacy. It is, for instance, the executive that provides the administrative support that enables the courts to function, and which stands ready to back court rulings with force if necessary.[2] But whilst judicial independence is a necessary feature of a successful court system, it brings a problem: the difficulty of holding judges to account

[1] Eoin Carolan, *The New Separation of Powers* (Oxford University Press 2009) ch 2; Aileen Kavanagh, 'The Constitutional Separation of Powers' in David Dyzenhaus and Malcolm Thoburn, *Philosophical Foundations of Constitutional Law* (Cambridge University Press 2016).

[2] The judiciary exercise significantly more control over the administration of the courts in Scotland than in England or Northern Ireland: Graham Gee, Robert Hazell, Kate Malleson, and Patrick O'Brien, *The Politics of Judicial Independence in the UK's Changing Constitution* (Cambridge University Press 2015) 231–34.

for their actions. Judges are powerful constitutional actors. At the systemic level, the courts play an important role in shaping and developing the law; like all other law-makers, their decisions and assumptions should be open to public criticism and debate, and, as unelected law-makers, their freedom to shape the law should be limited. More narrowly, in the context of particular litigation, judges exercise a great deal of power over the way in which a case is managed and decided: for the parties before the court, the judge is a figure of considerable power.[3] The power of the courts, and the risks this brings, present a paradox: how can judges be independent and yet accountable; autonomous and yet constrained?

9.1 COURTS: STRUCTURES

There are two aspects of the structure of the courts that require consideration: first, the overall structure of the court system and, second, the internal structure of courts. Both of these structures condition the ways in which the courts undertake their constitutional roles.

In terms of overall structure in the UK, the court systems broadly resembles a pyramid, with a large number of courts active at the low levels, narrowing to a single court, principally the Supreme Court, at the top. To one side of the UK's legal orders are the international courts in which UK citizens are able to bring cases: currently, the European Court of Human Rights and, until recently, the Court of Justice of the European Communities. As we progress up the judicial hierarchy, the number of court sittings and the overall number of judges decreases, whilst their power to make law increases. In Chapter 4 the rules of court hierarchy were discussed, and, in short, the higher the court is in the system, the greater its power to produce decisions that bind lower courts. Courts at the lowest levels have little or no power to make law, although they may have considerable discretion about how the law is interpreted and applied in a particular case. The Supreme Court, by contrast, has a far wider discretion over the creation

[3] As earlier writers on the separation of powers appreciated: Baron de Montesquieu, *The Spirit of the Laws* (Anna Cohler, Basia Miller, and Harold Stone (trs), Cambridge University Press 1989) bk 11 ch 6.

of law, although it is worth noting that it depends on the lower courts adhering to its decisions for those decisions to be effective.

A curiosity of the court system is that the number of judges sitting on a panel seems to be roughly correlated to the amount of judicial law-making discretion that court is likely to enjoy. So, at the lowest end of the spectrum, in the Crown and county courts, it is common for a single judge to hear cases, whilst the Court of Appeal has the capacity to field a bench of five in some cases, and in the Supreme Court as many as eleven justices may sit.[4] The international courts (the Court of Justice of the European Union and the European Court of Human Rights) are larger still.

There are at least two explanations for this aspect of the structure of the court system, a structure that sees a large overall number of judges (and magistrates) at its base, with ever smaller numbers as we progress up the judicial hierarchy.

First, this pyramid-like structure is partly explained by the dispute-resolving function of the courts. This structure places limits on the capacity of the higher courts to review the decisions of their lower counterparts: the system allows only a small number of cases to be appealed. Appeals are intended to be unusual: the objective of the court system is to end disputes, not to allow them to persist as they run up the appellate structure. A consequence of this is that lower court judges are placed in a position of considerable power, able to exercise both formal discretion, conferred by the law, and practical discretion, in that there is a broad range of conduct the judge can undertake without making an appeal of her decision likely.

Secondly, the structure of the court system is conditioned by the law-making function of the courts. As we progress down the pyramid the number of courts that hear cases increases, and the total number of judges who sit on those cases also grows. Whilst some courts in the lower half of the pyramid have the capacity to make decisions about the law that binds or persuades other

[4] Constitutional Reform Act 2005, s 42(1); see J Tomlinson, J Rylatt, and D Fairgrieve, 'And Then There Were Eleven: Some Context on the Supreme Court Sitting En Banc in the Article 50 Case' *UK Constitutional Law Blog* (9 November 2016) https://ukconstitutionallaw.org/2016/11/09/joe-tomlinson-jake-rylatt-and-duncan-fairgrieve-and-then-there-were-eleven-some-context-on-the-supreme-court-sitting-en-banc-in-the-article-50-case/ (accessed 11 March 2021).

courts, their sheer number inhibits their law-making capacity; the ability of lower courts to communicate their decisions is unavoidably constrained, as lawyers and other judges will not be aware of all the decisions they produce. Furthermore, with so many courts hearing such a high volume of cases, if these courts did attempt to develop the law in radical manner there is a significant risk that contradictory or incoherent pronouncements about the law would be generated as parallel courts heard similar cases. The need for clarity in judicial law-making helps explain why there are fewer courts at the top end of the pyramid, and why these courts are accorded more latitude in the creation of the law, binding those courts beneath them. Because higher courts produce fewer judgments, these decisions have greater salience than those produced by lower courts. Indeed, the need for clarity might also explain the larger numbers of judges that sit on the cases in higher courts. For instance, when the Supreme Court is being asked to depart from its own previous rulings, to resolve a conflict between its past decisions, or to decide a matter of public or constitutional importance, an unusually large panel may be assembled with up to eleven judges sitting.[5] Having such a large panel hear a case enables the court to make decisions about the law that are exceptionally clear; there is no risk that an alternative panel of Supreme Court justices would have reached a different conclusion and, as this is the Supreme Court, no risk that a higher court will unsettle the decision.

The hierarchal structure of the courts helps to further mitigate the tension between their dispute-resolving and law-making functions. Whilst it is the court system as a whole that develops the law, in many cases (perhaps the vast majority) the law applied by the lower court is reasonably clear and certain, and the claim by the court to be applying pre-existing law to the case before it is plausible. When a case is appealed from the lower courts over an issue of law, it will often mean that the law is unclear or, perhaps, that previous developments elsewhere in the law suggest a higher court might be willing to alter that law: when the court system is working well, changes in the law are, to a significant degree,

[5] Rules of the UK Supreme Court https://www.supremecourt.uk/procedures/panel-numbers-criteria.html (accessed 11 March 2021.

predictable. Consequently, when a higher court modifies or develops the law, it can often serve to clarify the law by ending a debate over the implications of a legal rule, bringing that area of law into line with broader legal principles. Even if it the court cannot be said to be applying pre-existing law to the case before it, it can still present its decision to the disappointed litigant as one which was predictable, in that it was guided by broader legal principles and necessary for the effective operation of the law.

The internal structure of courts takes a roughly triangular form, with a judge (or judges) at the top of this triangle, adjudicating between the two parties before her. This structure reflects the dispute-resolving role of the judges, and limits their law-making role in at least two respects. First, courts require a concrete dispute before they can hand down a judgment; they are a paradigmatically reactive, rather than proactive, institution. Secondly, courts rely on the parties before them for their information about the dispute and, more generally, for information about the implications of any changes to the law they might bring about. Courts in the UK have sought to mitigate each of these two constraints.

In respect of the need for a dispute, the courts have steadily widened the scope of those recognised as possessing standing, that is, those entitled to bring a case to the court. In private law actions standing is normally fairly straight-forward: the entitlement to bring an action is tied up with the assertion of the right. So, a person claiming damages for breach of contract or negligence must show that the party they are litigating against owed them a legal duty, and the breach of that duty caused them harm. At the heart of the claim is an assertion of a distinct legal relationship between the parties, a relationship that grounds special legal rights and duties that would not otherwise arise between individuals. In public law, by contrast, when a challenge is brought against a decision made by a state institution, standing can be harder to show. Under the Old Constitution, standing in public law tended to be interpreted relatively conservatively. Although the tests for standing varied considerably, it often required that a litigant show a special interest of some sort in the decision before a challenge was allowed; the decision had to impact on that person, causing some sort of special damage to justify the intervention of the court.[6] In the New Constitution, the test is far more generous. It seems that when the court is convinced that there is a strong public interest in its hearing the case, judges will allow the action to be brought.[7] The recent *Cherry* litigation over the prime minister's decision to prorogue Parliament is a good example of this more expansive approach.[8] Litigation was started by a private individual, Gina Miller, in the English courts, and by an MP, Joanna Cherry, in the Scottish system. Miller in particular could hardly claim to have been specially affected by the prorogation decision. The impact on her was identical to the impact on every other citizen of the UK, yet the court allowed her action to proceed.

By broadening standing the courts have made it more likely that someone will bring an issue to the court. This means that high-profile constitutional disputes are now more likely to end up being argued before judges and, as a corollary of this, that we are likely to see constitutional law develop at a more rapid pace. But the dispute-centred nature of the courts continues to limit their law-making role in many other areas. In most areas of law there are still strict limitations on who can bring a case, and, more broadly, the areas of law the courts can develop will depend on the willingness of affected individuals to litigate and on the chances of this litigation reaching the higher, law-making, parts of the court system. The capacity of the court system as a whole to develop law will thus be patchy. In some areas, especially those in which large sums of money are at stake, many cases will reach the higher courts. In other areas, far fewer cases will be heard.

The dispute-focused nature of the courts also limits the range of information that is provided to the judges. To a considerable extent, what the judges know about the case, and about the broader implications of the decisions they might reach, is dependent on the parties before them. This is defensible in terms of the dispute-resolving function of the courts, with the judge

[6] PP Craig, *Administrative Law* (8th edn, Sweet & Maxwell 2018) ch 25.

[7] *R v Inland Revenue Commissioners ex p National Federation of Self-Employed and Small Businesses Ltd* [1982] AC 617 (HL).

[8] *Cherry v Advocate-General for Scotland* [2019] UKSC 41, [2020] AC 373, discussed further in ch 4.

focusing tightly on the case before her, but this narrowness of focus may be problematic in terms of the law-making role of the judge.[9] Recalling the case of *Patel v Mirza*, discussed in Chapter 4, the Supreme Court handed down a decision on whether money paid on the basis of an unlawful agreement, which was unsuccessful, should be returned.[10] One of the key questions in the case was the impact of the decision on the likelihood of people entering into such agreements: by requiring the money to be returned, would the court encourage or discourage such conduct? The court had no reliable evidence on this question, and no means of obtaining such evidence; it just had to guess.

Once again, there have been attempts by the court to mitigate this constraint. The courts have become more willing to allow pressure groups to bring, or participate in, litigation. So for example, in *R v Inspectorate of Pollution ex p Greenpeace (No. 2)* Greenpeace was permitted to bring a challenge to the decision of the Inspectorate of Pollution to allow British Nuclear Fuels to discharge radioactive waste from one of its power stations.[11] Justice Otton, in deciding to allow Greenpeace to bring the action, asserted that Greenpeace was 'an entirely responsible and respected body with a genuine concern for the environment'.[12] Furthermore, Otton continued, if Greenpeace were not allowed to bring the action then the case might be brought by a less well-informed challenger who 'would not afford the court the assistance it requires in order to do justice between the parties'.[13] In effect, the court was hoping that Greenpeace would supply it with the information and technical expertise it needed to assess the merits of the inspectorate's decision properly.

Carol Harlow has warned against the role played by pressure groups in litigation.[14] As she notes, groups like Greenpeace pursue a political agenda. They are not impartial helpers of the court; if the judges perceive them as such, the integrity of the trial process

[9] Paul Yowell, *Constitutional Rights and Constitutional Design* (Hart Publishing 2018) ch 4.

[10] *Patel v Mirza* [2016] UKSC 42, [2017] AC 467.

[11] *R v Inspectorate of Pollution ex p Greenpeace (No 2)* [1994] 4 All ER 329 (QB).

[12] ibid 350. [13] ibid 351.

[14] Carol Harlow, 'Public Law and Popular Justice' (2002) 65 Modern Law Review 1.

is compromised, as the judge is now siding with one of the parties before her. The presence of pressure groups before judges might appear to mitigate the information problems created by the dispute-focused nature of the courts, but this mitigation might be illusory. There is no guarantee that the courts are able competently to assess the evidence given by these groups, and no guarantee that in any given case the spread of pressure groups before the court will reflect all of the societal interests at stake. Whatever ingenious mechanisms are introduced to mitigate the informational limits on the courts, their basic structure as dispute-focused institutions will inevitability limit their capacity to gather and process the full range of facts relevant to their law-making function, a limitation that should shape their law-making role.

9.2 COURTS: PEOPLE

In the Old Constitution, the appointment of judges was opaque. Key decisions about appointment were made by the Lord Chancellor in the English system, and the Lord Advocate in Scotland. Both were members of the executive, were political appointees, and made recommendations about judicial appointments after private discussions with judges and senior barristers. There was no formal application process, no set of public criteria for appointment, and, of course, no opportunity to scrutinise the process by which the judges were selected.[15] For the most senior judicial appointments, the final recommendation was made by the prime minister. This opacity, combined with the role played by members of the executive, brought with it the potential for political intervention. Lord Salisbury, prime minister at the start of the twentieth century, was quite open about his belief that party politics should shape judicial appointments. Vernon Bogdanor reports that Salisbury thought Conservatives made better judges than Liberals because, claimed Salisbury, Conservatives were more trustworthy.[16] Subsequent prime ministers were more discrete, but both Margaret Thatcher and John Major rejected the

[15] Technically, in each case, the appointment was made by the monarch, but she invariably followed the advice of her ministers.

[16] Vernon Bogdanor, *The New British Constitution* (Hart Publishing 2009) 67.

Lord Chancellor's first recommendation for a senior judicial post, preferring the second candidate on the list.[17] The extent of political interference in judicial appointments is unknowable, but, to the extent it occurred, its significance was mitigated by the constrained role played by the judges in the Old Constitution. The New Constitution, with the collapse of parliamentary sovereignty, the rise of human rights litigation, and the establishment of the devolution settlement, requires the judges to address politically controversial questions more frequently. Consequently, the mode of their appointment, the potential for political intervention, and, more broadly, the type of people who become judges, have become increasingly pressing questions.

Scotland and Northern Ireland were the first parts of the UK to move towards a more transparent system of judicial appointments, introducing appointments panels and opening the system to applications.[18] Reforms to the English system followed this model, and were established in the Constitutional Reform Act 2005.[19] Although there are differences between the processes, they adopt a similar structure. At its heart is an appointments board which oversees the process and makes recommendations about candidates. The board issues an open invitation for applications, and has a set of criteria against which applicants are assessed. For some posts, the board may require applicants to sit a test or submit written work. Members of the board are drawn from different groups, principally the judiciary, the legal professions, and the wider public, ensuring that the panel includes a range of members who interact with the legal system in different ways.[20] Once a decision has been made, the boards then send their recommendations to a senior judicial figure who, with a member of

[17] Robert Stevens, *The English Judges: Their Role in the Changing Constitution* (Hart Publishing 2005) 95.

[18] In Northern Ireland, this is the Justice (Northern Ireland) Act 2002. The Scottish Executive introduced a non-statutory advisory panel at about the same time as Northern Ireland. It was given a statutory foundation in the Judiciary and Courts (Scotland) Act 2008. See also Gee and others (n 2) 239–47.

[19] For a more detailed account of the English appointments process see Gee and others (n 2) ch 7.

[20] Constitutional Reform Act 2005, sch 12; Judiciary and Courts (Scotland) Act 2008, sch 1.

the executive (normally the Lord Chancellor or a minister of the Scottish Executive), conveys the recommendation to the Queen for formal approval. In most cases, the reviewing member of the executive has the power to reject the recommendation, but this power is rarely exercised.[21] The process varies for appointments to the higher courts and for senior judicial offices: here, a special appointments panel is convened, and the recommendation to the Queen is made by the prime minister.[22]

The modern process of judicial appointment is a significant improvement on the old system. It is easier for candidates to access, more transparent, and involves a wider range of people in its decisions. However, whilst the system draws the public and legal professionals into the process, the two principal players in judicial appointments are the judges and the executive. Although the precise balance between these two varies across the appointment processes, all require the two branches of state to work together: the judiciary is strongly represented on all of the appointment panels, with senior judges often playing a significant role in their operation, whilst the executive plays an important role in the selection of board members, and often holds a veto over the outcome of the process.

One reason for reforming the judicial appointments process was a concern over judicial diversity. At the end of the century, the figures were alarming: in 1995 there were no women sitting in the highest court in the UK system, then still the House of Lords, only one sat in the Court of Appeal, whilst there were just seven female judges in the High Court.[23] No judges in any of these courts came from a minority ethnic group.[24] By 2019, matters had improved somewhat: there were three women sitting on the Supreme Court, nine in the Court of Appeal, and twenty-six

[21] Graham Gee, 'Rethinking the Lord Chancellor's Role in Judicial Appointments' (2017) 20 Legal Ethics 4, 7–14.

[22] Although the Lord Chancellor is the effective executive officer.

[23] Gee and others (n 2) 161–62.

[24] Justice, *Increasing Judicial Diversity* (Justice 2017) 1.35 https://justice.org.uk/wp-content/uploads/2017/04/JUSTICE-Increasing-judicial-diversity-report-2017-web.pdf (accessed 11 March 2021).

in the High Court.[25] Two judges sitting in the Court of Appeal came from minority ethnic groups, with a further three sitting in the High Court.[26] To put this in perspective, this means in the senior English judiciary (the High Court and above) around a quarter of judges are female and about 3% are from a minority ethnic group, whereas in the population as a whole, around 50% are female and around 14% come from a minority ethnic group.[27] Furthermore, the senior judges are drawn from a narrow social background: in 2019 the Sutton Trust reported that two thirds of senior judges went to private school, only 13% went to a comprehensive school, and 71% had an Oxbridge degree.[28] In the population as a whole, around 7% go to a private school, and only a tiny fraction have an Oxbridge degree.[29] The problem of lack of diversity in the judiciary has been recognised in the statutory guidance given to the appointment boards. The legislation establishing the appointment commissions imposes a duty on those bodies to be take account of the need to encourage diversity in applications for the judiciary.[30] Since 2013 a very limited amount of positive discrimination has been permitted in the English system: the Judicial Appointments Commission has been permitted to take diversity issues into account when choosing between two candidates of equal merit.[31]

Lack of diversity in the judiciary is problematic because it indicates that certain groups are not getting a fair chance to hold

[25] Justice, *Increasing Judicial Diversity: An Update* (Justice 2020) para 2.1 https://justice.org.uk/wp-content/uploads/flipbook/21/book.html (accessed 11 March 2021).

[26] Justice, *Increasing Judicial Diversity: An Update* (n 24) para 2.28.

[27] Justice, *Increasing Judicial Diversity* (n 25) para 1.15.

[28] Sutton Trust, *Elitist Britain 2019* (Sutton Trust 2019) https://www.suttontrust.com/wp-content/uploads/2019/06/Elitist-Britain-2019.pdf (accessed 11 March 2021).

[29] Department of Education, *Schools, Pupils, and their Characteristics: January 2019* (Department of Education 2019) https://assets.publishing.service.gov.uk/government/uploads/system/uploads/attachment_data/file/812539/Schools_Pupils_and_their_Characteristics_2019_Main_Text.pdf (accessed 11 March 2021).

[30] Constitutional Reform Act 2005, s 64; Judiciary and Courts (Scotland) Act 2008, s 14; Justice (Northern Ireland) Act 2002, s 3(8).

[31] Constitutional Reform Act 2005, s 63(4), as amended by the Crime and Courts Act 2013, sch 10.

important, well-paid, public offices. But it might be thought, beyond this unfairness, that the failure of the courts to reflect the population they serve is unimportant. If the job of the judge is to apply the law, the race or gender of the judge is irrelevant: a competent black female judge should reach the same decision as her competent white male counterpart. In a lecture to the Bar Council, Lord Sumption, then a judge of the Supreme Court, countered arguments for positive discrimination in judicial appointments using reasoning of this type.[32] He noted that there was little evidence that judges of different races and genders reached different decisions because of these attributes. Indeed, as Sumption noted, if the court system is to be fair to the litigants who come before it then this must be the case: if the personal characteristics of the judge made a difference to its outcome, the equal application of the law would be undermined, rendering the system capricious.

Nevertheless, the force of Sumption's reasoning is limited, as it only engages with one aspect of the judicial function: the application of law to disputes. Reflection on the other two roles of the court, the judges' law-making and dispute-resolving roles, reveals further reasons for diversity in the judiciary—reasons connected to the institution of the court itself. In terms of the judges' law-making role, Sumption is right to warn of the dangers of trying to achieve a diverse panel of judges hearing each case, an attempt which would raise the problematic implication that judges of different races or genders would reach different decisions about the law. However, he is wrong to think that it is only in the confines of particular cases that diversity matters. People's understanding of the world is, in part, conditioned by those with whom they spend time: judges operating within the old judiciary, a group heavily dominated by white men of a similar social background, are likely to have had their assumptions and experiences shaped by, and reinforced by, this group. When these judges undertook their law-making role, these assumptions and experiences will have affected their understandings of the impact of the laws that they make. This might explain why, for example, until 1991 the

[32] Lord Sumption, 'Home Truths about Judicial Diversity' (Bar Council Law Reform Lecture, 15 November 2012).

law did not recognise a wife's capacity to refuse consent to sex with her husband,[33] or why early decisions protecting the employment rights of pregnant women did so by comparing the treatment of a pregnant woman with the supposed parallel of a sickly man.[34] In the case of marital rape, previous law-makers had focused on the risks of false allegations being made against husbands whilst failing to consider the dangers that such an exception posed to wives. In the example of pregnancy, the courts had adopted a male paradigm in discrimination cases, a paradigm that might have worked well enough in equal pay disputes, but which could not accommodate pregnancy. The point to take from these cases is not that the judges were consciously prejudiced (although doubtless some were) but rather that a non-diverse judiciary is a group in which even well-meaning individuals will fail to appreciate the needs or interests of parts of the broader community.[35] As Lizzie Barmes and Kate Malleson argue, judges, because they were operating in a homogenous environment, simply did not think about these issues; by making the judiciary as a whole more diverse, these unthinking assumptions are more likely to be exposed and reassessed.[36]

Reflection on the dispute-resolving role of the courts also grounds an argument for diversity. One reason people accept the decisions of state institutions is that they identify with those institutions. The lack of diversity amongst the judges may reduce people's capacity to identify with the institution, reducing the amount of confidence people have in the fairness of the process, and making it less likely that they will accept the courts as possessing a legitimate authority to resolve disputes in which they are

[33] It was not until *R v R* [1992] 1 AC 599 (HL) that a husband could be convicted of the rape of his wife.

[34] An approach firmly squashed by the European Court of Justice: Case C-32/93 *Webb v EMO Air Cargo (UK) Ltd (No 2)* [1994] ECR I-3567.

[35] A point made by Report of the Advisory Panel on Judicial Diversity (UK Judiciary 2010) 4 https://www.judiciary.uk/wp-content/uploads/JCO/Documents/Reports/advisory-panel-judicial-diversity-2010.pdf (accessed 11 March 2021). See also Caroline Criado Perez, *Invisible Women* (Chatto & Windus 2019) ch 1.

[36] Lizzie Barmes and Kate Malleson, 'Lifting the Judicial Identity Blackout' (2018) 38 Oxford Journal of Legal Studies 357.

involved. Once again, it is too simplistic to think this means that unless a judge is the same race and gender as the parties litigants will lack confidence in the system; rather, it is the judiciary as a whole, and so the entire court system, that must be relatable. As Lady Hale puts it, the public 'should be able to feel that the courts are their courts; that their cases are being decided and the law is being made by people like them, and not by some alien beings from another planet'.[37] Sumption failed to see that it is not necessary to have a diverse panel of judges sitting in every case for that court to benefit from diversity in the judiciary as a whole.

9.3 COURTS: POWERS, PROTECTIONS, AND ACCOUNTABILITY

Whilst many higher courts have the power to hand down rulings that develop the law, a capacity discussed in Chapter 4, the primary power of the court lies in its capacity authoritatively to determine people's legal position, identifying (amongst other things) their rights, duties and liabilities in the case before the judge. Having identified the legal position of the parties, the court may then require some remedy by, for example, obliging one party to pay damages to another, transferring the possession of an object, or, in a criminal case, requiring the defendant to pay a fine or spend time in prison. When the court orders a remedy, that remedy's efficacy is dependent on the support of the executive. This is obvious in criminal cases—when the judge hands down a prison sentence she relies on the executive to provide a prison and convey the convict to it—but is also true in private law cases. Most of the time when the judge requires an action from one of the parties in the court, the party, more or less reluctantly, complies with the order. However, if a party refuses to comply with an order of the court this would constitute contempt, potentially leading to the intervention of the police and, in some instances, imprisonment. Consequently, even private law

[37] Lady Hale, 'Women in the Judiciary' Fiona Woolf Lecture for the Women Lawyers' Division of the Law Society (London, 27 June 2014) https://www.supremecourt.uk/docs/speech-140627.pdf (accessed 11 March 2021).

decisions of the court are backed by the coercive power of the state, a power wielded by the executive branch.

If the judges are to make fair determinations of litigants' rights and duties, their decisions must turn on the facts before them and on their understanding of the requirements of the law. If there is an extraneous factor affecting the judge's decision, the judge will cease to be an independent arbiter, and it is hard to see why the disappointed party should then accept the ruling of the court. There are at least four possible sources of interference that threaten judicial independence: the state, private parties, other judges, and, finally, the judge herself.

The most commonly discussed threat to judicial independence comes from other state institutions, especially the executive branch. There are long-standing protections for the judges against interference from the government. First, judges in the higher English courts are hard to sack. They hold office on good behaviour and can only be dismissed following votes of the Commons and the Lords. This protection dates back to the Act of Settlement 1700, and is now found in the Constitutional Reform Act 2005.[38] Senior Scottish judges enjoy even greater protection: not only does there need to be a vote of the Scottish Parliament before removal, but a tribunal must be convened to investigate the judge's conduct, and must conclude that the judge is unfit for office.[39] Secondly, there are broad statutory duties resting on other constitutional actors to support and defend judicial independence. The Lord Chancellor and other ministers are under a statutory duty to protect the independence of the English judiciary.[40] There is a wider duty in Scottish law, with the obligation encompassing the First Minister, the Lord Advocate, the Scottish ministers, members of the Scottish Parliament, and, indeed, anyone else with responsibilities for the judiciary or the administration of justice.[41]

[38] Constitutional Reform Act 2005, s 33; Senior Courts Act 1981, s 11(3). In addition, judges have a compulsory retirement age (currently 70), and can be removed in cases of medical incapacity: Senior Courts Act 1981, ss 8–9. Furthermore, they can be suspended in some situations: Constitutional Reform Act 2005, ss 108–121.

[39] Scotland Act 1998, s 95(6)–(10); Judiciary and Courts (Scotland) Act 2008, ss 35–39.

[40] Constitutional Reform Act 2005, s 3.

[41] Judiciary and Courts (Scotland) Act 2008, s 1.

Northern Ireland follows the Scottish model, but does not extend the duty to members of the Northern Ireland Assembly.[42] These obligations may be more than window-dressing: potentially, a court could rely on these statutory duties whilst undertaking judicial review of an executive decision, either striking down a decision that undermined judicial independence or even requiring action to be taken to protect independence. Finally, the independence of the judiciary is protected through the restraint of other institutions. Under the rules governing debates in Parliament, parliamentarians should not criticise judges,[43] nor, in most circumstances, discuss matters that form the subject matter of current court cases.[44] Members of the executive also normally refrain from criticising judicial decisions, even when the judge decides against them.

The second source of potential interference comes from private parties: non-state actors seeking to pressure the judge. Judges are, of course, protected by the general criminal law, and threats of violence or attempts to blackmail them constitute criminal offences. In addition, they enjoy wide immunity from civil liability, which means disappointed litigants cannot sue the judge for negligence or slander.[45] But external pressure on the judge can come from sources other than the litigants: press criticism, for instance, may also risk influencing judicial decision-making. Following the High Court decision in the *Miller* case, a case which concerned the process for triggering Brexit, the *Daily Mail*'s front page consisted of photographs of the judges with the headline 'Enemies of the People' and, for a time, the *Mail*'s website identified one of the judges, Sir Terence Etherton, as an 'openly gay ex-Olympic fencer' in a context which implied that these were grounds for

[42] Justice (Northern Ireland) Act 2002, s 1.

[43] Save in the form of a substantive motion that enables the Commons to take a decision on the assertion: Thomas Erskine May, *Erskine May's Treatise on the Law, Privileges, Proceedings and Usage of Parliament* (David Natzler and others (eds), 25th edn, LexisNexis 2019) para 20.10 https://erskinemay.parliament.uk/.

[44] May (n 43) paras 12.19, 21.23, 20.11, and 25.74.

[45] *Scott v Stansfield* (1868) 3 LR Exch 220; *Trapp v Mackie* [1979] 1 WLR 377 (HL).

criticism rather than commendation.[46] It is hard to see how the law should respond, if at all, to criticism of this type. On the one hand, it seemed that the *Daily Mail* was seeking to intimidate the judiciary; *Miller* was on its way to the Supreme Court, and the Supreme Court justices might have worried that they would face the same type of attack if they found for Miller. On the other hand, judges are powerful constitutional actors who make decisions, like that in *Miller*, which affect the lives of millions of people. Just like politicians, it is important that judges can be subject to public criticism, and limiting that criticism, even if only by criminalising unfair attacks, risks inhibiting such debate.

The third threat to judicial independence is less commonly discussed: the risks that come from within the judiciary itself. It is very hard to sack a judge in the higher courts, but it is possible to side-line a judge or harm her judicial career.[47] Decisions about which judges sit on which cases generally are made by senior judges, and this power can be used to marginalise problematic judges, or could even be used to ensure that when the senior judge hears a case her colleagues will be favourably inclined towards her view of the law. Lord Denning, the Master of the Rolls from 1962 to 1982 and an innovative judge, picked the judges who would sit alongside him in important Court of Appeal cases with care.[48] And judges who are unpopular with their colleagues may find it harder to gain promotion: the views of the judiciary are taken into account when such promotions are made. This type of informal, internal, regulation brings some benefits: less able judges are confined to cases where they can do less damage, and eccentricity is discouraged. But there are also costs. Disagreement within the judiciary may be stifled, heightening the dangers that

[46] *R (Miller) v Secretary of State for Exiting the European Union* [2016] EWHC 2768 (Admin); J Slack, 'Enemies of the People' *Daily Mail* (4 November 2016). See Joshua Rozenberg, *Enemies of the People?* (Bristol University Press 2020) ch 2.

[47] Graham Gee, 'Judicial Conduct, Complaints, and Discipline in England and Wales: Assessing the New Approach' in Richard Devlin and Shelia Wildeman (eds), *Disciplining Judges: Contemporary Controversies* (Edward Elgar Publishing 2021). At the lower levels, judges have been removed: Gee reports 250 removals since 2006.

[48] Gavin Drewry, Louis Bloom-Cooper, and Charles Blake, *The Court of Appeal* (Hart Publishing 2007) 108.

judges will fall into those unthinking prejudices discussed in the previous section. The lack of transparency about these pressures makes them especially insidious; often a judge will not be aware that she has been deliberately excluded from a panel, or that negative evaluation of her conduct has been conveyed to senior colleagues. Consequently, there is little scope for the judge, or anyone else, to challenge these actions or assess their reasonableness.

The final threat to judicial independence comes from a surprising source: the judge herself. To give an extreme example, a judge whose judgment was motivated by a party's bribes would be unable successfully to accomplish any of the objectives of the court system: she would not be applying the law to the case before her, and there is little reason for anyone to accept her rulings as binding on them. There is little or no evidence of such simple corruption in the UK judiciary, but a lesser problem, that of judicial incompetence, can have a similar effect and can be harder to resolve.[49] The incompetent judge's personal failings undermine her capacity to succeed in the role of the judge: she lacks the skills necessary to succeed in this office. There are serious consequences for the parties before the court, who cannot be sure that the law will be fairly applied to their case. For example, Judge Peter Smith became notorious for his odd behaviour in the English High Court. Some of this was relatively innocuous, such as his decision to conceal a coded message in a judgment about Dan Brown's book, *The Da Vinci Code*, but other incidents were more problematic.[50] In a case involving British Airways, Smith interrupted proceedings to complain, at length, about his lost luggage and threatened to order BA's chief executive to come to the court to explain his missing suitcase.[51] After Lord Pannick QC wrote

[49] Gee (n 47).

[50] In *Baigent v Random House Ltd* [2007] EWCA Civ 247 [3], Lord Justice Lloyd wrote that Smith 'was prompted by the extensive use in [the book] of codes, and no doubt by his own interest in such things, to incorporate a coded message in his judgment, on which nothing turns. The judgment is not easy to read or to understand. It might have been preferable for him to have allowed himself more time for the preparation, checking and revision of the judgment'.

[51] *Emerald Supplies Ltd v British Airways* [2015] EWCH 2201 (Ch); David Pannick, 'A Case about Luggage that Carries a Great Deal of Judicial Baggage' *The Times* (3 December 2015).

an article in *The Times* criticising the judge, Smith wrote a letter to Pannick's chambers which was later described by the Court of Appeal as 'disgraceful' and which showed 'a deeply worrying and fundamental lack of understanding of the proper role of a judge'.[52] Smith's bizarre behaviour was such that any litigants who were allocated him as their judge would have had cause to worry that his decisions and behaviour would be erratic. They could justifiably worry that the law would not be fairly applied to them.

Whilst a corrupt judge can be investigated by the police, incompetent judges are harder to dislodge. The primary corrective for judicial incompetence is appeal, but appealing a decision is costly, and some forms of incompetence might not lead to the decision being overturned. Some types of complaints about the conduct of judges can be made outside of the appellate process.[53] The Judicial Office for Scotland, the Office of the Lord Chief Justice for Northern Ireland, and the Judicial Conduct Investigation Office in England and Wales can be contacted by unhappy litigants, and will undertake investigations into judicial conduct. However, the grounds on which these bodies will undertake investigations are narrow: complaints will not be investigated if they relate to the content of the decision or, in most instances, the handling of the case. In the end, in Judge Smith's case, a panel was convened by the Judicial Conduct Investigations Office (JCIO) to hear complaints against him, but he retired shortly before the panel was due to meet, after a decade of complaints about his competency.[54] If the panel had found against him, it would have been difficult to sack Smith—it would have required a resolution of each chamber of Parliament—but he might well have faced a prolonged suspension following the report of the JCIO, a penalty that the Lord Chancellor and Lord Chief Justice can jointly apply after a disciplinary hearing.[55]

[52] *Harb v HRH Prince Abdul Aziz bin Fahd Bin Abdul Aziz* [2016] EWCA Civ 556 [68] (Sir Martin Moore-Bick MR); Pannick (n 51).

[53] Gee and others (n 2) 237–39.

[54] O Rudgard, 'Judge Who Complained about Lost Luggage during Case Avoids Disciplinary Hearing by Retiring Two Days Beforehand' *The Telegraph* (27 October 2017).

[55] Constitutional Reform Act 2005, s 108; Judicial Discipline (Prescribed Procedures) Regulations 2014.

9.4 CONCLUSION

This chapter has considered the structure of the courts and court system, the type of people who sit in the courts, and the powers and protections they enjoy. Recalling the table in the previous chapter (Table 8.1), one of the questions the separation of powers raises is that of the unity of the elements within the columns; that is, why the structures, persons, and powers of each of the branches should be brought together. The unity of the judicial branch is explained by the roles of the judiciary: the combination of dispute-resolving, law-applying, and law-making functions is a combination of roles that explains the structures, skills, and capacities of the courts. At the core of almost every court case is a dispute. The first task of the judge is to bring closure to this dispute such that the parties will accept the outcome, even if they do not like it. In the vast majority of litigation this is done by applying pre-existing law to the disagreement, using the law to identify the relevant facts in the dispute and then deducing the parties' legal position from those facts. The judge can defend her conclusions to the parties as applications of the law: the decision does not rest on her own personal likes or dislikes. Instead, it rests on rules set by the state, the legal embodiment of the community in which the dispute arose. The type of person chosen to be a judge is connected to the structure of the court: judges are chosen because they are skilled in the law, and this expertise, combined with their independence, renders their claims to identify the relevant legal rules plausible.

There is a tension between the law-making role of the court and its other functions, but this tension is mitigated by the structure of the courts and, connectedly, by the manner in which judges justify the creation of law. First, law-making by the court occurs in the context of particular disputes. Legal rules are normally broad, designed to apply to a wide range of fact situations, and the courts are then required to apply these broad rules in specific cases. As a result, the judges are given a perspective on these rules that other constitutional institutions, especially the legislature, lack. The court is well-placed to resolve ambiguities in these general rules, making the general rule attractive in the context of the particular case, but is also well-placed to tailor rules when their application would appear to produce injustice; seeing the consequences of applying the rule in the case before her, the judge might conclude that outcome is sufficiently problematic to warrant changing the law. The dispute-focused nature of the courts therefore conditions—or should condition—the way in which the judge makes law. Secondly, the structure of the courts limits the law-making power of any given judge. Whilst the courts as a whole are a powerful law-making institution, individual judges, even very senior ones, have limited law-making power. To be effective, they must persuade their colleagues of the merits of their interpretation of the law. These two structural features of the courts, their focus on a specific dispute and the limited capacity of any single judge to change the law, reflect the two audiences that a judge addresses when handing down her decision: the parties before the court, and her fellow judges. When the judge makes, as opposed to merely applies, the law, she must do so in a way that will persuade both of these groups. To do this, she must show that her development of the law fits with the broad trends of the law; it can be squared with past cases and shown to be consistent with underlying legal principles. Even if the law is changing, it is changing in a predictable way, one that the parties before the court could have anticipated and which sits comfortably with the views of other judges about the content of the law.

10
LEGISLATURES

In much of the classic literature on the separation of powers the legislature is presented as a law-making institution, as the body that legislates and sets the broad policy direction of the state. Whilst this is certainly one of its functions, in parliamentary systems the legislature also has a close relationship with the executive branch. Part of this relationship is one of scrutiny and challenge, whereby the legislature examines the conduct of the executive, reviewing and criticising its operation. But it is also one of support: it is the legislature's responsibility to ensure that the executive functions well. It acquits this task by ensuring that the executive is headed by a government that is able to govern, and by providing the executive with the money it needs to operate. Although rarely included in the list of the legislature's duties, its selection of a prime minister (or first minister, in the case of the devolved institutions), the consequent appointment of governmental ministers, and its support of the government once in office, are amongst the most important of its tasks. These three tasks, of setting policy, applying scrutiny, and providing support, combine to a requirement of control: in parliamentary systems, the legislature should exercise control over the executive, setting the goals for that body, providing it with the means to achieve those goals, and reviewing its conduct to ensure these goals are being achieved. This chapter will focus on Parliament, but Parliament is not the only legislative body in the UK. There are also legislatures in Scotland, Wales, and Northern Ireland, and bodies similar to legislatures also operate in many local government units. Much of the discussion in this chapter is relevant to these other institutions, whilst the special features of the devolved legislatures will be discussed in later chapters.

The interaction between the formal structures of the constitution and the political organisations operating within those structures is important throughout the UK constitution, but it is

The United Kingdom Constitution. N. W. Barber, Oxford University Press. © Nick Barber 2021.
DOI: 10.1093/oso/9780198852315.003.0010

especially important when we turn to examine the legislature. In Chapter 6 we examined the role of constitutional conventions, non-legal constitutional rules, in the constitution. In this chapter we will examine the role played by political parties and, by implication, the rules that constitute these entities. These rules are not ordinarily thought of as conventions because political parties are normally considered to stand outside of the constitution: they are private, or quasi-private, entities that are not parts of the state. Nevertheless, political parties play a central role in the operation of legislatures, and many of the formal structures of the legislature presuppose functioning political parties. Perhaps because of the significance of these non-state bodies for the operation of state institutions, there is a long-standing scepticism over the value of political parties in UK constitutional scholarship. Most recently, Adam Tomkins has called for the banning of the whips (the party officials who maintain party discipline within Parliament) in the hope of reducing the influence of parties within Parliament.[1] One of the most important questions raised by this chapter turns on the relationship between political parties and the legislature: are political parties a constitutional boon, a regrettable necessity, or, as Tomkins argues, an impediment to the proper functioning of the legislature?

10.1 STRUCTURES

The three roles of the legislature identified at the start of this chapter correspond to three sets of structural features: those that relate to the making of law, those that enable the scrutiny of the executive, and those that facilitate Parliament's support of the executive.

10.1.1 Law-Making

The formal law-making structures of Parliament turn on the relationship of its two chambers: the House of Commons and the House of Lords.[2] Most bills become laws after obtaining the

[1] Adam Tomkins, *Our Republican Constitution* (Hart Publishing 2005) 136–39.

[2] What follows is a greatly abbreviated account. For a fuller explanation see Meg Russell and Daniel Gover, *Legislation at Westminster: Parliamentary Actors and Influence in the Making of British Law* (Oxford University Press 2017) ch 2.

agreement of each House and the assent of the monarch, although in modern times the grant of royal assent has become a formality. In principle, a bill could be brought forward by any member of the Commons or Lords, but in practice most bills with a chance of becoming a statute are backed by, and were drafted within, the government, have a minister as a sponsor, and start life in the Commons.[3] Until 1911, the Lords had the capacity to prevent a bill from becoming a statute, but this changed with the enactment of the Parliament Act 1911, which enabled the Commons to legislate without the consent of the Lords after a two-year delay. This was modified by the Parliament Act 1949, which reduced the Lords' capacity to delay to a single year.[4] Although the House of Lords plays a significant role in legislation, and its power to delay can be used as a negotiating tactic to secure amendments to the bill or even stall the legislative process, the Commons is by far the most important player in the legislative process.

When a political party has a majority in the Commons, it is rare for it to suffer a defeat in that chamber, and the larger its majority, the rarer the chances of defeat become. For some, the rarity of defeats is a cause for concern, a demonstration that the government is able to dominate the legislature.[5] Part of this control is mediated through the whipping system. Whips are members of the Commons or Lords appointed by the government to maintain party discipline in Parliament. One of their tasks is to get government business through Parliament, encouraging members of the Commons and Lords to vote with their party. In addition, the government exercises significant control over the business of the Commons and, to a lesser degree, the Lords, and is able to schedule debates and votes. Using the whipping system and its capacity to control the process of Parliament, the government

[3] On the role of private members' bills see Robert Hazell and Fergus Reid, 'Private Members' Bills' in Cristina Leston-Bandeira and Louise Thompson (eds), *Exploring Parliament* (Oxford University Press 2018).

[4] The Parliament Acts are discussed further in ch 5.

[5] See eg Lord Hailsham, *The Dilemma of Democracy* (Collins 1978) ch 20 and Anthony King, *The British Constitution* (Oxford University Press 2009) 331–41. Philip Norton provides a brief survey of the many similar claims made over the decades: Philip Norton, 'Is the House of Commons Too Powerful?' (2019) 72 Parliamentary Affairs 996.

is able to exercise considerable control over the legislative process. However, this control is dependent on the party (or parties) in government having the support of the majority of Members of Parliament (MPs) in the Commons. In the latter half of 2019, Boris Johnson's government lost its majority. Lacking the support of the majority of MPs, the government lost both its capacity to win votes in the Commons and its control over the business of the House, and faced regular defeats in the chamber.[6]

The last days of 2019 might look pathological, an aberration from the normal functioning of Parliament, but it exposed the political pressures that always operate under the surface of Parliament's formal law-making structures. When a government has a majority, it wins votes and controls the business of the Commons because it has the support of its party: the party in Parliament approves of the broad policy objectives of the government. One of the jobs of the whips is to ensure this approval continues. The whips may pressure MPs to support the government, but they also inform the government of the resistance their proposals will face within their party.[7] So, even whilst a governing party enjoys a majority in the Commons, the whips will still warn when a proposal is unpopular within the party, and, as a result, these proposals may be abandoned or changed.[8] By the time a legislative proposal is introduced in the Commons, the government should know that it has a majority of MPs who are willing to support it because its whips have undertaken soundings in the party in Parliament, and, if necessary, the legislation has been modified in response to those soundings. During the parliamentary crises of 2019, these inner-party pressures that are normally hidden became public: it was plain that the government was negotiating

[6] This occurred on 3 September 2019, when Boris Johnson withdrew the whip from 21 Conservative MPs, but the government's power had been ebbing away for over a year, with the whips finding it increasingly difficult to maintain party discipline.

[7] Philip Norton, 'The Political Organisation of Parliament' in Cristina Leston-Bandeira and Louise Thompson (eds), *Exploring Parliament* (Oxford University Press 2018) 16.

[8] The mooted privatisation of the forests by the Cameron government in 2011 came to an end without the need for rejection in Parliament once the depths of opposition to the proposal became apparent: Russell and Gover (n 2) 20–21, 192.

with its own MPs (and MPs in other parties) for support. This form of negotiation goes on all the time, but privately, and within party structures, structures which had broken down because the government's most important policy, Brexit, cut through party allegiances. The government found itself unable to govern because a substantial portion of its party in Parliament no longer judged that the benefits of supporting its government in power outweighed the costs; Brexit was just too significant a policy and, in their eyes, too harmful to the country.

10.1.2 Scrutiny

The second task of the legislature is that of scrutiny; examining decisions of the executive and the broad policy objectives it pursues. At the formal level, this scrutiny occurs through questions and through investigation by select committees. MPs and Lords ask questions of ministers, both orally, in the chambers, and in written form.[9] There are a range of select committees which scrutinise government departments and also consider policy matters relating to their areas, producing reports on issues within their remits. Party control extends to the membership of these committees. Whilst the chairs of the select committees are chosen by secret ballot, the other members are picked by the Commons Committee of Selection, a body largely consisting of government and opposition whips.

Underpinning these mechanisms lies the convention of ministerial responsibility.[10] Ministerial responsibility requires that ministers take responsibility for their departments. Responsibility has two aspects: first, that ministers exercise control over their departments, and, second, that they account to Parliament for their department's operation. Some aspects of this convention have been codified in the Ministerial Code, a document produced under the authority of the prime minister. From time to time, scholars have expressed scepticism about the existence or efficacy

[9] Although the capacity to challenge ministers who give inadequate answers is limited in the Commons, the Procedure Committee monitors the responses given to questions, and will criticise departments who fail to provide timely answers that are of a satisfactory quality.

[10] Matthew V Flinders, *The Politics of Accountability in the Modern State* (Ashgate Publishing 2001) ch 1.

of this convention. The classic, and often repeated, example of the convention is the Crichel Down affair, back in 1954: a public inquiry exposed incompetency within the Ministry of Agriculture, and the minister, Sir Thomas Dugdale, resigned as a result.[11] However, since 1954 it is hard to find examples of errors that have caused resignation. It is this supposed connection—linking error and resignation—that has led to doubts over the continued existence of ministerial responsibility; perhaps the failure of ministers to resign promptly shows it to be a fiction. As Adam Tomkins has argued, this scepticism is unjustified.[12] First, it misunderstands the primary purpose of the convention. Rather than punishing failing ministers, the point of the convention is to ensure Parliament exercises control over the executive: ministerial responsibility requires that ministers succeed in controlling their departments, that they are able to ensure that their departments operate effectively and apply government policies. To an extent, this aspect of the convention does not need to be backed by sanctions as it requires ministers to do what they would want to do in any event; this is the reason why they wished to become a minister. Secondly, it misses the underlying political pressures that render the convention effective. As we saw in Chapter 6, breach of convention will normally lead to a reduction in a minister's political capital; their standing within the political community will be reduced. Whilst it is rare for a minister who breaches convention to resign as a consequence of that breach, modern political history is full of ministers who performed badly and then found themselves outside government at the next Cabinet reshuffle, or, perhaps, did not receive the promotion they were expecting. Once again, it is worth drawing attention to the role of political parties in rendering the convention effective. The most important audience for the minister, the group that has the most immediate impact on her career, is her party, and in particular, those members of her party who sit in Parliament.[13]

[11] John Griffith, 'Crichel Down: The Most Famous Farm in British Constitutional History' (1987) 1 Contemporary Record 35.

[12] Adam Tomkins, *Public Law* (Oxford University Press 2003) 140–59.

[13] Flinders (n 10) 115–19.

10.1.3 Support

Choosing a prime minister is one of the most important tasks of the Commons. It is the responsibility of the Commons to identify the person who commands the support of the largest number of MPs in the House, enabling the monarch to invite that person to form a government. In older constitutional scholarship this task would have been presented the other way around: as the monarch's duty to pick out the potential prime minister. However, when the Commons is functioning well, the monarch has no discretion.[14] Yet again, it is the party structures within Parliament that enable the Commons acquit this duty and select a prime minister. By identifying themselves as members of a party, MPs commit to accept their leader in the Commons as prime minister if their party secures a majority of seats. Where no party gets a majority, multiple parties may come together to form a coalition government, agreeing on a future prime minister. If this cannot be accomplished, a minority government can be formed if a majority in the Commons is willing to accept its creation (given that a minority government can only survive if the majority of the Commons refrain from holding a vote of confidence that would then trigger a new election). Those rare occasions when the monarch has exercised some personal discretion in picking the prime minister arise when party structures have failed to identify a leader in the Commons.[15]

In addition to identifying a prime minister, Parliament provides the executive with the support it needs to govern. This is partly a matter of money. Parliament enacts legislation that enables the collection of taxes, approves, on an annual basis, the levels of tax to be set, and votes through a series of supply statutes that authorise the government to expend this cash.[16] More generally, Parliament enacts legislation proposed by the government, enabling the production of new laws. Of course, Parliament is not failing in its

[14] Anne Twomey, *The Veiled Sceptre: Reserve Powers of Heads of State in Westminster Systems* (Cambridge University Press 2018) 116–17.

[15] Twomey (n 14) 121–23.

[16] Terence Daintith and Alan C Page, *The Executive in the Constitution: Structure, Autonomy, and Internal Control* (Oxford University Press 1999) 104–109; Tony Prosser, *The Economic Constitution* (Oxford University Press 2014) chs 4 and 5.

constitutional function if it, from time to time, rejects a legislative proposal advanced by the government. But if it is persistently rejecting these proposals, something has gone wrong; the government is out of line with the legislature and there needs to be a new prime minister and a new administration installed. During the 2019 Brexit crisis, when the Johnson government lost its majority and its capacity to get legislation through Parliament, this stalemate was often seen as a failure of government, but it should, perhaps, have been seen as a failure by Parliament, in particular the House of Commons, to provide the support that the government needed in order to govern.[17] If the Commons was unable to support the Johnson government, it should either have identified an alternative prime minister it could support, enabling that person to form a new administration, or it should have passed a motion of no confidence in Johnson, triggering an election. By simultaneously denying Johnson its support and refusing to take the steps necessary for a new, and effective, government to take office, the Commons failed in one of its core constitutional responsibilities.

Part of the difficulties faced by the 2019 Johnson government stemmed from the Fixed-term Parliaments Act 2011. Prior to this statute, the prime minister could ask the monarch to dissolve Parliament and hold an election, advice that the monarch would almost invariably accept. As its title suggests, the Fixed-term Parliaments Act provides a means for calculating the date for the next election, removing the prime minister's discretion.[18] An early election can be held in two situations. First, where there is a motion passed by two-thirds of MPs calling for an early general election. Secondly, where there is a vote of no confidence in the government, after which, if the Commons fails to pass a motion expressing confidence within fourteen days, an election will be held. The Fixed-term Parliaments Act is easy for a majority government to evade, as it could pass a motion of no confidence in itself (or, indeed, simply ask the opposition to join it in calling for

[17] Timothy Endicott, 'Making Constitutional Principles into Laws' (2020) 136 Law Quarterly Review 175, 176. See also Norton (n 5) 1009–11.

[18] According to s 1(3), an election is to be held on 'the first Thursday in May in the fifth calendar year following that in which the polling day for the previous parliamentary general election fell'.

an election, something any opposition party would find hard to resist). Its principal utility arises during coalition governments, where it removes the prime minister's capacity to call for an election to prevent a new coalition being formed. But where there is a minority government, such as Johnson's, it can have the effect of trapping a government in office, with the opposition refusing to support an election, but also preventing the government from functioning effectively. Before the Fixed-term Parliaments Act, a prime minister of a minority government had a threat she could use against Parliament: if the opposition parties made her position too weak, she could call an election.[19] Opposition parties would then have to weigh either giving the government just enough support to make it worthwhile for it to continue, or to call the prime minister's bluff in the hopes that their party might gain power in a fresh election. The Fixed-term Parliaments Act, passed during a period of coalition government, failed to consider the consequences of its restrictions for minority administrations.[20]

10.2 PEOPLE

The UK Parliament is divided into two chambers: the House of Commons and the House of Lords. The Commons is elected, whilst the Lords is largely appointed.

10.2.1 The Commons

In the 2019 General Election, 650 seats were contested. Table 10.1 shows the outcome of the vote, and contrasts the number of seats won under the UK's present electoral system with a rough assessment of how many would have been won under a proportional system. As can be seen from the table, the outcome of the 2019 election was a sizeable Conservative majority, whereas under a proportional system it is likely that some deal, possibly a formal

[19] Philip Norton, 'The Fixed-term Parliaments Act and Votes of Confidence' (2016) 69 Parliamentary Affairs 3.

[20] The government has proposed a bill that would effectively restore the power of the prime minister to call an election: Cabinet Office, *Draft Fixed-term Parliaments Act 2011 (Repeal) Bill* (2020).

Table 10.1 Seats and Percentage vote in 2019 General Election[a]

Party	Percentage Vote UK	Seats	Seats if Proportionate to UK Vote
Conservative	43.6	365	283
Labour	32.2	203	209
SNP	3.9	48	25
Lib Dem	11.5	11	75
Democratic Unionist	0.8	8	5
Sinn Féin	0.6	7	4
Plaid Cymru	0.5	4	3
SDLP	0.4	2	3
Green	2.7	1	18
Alliance	0.4	1	3
Brexit Party	2.0	0	13

[a]'Election 2019: Results' *BBC News* https://www.bbc.co.uk/news/election/2019/results (accessed 18 February 2021.

coalition, would have had to be struck between the Conservative and Lib Dem parties.

The disparity between the percentage of votes won and the number of seats gained is caused by the UK's electoral system. The UK is divided into 650 regional constituencies, with parliamentary elections conducted under a 'first past the post system', with the candidate who achieves the most votes in a constituency becoming the MP. This means that it is possible that a candidate may secure a relatively small percentage (sometimes as low as one-third) of the total votes cast in the constituency, and yet still win, if the other candidates gain even smaller percentages of the vote. The system favours parties that perform strongly in particular seats and discriminates against parties whose vote is spread more thinly across the UK. So, looking at the table, the SNP secured a far greater number of seats than the Lib Dems despite getting a far smaller percentage of the total vote. This is because the SNP's votes were concentrated in Scottish constituencies whilst the Lib

Dem vote was spread throughout Britain.[21] This feature of the system can serve to exclude smaller national parties entirely: the Brexit Party won about half the votes of the SNP but did not gain a single seat.

Maurice Duverger has argued that first past the post systems lead to fewer political parties.[22] Because smaller parties cannot win seats under this system, voters are encouraged to plump for the larger parties that have a chance of victory, and feedback loops emerge: within constituencies, as more voters vote for the larger parties, voting for smaller parties looks decreasingly attractive. Duverger's reasoning applies most cleanly within constituencies rather than at a national level; there may be more than two parties that profit from the pressures of the electoral system, with different rivals emerging in different areas. Indeed, looking at the allocations of seats in 2019, it is noticeable that the smaller parties that do best are regional parties, suggesting that in some constituencies these regional parties are able to present themselves as one of the two capable of winning the seat. But where two parties enjoy significant support across a country, the phenomenon identified by Duverger may also operate at a national level, with first past the post acting to protect, or foster, a system in which two parties will tend to dominate the legislature: voters may come to regard elections as a binary choice between two national parties, a perception that might then shape their conduct in constituency elections, giving a boost to the national rivals in local polls. The dominance of the two parties in Westminster is not unshakable and it is possible that we will see coalitions and minority governments in the future, forcing the two larger parties to negotiate with their smaller counterparts, but the UK's electoral system does seem to marginalise smaller parties, making the chances of one party gaining a parliamentary majority higher than it would be in a more proportionate system.

[21] The Lib Dems, like the Labour Party, do not contest seats in Northern Ireland.

[22] Maurice Duverger, *Political Parties: Their Organisation and Activity in the Modern State* (Methuen 1954), discussed further in Alan Renwick, 'Voting Behaviour and Electoral Outcomes' in Richard Heffernan and others (eds), *Developments in British Politics, vol 10* (Palgrave 2016).

A further possible consequence of the first past the post system is that it may encourage homogeneity within the Commons. There could be characteristics that make candidates more likely to be elected, and if these preferences are common throughout the country, they may have a significant impact within a first past the post electoral system. Some of these characteristics may be commendable—that the electorate tend to prefer honest and intelligent candidates would be a good thing—but others may be problematic. If there are widespread prejudices against candidates of a particular gender or race, for example, or if, perhaps, a significant proportion of people did not believe someone with a disability could operate as an MP, these groups might be radically underrepresented in the Commons. These prejudices might be enough to tip the balance in some seats and, even if this is not the case, when parties select candidates to run in constituencies they might do so defensively: anticipating prejudice, even if that prejudice might not have manifested in the election. After the 2019 election, 220 MPs were women, approximately one-third of the total number of MPs, and sixty-five MPs came from an ethnic minority, about 10% of the total.[23] If the gender and racial balance of the Commons mirrored that of the population, there would be around 325 women MPs and around ninety-one MPs from an ethnic minority. Nevertheless, the 2019 figures were a significant improvement on the position at the turn of the century. In the 1997 Parliament, there were only 120 women MPs, 18 percent of the total (itself a big improvement on the previous election), and nine ethnic minority MPs, one percent of the total.[24] More remarkably still, from 1929 to 1987 not a single ethnic minority MP sat in the Commons.[25]

The extent to which diversity in the Commons matters will depend on the form of representation we want to establish within

[23] Daniel Dunford and others, 'Election 2019: Britain's most diverse Parliament' *BBC News* (7 December 2019) https://www.bbc.co.uk/news/election-2019-50808536 (accessed 18 February 2021).

[24] Elise Uberoi, Chris Watson, and Esme Kirk-Wade, *Women in Parliament and Government* (CBP 01250, House of Commons Library, 25 February 2020); Elise Uberoi and Rebecca Lees, *Ethnic Diversity in Politics and Public Life* (CBP 01156, House of Commons Library, 22 October 2020).

[25] Uberoi, Watson, and Kirk-Wade (n 25); Uberoi and Lees (n 25).

the constitution. There are three broad types of representative institution, characterised by three broad types of representation: descriptive, mandate, and trusteeship.[26] The decision about which of these three should characterise the Commons has implications for the type of person we want as an MP. *Descriptive representation* exists when an institution is a scale model of the group it represents; the institution's characteristics map those of the group represented. *Mandate representation* requires representatives to carry out the instructions of those they represent; the representatives should do as they are told. *Trustee representation* requires the representatives act in the best interests of those they represent, which may or may not track the wishes of the voters. Only one of the three types of representation, descriptive representation, requires the Commons to mirror the population. If we wished to achieve descriptive representation, the Commons would not be chosen through election but through lot, by random draw. That the Commons is elected amounts to a rejection of descriptive representation: by choosing the Commons through election, the constitution gives voters chance to select representatives they believe will do a good job in the chamber; hopefully rising above the average level of capacity we would expect from a randomly selected group. The point of choosing election as a selection process is to ensure that the legislature does not mirror those being represented, but, instead, consists of representatives best able, in some sense, to advance the interests of those they represent.

This leaves open the two forms of representation, mandate and trustee. Under the mandate model, questions of diversity are an irrelevance. The job of the representative is to convey the demands of their electorate, and the personal characteristics of the representative should not impact on this task. The mandate model of representation has not proved popular in discussions of the role of Parliament: following the trustee model, representatives are expected to do their best to advance the interests of those they represent, even if this runs against the wishes of their electorates. When it was mooted that voters be given the capacity to recall MPs, requiring that a fresh election be held in the constituency,

[26] Hanna Pitkin, *The Concept of Representation* (University of California Press 1972).

Edmund Burke was frequently cited: as Burke put it in a speech to the voters of Bristol, their representative owed them 'not his industry only, but his judgment; and he betrays, instead of serving you, if he sacrifices it to your opinion'.[27] Following the trustee model of representation, an MP who is acting contrary to the wishes of the majority of her constituents may, nevertheless, be acquitting her constitutional obligations.[28] Similarly, attempts to argue that party manifestos are legally binding have not swayed the courts. Indeed, in one local government case Lord Diplock argued that representatives who regarded themselves as irrevocably bound to their manifesto, and refused to consider new factors relevant to the best interests of their electors, might be acting unreasonably, and their decision overturned for this reason.[29] However, in recent times the mandate theory of representation has enjoyed something of a revival, although in a limited area. Many interpreted the Brexit referendum as amounting to a mandate to leave the European Union given by the electorate: the people had spoken, and the duty of parliamentarians was to follow their decision. In Parliament, however, a portion of MPs regarded Brexit as contrary to the best interests of those they represented and continued to fight against it. A small portion of the controversy over Brexit may have been generated by these competing understandings of representation and their implications for the conduct of MPs.

If the duty of MPs is to act for the interests of those they represent, and process of election exists to enable the electorate to pick those they think will acquit this task well, that the Commons

[27] Edmund Burke, 'Speech at the Conclusion of the Poll at Bristol' in Jesse Norman (ed), *Reflections on the Revolution in France and Other Writings* (Everyman 2015) 151.

[28] Tony Wright, 'Recalling MPs: Accountable to Whom?' (2015) 86 Political Quarterly 289. The resulting statute, the Recall of MPs Act 2015, is heavily circumscribed, and requires wrongdoing before a recall petition can be launched. See Jonathan Tonge, 'The Recall of MPs Act 2015: Petitions, Polls, and Problems' (2019) 90 Political Quarterly 713 for an analysis of its use.

[29] *Bromley London Borough Council v Greater London Council* [1983] 1 AC 768, 830–31 (HL) (cf 795–96). There is a valuable, and rare, discussion of the constitutional status of manifestos by Dawn Oliver: Dawn Oliver, 'The Parties and Parliament: Representative or Intra-Party Democracy?' in Jeffrey L Jowell and Dawn Oliver (eds), *The Changing Constitution* (Clarendon Press 1985).

does not mirror the electorate is unsurprising. But diversity still matters under the trustee model, although indirectly. As Edmund Burke acknowledged, diversity within the chamber is essential if the Commons is to play its trustee role, making decisions that successfully track the interests of those MPs represent.[30] Diversity ensures that a range of different experiences are brought to bear on the tasks of the legislature. Representatives with different characteristics, whether these relate to gender, race, religion, social class, or some other factor, may have different understandings of the needs that statutes should address or of the impact of government policies. Sometimes there will be disagreement about whose interests should be given priority and these different understandings will cause debate, but sometimes, perhaps often, these different understandings will enrich the legislative process, identifying considerations that would otherwise have been overlooked. A homogenous legislature, no matter how well-intentioned and competent, may miss issues that would be raised in more diverse assembly. Furthermore, recalling the discussion in the last chapter, if the composition of the Commons appears radically out of line with the community it should serve, its capacity to resolve disputes within that community may be impaired. Why should members of a section of society accept the decisions of Parliament when it appears they have been excluded from participating in those decisions?

10.2.2 Lords

The House of Lords is a bit of an oddity. A weakness, and sometimes a strength, of the UK constitution is that its longevity allows elements of superseded conceptions of constitutionalism to persist in its current structures. The House of Lords is grounded in the medieval idea of a mixed constitution, a distant ancestor of the modern principle of the separation of powers.[31] In the mixed constitution, the different classes of society come together to agree

[30] Edmund Burke, 'Letter to Sir Hercules Langrishe' in Jesse Norman (ed), *Reflections on the Revolution in France and Other Writings* (Everyman 2015) 766–68; Pitkin (n 27) 173–80.

[31] Maurice Vile, *Constitutionalism and the Separation of Powers* (2nd edn, Liberty Press 1998) ch 3.

the rules that will govern the community: the Commons represents the ordinary people, the Lords represents the aristocracy, and, finally, the monarch's agreement is required before a statute is enacted.[32] Many modern constitutions contain legislatures with two chambers, but, in contrast to the UK, these are not intended to represent different social classes; social groups are expected to interact within the same chamber. The House of Lords, even in its current form, is a sharp reminder of the inequalities within the UK constitutional order and its society more generally.

Members of the House of Lords can be split into three groups: bishops, hereditary peers, and life peers.[33] There are twenty-six bishops in the Lords, some of whom, such as the Archbishop of Canterbury, automatically get a seat in the chamber, whilst the others must wait their turn, with places in the Lords being allocated on the basis of seniority.[34] In addition, there are eighty-five hereditary peers currently sitting in the chamber, and a further 692 life peers, who make up the bulk of those sitting in the Lords.[35]

The selection of the hereditary peers is complex, and this complexity is partly the result of an accident. When the Labour Party undertook the last major reform of the House of Lords in 1999, the majority of hereditary peers lost their capacity to sit in the Lords, but ninety-two were allowed to remain.[36] Two of the hereditary peers got a seat by virtue of inheritance, whilst the remainder were elected by the hereditary peerage. This was a compromise: the government was confident that it would soon be creating an elected second chamber, and so was willing to accept a hereditary element before this more radical reform was

[32] Measures of the Church of England, which are a form of primary legislation, must be passed by the General Synod in addition to the Commons and Lords, before receiving royal assent. Here the clergy is treated as a further sector of society whose consent is required before legislation can be made.

[33] There is also a small, and diminishing, group of Law Lords, appointed under the Appellate Jurisdiction Act 1876; contemporary justices of the Supreme Court are no longer members of the House of Lords.

[34] Again, the medieval model of the constitution persists, with the clergy given a role in the legislative process.

[35] See 'Lords membership: by peerage' (UK Parliament) https://members.parliament.uk/parties/lords/by-peerage (accessed 18 February 2021).

[36] House of Lords Act 1999.

completed. However, the anticipated reform did not materialise, and it became necessary to fill vacancies in the pool of hereditary peers as they arose. To avoid altering the political balance of the hereditary group, the peers are subdivided into groups affiliated to parties or cross-benchers, which are tied to groupings within the wider set of hereditary peers entitled to stand for election to the Lords. When a hereditary peer leaves the Lords, a by-election is held within the group of which she is a member, and a new peer is appointed to the chamber.[37] Some of the subgroups that undertake this election are tiny, and the new legislator can be picked by a handful of voters.

The bizarre and complicated nature of the selection of the hereditary peers is a function of the strange, if politically explicable, decision to include an element in Parliament that is chosen by birth. It is a small part of the constitution, but throws up a number of interesting conundrums. For instance, are the elected peers supposed to be representative, and, if so, representative of whom? Members of the Commons are elected by the people, and so can be said to represent them, but the hereditary lords are elected by other peers; is this the constituency they are supposed to represent? If, on the other hand, it is argued that the elected peers are chosen to represent the country as a whole, is this really a form of 'representation' at all, as it is one group picking someone to help govern another group? And what is to be said about the political groupings in which the elections are held? These are the only legislative posts allocated to parties as of right in the UK constitution; normally, we would see the potential for party competition as a necessity for a valid election to the legislature.

By far the largest group of peers consists of those with a life-peerage. The capacity for life peers to sit in the House of Lords is established by statute, the Life Peerages Act 1958. The appointment of life peers is overseen by the House of Lords Appointments Commission, which was established in 2000 as part of Labour's project to reform the Lords. The Commission was set up by the prime minister, then Tony Blair, and continues

[37] Thomas Erskine May, *Erskine May's Treatise on the Law, Privileges, Proceedings and Usage of Parliament* (David Natzler and others (eds), 25th edn, LexisNexis 2019) para 1.15.

to advise the prime minister on recommendations for peerages. The Commission nominates potential life peers directly, and vets candidates proposed by the prime minister and other party leaders. It is the prime minister who decides the number of life peers who will be appointed to the Lords, including the number that can be nominated by other party leaders, and, ultimately, it is the prime minister who decides whether to accept the decisions of the Commission. Generally, the Commission's decisions are followed, but in 2021 Boris Johnson decided to appoint Peter Cruddas, a former Conservative Party Chairman and donor, to the Lords despite the Commission's rejection of his nomination.[38] The incident underlined the remarkable degree of control over appointments possessed by the government: a prime minister could, if she wished, dissolve the Commission and recommend whomever she liked for appointment to the Lords, even seeking to flood the House with members of her own party.[39]

That the House of Lords is largely appointed makes it an outlier in terms of democratic constitutions, and it is hard to imagine any modern democratic state seeking to replicate it, but its appointment processes could be used to counterbalance some of the inequalities in the Commons, with appointments being drawn from underrepresented groups. Unfortunately, in terms of race and gender, the Lords actually fares worse than the current Commons. As to gender, about 28% of the Lords are female compared to 34% of the Commons, and as to race, about 6% of the Lords come from a minority ethnic group compared to 10% of the Commons.[40] Social diversity is harder to measure, but the Sutton Trust and the Social Mobility Commission jointly calculated that 57% of the Lords are privately educated, compared to 29% of the

[38] Justin Parkinson, 'Peter Cruddas: PM Overrules Watchdog with Tory Donor Peerage' *BBC News* (22 December 2020) https://www.bbc.co.uk/news/uk-politics-55414981 (accessed 18 February 2021).

[39] It is an open question how the monarch should respond to such an attempt: see chs 6 and 22.

[40] Gender information is available here: 'Lords membership: by gender' (UK Parliament) https://members.parliament.uk/parties/lords/by-gender (accessed 18 February 2021). Data on ethnic minorities can be found in Uberoi and Lees (n 25) s 2.2.

Commons, and only 7% of the population as a whole.[41] It can be argued, however, that the House of Lords contains a broader range of expertise than is found in the Commons. Many members of the Lords gained their seats after a successful career outside of politics. There are lawyers, business people, people who have run charities, medical professionals, and so on.[42] This can prove a strength when the Lords scrutinises government conduct or reviews legislation; the Lords will often have a pool of expertise larger than that of the Commons. Although the expertise in the Lords is often, and justly, celebrated, the appointment process allows other considerations to come into play that are less attractive. Former members of the Commons are strongly represented in the Lords, with just under 10% of Lords being former MPs.[43] Many of these appointments may have been made on merit, but it could be that in some cases the prospect of a peerage has been used to encourage an MP to give up her seat in the Commons, or, perhaps, as a reward for supporting her party's frontbench. More worryingly still, whilst it is illegal to sell a peerage, there is a correlation between the generosity of donors to political parties and the award of a seat in the Lords.[44]

10.2.3 A Note on Electoral Reform and House of Lords Reform

The processes whereby members of the Commons and Lords are selected seem ripe for reform, yet the enthusiasm for change within the two leading parties is muted. The closest that we have

[41] Sutton Trust and Social Mobility Commission, 'Elitist Britain: 2019' (2019) https://www.suttontrust.com/wp-content/uploads/2019/12/Elitist-Britain-2019.pdf (accessed 18 February 2021).

[42] Pete Dorey and Matt Purvis, 'Representation in the Lords' in Cristina Leston-Bandeira and Louise Thompson (eds), *Exploring Parliament* (Oxford University Press 2018) 246–48.

[43] 'Members of the House of Lords who were once MPs' (UK Parliament) https://www.parliament.uk/about/faqs/house-of-lords-faqs/lords-once-mps/ (accessed 18 February 2021).

[44] Simon Radford, Andrew Mell, and Seth Alexander Thevoz, '"Lordy Me!" Can Donations Buy You a British Peerage? A Study in the Link Between Party Political Funding and Peerage Nominations, 2005–2014' (2020) 15 British Politics 135. The Honours (Preventions of Abuses) Act 1925 renders the sale of honours a criminal offence.

come to major change in this area over the last few years were the reforms proposed by the Coalition government. The Coalition Agreement committed the government to a referendum on the adoption of the Alternative Vote system of election for the Commons and to bring forward proposals making the House of Lords a wholly or mainly elected chamber on the basis of proportional representation.[45] The Alternative Vote mechanism would have allowed voters to rank candidates, with second preferences being examined if no candidate won an overall majority. Alternative Vote is not a form of proportional representation, and probably would have had a limited impact on the disparity between the overall percentage of the vote and seats won in the Commons.[46] In a referendum the Alternative Vote system was decisively rejected, with about 68% voting against the proposal.[47]

The proposed reforms of the House of Lords fared little better. The House of Lords Reform Bill presented an exceptionally complicated plan for the Lords, which combined appointed and elected representatives.[48] The appointed element would have included bishops, a group of peers chosen by the prime minister, and a further set of peers chosen by the House of Lords Appointments Commission. On the elected side of the House, voters could choose between voting for an independent candidate, a party, or a party candidate. The constituencies would have been very large and multiple members would have represented each territory.[49] Elected members of the chamber could serve for fifteen years, but could not then stand for re-election. The bill was abandoned when a significant number of Conservative MPs refused to support it.

[45] Cabinet Office, *The Coalition: Our Programme for Government* (2010) https://www.gov.uk/government/publications/the-coalition-documentation (accessed 18 February 2021).

[46] Renwick (n 23) 54–56.

[47] 'Vote 2011: UK rejects alternative vote' *BBC News* (7 May 2011) https://www.bbc.com/news/uk-politics-13297573 (accessed 18 February 2021).

[48] House of Lords Reform HC Bill (2012–13).

[49] To add to the complexity, a different electoral system would have applied to Northern Ireland, and a further, distinct, mechanism would have been invoked when a vacancy arose.

The failure to reform the processes for selection to the Commons and Lords should not surprise us. All attempts at reform in this area face a paradox: the constitutional actors tasked with bringing forward the reforms are the beneficiaries of the old system which put them into their positions of power. As we have seen, both of the two major parties have reason to want to keep first past the post, both because it can reward them with disproportionate majorities and because in a proportionate system it is likely they would fragment, with multiple parties emerging. Similarly, there is little incentive for the Commons and government to turn the Lords into an elected second chamber; it risks creating a rival to the Commons, making it harder for the government to get its business through. The decision to include an appointed element in the 2012 Bill, even keeping the bishops in the House, might have been motivated by a desire to make it clear that the Lords' legitimacy was less than that of the elected Commons.

10.3 LEGISLATURES: POWERS, PROTECTIONS, AND ACCOUNTABILITY

The classic power of the legislature is, of course, that of legislation. The legal rules that render this power effective were discussed in Chapter 5, but it is worth noting that, like the courts' power to decide cases, the legislature's power to legislate depends on the support of the other branches of the constitution. The legislature relies on the courts to apply the statutes in the event of disputes and its capacity to legislate is constrained by the extent to which judges adhere to the meanings of the statutes as enacted. When courts ignore statutes, or depart from the enacted meaning of those instruments, Parliament's legislative capacity is reduced. In addition, the legislature's ability to create statutes relies on the support of the executive. We have already seen that it is normally the executive that drafts bills put before Parliament, with government ministers introducing them in the Commons, but it is also the executive that administers and enforces statutes once they are enacted. Indeed, the effectiveness of many statutes will depend, to a significant extent, on the extent to which the executive is willing to invest its energies in their application. Whilst the power of legislation is often seen as central to the legislature, the success of its legislation depends upon the support of the other branches.

A second, and equally important, set of powers possessed by the legislature relate to its control of the executive. The power to control the budget of the executive is often held up as a key aspect of this control: the legislature's capacity to restrict, or even refuse, the executive's funding facilitates the legislature's scrutiny of the executive, and obliges the executive to be sensitive to the wishes of the legislature. However, it is the capacity of the legislature to select the prime minister that is probably the most important power that body possesses. By controlling the selection of prime minister, Parliament is able to exercise indirect control over the appointment of the whole government, the political element of the executive. One way that the prime minister maintains the confidence of the Commons, and ultimately her position, is through her choice of ministers. Although different prime ministers have different degrees of latitude, the prime minister must pick ministers who, broadly, will be endorsed by her party within the Commons; ministers who are perceived as competent and who reflect the various political strands of her party. If she fails to choose her ministers wisely, the prime minister's own position may be called into question if her party loses confidence in her.[50] Consequently, the capacity to select the prime minister brings with it a broader capacity to regulate the government which, in its turn, regulates the remainder of the executive branch.

When exercising these powers, legislators are required to act in the best interests of those they represent. Legislators may face pressure to act contrary to this duty from at least two sources: externally, from private actors in society, who may seek to use their power to distort the legislative process, and internally, from other parts of the constitution and, crucially, from their own parties, who may pressure legislators to stick to the party line. A challenge when gauging the types and level of protection that legislators should be given is distinguishing unjustified pressures, which need to be curbed, from the ordinary and valuable pressures of

[50] An example of what Tony King called 'intra-party' control: Anthony King, 'Modes of Executive-Legislative Relations: Great Britain, France, and West Germany' (1976) 1 Legislative Studies Quarterly 11, 15–16.

political life. After all, legislators are supposed to have a close relationship with the people for whom they legislate, and legislatures can only operate effectively if their conduct is, generally, conditioned by constitutional and party structures. That legislators often feel constrained by these forces may be a positive, even essential, feature of their role.

The most obvious protection enjoyed by legislators is found in Article IX of the Bill of Rights 1689, the Claim of Right Act 1689, and the broader doctrine of parliamentary privilege.[51] Amongst other things, these provisions prevent legislators from being sued for statements made within Parliament; legislators enjoy absolute freedom of expression within the chambers. This aspect of privilege provides protection against those who would use the courts to put pressure on legislators. In modern times, this aspect of privilege is generally presented as providing protection for legislators against powerful private actors, who might try to use the libel laws to inhibit debate in Parliament. In earlier times, it was more commonly presented as protecting legislators from pressure brought by the Crown, or the executive, through the courts.[52] In either case, privilege removes one possible source of pressure—litigation based on speech—that might otherwise be exerted against legislators.

A further, and more insidious, threat to the conduct of legislators comes from the inducements they receive, or may come to receive, from private actors. Members of the Commons are now required to disclose any payments they receive above a certain level, currently £100, and any donations made to support their work as an MP of over £1,500, and must not act as lobbyists for organisations—although they can act as consultants or advisers.[53] There is a similar register for peers, but it is less explicit about the sums received.[54] A look at these documents reveals that many

[51] See ch 4.

[52] 1 Blackstone Comm 159; Josh Chafetz, *Democracy's Privileged Few: Legislative Privilege and Democratic Norms in the British and American Constitutions* (Yale University Press 2007) ch 1.

[53] House of Commons, *The Code of Conduct together with the Guide to the Rules relating to the Conduct of Members* (HC 2017–19, 1882).

[54] House of Lords, *Code of Conduct for Members of the House of Lords* (HL 2019–21, 99).

legislators receive money from outside sources such as companies, trade unions, and individuals. Perhaps even more worrisome is the propensity of former ministers (and prime ministers) to take up lucrative posts within the sectors that used to be covered by their ministries.

A second source of pressure exerted over representatives comes from within Parliament, and, in particular, from within their own parties. As we saw at the start of this chapter, it was this pressure that led Adam Tomkins to recommend the banning of the whips: a ban, if it worked, that would dissolve party structures in Parliament, or, at least, significantly reduce their efficacy. In the Commons, and to a lesser extent the Lords, the parties have considerable sway over their MPs. The ultimate sanction that can be applied is expulsion from the parliamentary party, withdrawal of the whip. Once the whip has been withdrawn, the MP cannot stand as the party's candidate in elections; if she wants to seek re-election she must join another party or stand as an independent candidate. As many voters cast their votes based on party, rather than on the personality of the candidate, the expelled MP's chances of re-election are reduced. Short of this extreme, parties also exercise significant control over an MP's political career, often determining which posts she will hold. There is minimal protection provided against pressures of this type; what legal regulation there is of political parties focuses almost entirely on their operation outside of the legislature. And perhaps it would be unwise to seek to provide protection even if the power of parties is abused: as we have seen, parties are needed if the legislature is to perform its constitutional role successfully, and party discipline is needed if parties are to function effectively. Tomkins himself may have had second thoughts about the value of political parties: a few years after advocating the banning of whips, he was elected to the Scottish Parliament and sat as a Conservative MSP from 2016 to 2021.

Although there are few specific legal protections for legislators, aside from the rules of privilege, they enjoy one very important bulwark against external pressures: it is very hard to remove a legislator from Parliament except at an election. In the period between votes, legislators can be confident of keeping their posts.[55]

[55] Members of the Commons and Lords can be expelled, but such expulsions are exceptionally rare: Erskine May (n 38) paras 11.33, 11.38.

The flip side of this protection is that between elections the formal accountability mechanisms that apply to legislators are weak.[56] The Code of Conduct for MPs principally focuses on the financial affairs of MPs, seeking to draw a line between the private renumeration of MPs and their public function.[57] Complaints about breaches of the Code can be made to the Parliamentary Commissioner for Standards, who reports to the Commons, which can, in its turn, impose sanctions on the MP.[58] There are currently moves to expand the Code to include bullying, harassment, and sexual harassment. A similar internal structure exists in the House of Lords. That the structures for disciplining members of the Commons and Lords are relatively weak should not come as a surprise. Any internal mechanism that might lead to the suspension or expulsion of legislators brings a risk that it will be used in the political struggles in the chamber.

10.4 CONCLUSION

Under older accounts of the separation of powers, the unity of the legislative column presented a puzzle. The structures of the legislature, and the qualifications of those who legislate, did not appear to align with the powers given to that body: how could an institution, which often consists of hundreds of people, many of whom possess no training in law-making, management, or public policy, hope to determine the policy direction of the state through the production of coherent statutes and by exercising control over the executive? The answer lies in the semi-hidden structural feature of legislatures: political parties. It is political parties that provide the internal structures of legislatures that enable those bodies to function; once we see legislatures as including parties, the elements of the legislative column start to make sense. Political parties enable like-minded people to work together,

[56] Although, again, it is worth noting that parties exercise some ongoing control, and a legislator who hopes for a political career that extends beyond the next election will be sensitive to her party's view of her conduct.

[57] House of Commons, *The Code of Conduct* (n 54).

[58] The regulation of MPs' expenses claims is conducted by the Independent Parliamentary Standards Authority, a body established by the Parliamentary Standards Act 2009.

formulating policies and identifying leadership teams. Within the legislature, parties act as the first forum through which policies for legislation are identified and developed, and it is parties that identify candidates for prime minister and which, indirectly, shape the government by providing ministers to oversee the executive. It is party structures that enable the creation of the government and which tie the government to the legislature.

Parties are also crucial to the connection between the legislature and the voters. First, because at election time they present voters with broad policy platforms and leadership teams that voters can choose between; it is rarely the case that voters know, or could know, the personalities of the candidates in their areas. When we think about the people who populate legislatures, party affiliation is normally part of the reason for their election, and, in consequence, part of their qualification to sit in the chamber. Secondly, parties act as a bridge between Parliament and the voters between elections. Whilst individual legislators come and go, parties are normally in politics for the long term. This means that parties provide an opaque but essential constraint on their leadership when in power. The extent to which the government can diverge from the wishes of the people will be limited by the party: even if the prime minister plans to leave politics at the next election, her party will always have an eye on re-election. A government that becomes radically unpopular may find that it loses the support of its party and the prime minister is changed during the Parliament.[59] Because political parties are commonly considered outside of the constitution, private, or quasi-private, bodies, the crucial role of these bodies has often been overlooked, but it is parties that enable the legislature to fulfil its constitutional roles by providing it with the internal structures that are essential to its operation.

[59] As was the case with Margaret Thatcher in 1990 and Theresa May in 2019.

11

EXECUTIVE

The executive is, quite literally, the most powerful branch of the state. It possesses the capacity to make changes to the world; to move and harm things and people; to buy property and to employ; to cajole, threaten, and encourage. It is the executive that reshapes society to match the demands of statutes and which provides the threat of coercion that backs up judicial decisions. To undertake this task, the executive needs to be both large and complex. In the United Kingdom (UK), several million people are employed by the executive, distributed across a complex variety of forms of institutions and structures.[1] Some parts of the executive operate at a national level, such as the core government departments, whilst others operate at a regional level, such as police authorities or civil servants working in local government. Some of the executive is under tight political control, whilst other parts are carefully insulated from political interference. And the ways in which these bodies carry out their tasks is also radically diverse: from soldiers fighting overseas, to teachers in primary schools, the executive encompasses an enormous range of skills and modes of working, a diversity that enables the state to realise its policies in the world.

That the executive is characterised by its possession of, and capacity to exercise, power, raises a pair of connected challenges, each of which turn on the question of control. First, in a democratic country, such as the UK, the executive should be regulated by the decisions of the legislature and the courts. Whilst the executive has a role in setting policy and determining people's entitlements, it should be the legislature that determines the broad policy direction of the state, and the courts that have the final say about people's legal rights. If the executive is not bound by law,

[1] See Office for National Statistics, 'Public Sector Employment, UK: September 2019' (17 December 2019) www.ons.gov.uk/employmentandlabourmarket/peopleinwork/publicsectorpersonnel/bulletins/publicsectoremployment/september2019 (accessed 17 February 2021).

The United Kingdom Constitution. N. W. Barber, Oxford University Press. © Nick Barber 2021.
DOI: 10.1093/oso/9780198852315.003.0011

if it is not tied to the decisions of the legislature and the courts, the democratic structures of the state become meaningless. But this raises a paradox: the executive must be constrained, but the bodies in the constitution that can make these constraints effective, police, auditors, inspectorates of various sorts, are parts of the executive itself. Secondly, and relatedly, whilst constrained, the executive also needs to be effective; it must possess the capacity to act if it is to achieve anything at all. Here, the size and complexity of the executive becomes a challenge: if the internal structures of the executive branch are weak, the executive will function poorly.

11.1 STRUCTURE

Identifying a discrete constitutional institution, delineating it from other, near-by, bodies, is often as much a matter of convenience as hard legal analysis. It is possible, and sometimes useful, to present the entirety of the executive branch as a single institution. As an institution, the executive has an objective and means of action, together with a structure suited to realising its objective through these means. The executive's objective is to realise the policy goals of the state, it achieves this objective through the exercise of power, and it wields this power through a collection of task-focused offices, groups of people who are charged with bringing about changes in the world. But if we open up the executive, these task-focused offices can be seen as distinct institutions of their own. And, pulling back another layer, these entities often contain groupings that could also be considered to be distinct institutions. Deciding whether a given action is attributed to the UK executive, the Department of Work and Pensions, the Pension Service, or, indeed, to the Wolverhampton branch of the Pension Service, may depend on the purpose of the attribution.

There are many ways the internal structures of the executive could be distinguished, but perhaps the two most significant criteria turn on the extent of political control over activities of bodies and the extent of the regionalisation of their jurisdiction. Taking political control first, four contrasts can be drawn: between the political and apolitical parts of the executive; between core government departments and agencies and offices within those departments; between government departments and non-departmental public bodies that remain under the supervision of that department; and, finally, between public bodies and those private bodies that are used by the executive to achieve some of its objectives.

11.1.1 Degrees of Autonomy

Though the definition given to the term varies, in this book 'government' is taken to encompass the political side of the executive; that is, those individuals who hold posts tied to executive departments, who have been selected by the prime minister or her devolved equivalents, and who also, almost invariably, have seats in a legislature. At the national level, the government consists of secretaries of state and ministers of state.[2] The Cabinet, chaired by the prime minister, sits as the decision-making body of the government as a whole; under the convention of collective responsibility, once the Cabinet has made a decision, all members of the government are bound to support the policy. Though the Cabinet may be the highest committee of state, most governmental decision-making goes on within government departments.[3] Inside these departments sit teams of ministers, normally headed by a secretary of state. The secretary of state is responsible for the department as a whole, whilst the other ministers in her team have narrower sets of responsibilities, focusing on particular areas of the department's activities. Within the confines of the law and the decisions of Cabinet, these ministers determine the policy objectives of their department and oversee its operation. Inside government departments, often working alongside ministers, are civil servants. The leading civil servant within the department is the permanent secretary, with other civil servants reporting to her. Like the rest of the executive branch, these civil servants are apolitical; that is, they are not appointed on the basis of their

[2] There are also parliamentary private secretaries, but these are not regarded as members of the government, although their functions overlap with those of the government: Cabinet Office, 'Ministerial Code' (August 2019) paras 3.6–3.12 www.gov.uk/government/publications/ministerial-code (accessed 17 February 2021).

[3] Terence Daintith and Alan Page, *The Executive in the Constitution: Structure, Autonomy, and Internal Control* (Oxford University Press 1999) 29–32.

political beliefs, and are expected to work under governments of different political complexions.

Internally, departments can be divided between the core department and agencies operating within the department. Inside the Department for Work and Pensions, for example, can be found the Pensions Service and the Child Maintenance Service. Whereas the core department is under the direct supervision of the permanent secretary, these agencies enjoy significant freedom of action, although the extent of this freedom varies from agency to agency. They are established under framework documents that set targets and delineate their relationships with the core government department. Each agency is headed by a chief executive, who is responsible to a minister for its day-to-day operation, and to the permanent secretary for its use of public funds.[4] The chief executive is directly accountable to Parliament for the running of the agency, but the agency remains part of the department, does not possess a separate legal identity, and ministers remain responsible to Parliament for its operation.

These internal agencies trace their origins back to a report produced in 1988, entitled *Improving Management in Government: The Next Steps*, and were historically called 'Next Steps' agencies.[5] These agencies are established where there is an area of departmental work of significant size that involves the delivery of a specialised service distinct from the core function of the department.[6] The hope is that these agencies will be more tightly focused on the tasks delegated to them than would be the case if the task was undertaken by the core department directly. When the agency structure was introduced, it was thought that the new structure would lead to a division of responsibility between

[4] Cabinet Office, 'Public Bodies Handbook Part 3: Executive Agencies: A Guide for Departments' (2018) https://assets.publishing.service.gov.uk/government/uploads/system/uploads/attachment_data/file/690636/Executive_Agencies_Guidance.PDF (accessed 20 February 2021), 3.

[5] Kate Jenkins, Karen Caines, and Andrew Jackson, *Improving Management in Government: The Next Steps* (Her Majesty's Stationery Office 1988); June Burnham and Sylvia Horton, *Public Management in the United Kingdom: A New Introduction* (Palgrave MacMillan 2013) 52–55.

[6] Cabinet Office, 'Executive Agencies' (n 4) ch 3; Paul Craig, *Administrative Law* (8th edn, Sweet & Maxwell 2016) 76–79.

ministers and chief executives: ministers would be responsible for setting the policies followed by the agencies, whilst chief executives would be responsible for their implementation, and the continued accountability of chief executives to Parliament is a legacy of this distinction.[7] In the early days of the agency structure, ministers sought to invoke the divide to limit their responsibility to Parliament. Notoriously, in 1995 the Home Secretary, Michael Howard, attempted to draw a line between policy and operational matters, seeking to avoid responsibility for the escape of prisoners. Howard argued that the prisoners' breakouts fell within the responsibility of the chief executive of the Prison Service.[8] Such a sharp divide proved politically unattractive, and Howard's attempt to recraft the convention of ministerial responsibility failed; subsequent ministers made it clear that they remained responsible to Parliament for the operation of their departments, including the operation of agencies within the department.

A more radical form of distancing places the agency outside of the formal structures of the department, through the establishment of a non-departmental public body (NDPB). These entities are also sometimes known as quangos, quasi-independent non-governmental organisations. In contrast to Next Steps agencies, NDPBs mostly possess a distinct legal identity from the department, are normally established under legislation or the prerogative rather than by an administrative decision, and are not ordinarily staffed by civil servants. NDPBs are 'sponsored' by a government department, with ministers responsible for the appointment of key personnel in the NDPB and possessing varying levels of control over the functioning of the NDPB, depending on the instrument founding the body.[9] Whilst NDPBs possess significant autonomy, ministers remain accountable to Parliament for their operation.[10]

[7] Daintith and Page (n 3) 39; Matthew Flinders, *The Politics of Accountability in the Modern State* (Ashgate 2001) 49–55.

[8] Flinders (n 7) 48.

[9] Appointment decisions made by ministers are now heavily regulated: Craig (n 6) 91.

[10] Cabinet Office, 'Public Bodies: A Guide for Departments' (June 2006) ch 2 www.gov.uk/government/publications/non-departmental-public-bodies-characteristics-and-governance (accessed 17 February 2021).

By establishing an institution as an NDPB, the department gives the institution a significant degree of independence, and, equally importantly, the appearance of independence. This independence is attractive when the body is intended to act in a non-political way. So, for example, the Department of Work and Pensions sponsors bodies such as the Pensions Regulator, the Social Security Advisory Committee, and the Pensions Protection Fund. In each case, there are reasons why the body is held at arm's length from the Department. The Pensions Regulator plays a policing role, regulating and investigating the operation of pension funds, and, just as the police are insulated from political control to reduce the risk that politicians will use them inappropriately, regulatory bodies are commonly kept at a distance from the political side of the executive. The Social Security Advisory Committee exists to provide the Department with advice on social security matters, providing scrutiny of the detailed secondary legislation that supports the social security system. As a body that exists, in part, to hold the Department to account, distance from the Department is necessary for it to accomplish its objectives. Finally, the Pensions Protection Fund protects those who pay into private pension schemes covered by the fund; if their provider becomes insolvent, the fund takes over the running of the scheme. Private schemes pay a levy to the fund, which currently manages over £30 billion worth of assets, paying pensions to about a quarter of a million people. One reason for creating the fund was to encourage people to pay into private pensions, knowing that the state would support pensioners in the event of insolvency. Making the fund a NDPB facilitates long-term decision-making by reducing the risk politicians will be able to manipulate investment decisions and the coverage of the fund.

A final, shrinking, set of NDPBs exist in the form of tribunals. Tribunals are dispute-resolving bodies that closely resemble courts in form and operation. In contrast to the courts, tribunals tend to be less formal, cheaper to access, and possess specialisms in particular areas, often with experts from the area regulated by the tribunal sitting on the bench. Whereas courts have only a limited jurisdiction to review administrative decisions, tribunals can often take the decision afresh: they can assess the merits of an issue, reaching conclusions that then bind government departments. Historically, tribunals have had a close connection to the executive branch; whilst possessing a statutory base, they were often established at the instigation of the government, and, because their decisions turn on the merits of an issue, were regarded as making decisions that would otherwise be the province of government departments, not courts. Over the last sixty years, tribunals have become steadily more distanced from the government. The Franks Report in 1957 decided that tribunals should be seen as adjudicative, rather than administrative, institutions; Franks required that tribunal chairs be appointed through a process analogous to that used to appoint judges, and that the potential for appeals being made from tribunals to ministers be brought to an end.[11] The Leggatt Review in 2001 continued this process: following that review, most tribunals were split from their sponsoring departments and are now administered by HM Courts and Tribunals Service, an executive agency within the Ministry of Justice.[12] The majority of tribunals are now no longer NDPBs, but are their own, distinct, constitutional entity.[13] Tribunals should probably now be considered parts of the judicial rather than executive branch, an aspect of the constitutional order that has shifted its constitutional identity over time.

A further form of arm's length agency, the non-ministerial department, is yet further removed from the control of the political part of the executive. Non-ministerial departments, like most NDPBs, are creations of statute but, in contrast to NDPBs, are not attached to a government department. They still have a sponsoring minister, who represents the body in Parliament and has overall responsibility for the body's statutory framework, but these bodies are headed by a civil servant, their funding is not channelled through a government department, and they are

[11] Committee on Administrative Tribunals and Enquiries, *Report of the Committee on Administrative Tribunals and Enquiries* (Her Majesty's Stationery Office 1957); Craig (n 6) 233–34.

[12] Sir Andrew Leggatt, *Tribunals for Users: One System, One Service* (Stationery Office 2001).

[13] Cabinet Office, 'Public Bodies Handbook Part 1: Classification of Public Bodies: Guidance for Departments' (April 2016) 13 www.gov.uk/government/publications/classification-of-public-bodies-information-and-guidance (accessed 17 February 2021).

directly accountable to Parliament for their actions, reporting to Parliament and monitored by Select Committees. Non-ministerial departments tend to be created where the body plays a regulatory role, such as the Charities Commission or Crown Prosecution Service, and political interference might undermine the body's operation.

In addition to these varying constitutional forms, public bodies may also take on the legal structures of private institutions, becoming charities or companies. The Victoria and Albert Museum, for instance, is both a NDPB[14] and a charity; its trustees are appointed by the prime minister and a significant portion of its income comes from government.[15] Other public bodies are structurally identical to private companies: they are owned by shareholders who have limited liability for their debts.[16] Some of these companies are entirely state-owned: the British Business Bank, for instance, is a public limited company wholly owned by the state, but which could also be considered a NDPB, as it is sponsored by the Department for Business, Energy and Industrial Strategy. Sometimes, these companies are part-owned by the state, with a government department exercising control over the company, but with private investors holding a portion of shares in the organisation.[17]

It might be asked why the executive would choose to create a charity or a company, legal forms that bring with them additional regulation, when the entity could simply be constituted as an ordinary public body. One of the reasons for so doing is that the form given to the institution shapes the way it behaves, and, in consequence, the ways others treat it. The legal framework that establishes these bodies shapes their range of concern: charities

[14] It is sponsored by the Department of Digital, Culture, Media and Sport.

[15] In 2017–18, over one-third of the museum's income came from the state: Victoria and Albert Museum, *Annual Report and Accounts 2017-2018* (HC 1263, Her Majesty's Stationery Office 2018).

[16] See National Audit Office, 'Companies in Government' (December 2015) www.nao.org.uk/wp-content/uploads/2015/12/Companies-in-Government_updated.pdf (accessed 20 February 2021).

[17] For instance, the state owns 49% of shares in NATS Holdings (which provides air traffic control) and a 'golden share' giving the government special voting rights.

are required to spend their money on their charitable objectives, directors of public limited companies are required to make decisions that will promote the success of the company.[18] By placing a public body into one of these forms, the executive reassures those engaging with it that the scope of the body's concern is restricted. So, people can donate money to the Victoria and Albert Museum knowing that the money will be spent on the Museum and not diverted elsewhere, or they can buy shares in a company established by the state knowing that those running the company will strive to make it profitable. More broadly, the form that the body adopts shapes how it behaves and how those operating it understand their roles. For instance, when the state establishes an entity as a company, it expects those who operate it to act in a commercial manner, competing for business in the marketplace, and it is not uncommon for these companies, even when wholly owned by the state, to compete with privately-owned companies for public contracts.[19]

We have now reached the edge of the executive branch; at this point, the line between the public and private, however sharp in theory, becomes vague in practice. It may be a matter of chance whether the institution used to pursue the policies of the state is a public body or a private body. Sometimes, the control that a department exercises over a private body through an ordinary contract may be as great as, or greater than, the control it exercises over a NDPB; indeed, sometimes those engaging with that private body may be unaware that it is not part of the public realm. Moreover, institutions can shift their identity over time, being spun off into the private sector by the state, becoming a purely private company, and then later being renationalised if necessary. The boundaries of the executive can shift and blur.

The progression from core government departments through executive agencies, NDBPs, and state-owned companies, traces a collection of institutional forms with different levels of autonomy, elements of the executive radiating outwards from parts which are subject to close, day-to-day, political control, to those over which political control is more remote. This structure

[18] Charities Act 2011; Companies Act 2006, s 171.

[19] Burnham and Horton (n 5) 27–38.

reflects a tension within the executive branch between democratic control and technical expertise, two potentially competing modes of legitimacy. Political actors within the executive are, directly or indirectly, democratically accountable; their legitimacy turns on election. The apolitical part of the executive, in contrast, is appointed on the basis of technocratic ability; what autonomous legitimacy it possesses is grounded in its capacity to identify and pursue the most effective way of achieving the goals of the state. Ideally, these two modes of legitimacy complement each other, but there is the potential for conflict. Political actors may enjoy democratic legitimacy but, almost invariably, they lack the knowledge and experience required to operate executive institutions effectively. The degrees of autonomy granted to executive institutions embody a balance: seeking to protect those with technical expertise from interference by inexpert, yet democratically mandated, politicians, whilst also ensuring that, ultimately, the democratic side of the constitution remains in control.

11.1.2 Regionalisation

Cutting across these institutional forms is the regionalisation of the executive, the spread of these institutions throughout the country. There is regionalisation of the political executive, with political control exercised at the level of national government, the devolved assemblies, and through local government, with each of these levels of government having its own distinct set of officials and executive institutions. In addition, these executive institutions often contain regional sub-units, local offices, and even officials within those local offices who are responsible for a yet smaller area. The characteristic means employed by the executive, the exertion of power, requires this radical regionalisation. Whilst a degree of regionalisation is desirable for the legislative and judicial branches, it is essential for the executive branch and, moreover, must be realised to a far greater extent: to control its territory, to vindicate its claim to sovereignty, the state needs to have executive officials close to its people.

11.2 PEOPLE

Those working in the executive can be divided into two broad, if unequal, groups: those who gain their position through the operation of the democratic process, and those who are appointed as a result of their technical expertise.

The political side of the executive consists of politicians who are, directly or indirectly, democratically accountable. At the national level, the government consists of members of the House of Commons and, less frequently, the House of Lords. The number of paid ministers is capped by the Ministerial and other Salaries Act 1975 at 109, and the House of Commons Disqualification Act 1975 limits the number of ministers who can sit in the Commons to ninety-five.[20] Of these, around twenty-one sit in the Cabinet. Cabinet members are, normally, secretaries of state, and are the most senior ministers attached to their government departments. As we saw in the last chapter, appointments to government are made by the prime minister, although her freedom of choice is limited by the need to maintain the support of her party. Appointments to the Scottish and Welsh governments are undertaken in a similar fashion, although in Scotland the Scottish Parliament must agree to ministerial appointments before they are finalised.[21] The position in Northern Ireland is different, and is discussed in Chapter 16.

The second group of members of the executive are appointed on the basis of their technical expertise, expertise that should be relevant to the particular executive institution to which they belong. Because the basis for their appointment is grounded in their technical skills, they are expected to set aside party-political beliefs whilst at work. According to the Office for National Statistics, in 2019 there were around 5.44 million people employed by the state, compared to 27.55 million people working in the private sector. Central government employed around 3.2 million people in total, and local government employed about 2.1 million.[22] The largest single public sector employer was the National Health

[20] House of Commons Disqualification Act 1975, s 2.
[21] Scotland Act 1998, s 47.
[22] Office for National Statistics (n 1).

Service (NHS) with 1.73 million workers, almost one-third of the total public workforce. For comparison, the armed forces and police each employ around 150,000.

Around 500,000 of those employed by the state are civil servants.[23] The Civil Service includes the administrators who work most closely with the political side of the executive, and many of the staff of government departments. Civil servants are appointed on the basis of merit: one of the great constitutional reforms of the Victorian period was to end patronage within the service, instead appointing people on the basis of ability.[24] The Civil Service Code, which now has a statutory underpinning and forms part of the Civil Service contract of employment, identifies the values that civil servants are expected to uphold.[25] The core values it picks out are integrity, honesty, objectivity, and impartiality; civil servants are expected to put public service ahead of their own interests, base the advice they give and decisions they take on evidence, and remain politically impartial, supporting governments of all political persuasions.[26] To achieve political impartiality, and, perhaps, to bolster the appearance of impartiality, civil servants cannot stand for election to the Commons, and those in higher grade posts are barred from holding offices in political parties and expressing views on matters of political controversy.[27]

Whilst members of the Civil Service constitute an important subset of members of the executive, they are in a minority. Most people employed by the state are not, formally, classed as civil servants. Beyond the Civil Service, there is a huge range of different forms of employment across the public sector: from curators in museums to generals in the army, from nurses working

[23] This figure includes the Northern Ireland Civil Service (which has around 25,000 employees) and the Diplomatic Service (with around 14,000 employees).

[24] Constitutional Reform and Governance Act 2010, s 10; Daintith and Page (n 3) 78–80; Burnham and Horton (n 5) 23–27.

[25] UK Government, 'Civil Service Code' (2015) www.gov.uk/government/publications/civil-service-code/the-civil-service-code (accessed 20 February 2021); Constitutional Reform and Governance Act 2010, s 5. There are similar codes for the Diplomatic Service and the Northern Ireland Civil Service.

[26] Daintith and Page (n 3) 89–91.

[27] House of Commons Disqualification Act 1975, s 1(1)(b); UK Government, 'Civil Service Management Code' (2016) s 4.4 www.gov.uk/government/publications/civil-servants-terms-and-conditions (accessed 20 February 2021).

in hospitals to teachers in schools. It is not possible to survey all of these different types of office within the executive, but they share some important features with the Civil Service: all rest on technical ability, all are apolitical roles, and all, ultimately, exist to further the policies of the state.

In the chapters on the courts and legislature, some space was devoted to discussing the diversity of those institutions. Assessing the diversity of the executive is a far harder task because of the wide range of different institutions within that body. The Race Disparity Unit, a body within the Cabinet Office, produced a report in 2019 which surveyed the ethnic diversity of public sector bodies, and revealed enormous variations across executive institutions.[28] The NHS, for example, draws 44.4% of its staff from ethnic minority groups, whilst firefighters are the least diverse, with 4.1% from an ethnic minority, and the police are at 6.9%. In the Civil Service, around 12% came from an ethnic minority group, but only about 6% of senior civil servants fell into this category. In terms of gender, in the NHS, about 58.3% of employees are female, but there are significantly more women than men working in lower-paying jobs.[29] In the Civil Service, 53.9% are female but, as with the NHS, at the senior level that percentage reduces to 45.2%.[30]

11.3 POWERS, PROTECTIONS, AND ACCOUNTABILITY

When constitutional lawyers consider the powers of the executive branch, they tend to focus on the legal rules that empower the executive to act.[31] Depending on how things are categorised,

[28] Race Disparity Unit, 'Ethnic Diversity of Public Sector Workforces' (18 July 2019) www.ethnicity-facts-figures.service.gov.uk/summaries/public-sector-workforces (accessed 20 February 2021).

[29] NHS, 'Gender Pay Gap Report 2017 to 2018' https://improvement.nhs.uk/documents/5109/NHSI_Gender_pay_gap_report_201718.pdf (accessed 20 February 2021).

[30] Cabinet Office, 'Civil Service Diversity and Inclusion Dashboard' www.gov.uk/government/publications/civil-service-diversity-inclusion-dashboard/civil-service-diversity-and-inclusion-dashboard (accessed 20 February 2021).

[31] Daintith and Page (n 3) 3.

there are either two or three sets of legal powers available to the executive. Statute and the prerogative both confer on the executive legal powers to take decisions, spend money, and apply force in particular situations. Of these two types of legal power, statute is by far the most important in the modern state, with most of the executive's legal powers grounded in legislation. Alongside these two categories stands a possible 'third source', as Bruce Harris has styled it, of legal powers: those powers that the executive possesses simply by virtue of being a legal person.[32] As we saw in Chapter 7, the Crown is regarded as a corporation sole and, as such, is recognised by the law as able to act and form legal relations.[33] Harris argues that some of the legal powers of the executive, such as its capacity to form contracts, fall into this 'third source'. The attractions of this argument depend on how the scope of the prerogative is defined. If we follow A. V. Dicey and treat the prerogative as comprising all the legal powers possessed by the state that are not conferred by statute, much of Harris' third source should be considered parts of the prerogative.[34] If, in contrast, we follow William Blackstone and treat the prerogative as encompassing only those special legal powers the Crown possesses that private persons lack, the prerogative is drawn more narrowly, and there is space left for Harris' third source. In addition to these legal powers, Harris argues that the 'third source' also includes other activities undertaken by the state that are also undertaken by private persons, such as giving advice and providing information.[35] Here, Harris may be over-extending the reach of what requires legal authorisation. Some of the activities of the executive do not require a legal basis because they have no direct legal implications. When state officials deliver advice—or make apologies or admonish bad behaviour—they are often treated as speaking in an official capacity, and, as a result, their statements may shape people's conduct, even though no legal power has been exercised

[32] BV Harris, 'The "Third Source" of Authority for Government Action' (1992) 108 Law Quarterly Review 626.

[33] *R (New London College Ltd) v Secretary of State for the Home Department* [2013] UKSC 51, [2013] 1 WLR 2358.

[34] AV Dicey, *Introduction to the Study of the Law of the Constitution* (10th edn, Macmillan & Co 1959) 424–25.

[35] Harris (n 32) 627.

that brings about this effect. These powers of the executive exist outside of the law.[36]

Determining whether any given action of the executive falls within these categories of lawful action is one of the primary tasks undertaken by lawyers, but there is a broader question to be addressed about executive power: irrespective of the source, the range of these powers merits consideration. The executive has many different tools it uses to shape people's conduct, from the raw exertion of force, to the application of economic pressure, from the creation of new legal rules, to the giving of advice and encouragement.

First, and most basically, the executive possesses the capacity physically to compel. Through the police, army, and other enforcement agencies, it can move people against their will, harming them, seizing them, confining them for periods of time. It can break down doors to enter buildings, confiscating or destroying things that it finds, or it can take money out of people's bank accounts and dock their wages. As was noted in previous chapters, it is this raw ability to coerce that provides the foundation of all state power, making the legal system possible and enabling the courts and legislature to function effectively. More broadly still, even when not exercising compulsion, the executive has a wide capacity to make a physical difference to the world. It can put up signs, operate on the sick, teach children, and undertake a myriad of other activities.

Secondly, the executive uses economic pressure to shape conduct. Some of the economic tools available to the executive operate at the macro-economic level. For instance, the Bank of England sets the base rate, the level of interest it will pay commercial banks whose money it holds, and regulates the supply of money in the system. These capacities enable the executive to influence the price at which commercial banks lend and, more broadly, the level of inflation in the economy. More prosaically, the executive exercises an enormous amount of economic power through contracting. The executive spends hundreds of billions of pounds each year, buying goods and services, and employing workers. These contracts are powerful policy tools. The overarching aim

[36] The capacity of the state to act outside of the law is discussed further in ch 20.

of public procurement is 'value for money',[37] but, under the Public Contracts Regulations 2015, public bodies are permitted to include social and environmental requirements in contracts in some situations.[38] Because of the sheer volume of executive contracting, decisions about the types of companies that executive bodies will contract with, and the obligations that are inserted into those contracts, will have a significant effect on society. If the executive chose to, these contractual relations could be used to have an even bigger impact on society than is currently the case.

Thirdly, the executive creates laws. In terms of statutes, it is normally the executive that develops the policy behind legislation and drafts the bills that go before Parliament. There is an interplay between the political and apolitical parts of the executive in these tasks. Whilst it is government ministers who, ultimately, determine the policy direction and contents of the bills put before Parliament, civil servants give advice about the objectives, means, and wording of legislation. Though the relationship between technocratic civil servants and democratic ministers can sometimes be tense, civil servants are well-placed to advise ministers on the practicalities and implications of potential legislation.[39]

As well playing a part in the production of statutes, the executive can also enact law where that legislative capacity has been conferred on it by statute or the prerogative. There is a range of types of executive legislation, but perhaps the most important form is the statutory instrument, a type of legislation produced under a power conferred by statute. The Hansard Society counted 757 statutory instruments in the 2015–16 parliamentary session, which amounted to 7,783 pages of new legislation.[40] It noted that 'most of the United Kingdom's general public law is made not

[37] HM Treasury, 'Guidance: Public Procurement Policy' (8 January 2021) www.gov.uk/guidance/public-sector-procurement-policy (accessed 20 February 2021).

[38] The latitude of local government to include similar requirements in its procurement contracts is more limited: Local Government Act 1988, s 17.

[39] On the tensions see Anthony King, *The British Constitution* (Oxford University Press 2007) ch 9.

[40] Hansard Society, 'Parliament and Delegated Legislation in the 2015–16 Session' (2017) https://assets.ctfassets.net/rdwvqctnt75b/21cT0OJLzGIycKwosYqwyu/c321fc7534e1f357eae8c9a3ec939a6f/publication__westminster-lens-2017.pdf (accessed 20 February 2021).

through Acts of Parliament but through delegated legislation'.[41] Though these figures are remarkable enough, they do not capture the full extent of the law-making power of the executive. The executives of Scotland, Wales, and Northern Ireland also have powers to issue statutory instruments in some areas. In addition, executive legislation may be enacted under the royal prerogative, rather than a statute, and so count as a type of primary legislation.

The executive's capacity to legislate does not exhaust its capacity to make effective rules. Alongside legislation, executive institutions also produce policies that regulate their exercise of discretion. Whilst an executive body should not adopt a policy that runs contrary to law, it often has latitude to create rules that shape how it makes decisions, both in terms of the process of decision-making and the factors it will consider when making the decision. Given that these policies are normally made public, they have the capacity to guide the conduct of those who wish to apply for a benefit or who fear prosecution. Functionally, the creation of policy can differ little from the enactment of legislation.

Finally, the use of policy as a means of influencing behaviour shades into less formal modes of influence. For instance, the executive also shapes conduct by issuing advice. Some of this advice looks similar to legislation. The Highway Code, for example, takes the form of a set of rules that road users should follow, yet the Code itself is not a source of legal obligation. The rules in the Code either draw attention to legal duties grounded elsewhere or set out what the Department of Transport thinks constitutes good practice on the roads. Though the latter rules have no direct legal force, drivers still need to know them to pass their test, and, moreover, these non-binding rules may also be invoked in court if a driver is accused of behaving recklessly or negligently. As well as codes of this type, members of the executive, particularly the political side of the executive, often issue advice in interviews and speeches, or just by seeking to lead through example. During the 2020 coronavirus crisis, there was a procession of ministers encouraging people to phone elderly relatives, to volunteer to ferry around food parcels, and praising, and encouraging the rest of us to praise, NHS staff.

[41] ibid 6.

It is tempting to imagine that policies are produced under the direction of ministers, who, in turn, are responsible to Parliament for the policy decisions of their departments.[42] In *Carltona Ltd v Commissioners of Works* this fiction became a legal presumption.[43] Under the *Carltona* principle, where a statute gives a power to a minister, that power can be exercised by civil servants within the minister's department unless the statute explicitly states otherwise. Carol Harlow and Richard Rawlings note that the fiction embodied in *Carltona*, of top-down policy creation, is often inaccurate.[44] Frequently, policy is created from the bottom up, with the practices of low-level civil servants forming its basis. Recalling our discussion of the diversity of executive institutions at the start of this chapter, policies are formulated in all institutions, and often at multiple levels within those institutions. The democratically accountable minister, who is constitutionally responsible for these policies, may be far-removed from the actual decision-maker, and might have no knowledge of the decision.

In the chapters on the courts and legislatures, the legal immunities accorded to those who work within those institutions were examined. Whilst some of the institutions within the executive, in particular those that are regarded as aspects of the Crown, are accorded special legal privileges and immunities, those who work within the executive, with the exception of the monarch, do not enjoy any general protections from the ordinary operation of the law. Indeed, for members of the executive, the position is inverted: by virtue of their membership of the executive, officials are often able to exercise legal powers ordinary citizens lack, and, for this reason, can undertake actions that would otherwise ground civil or criminal liability. The immunities they enjoy are the counterparts of the powers they possess. For example, a police officer has wider powers of arrest than an ordinary citizen; she is able to detain people in situations that would otherwise trigger criminal and tortious liability.

[42] As Flinders notes, when the convention of Ministerial Responsibility first emerged, in the mid-nineteenth century, a competent minister could exercise personal control over the whole department: Flinders (n 7) 42–47.

[43] [1943] 2 All ER 560 (CA).

[44] Carol Harlow and Richard Rawlings, *Law and Administration* (3rd edn, Cambridge University Press 2009) 196; Daintith and Page (n 3) 5.

That the executive possesses extensive powers, both legal and practical, raises the challenge of control, of ensuring these powers are exercised in a constitutionally appropriate fashion. There are at least three modes of control over the executive: political control, from the legislatures; legal control, from the courts; and internal control, from within the executive itself. The controls exercised by the legislature over the executive were discussed in the previous chapter, and centre on the convention of ministerial responsibility and Parliament's control of the budget. As to legal controls, applied by the courts, these are the province of administrative law, a specialised subset of constitutional law, and one which requires more extensive treatment than can be provided here. In short, the courts require that the executive act within the scope of its lawful powers, that those subject to the executive's decisions are able to participate in the making of those decisions, and that the executive consider and properly weigh the reasons relevant to each decision.

Though these formal structures are important, there is a further challenge, lying just beneath the surface: whilst each of the branches of state depends on the others to an extent, the reliance of the courts and legislatures on the executive is especially profound. It is the executive that has the physical capacity to make the legislation of legislatures and the judgments of the courts effective, and if the executive is not prepared to apply these decisions, their practical force is radically diminished or even negated. Political scientists talk of 'veto players' within constitutional orders.[45] Veto players have the capacity to stop things from happening; this might be because the constitution grants them a capacity to exercise a veto (and this capacity is effective), as with the Commons' capacity to reject a legislative proposal, but it can also be because the veto player has a practical capacity to refuse to execute the decision. So, for example, laws might be passed prohibiting the possession of cannabis, but if the police decide they have better things to do than enforce them, the laws will become a dead letter. The police, in this instance, act as veto players.

[45] George Tsebelis, *Veto Players: How Political Institutions Work* (Princeton University Press 2002); Iain McLean, *What's Wrong with the British Constitution?* (Oxford University Press 2010) ch 2.

The concept of a veto player requires a couple of qualifications. First, whilst relatively few constitutional entities possess an absolute veto power which is not backed by formal constitutional authority, a great many possess the power to make a proposal more difficult to realise. So, the police's reluctance to arrest cannabis users might be overcome if there is continued pressure from the Home Secretary, but applying this pressure comes at a cost, diverting her energies from other issues and potentially creating resentment within the institutions she exerts pressure against. The question of whether a body is a 'veto player' may be a matter of degree rather than an absolute, enabling one institution to require another to pay a price for its obedience; the veto can be overcome, but at a cost. Secondly, recalling the structure of the executive in the first part of this chapter, the nested nature of institutions within the executive entails that whether 'the executive' has the capacity to veto may vary depending on the parts of the executive that are included in the assessment. Taken as a whole, the capacity of the executive branch to veto the proposals of courts and legislatures is almost unlimited, but the capacity of a single institution within the executive to veto is far more constrained. The executive's position as a veto player underlines the challenge of control. How can the constitution ensure the executive is constrained by, and applies, the decisions of courts and legislatures, when these institutions rely on the executive for their effectiveness?

In the UK constitution, at least two practical devices can be identified that serve to mitigate the risks possessed by the power of the executive branch to regulate itself. First, the internal divisions of the executive, its fragmentation into many smaller, often strongly autonomous, units, makes it less likely that the executive will have the capacity, or the will, to act as a united force. It divides power, enabling multiple institutions to be engaged on related tasks, and creates the possibility of internal checks within the executive branch. Secondly, the culture of executive institutions plays a part in shaping their conduct. The idea of an institutional culture is hard to pin down, but seeks to capture the self-understanding of the organisation: crucially, what the organisation, and those within it, define as success. Institutional culture is often shaped by law, by the legal obligations of the body, but it is determined by the shared expectations and assumptions of those operating within the organisation, which may or may not track these legal duties. If support for the other branches of the constitution is seen as a criterion of success by those working within the institution, and if those officials regard the success of their institution as of personal importance to them, the institution is likely to comply with the decisions of the courts and legislature. It is, perhaps, unsurprising that executive organisations which possess the most significant power to challenge the decisions of other bodies, to act as veto players, are often the most heavily laden with symbolism and tradition. That the armed forces and police wear uniforms, sport badges, swear oaths of allegiance, and take part in elaborate ceremonies and parades, might, in part, amount to an attempt to shape the culture of these organisations, to persuade their members that their duty is to support the state's constitutional structures, not to undermine them.

11.4 CONCLUSION

The links between the structures, people, and powers of the executive branch are harder to discern than those that tie together these elements in the legislative and judicial branches. This may be, in part, because it is harder to capture the tasks and operation of the executive at an abstract level. Any description of an institution that is general enough to encompass soldiers, teachers, surgeons, park wardens, and the Permanent Secretary to the Treasury, is likely to appear unsatisfying; these are very different types of office, requiring different skills and powers, and operating within different organisational structures. But, despite this diversity, some factors that unite them can be discerned. Starting with the type of person found in the executive (and setting aside government ministers for the moment) these are apolitical, technocratic, offices. Those holding them should not, whilst at work, make decisions based on their party-political beliefs, and are expected to carry out their tasks under governments of varying political complexions. Members of the executive are appointed because of their technical skills in a particular area, in contrast to members of the legislature, who are elected, and members of the judiciary, who are skilled in law. The executive is then structured in such a way that enables these technical skills to be deployed in the service of the policy objectives of the state, with nested institutions that enable officials to focus on particular tasks, and to apply the tools appropriate to these undertakings. These tools, the powers used by the executive, reflect the skills of the officials and the tasks their offices are oriented towards. There are good reasons why the executive consists of technically competent people, working within institutions that are focused on tasks appropriate to their technical competences, and using powers that enable them to bring these capacities to bear on the world.

A further reason for the lack of clarity around the executive is the profound divide between the political side of the executive branch, the government, and the apolitical side of the executive. The political side of the executive branch is, of course, political; it is partisan. The entitlement of its members to occupy their positions is, however indirectly, grounded in election and, as a consequence, members of the government need not have any technical expertise in the areas they supervise. The radically different natures of the political and apolitical sides of the executive presents us with a choice. First, we could conclude that the executive should be split, that it contains two, very different, constitutional elements with only superficial similarities. Secondly, perhaps it is a mistake to assign the government to the executive branch, and the government should be thought of as an emanation of the legislature, as a committee of Parliament (or of the other legislative bodies) that provides democratic supervision of the executive branch. This second possibility will be explored further in the next chapter, which considers the ways in which the principle of the separation of powers is realised within the UK constitution.

12

REALISING THE SEPARATION OF POWERS

For much of the twentieth century, those writing on the UK constitution were sceptical of the significance of the separation of powers. In part, this scepticism was motivated by a broader doubt about the utility of constitutional principles: UK scholars tended to present the constitution as a collection of narrowly drawn rules, and were uncomfortable with the ambition and vagueness of principles.[1] But there was also scepticism about the applicability of separation of powers to parliamentary-style constitutions: parliamentary systems, in contrast to their presidential counterparts, were, it was said, based on a fusion, not a separation, of powers.[2] Over the last twenty years, the idea of constitutional principles and, connectedly, the attractions of the separation of powers, have undergone a reassessment. It has become common to argue that the separation of powers, in some form, is a feature of the UK constitutional order; as Roger Masterman and Se-shauna Wheatle have put it, the separation of powers has experienced a 'rehabilitation' in UK constitutional discourse.[3]

12.1 THE SEPARATION OF POWERS AS A FEATURE OF THE UK CONSTITUTION

In presidential systems the president is elected and, as such, possesses her own democratic mandate; she is entitled to pursue her own policies even when these clash with those of the legislature.

[1] See eg Geoffrey Marshall, *Constitutional Theory* (Clarendon Press 1971) 124.

[2] Walter Bagehot, *The English Constitution* (Watts & Co 1964) ch 1; SA de Smith, 'The Separation of Powers in New Dress' (1966) 12 McGill Law Journal 491; O Hood Phillips, 'A Constitutional Myth: Separation of Powers' (1977) 93 Law Quarterly Review 11.

[3] Roger Masterman and Se-shauna Wheatle, 'Unpacking Separation of Powers: Judicial Independence, Sovereignty and Conceptual Flexibility in the United Kingdom Constitution' [2017] Public Law 469, 470.

The United Kingdom Constitution. N. W. Barber, Oxford University Press. © Nick Barber 2021.
DOI: 10.1093/oso/9780198852315.003.0012

The constitution protects the president from the other branches, making it difficult for the legislature to remove her, and grants her autonomous power. The president also exercises control over the appointment of the civil servants who work under her, frequently picking officials with whom she is ideologically aligned. Consequently, in presidential systems the separation of powers is obvious: there is a very clear and explicit distinction between the legislative and executive branches. Indeed, in the paradigmatic example of a presidential system, the USA, the first three articles of the Constitution are devoted to establishing the separation of powers structure, with each article devoted to a separate constitutional branch. In parliamentary systems, in contrast, the executive and the legislature appear tightly bound together. In the UK, the prime minister depends on Parliament for her position and her power, and this relationship conditions her actions, shaping both her appointments to government posts and the policies her government pursues. In short, the American president depends on the people for her position, whereas the UK prime minister depends on Parliament.

The apparent fusion of the legislative and executive branches is the strongest argument against the applicability of the separation of powers to the UK. Perhaps, it might be argued, the UK system could only fully realise the demands of the principle if it shifted to the presidential mode; only once the head of the executive is elected, and possesses her own, discrete, democratic legitimacy, will the UK be characterised by the principle. However, an alternative view, one which questions the apparent bonding of the legislative and executive branches, can be drawn from an unlikely source. Amongst the many constitutional arguments Walter Bagehot is famous for is his attack on the principle of the separation of powers: Bagehot claimed that the constitution's 'efficient secret' was the 'close union, the nearly complete fusion, of the executive and legislative powers'.[4] Yet later in the same paragraph from which this quotation is drawn, Bagehot describes the Cabinet as a 'committee of the legislative body selected to be the executive body'.[5] There are two claims here. First, Bagehot equates the Cabinet with the executive as a whole. Few modern

[4] Bagehot (n 2) 65. [5] ibid.

scholars would adopt this usage; as we saw in the previous chapter, the executive is a far more extensive than the twenty or so people who make up the Cabinet. But Bagehot's second claim, that the Cabinet should be seen as a committee of the legislature, is more plausible. Perhaps it was a mistake to locate the Cabinet, and the government more generally, within the executive branch? The difference between the political and apolitical executive is profound. The political side owes its position, directly or indirectly, to election, and its task is to ensure that those policies that have the support of the legislature are pursued by the executive branch. Seeing the government as a committee of the legislature captures this role; the government is not the executive's agents in the legislature, but rather the legislature's agents supervising the executive.

If the government is conceptualised as part of the legislative branch, the division between the legislative and executive branches in parliamentary systems is, if anything, more profound than in presidential systems. In presidential systems the executive and legislative branches share a common mode of legitimation: they are each elected. In parliamentary systems the executive's legitimacy is primarily (although not exclusively) derivative, resting on its implementation of the decisions of other constitutional bodies combined with its technical capacity to realise these decisions. As a result, there is also a greater division in terms of the partisanship of executive officials. In the presidential structure administrative officials, at least at the higher levels, are chosen, in part, because of their political beliefs and are expected to make decisions on this basis. In the parliamentary structure even the most senior civil servants are required to work with whatever political party or parties have received a mandate to govern; administrative officials are required to take policy decisions, but are not expected to base these on their political beliefs.

Whether the government is located in the legislative or executive branch is a matter of presentation, a question of which analytical division of the UK constitution is the more illuminating. But the substance of UK constitution has also moved towards the principle of the separation of powers in recent years, removing some of the institutional overlaps cited by earlier scholars. The most obvious and widely discussed constitutional reform linked to the separation of powers has been the ending of the judicial role of the House of Lords and the creation of the Supreme Court by the Constitutional Reform Act 2005.[6] Alongside the creation of a supreme court, the Constitutional Reform Act also curtailed the role of the Lord Chancellor, an official who formerly held offices in all three branches of state: acting as a member of Cabinet, as speaker of the House of Lords, and handing down judgments in the judicial committee of the House of Lords. The position still exists, but now more closely resembles a minister for justice; a Cabinet member with special responsibility for the courts and the legal process. Older writers cited the Lord Chancellor as a one-man refutation of the relevance of the separation of powers to the British constitution: following the Constitutional Reform Act 2005, this charge can no longer be made.[7]

12.2 THE MECHANICS OF THE SEPARATION OF POWERS IN THE UK

The last three chapters have sought to illuminate and explain the connections that exist between the structures, people, and powers of the three branches of the state, unpacking the reasons for the unity of the elements found in the columns of Table 8.1. As well as this unity, the separation of powers speaks to the interaction of the elements across the rows of the table; the reasons why there should be a distinction between the elements ascribed to each branch and, connectedly, the relationships that should exist between these elements. At the heart of the separation of powers lies a test of suitability, with the structures, persons, and powers each well-suited to the other two elements, and the overall combination of features well-suited to the branch succeeding in its role within the state. The explanation of the divisions between the columns is the other side of this argument: mixing the elements would result in ill-suited linkages. For instance, the structures

[6] Lord Steyn long advocated such a reform, linking it to the principle of the separation of powers: Lord Steyn, 'The Case for a Supreme Court' (2002) 118 Law Quarterly Review 382.

[7] Trevor C Hartley and JAG Griffith, *Government and Law* (2nd edn, Weidenfeld & Nicolson 1981) 179, discussed in Masterman and Wheatle (n 3) 471.

and persons of the legislature would be ill-suited to the exercise of judicial power, with MPs lacking the legal skills to decide cases according to law, and a chamber of 650 or so persons badly placed to undertake the questioning and reasoning we would expect of a judge. Or, to give another example, the courts are poorly placed to enact statutes: judges lack a democratic mandate and the court structure would struggle to allow the diversity of views and information relevant to statute creation that can be processed within legislative structures.

Models of the separation of powers that focus tightly on liberty, on the prevention of over-bearing state power, present the relationships between the institutions as primarily characterised by friction: it is the task of each branch to check the other, challenging and slowing the processes of the constitution. The model of the separation of powers developed over the last three chapters, in contrast, has presented the distinctions between the branches as complementary: the three branches of state undertake different tasks, but these are oriented towards a shared overarching goal: the successful execution of the policies of the state, and, through this, the improvement of the lives of its people. The primary mode of interaction between the branches is characterised by cooperation and comity.[8] The relation is cooperative, as the branches work together towards a shared goal, and characterised by comity, as they respect the contribution made by the other branches. As a number of scholars, in particular Eoin Carolan and Jeremy Waldron, have argued, the different branches of state are sensitive to different groups of reasons that apply to state action.[9] The legislature is well-placed to consider the overall good of the community, the courts well-placed to assess the impact of general laws on individuals, and the executive well-placed to consider the technical impacts of laws and their impact on industries and other

[8] On comity and the separation of powers see Timothy Endicott, *Administrative Law* (4th edn, Oxford University Press 2018) 9–11 and Aileen Kavanagh, 'The Constitutional Separation of Powers' in David Dyzenhaus and Malcolm Thoburn (eds), *Philosophical Foundations of Constitutional Law* (Oxford University Press 2016) 234–37.

[9] Eoin Carolan, *The New Separation of Powers* (Oxford University Press 2009); Jeremy Waldron, 'Separation of Powers and the Rule of Law' in Jeremy Waldron (ed), *Political Political Theory* (Harvard University Press 2016).

social groups. The structures of the constitution, the mechanics of the separation of powers, serve to combine these partial perspectives into a coherent whole.

It is pointless to pick out the legal and, more broadly, the constitutional structures that embody and facilitate these relationships of cooperation and comity; these are the basic structures of the constitution that are explored throughout this book. Most of the time, in the UK system, institutions work together successfully: the legislature produces statutes which are applied by the executive, and, when there is a dispute over the legislation, the courts interpret it in a way that is faithful to the legislature's intentions.[10] Studying constitutional law can obscure this boring truth because, understandably, lawyers focus on the pathological situations in which these relationships break down rather than the day-to-day interactions in which the relationships work successfully. Moments when problems arise between institutions should be placed in the context of the vast amount of activity undertaken by the state: state action is not normally characterised by inter-institution friction and dispute, although when such disputes do arise they tend to attract attention.

However, whilst cooperation and comity might set the primary mode for institutional interaction within the separation of powers, it would be a mistake to structure the constitution on the assumption that such interactions will always be positive. Mistakes will be made, and, given the different focuses of the branches, it is likely that they will, from time to time, come into conflict. More generally, there is the risk that relationships between institutions will deteriorate and mechanisms will be needed to protect one branch against another. The UK constitution includes a range of devices that serve to mitigate and channel friction between institutions, devices that help maintain the separation of powers. Some of these bolster the principle by reinforcing the divisions with legal, or more broadly, constitutional rules. On occasion, these take the form of absolute restrictions: civil servants cannot stand for Parliament, legislators cannot act as full-time judges.

[10] See *Duport Steel Ltd v Sirs* [1980] 1 WLR 142, 157 (HL), where Lord Diplock stated that the constitution 'is firmly based on the separation of powers; Parliament makes the law, the judiciary interpret them'.

Sometimes the requirements are more subtle, allowing persons from one branch to make decisions in another, provided they alter their mode of decision-making. When a government minister makes an administrative decision, the range of reasons she can rely on is more limited than when she makes a legislative decision: the courts will review her decision to test its rationality, but would not apply the same test to legislation. Sometimes the constitution protects institutions by providing what might be called 'self-defence' mechanisms, devices that either provide a shield for one institution against another, or provide a weapon that can deter overreaches of power.[11] To give some examples, in terms of shields, there are rules such as those of parliamentary privilege, which protect members of Parliament from the attentions of the court for statements made in the Chamber, and the protection of judicial tenure, which makes it unusually hard to dismiss a judge.[12] Whilst in terms of weapons, the legislature controls the executive's budget, and could refuse to fund its activities, whilst the judges have mooted that they might have the power to strike down statutes that restricted access to the courts.[13] These constitutional weapons need not be deployed to have effect; that they *might* be invoked could be enough to instil caution and respect in the other branch, even if it is unclear how effective they would ultimately prove.[14]

12.3 CONCLUSION: SEPARATION OF POWERS IN THE UK CONSTITUTION

There is no legal principle labelled 'the separation of powers' in the UK constitution, but perhaps we should not be surprised by

[11] The term comes from an article written with Alison Young: NW Barber and Alison L Young, 'The Rise of Prospective Henry VIII Clauses and their Implications for Sovereignty' [2003] Public Law 112; and is explored further in NW Barber, 'Self-Defence for Institutions' (2013) 72 Cambridge Law Journal 558.

[12] See ch 9. [13] See chs 5 and 20.

[14] For a possible example see John McGarry, 'Parliamentary Sovereignty, Judges and the Asylum and Immigration (Treatment of Claimants etc) Bill' (2005) 26 Liverpool Law Review 1; Dawn Oliver, 'Constitutional Scrutiny of Executive Bills' (2004) 4 Macquarie Law Journal 33.

this omission.[15] The separation of powers speaks to the structuring of the constitution, and, as such, it is to be found in the rules that establish constitutional institutions and which govern their relationships. Whilst states can have legal versions of the principle, with the 'separation of powers' standing for a rule used by the judges to assess legislation or review executive acts, even where such a legal principle exists, it is unlikely that it will precisely track the constitutional principle of the separation of powers. Indeed, the point could be made more strongly: it might be unwise for a constitution to allow the judges such a far-reaching power. As the separation of powers speaks to the limitation of the courts, as well as to the other branches of state, it would run contrary to the separation of powers for the judges to be given a free hand in the interpretation and application of the principle; the UK may, then, be characterised by the separation of powers even if this characterisation is not explicit. The last three chapters have argued that Montesquieu was broadly right: the UK's constitution can be considered to embody a form of the separation of powers. The unities required by the principle, the connection of the different types of structure, persons, and powers, are present, but so too are the divisions. If the government is seen as part of the legislative, rather than executive, branch, the divisions within parliamentary systems are even more profound than those in presidential constitutions.[16] Parliamentary models of the separation of powers differ from their presidential counterparts in significant respects, but the three basic branches of state can still be discerned.

[15] Although the principle has been invoked by judges from time to time: see Masterman and Wheatle (n 3).

[16] Bruce Ackerman, 'The New Separation of Powers' (2000) 113 Harvard Law Review 633, 699–702.

III

SUBSIDIARITY

13

INTRODUCTION TO THE REGIONALISATION OF POWER

Regionalisation of state power raises two questions: why should state power be regionalised, and, assuming it should, how should this be accomplished? This part of the book examines these questions in the context of the UK constitution. The bulk of the following chapters will focus on the constituent territories of the UK: Wales, Scotland, Northern Ireland, and England. These territories can be described as 'constituent' for two reasons. First, because they each had, in some form or other, a constitutional identity before becoming part of the UK and, moreover, this constitutional identity persisted after the UK was formed. Secondly, and relatedly, because these territories arguably possess a constitutional right to exit the Union. Whilst the devolved assemblies of Wales, Scotland, and Northern Ireland are the most visible forms of regionalisation of power within the UK constitution, they are far from its only forms. As we saw in previous chapters, there is significant regionalisation within institutions, with both the judicial and executive branches containing institutions with regional jurisdictions, and, of course, there are also local government units, county councils, and city councils operating within each constituent territory.

13.1 WHY REGIONALISE STATE POWER?

There are many good reasons to regionalise state power. Most basically, administering government at a local level is often more efficient. Sometimes institutions are given a limited territorial jurisdiction to help divide up the work they undertake: some courts, for instance, have a limited territorial reach to facilitate the division and channelling of litigation. On other occasions, territorial divisions exist simply to enable bodies to focus their attention: the police, for instance, have clear regional divisions.

The United Kingdom Constitution. N. W. Barber, Oxford University Press. © Nick Barber 2021.
DOI: 10.1093/oso/9780198852315.003.0013

These are both good, practical, reasons for regionalising state power, but the regionalisation of democratic units, the creation of legislative bodies with accompanying executive institutions, is often backed by more ambitious arguments, grounded in the nature and operation of democracy. These arguments can be divided into two broad groups. First, there are arguments grounded in national identity: claiming that national groups are entitled to govern themselves, and that the boundaries of democratic units should, as far as possible, track the boundaries of these peoples. Secondly, there are arguments based in subsidiarity. Subsidiarity, in this context, contends that it should be those who are affected by a decision of the state who get to make that decision, and the boundaries of democratic units should track, as far as practicable, these groups. Both nationalism and subsidiarity seek to provide an answer to what political theorists call the 'boundary problem'.[1] Democracies need a *demos*, a people, who vote in elections. But the boundaries of the *demos* cannot always be determined democratically: we need to know who is entitled to vote before creating institutions through which that entitlement can be exercised.

Nationalist arguments for the regionalisation of power come in many forms. Some of these are crude, resting on belief in the moral superiority of an ethnic or religious group. Other types of nationalist argument are far more subtle. Neil MacCormick, a staunch supporter of Scottish independence, argued for a form of liberal nationalism resting in the value of a culture.[2] MacCormick's work skilfully combined two arguments for the constitutional recognition of national groups. First, he contended that national identity is key to individual well-being: people only flourish within communities, and successful communities take the form of national groups, characterised by a unifying culture and history. Given that these national groups are necessary for well-being, the body charged with making decisions about the

[1] Fredrick Whelan, 'Prologue: Democratic Theory and the Boundary Problem' in JR Pennock and JW Chapman (eds), *Nomos 25: Liberal Democracy* (New York University Press 1983).

[2] Neil MacCormick, 'A Kind of Nationalism' in Neil MacCormick (ed), *Questioning Sovereignty* (Oxford University Press 1999).

community, the state, must protect and foster these identities.[3] Secondly, he argued that the social prerequisites of a flourishing democracy only, or, perhaps only commonly, exist when the formal structures of state map on to the social structures of a national group.[4] It is the social connections between members of national groups that establishes a sense of social solidarity which prevents politics becoming a zero-sum game: that sense of solidarity leads members to accept collective decisions with which they disagree, and the existence of the national group then underpins the integrative function of the state.[5] These two arguments combine to ground an entitlement for the constitutional recognition of national groups. National groups require constitutional recognition to ensure that state policies do not undermine them and, more widely, to permit them to flourish; the preservation of these communities becomes a matter of political concern.[6] Drawing the boundaries of democratic units along broadly national lines enables groups to protect and develop their own identities through constitutional institutions, and, moreover, helps ensure strong and effective democratic units, resting on the social foundations provided by national groups. In the constitutional context, nationalists often argue for independence, for national self-determination, but, as MacCormick noted, political recognition need not be equated with sovereignty; sometimes regional autonomy within a larger constitutional framework is sufficient. Indeed, MacCormick himself argued for an independent Scotland located within the broader constitutional structures of the European Union.[7]

MacCormick's case for nationalism provides instrumental arguments for the constitutional recognition of national groups. Rather than endorsing the claims made by national groups, which may turn on all manner of beliefs about the group's culture, race, or history, MacCormick's arguments point to the

[3] An argument further developed by Will Kymlicka. See Will Kymlicka, *Multicultural Citizenship* (Oxford University Press 1995).

[4] An argument further developed by David Miller. See David Miller, *On Nationality* (Oxford University Press 1997).

[5] MacCormick (n 2) 168, 186.

[6] MacCormick (n 2) 183, 186.

[7] Neil MacCormick, 'Is There a Constitutional Path to Scottish Independence?' (2000) 53 Parliamentary Affairs 721.

benefits that flow from having groups that are bound together by such beliefs: principally, the social solidarity they can engender. Whilst these instrumental arguments need not endorse the beliefs of those groups, they do have implications for those beliefs. If we accept MacCormick's factual premises, if it is true to say that the existence of a national group is necessary for, or conducive to, democracy or individual flourishing, we will have reason to want to support and maintain these groups. And this has implications for the core beliefs that help define the group's identity: all else being equal, these beliefs should be fostered and preserved. Consequently, a subscription to nationalism, even in the form advocated by MacCormick, will have implications for state policies in areas that relate to the group's beliefs, potentially affecting language rights, the provision of education to children, immigration, and a host of other areas which might have ramifications for the strength and maintenance of the group.

Subsidiarity provides a less ambitious justification for regional autonomy. It starts from a simple premise: that those who will be affected by a public decision are entitled to take part in its making. The constituencies that elect legislatures should, as far as possible, map on to the groups of people who are affected by the decisions of those bodies. Qualifying this demand are the practical limits on the number of legislative units that can be created: if we want voters to engage with legislatures, to have some knowledge of the issues being decided in these bodies and some connection with their representatives, only a small number of such units can be created. For subsidiarity to produce vibrant democratic units, decisions about state action must be clustered together, with legislatures legislating across a range of issues. Whilst this means that subsidiarity can never hope to provide a precise delineation of constitutional powers, and constituencies will always be both under- and over-inclusive, the principle can provide clear answers in some cases. For instance, one mooted solution to the lack of representation in the British Empire was that an Imperial Parliament should be created to represent the peoples of the Empire.[8] But such an institution would not accord with the principle of subsidiarity. There are too few issues that affect, say,

[8] Duncan Bell, *The Idea of Greater Britain* (Princeton University Press 2007).

Indians and Britons, to justify its creation; subsidiarity requires that these be wholly separate democracies, not combined into a single polity. To give another example, there are a large number of issues that have a significant impact on the people of Scotland but have a more limited impact on the people of England and Wales. Here, subsidiarity pushes for some form of regionalisation of power: a UK-wide democratic unit is still needed, but a regional democratic unit in Scotland is also required. As these examples show, subsidiarity and nationalism often argue for the same outcome. But the reasons underpinning these outcomes differ: those who subscribe to subsidiarity need not endorse the value of national groups and need not embrace cultural policies that aim to preserve the vitality of these groups.

Elsewhere I have argued that subsidiarity is a more attractive principle of democratic ordering than its nationalist counterparts: nationalist arguments for constitutional autonomy, in all of their forms, bring with them a division between members of the national group and members of the constitutional unit. This gap emerges because the national group has an existence separate from the state and, however inclusively the national group is drawn, it cannot exactly track those entitled to participate in public decision-making. The cultural aspect of the national group, a dimension which must be present to make the idea of a national group meaningful, is an element that will not be shared by all of those within the constitutional unit. Both nationalism and subsidiarity are, unavoidably, exclusive, in that whilst creating a set of group members they simultaneously create a set of those outside of the group, but subsidiarity binds this divide to the boundaries of the constitutional unit. Nationalists may be correct to claim that states need cultural elements to ground the social solidarity necessary for democracies to flourish, but they might be wrong in assuming that states need to endorse or co-opt a single, or unified, cultural vision to achieve this end.

13.2 FORMS OF REGIONALISATION

Although the regionalisation of power can take many forms, states can be divided into two groups: unitary states and federations. In a unitary state, constitutional power is vested at the national level. Commonly, although not necessarily, unitary states contain a legislature with unlimited law-making powers. Within a unitary state there is often regionalisation of law-making, but this is accomplished through a capacity granted by the centre: legislative powers are devolved from the national legislature to regional assemblies and can be later modified or removed by the national body. In a federation, in contrast, the constitution allocates powers between the centre and the regions: both the federal and local level are exercising delegated powers.[9] In a unitary state, in the event of a conflict the final say about an issue lies in the hands of the national institutions, whilst in a federal state power is divided such that each level of government has the final decision over some matters.[10] In addition, federal states normally have written constitutions that are difficult to amend, constitutional courts to police the boundaries between the regions and the centre, and bicameral legislatures, one chamber of which represents the regions.[11]

A further form of polity, the confederation, provides a structure through which states can act collectively. Confederations are generally understood as political entities where the central government is subordinate to the regional units.[12] In confederations the centre and the regions lack the unifying constitution of a federation: the centre has its own constitution, and each of the constituent states has its own, distinct, underived, constitution.[13] Confederations are not themselves states; sovereignty remains vested in the constituent states. As a consequence, a confederation only possesses the powers given to it by its members, and those states, as sovereign entities, can leave at any time. In constitutional terms, confederations are the mirror image of devolution settlements: power has been devolved up to the international level, rather than down, to the state's regions.

The line between unitary states with devolved power, federations, and confederations may be sharp in theory, but is fluid in practice.[14] The formal rules of the legal order only tell part of

[9] Daniel Elazar, *Exploring Federalism* (University of Alabama Press 1992) 39–41.

[10] KC Wheare, *Federal Government* (4th edn, Oxford University Press 1963) 33.

[11] Arend Lijphart, *Patterns of Democracy* (Yale University Press 1999) 186–91.

[12] Wheare (n 10) 33. [13] Elazar (n 9) 3, 50–54.

[14] Wheare (n 10) ch 2.

the story. It could be that the practical significance of these rules changes over time, either through the emergence of conventions that condition the exercise of legal powers or, more basically, through the operation of political pressure that determines the balance of power between the centre and the regions. In a devolved settlement the centre might not, for political reasons, be able to remove or interfere with the powers of the regions: what appears to be a unitary state might, in effect, be more like a federation. On the other hand, it is possible that the real power in a federal state might vest in the centre: if the regions are wholly reliant on the discretion of the centre for their funding, their apparent constitutional autonomy might be little more than a façade. Finally, it is also possible that there are rival legal conceptions of the relationship existing within the polity. As we have seen, it is conceivable that the Scottish legal order has a different understanding of the fundamental constitutional structure of the UK to that held by the English legal order. Indeed, it is strongly arguable that the European legal order (which tends to present the European project in federal terms) has a different conception of its constitutional identity to that held by Member States (which see the European Union as a confederation).[15]

13.3 CONCLUSION

The remainder of this part of the book will consider the constitutional position of the UK's constituent territories. These chapters will examine whether the description of these regions as 'constituent' is accurate, asking whether their membership of the UK rests on consent, and whether they possess a constitutional right to exit. The current constitutional autonomy given to these territories will also be examined. Whilst in form the UK remains a unitary state, with the devolved assemblies granted a limited law-making power by the Westminster Parliament, a grant which could be revoked, in substance aspects of the UK's constitutional settlement appear more federal, with Westminster having

[15] NW Barber, 'The Two Europes' in N W Barber, Maria Cahill, and Richard Ekins (eds), *The Rise and Fall of the Draft Constitution* (Hart Publishing 2019).

limited power to alter the settlement without the agreement of the regions.

The creation of the devolved assemblies in three of the constituent territories of the UK is certainly the most important constitutional development of the last twenty years, and is arguably the most significant since the expansion of the franchise in the early twentieth century. This is the area in which the major constitutional crises of the next few decades will arise, generated by the unstable nature of the devolution settlement. A number of factors have combined to put the survival of the Union under pressure. First, the elements that served to unite the UK have weakened. In her book on the birth of the UK, *Britons*, the historian Linda Colley identifies a combination of elements that bound the UK together.[16] She picks out the shared Protestantism of England, Wales, and Scotland, the economic benefits that the emerging Empire offered to people within those regions, and the external threat posed by France, as factors that drew these territories together during the eighteenth and early nineteenth centuries.[17] All of these factors dissipated during the second half of the twentieth century, a period that, probably not coincidentally, showed a renewed interest in Scottish and Welsh nationalism. Secondly, Brexit and, in Northern Ireland, long-term demographic changes have put pressure on the Union. Both Scotland and Northern Ireland voted against Brexit, and if those regions wished to rejoin the EU, they would need to leave the Union. Whilst in Northern Ireland the Protestant section of the population, which has tended to support the Union, is shrinking whilst the Catholic section, which has tended to support Irish unification, is growing. Finally, the structure of the 1998 devolution settlement is flawed: the opportunity to have a UK wide conversation in the late 1990s about a new regional structure was missed, with England left out of the scheme. The lack of regional representation for England means this territory is governed by the UK

[16] Linda Colley, *Britons: Forging the Nation 1707–1837* (rev edn, Yale University Press 2005).

[17] With, we could add, Germany replacing France as a threat in the first half of the twentieth century.

legislature and executive, a disparity that might, one day, become problematic. All of these factors have served to render the Union more fragile, and it is likely that one or more of the UK's constituent territories will leave the Union over the next twenty or so years.

14
WALES

Of all the devolved regions, Wales is the one that has caused Westminster least trouble. This might reflect the close and long-standing ties between England and Wales, territories which have been constitutionally bound together in some form for over a millennium. Moreover, over the course of this period, England pursued a conscious policy of colonisation and assimilation, developing legal structures that reduced Wales' autonomy. Many of the strategies used by the English to exert control over Wales foreshadowed the strategies used by the British to control the Empire: English settlers were given Welsh lands, indigenous leaders were removed or assimilated into the English aristocracy, the indigenous Welsh legal order was extinguished, and the Welsh language marginalised. For centuries, Wales, as a constitutionally significant unit, had only a fragmentary existence, and the 1998 devolution settlement brought Wales greater constitutional autonomy than it had enjoyed in over 800 years. It is evidence, perhaps, of the effectiveness of the English imperial project that when a referendum was held in 1997 on the creation of the Welsh Assembly, the vote was won by an exceptionally narrow margin. Since then, Wales has experienced a constitutional revival. The powers of the Welsh Assembly have steadily expanded, and in 2020 it was renamed as Senedd Cymru—the Welsh Parliament, a name that reflects both the increased powers exercised by the body, and Wales' commitment to bilingualism. This chapter examines Wales as a constitutional entity. It begins by looking at the entry of Wales into the Union and the measures taken by the English state to exert control over the Welsh people and territory. The next section charts the constitutional rebirth of Wales after the 1998 devolution settlement. The chapter concludes by examining the extent to which Wales can still be considered a constituent territory of the Union; that is, whether Wales possesses a constitutional right to secede.

The United Kingdom Constitution. N. W. Barber, Oxford University Press. © Nick Barber 2021.
DOI: 10.1093/oso/9780198852315.003.0014

14.1 JOINING

The histories of Wales and England are tightly intertwined, and Wales has rarely enjoyed the level of constitutional autonomy possessed, at points in their history, by Ireland or Scotland. From the tenth century onwards, English kings asserted, and Welsh rulers generally accepted, with varying degrees of enthusiasm, over-lordship: Welsh rulers paid homage to English kings and, in principle at least, accepted their overarching authority.[1] Wales' constitutional story between the tenth century and the sixteenth is one of a gradual transition from a territory that was under English imperial control to a territory that was part of the English Kingdom. The relative strengths of the English kings and Welsh rulers varied across localities and time: on occasion, Welsh rulers were effectively independent and their allegiance to the English little more than a gesture, whilst sometimes the relationship tipped the other way and the Welsh rulers became little more than agents acting on behalf of the king.

The Normans undertook the first wave of colonisation around 1100. Large estates within Wales were given to Norman lords who became known as the 'Marcher Lords', and who governed regions of Wales for the next 400 years.[2] Allied to this, the Normans moved English peasants into Wales, establishing new towns and communities. As with much of the early history of Wales, there are foreshadowings of the later strategies adopted by the British state to subdue its imperial territories. The use of the Marcher Lords to govern parts of Wales could be seen as an early form of contracted-out government, with the state making use of private actors to achieve its ends; rather than the state, the king, governing directly, powerful private actors were given wide latitude to govern the territories. Centuries later, this model was replicated throughout the British Empire, with, for example, the East India Company governing Indian territories and Cecil Rhodes'

[1] John Davies, *A History of Wales* (rev edn, Penguin 2007) 83; RR Davies, *The First English Empire: Power and Identity in the British Isles 1093–1343* (Oxford University Press 2000) ch 1.

[2] Davies, *A History of Wales* (n 1) 104–107; Glanmor Williams, *Renewal and Reformation: Wales c.1415–1642* (Oxford University Press 1993) 36–39.

British South Africa Company governing swaths of Africa. As with the Marcher Lords, the relationship between the state and these private bodies was a fractious one, with an unstable and uncertain balance of power. The use of settlers to shore up English rule, described by Geraint Jenkins as, in some areas, amounting to a form of 'ethnic cleansing',[3] was also a policy widely applied in imperial territories, with territories such as Australia and Kenya seeing an influx of settlers.

The balance of power between the Marcher Lords, the local Welsh rulers, and the English kings fluctuated. The high point of Welsh autonomy was arguably reached in the Treaty of Montgomery in 1267, which recognised Llywelyn ap Gruffudd as Prince of Wales and identified Wales as a principality, a distinct constitutional unit. The Treaty did not, however, challenge the overlordship of the English Crown: Llywelyn conceded that those holding the office of Prince of Wales would continue to owe fealty, homage, and service to the kings of England.[4] This relative constitutional autonomy was brief. Following the accession of Edward I in 1272, a harder line was adopted towards Wales; Edward ultimately decided that English control needed to be reasserted.[5] Following a war involving an English army larger than any seen in Britain since 1066, England formally annexed Wales by the Statute of Wales 1284, a royal pronouncement also known as the Statute of Rhuddlan.[6] Wales became part of the realm of England, and English law was extended to most of the territory and to most areas of law.[7] Edward's government coupled these measures with direct exertions of power designed to bolster his rule: a string of castles was constructed across Wales, a further wave of colonisation undertaken, new Marcher lordships created, and the Welsh were systematically excluded from senior administrative posts.[8] Edward also sought to weaken the

[3] Geraint H Jenkins, *A Concise History of Wales* (Cambridge University Press 2007) 70.

[4] Davies, *A History of Wales* (n 1) 142–50.

[5] Marc Morris, *A Great and Terrible King: Edward I and the Forging of Britain* (Windmill Books 2008) ch 5.

[6] Davies, *A History of Wales* (n 1) 151.

[7] Jenkins (n 3) 103; Williams (n 2) 34–35. Edward later made it clear that the king's authority extended over the Marcher Lords: Morris (n 5) 255–56.

[8] Jenkins (n 3) 105.

cultural identity of the Welsh: the *Croes Naid*, part of the Welsh princely regalia, was confiscated and taken to London along with other cultural icons.[9] Once again, these measures presaged later strategies of British imperial rule. In the eighteenth and nineteenth centuries, common law was deployed in many territories throughout the British Empire, replacing or constraining indigenous legal orders.[10] And the confiscation of cultural icons was commonplace: the beautiful Trophy Head, taken from the Asante royal place in Kumasi, is now in the Wallace Collection in London, whilst those wishing to see the bronze panels that decorated Benin's royal place can view them in a basement in the British Museum, following their seizure in a 'punitive expedition' by British forces in 1897.[11]

The last few paragraphs have devoted some space to the 1284 Statute of Wales and the events surrounding it. This might seem surprising, as the union between England and Wales is commonly dated to a series of statutes enacted in the first half of the sixteenth century in the reign of Henry VIII.[12] The Laws in Wales Act 1535 and 1543 are sometimes labelled 'Acts of Union', drawing comparisons with the later statutes joining England and Scotland, and then Britain and Ireland. In the words of the 1535 statute, Wales was 'incorporated, united and annexed to and with' England.[13] Common law was to apply in the territory, and English was to be used in the courts and administration.[14] Whilst these measures might appear oppressive, a reinforcement of measures to guarantee English rule in Wales, it seems that their reception in Wales at the time was more equivocal; indeed some historians have argued the statutes were positively received.[15] In a number of respects, the Tudor statutes improved the position of the Welsh. In particular,

[9] ibid 102.

[10] Jörg Fisch, 'Law as a Means and as an End: Some Remarks on the Function of European and Non-European Law in the Process of European Expansion' in Wolfgang J Mommsen and Jaap A de Moor, *European Expansion and Law: The Encounter of European and Indigenous Law in 19th- and 20th-Century Africa and Asia* (Berg 1992).

[11] Dan Hicks, *The Brutish Museums* (Pluto Press 2020).

[12] See the discussion in Williams (n 2) 272.

[13] Laws in Wales Act 1535, s 1.

[14] Williams (n 2) ch 11.

[15] Davies, *A History of Wales* (n 1) 231; Jenkins (n 3) 144.

the powers of the Marcher Lords were radically curtailed, and the Welsh were given legal equality with the English, with official posts opening to the Welsh gentry and Welsh representatives becoming entitled to sit in Parliament on a regular basis. Aspects of the Tudor statutes that now appear oppressive and attract the attention of a modern reader might, to contemporaries, either have appeared as declarations of pre-existing features of Welsh life, features brought about by Edward I a couple of centuries earlier, or as liberalisations of the constraints that burdened Wales. After all, by the time of the Laws in Wales Acts, Wales had been annexed to England for more than 200 years, and the two provisions that strike the modern reader as most significant, the abolition of Welsh Law and the proscription of the Welsh language in court and administrative proceedings, may not have appeared as significant to contemporaries as they do today. The abolition of Welsh Law (the Law of Hywel Dda) had been largely accomplished by Edward I; the Tudor statutes, by removing the vestiges of that system, removed what had become anomalies within the legal order.[16] As for the imposition of English as the language of government, many of the Welsh gentry already spoke English, and beyond the courts and administration there was no effort by the state to eradicate the Welsh language.[17]

If the Tudor period is presented as the moment at which Wales entered the Union, it is, as the above paragraph explains, possible to argue that this union was based on consent. Although it is a question for historians rather than constitutional lawyers, it is arguable the Laws in Wales Acts were welcomed by some of the Welsh at the time. But even if the Tudor reforms were positively received, this welcome came, in large part, because they mitigated hardships caused by previous English engagement in Welsh affairs. The Marcher Lords, the atrophying of the residual elements of Welsh Law, the exclusion of the Welsh from offices of state and, more generally, the broader legal discrimination faced by the Welsh, were the products of English policies, and the support found in Wales for the Tudor reforms needs to be

[16] Davies describes Welsh Law as becoming 'increasingly moribund' over the thirteenth and fourteenth centuries: Davies, *A History of Wales* (n 1) 164.

[17] Williams (n 2) 278; Davies, *A History of Wales* (n 1) 229.

placed in this context. If, in contrast, we take 1284 as the moment of union, the linking of Wales and England is more problematic, and is clearly one of domination and conquest. Although it is tempting, and comforting, to date the Union from the Tudor statutes, it is Edward I's conquest of Wales which may provide the true story of Wales' entry into the Union. On balance, Wales' entry into the UK should be understood as the product of conquest, colonisation, and annexation; a precursor to the imperial projects of later centuries.

14.2 THE DEVOLUTION SETTLEMENT

Describing Wales as 'England's first colony', Richard Rawlings writes that 'no-where in the common law globe has the process of legal, political and administrative assimilation been deeper or more thoroughgoing'.[18] For close to 500 years, Wales received little recognition as a constitutional unit. Of course, Wales had local government—and for much of the nineteenth and early twentieth centuries local government played a far bigger role in people's lives than it does today—but at the level of Wales as a whole, few constitutional institutions existed. It had some autonomy within the court structure, and, from 1964, some administrative recognition within the national government through the creation of the Welsh Office, but these were of limited significance.[19] It may have been the persistence of the Welsh language that was key to the maintenance of a distinct sense of Welsh identity over this period, a significance that extended beyond Welsh-speakers.[20] Even those who could not speak Welsh were aware that Wales had its own culture, its own literary tradition, that set it apart from its English neighbour; due more to cultural than legal factors, Wales remained distinct.

[18] Richard Rawlings, 'The Welsh Way/Y Ffordd Gymreig' in Jeffrey Jowell and Colm O'Cinneide (eds), *The Changing Constitution* (9th edn, Oxford University Press 2019) 300.

[19] Jenkins (n 3) 221; James Mitchell, *Devolution in the UK* (Manchester University Press 2009) ch 3.

[20] Linda Colley, *Britons: Forging the Nation 1707–1837* (rev edn, Yale University Press 1992) 13.

The Welsh people's limited appetite for a distinct constitutional identity can be seen in the results of the 1997 referendum: 50.3% voted for the creation of a Welsh Assembly, with a turnout of just 50.1% of eligible voters.[21] This caution over devolution was reflected in the initial allocation of law-making powers to the Welsh Assembly.[22] Under the Government of Wales Act 1998, the Welsh Assembly's powers were largely limited to those previously exercised by the Secretary of State for Wales. In legislative terms, this meant that the Assembly only exercised powers over the delegated legislation that had previously fallen within the jurisdiction of the minister. From the beginning of the devolution settlement, it was recognised that the powers of the Welsh Assembly would evolve; in the often-quoted words of Ron Davies, devolution was 'a process' and 'not an event'.[23] In 2002, the Richard Commission was established to review the Assembly's powers; it presented its report in 2004.[24] It concluded that the Assembly should be given primary law-making power and, following the model of the Scottish Parliament, rather than its empowering statute specifying the areas in which the Welsh Assembly *could* legislate, the statute should specify those areas that were reserved to Westminster, in which the Welsh Assembly *could not* legislate. The Government of Wales Act 2006 adopted, in modified form, these proposals. First, it empowered the Welsh Assembly to make primary laws (known as 'Assembly Measures') in the Assembly's devolved areas of competence. However, these measures required the approval by each House of Parliament before they became law, a serious constraint on the efficacy of the process. Secondly, it established the potential for a more radical enhancement of the Assembly's powers: if approved by referendum, the Assembly would be empowered to enact primary legislation without requiring the approval of the Commons and Lords. In 2011, a referendum was held and 63.5% of

[21] Mitchell (n 19) 155. This was an improvement on the results of an earlier referendum, held in 1979, when only 20.3% supported the proposal.

[22] David Torrance, *'A Process, Not an Event': Devolution in Wales 1998–2020* House of Commons Briefing Paper CBP-8318 (6 April 2020).

[23] Ron Davies, *Devolution: A Process, Not an Event* (Institute of Welsh Affairs 1999) 15.

[24] Ivor Richard, *Report of the Richard Commission: Commission on the Powers and Electoral Arrangements of the National Assembly for Wales* (National Assembly 2004).

those voting supported the expansion of the Assembly's powers. The wider structural proposal made by Richards, the shift from a conferred-powers to a reserved-powers model, was not adopted. A second commission, the Silk Commission, conducted a further review of the Assembly's legislative powers, reporting in 2014. Following the Richards Commission, the Silk Commission also proposed that Wales shift to a reserved-powers model of devolution, where the Assembly would be empowered to legislate on any area of law, save for those areas reserved to Westminster. The Wales Act 2017 implemented this proposal, modifying the Government of Wales Act 2006, and Wales, like Scotland, now follows the reserved-powers model of devolution.[25] Reflecting this expansion of power, in 2020 the Welsh Assembly renamed itself Senedd Cymru—the Welsh Parliament.[26]

Elections to the Senedd are undertaken through a version of the additional member system, a different process to the simple first past the post system used in Westminster.[27] Voters are given two votes: the first is for a constituency member; the second is for a regional member. Constituency members are elected through the first past the post system; as in Westminster, the candidate who receives the most votes in the constituency wins. The election of regional members is more complicated. Regions are larger than constituencies, electing multiple representatives, and a form of proportional representation is used. The total number of regional member votes cast is then divided by the number of constituency seats (plus one) that the party has secured. The parties provide ranked lists of candidates, and the party which, after division, has the most votes, is awarded a regional seat. The process is then repeated until all four seats in the region are filled, with the winning party having an extra seat added to their count before each subsequent division takes place. The mechanism seems complex, but its aim is simple: it draws the total balance of seats awarded closer to the proportion of votes cast for different parties. In a further

[25] Richard Rawlings, 'The Strange Reconstitution of Wales' [2018] Public Law 62, 73–84.

[26] Senedd and Elections (Wales) Act 2020 (anaw 1).

[27] Government of Wales Act 2006, ss 3–9.

contrast to Westminster, in 2020 the Senedd lowered the voting age in Wales to 16.[28]

As with its legislative powers, Wales' tax-setting capacity has also steadily expanded. Wales' original power to raise funds was exceptionally limited. In the 1998 settlement the Welsh Assembly only had the power to vary charges that had fallen within the jurisdiction of the Welsh Office, using this power to freeze, and later abolish, prescription charges, and to subsidise student fees. The Assembly had no power, however, to levy or vary taxes. The Wales Act 2014, building on proposals made by the Silk Commission, modified this position, devolving control over some taxes to the Welsh Assembly: stamp duty, landfill tax, and business rates now fell within its jurisdiction. This statute also created the potential for the Welsh Assembly to vary income tax rates, but tied this variation to a referendum. A few years later the requirement to hold a referendum was dropped, and the Wales Act 2017 gave the Welsh Assembly the capacity to raise or lower income tax rates by up to 10%, mirroring the tax-powers possessed by the Scottish Parliament at that time. Whilst this amounts to a radical expansion of the Assembly's powers, the revenue controlled by the Assembly is only a small percentage of the total Welsh budget. To give some idea of the degree of Welsh autonomy in the area of tax, the Welsh budget in 2019–2020 was set at £17.2 billion. The fully devolved taxes (landfill tax and so forth) brought in about £298 million; the Senedd now controls £2.1 billion of income tax; £1.1 billion comes from non-domestic rates; and the remainder, £13.7 billion, comes from the UK government.[29] So far, the Senedd has chosen to stick with the same level of tax as applied in England, but in the future it could choose to raise or lower taxes, adopting a different view about the balance between the economy, taxation, and public expenditure to that struck in Westminster.

[28] Senedd and Elections (Wales) Act 2020.

[29] Auditor General for Wales, 'Fiscal Devolution in Wales: Devolved Taxes and Welsh Rates of Income Tax' (December 2018) 6 www.audit.wales/publication/fiscal-devolution-wales-devolved-taxes-and-welsh-rates-income-tax (accessed 28 February 2021).

The Senedd has exercised its powers in a wide range of areas, but perhaps the most interesting are language rights and the creation of a Welsh legal jurisdiction. That these areas have been seen as priorities links back to the first half of this chapter: the proscription of Welsh as a language of government and the abolition of Welsh Law were two of the key measures adopted in the process of the annexation of Wales.

The Tudor laws preventing the use of Welsh in courts and administration persisted until the Welsh Language Act 1967, which permitted the use of Welsh in court proceedings and enabled ministers to publish documents and forms in Welsh. The 1967 Act was a pivotal moment: after that statute Welsh steadily gained legal recognition, and the attitude of the UK towards the language shifted from one of toleration to active support. The Education Reform Act 1988 made the teaching of Welsh compulsory in schools, whilst the Welsh Language Act 1993 established the Welsh Language Board,[30] an institution tasked with promoting and facilitating the use of Welsh and, more broadly, required that Welsh and English be treated on a basis of equality.[31] The Welsh Assembly built on these provisions in the Welsh Language (Wales) Measure 2011 (nawm 1). This statute conferred official status on the Welsh language for the first time, and imposed a broad range of duties on public, and, in some cases, publicly funded, bodies to use and support the language.[32] Now people have a right to speak Welsh in court proceedings and to use the language in interactions with administrative bodies: an inversion of the position set out in the Tudor statutes. Despite these measures, Welsh remains a minority language. In the 2011 census, 19% of people declared themselves able to speak Welsh, 14.6% were able to read, speak, and write in Welsh, whilst almost three-quarters had no Welsh language skills.[33]

[30] Now replaced by the Welsh Language Commissioner: Welsh Language (Wales) Measure 2011 (nawm 1).

[31] Welsh Language Act 1993, s 3(2)(b).

[32] Finding bilingual statutory drafters proved a challenge: Alan Greer, 'Reflections on Devolution: Twenty Years On' (2019) 90 Political Quarterly 553, 556.

[33] Office for National Statistics, 'Language in England and Wales: 2011' (4 March 2013) www.ons.gov.uk/peoplepopulationandcommunity/culturalidentity/language/articles/languageinenglandandwales/2013-03-04 (accessed 28 February 2021).

Following the Wales Act 2017, yet another commission was established to review Welsh devolution: the Thomas Commission.[34] This Commission focused on issues relating to the legal system and justice within Wales, publishing its report in 2019.[35] The Thomas Commission delivered a broad range of proposals, but perhaps the most notable were the recommendations that there be full devolution of the justice system to Wales and that the laws applicable to Wales should be recognised as the 'law of Wales', by analogy with Scots Law and the law of Northern Ireland. The identification of Welsh Law as distinct from English Law would have implications for the court system and for legal education. The Thomas Commission called for the creation of a Welsh High Court and Welsh Court of Appeal, and for Welsh Law to be an aspect of the core syllabus in Welsh universities and to be a part of professional legal training. Presumably, the creation of a Welsh High Court and Court of Appeal would permit a similar degree of autonomy in the Welsh legal system to that found in Northern Ireland: below the level of the Supreme Court, English and Welsh courts could take different positions on the interpretation of statutes and the contents of the common law. An advantage of this approach would be that it allows Welsh courts to tailor the law to fit Welsh needs and, potentially, to align the law with the broader moral commitments of the Welsh community where these diverge from the English.[36] The cost, however, is that this builds uncertainty and complexity into the legal system. Litigants cannot be sure whether the Welsh courts will adopt the same view of the law as their English counterparts, and lawyers must spend time studying the differences between the two systems. The Thomas Commission drew repeated parallels between Wales, on

[34] For the background to the Thomas Commission, see Rawlings, 'The Welsh Way' (n 18) 315–20.

[35] Commission on Justice in Wales, *Report: Justice in Wales for the People of Wales* (October 2019) https://gov.wales/commission-justice-wales-report (accessed 28 February 2021).

[36] Tom Hannant, 'Justifying a (Welsh) Legal Jurisdiction' [2019] Public Law 665, 674–78; Sarah Nason, 'The "New Administrative Law" of Wales' [2019] Public Law 703.

the one hand, and Northern Ireland and Scotland, on the other. However, whilst it is true to argue, as the Thomas Commission did, that Wales enjoys a long legal tradition, it does not enjoy the sort of continuity of legal tradition found in the other territories, and, as we saw in Chapter 4, the legal distinctions between the English, Northern Irish, and Scots systems have historical explanations; they are products of that continuity. The legal autonomy enjoyed by the courts of Northern Ireland and Scotland might not be something we would wish to create if we were starting from scratch.

Recalling the discussion of nationalism and national identity in the last chapter, these two policy areas, of language and law, could be seen as underpinnings of Welsh national identity. The culture of Wales should not be reduced to literature produced in Welsh, but the Welsh language, which has been extensively used by artists and scholars for centuries, constitutes a defining cultural attribute that helps distinguish Welsh culture from its English neighbour.[37] Similarly, Welsh Law provided a formal mechanism for the articulation of the moral values of the Welsh people; although it would be wrong to overstate the control which ordinary folk exercised over the content of the medieval Code of Hywel, this set of laws purported to be grounded in the customs of the Welsh people, and enabled the Welsh community to express its views about how its members should treat each other. Viewed in this way, it is unsurprising that disputes over language and law have been central to both the attempts, from the English side, to assimilate Wales into the Union, and have once more become key constitutional issues as elements within Wales seek to restore and foster constitutional autonomy.[38] After all, for those drawn to

[37] Plaid Cymru, the most significant political party campaigning for Welsh independence, started out as a movement to preserve the Welsh language: Vernon Bogdanor, *Devolution in the United Kingdom* (Oxford University Press 1999) 153.

[38] For a broader discussion of the invocation of 'Welshness' by political parties, showing parties attempting to depict their ideologies as manifestations of Welsh national values, see Jonathan Bradbury and Rhys Andrews, 'State Devolution and National Identity: Continuity and Change in the Politics of Welshness and Britishness in Wales' (2010) 63 Parliamentary Affairs 229, 236–38; Sophie Williams 'The Politics of Welshness: A Response to Bradbury and Andrews' (2018) 71 Parliamentary Affairs 305, 312–19.

nationalist thought, it is national identity that both justifies and underpins the devolution settlement: Wales needs its own constitutional structures to protect and enable the flourishing of its national group; relatedly, the success and effectiveness of those structures depends on the vitality of that national group. The nationalist would see this as a virtuous circle: the existence of a national group warrants the creation of political institutions, and these institutions then adopt measures to protect and bolster the existence of the national group.

14.3 LEAVING

As we shall see in the subsequent chapters, both Northern Ireland and Scotland possess, in different ways, a right of exit from the Union. Wales' position is slightly less clear, primarily because the appetite for independence in Wales has been less than in these other territories and so the question has not yet needed to be addressed. However, it could be that support for independence is growing: at the start of June 2020, YouGov reported that a quarter of those surveyed by its pollsters supported independence.[39] Wales' case for a right of exit appears as strong as these other territories. Indeed, it could be argued that as Wales was originally incorporated into the Union through annexation, it has an even stronger claim, given that Scotland's and Northern Ireland's entry into the Union was arguably based on consent. Whilst there is no formal mechanism through which an independence vote can be triggered, it would be hard for Westminster to avoid holding a referendum if a majority within the Senedd voted in favour of a such a poll.

[39] The survey can be found at https://docs.cdn.yougov.com/wkgo1h4rcp/Results_WelshBarometer_MayJune2020_W.pdf (accessed 28 February 2021).

15

SCOTLAND

In contrast to Wales and Northern Ireland, Scotland had a strong and clear history as an independent state well before entering the Union.[1] Because of this history, at the time of union Scotland possessed its own constitutional institutions, in particular, its own parliament, which provided structures through which the Treaty of Union 1707 could be negotiated and then ratified. Although it remains a matter of debate amongst historians, it is arguable that by the standards of the time, the Union of 1707 was based on consent; whilst the story of Wales' accession to the Union is one of conquest and annexation, Scotland's story is one of negotiation based on a recognition, by some on each side, of the advantages of England and Scotland joining to become a single state. Scotland's constitutional autonomy persisted after 1707, as it maintained a separate legal system, its own court structure, and possessed many administrative bodies that served Scotland as a whole. Pressure for some sort of autonomous legislature for Scotland grew in the second half of the twentieth century, and when a referendum was held on devolution in 1997 there was strong support for the creation of a new Scottish Parliament. At the time, some hoped that the creation of this Parliament would satiate the Scottish appetite for autonomy, but this hope does not seem to have been realised: the Scottish National Party quickly established itself as the largest party in the Scottish Parliament and, in 2014, a referendum on independence was held.[2] Scotland voted to remain within the Union, but only by a moderate, if clear, majority. The issue of Scottish independence remains open: sooner or later, it is likely that the question will, once again, be put to the Scottish people.

[1] RR Davies, *The First English Empire: Power and Identity in the British Isles 1093–1343* (Oxford University Press 2002) 78–83.

[2] Aileen McHarg, 'Devolution in Scotland' in Jeffrey Jowell and Colm O'Cinneide (eds), *The Changing Constitution* (9th edn, Oxford University Press 2019) 280.

The United Kingdom Constitution. N. W. Barber, Oxford University Press. © Nick Barber 2021.
DOI: 10.1093/oso/9780198852315.003.0015

15.1 JOINING

As with Wales, English kings asserted overlordship over Scotland from around the tenth century.[3] There were periods in which English kings did succeed in dominating the Scots, and this assertion amounted to something more than a mere claim. In 1072, for instance, King Malcolm III signed the Treaty of Abernethy, acknowledging William I as his overlord, whilst in 1296 Edward I, pausing only to loot the Stone of Scone, an artefact used in the coronation of the Scottish kings, briefly managed to hold the territory.[4] For the most part, however, Scotland operated as an independent state, with its own kings who rejected, more or less effectively, English claims over their lands.

The first step towards the British state came with the Union of the Crowns in 1603. James VI of Scotland inherited the English crown, becoming king of both Scotland and, as James I, of England and Ireland. It is, perhaps, worth emphasising that by this point James had already been King of Scotland for over thirty years; the 1603 Union was the product of dynastic accident, and not an English power-grab. Whilst James wanted a closer union between the two kingdoms, combining them into a single state with a common set of laws, he was unable to make much progress towards this end, primarily because of opposition from the English side.[5] Scotland and England remained separate states, although with the same person as monarch. However, the Union of the Crowns went beyond merely having a single person occupying two offices; it also had implications for the rights of those born within the kingdoms. In *Calvin's Case*, the Court of Exchequer Chamber concluded that a child born in Scotland after the Union of the Crowns was entitled to own land in England, a

[3] Colin Kidd, *Unions and Unionism: Political Thought in Scotland, 1500–2000* (Cambridge University Press 2008) 93–95; Davies (n 1) ch 1.

[4] Marc Morris, *A Great and Terrible King: Edward I and the Forging of Britain* (Windmill Books 2008) ch 9. The Stone of Scone was returned by John Major's government in 1996. The hope was that the gesture would quell pressure for devolution: it didn't.

[5] Kidd (n 3) 53–60; Conrad Russell, 'Topsy and the King: The English Common Law, King James VI and I and the Union of the Crowns' [2005] Public Law 336.

right not normally available to foreigners; the common law saw Calvin not as an alien, but as a subject of the king.[6] As a result of this case, James achieved through the courts a portion of what he had been unable to achieve through the English Parliament.[7] Scots born after 1603 were entitled to the benefits of (English) common law: they could sue in English courts and exercise rights within the English legal system; consequently, the legal significance of the distinction between James' English and Scottish subjects was reduced.[8] The outcome of *Calvin's Case* was not inevitable: recalling our discussion of the Crown in Chapter 7, the court could have concluded that Calvin owed allegiance to the Scottish Crown, that is, to the office, and not directly to James, the person who occupied the role.[9] Once again, the common law was reluctant to draw a sharp divide between the office of the Crown and the person of the monarch.

Whilst the decision in *Calvin's Case* may have reduced some of the inconveniences caused by having a Union of Crowns rather than states, it did not entirely remove them.[10] On the one side, the English worried about the instability brought by an independent Scotland. The Scottish Parliament enjoyed significant power and autonomy. As evidence of this, in 1688 it, alongside the English Parliament, had voted for the Crown to pass to William of Orange, ejecting the Stuart dynasty. That the continuation of the Union of the Crowns turned, at that moment, on the Scottish Parliament's consent in combination with the English Parliament's, underlined the fragility of the Union.[11] Furthermore, the English feared an independent Scotland might provide a bridgehead for a

[6] Polly J Price, 'Natural Law and Birthright Citizenship in *Calvin's Case* (1608)' (1997) 9 Yale Journal of Law and the Humanities 73; Margaret Franz, 'Legal Rhetoric and the Ambiguous Shape of the King's Two Bodies in *Calvin's Case* (1608)' (2017) 20 Advances in the History of Rhetoric 262.

[7] Franz (n 6) 265–66; Price (n 6) 97–102.

[8] The parallel question in Scottish law (that is, the rights of those born in England) was answered by a statute enacted by the Scottish Parliament: Price (n 6) 119.

[9] Price (n 6) 84–86, 103–105.

[10] The English Parliament eventually threatened the statutory reversal of *Calvin's Case* to push the Scots into negotiations towards a full union: Alien Act 1705.

[11] TM Devine, *The Scottish Nation: A Modern History* (Penguin 2012) 4–7.

French invasion.[12] On the other side, some in Scotland began to see economic advantages in a tighter union. Scotland's attempts to build its own empire by founding a colony in Central America had failed, and a closer union with England would bring access to the English colonies.[13] Iain McLean and Alistair McMillan describe the Union of England and Scotland in 1707 as 'a genuine treaty, conducted by two bargainers of unequal power; however the weaker partner (Scotland) had enough to force the English to the table and to extract some concessions from them'.[14] Most notably, the Scots were able to ensure that provisions were included to protect Scottish institutions, such as the Scottish legal system, and to guarantee Scottish representation in a new, British, Parliament.[15] Furthermore, in a statute enacted alongside the Acts of Union, the Church of Scotland was given special protection, a concession from the English side that helped secure a majority in the Scottish Parliament for the Union.[16]

Whilst McLean and McMillan are right to present the Treaty of Union 1707 as a genuine agreement, with each side gaining something and each making concessions, the process by which this agreement was reached and ratified would not meet modern expectations. There was significant use of bribery, and had the proposed union been put to the Scottish people in a referendum it is likely that the Treaty would have been rejected; the historian Tom Devine writes of 'overwhelming popular opposition to the loss of the parliament and angry hostility to the whole idea of an 'incorporating' union'.[17]

Of course, to criticise those responsible for the Union of 1707 for not holding a referendum would be anachronistic; the idea of holding an inclusive vote, one in which all adults, on both sides

[12] Iain McLean and Alistair McMillan, '1707 and 1800: A Treaty (Mostly) Honoured and a Treaty Broken' in Iain McLean (ed), *What's Wrong with the British Constitution?* (Oxford University Press 2009) 49; Devine (n 11) 8–9.

[13] McLean and McMillan (n 12) 48.

[14] McLean and McMillan (n 12) 47.

[15] The significance of the Acts of Union 1707 for the Scottish legal system are discussed further in ch 3.

[16] Protestant Religion and Presbyterian Church Act 1707 (Scottish Parliament); Devine (n 11) 12, 73; McLean and McMillan (n 12) 70–71.

[17] Devine (n 11) 16.

of the border, could participate, would have seemed ridiculous to those engaged in the negotiations. But when, over three hundred years later, a referendum was held, at least on the Scottish side, the vote in favour was clear, with around 55% voting to remain within the UK. Even if questions of legitimacy could be raised about the 1707 process, the 2014 independence referendum firmly grounded the Union in an act of consent by the Scottish people.

15.2 THE DEVOLUTION SETTLEMENT

Whilst there were always voices of opposition to the Union between England and Scotland, during the nineteenth century pressure for Scottish independence was muted. Recalling Linda Colley's comments about the sources of stability in the UK, discussed in Chapter 13, it could be that it was access to imperial offices and the capacity to trade with imperial territories that rendered the Union attractive.[18] From the second half of the eighteenth century, Scots played a significant role in the empire, holding a range of prominent posts.[19] With imperial money flowing in, Scotland enjoyed a period of affluence.[20] But as the British Empire came to an end, support for Scottish constitutional autonomy grew.[21] The Scottish National Party, formed in the 1930s, became increasingly politically significant in the 1960s and 1970s.[22] This political shift was compounded by the experience of the Thatcher government of 1979–1990, which, to many Scots, appeared to be an English government governing the UK in the interests of England.[23] In 1989, the Scottish Constitutional Convention was established, a body which included representatives from a range of political parties (with the notable exception of the Conservatives) and civic institutions.[24] In *Scotland's*

[18] Linda Colley, *Britons: Forging the Nation 1707–1837* (rev edn, Yale University Press 2009) ch 2.

[19] Niall Ferguson, *Empire: How Britain Made the Modern World* (Penguin 2004) 39–40; Devine (n 11) 25–26, 59–63; Colley (n 18) 127–32.

[20] Colley (n 18) 122–23.

[21] Devine (n 11) ch 26.

[22] Vernon Bogdanor, *Devolution* (Oxford University Press 1999) 119–20.

[23] Devine (n 11) 599–609; McHarg (n 2) 276–79.

[24] Devine (n 11) 609–13.

Parliament, Scotland's Right, published in 1995, the Convention set out a blueprint for devolution.[25]

Whereas the majority in Wales that voted for devolution in 1997 was fractional, in Scotland it was sizeable. With a 60% turnout, 74.3% voted to create a Scottish Parliament, and, in the same referendum, 63.5% voted in favour of giving that body limited tax-raising powers. That Scotland preserved a strong, autonomous, constitutional identity after 1707, both through the Scottish legal system and through other administrative structures, may partly explain why the pressures for devolution were greater than in Wales.[26] Furthermore, as Aileen McHarg notes, even though the devolution settlement was brought about by an act of the UK Parliament, the work of the Scottish Convention in the years prior to devolution gave the Scottish Parliament a 'strongly autochthonous quality'; it was the product of the Scottish people, rather than a scheme dreamed up in Westminster.[27] The work of the Convention may have helped build consensus in favour of the project, with most of the key political actors in Scotland engaged in the process.

When the Scottish Parliament opened on the 12th of May 1999, Winnie Ewing, chairing the session, announced it as a reconvention of the Scottish Parliament that had been adjourned in 1707.[28] This was a piece of constitutional romanticism: the new Scottish Parliament is a radically different constitutional institution. Unlike the 1707 Parliament, the 1999 Parliament is a creature of statute, established by an act of the UK Parliament. The Scotland Act 1998 conferred a limited, if broad, legislative power on it, whereas the pre-1707 Parliament had an inherent power to legislate.[29] In contrast to Wales, the Scottish Parliament's

[25] Scottish Constitutional Convention, *Scotland's Parliament, Scotland's Right* (1995).

[26] Neil MacCormick, 'A Kind of Nationalism' in Neil MacCormick (ed), *Questioning Sovereignty* (Oxford University Press 1999) 183–84; McHarg (n 2) 271.

[27] McHarg (n 2) 278.

[28] 'Winnie Ewing's Speech to the reconvened Scottish Parliament, 1999' *YouTube* (11 May 2019) https://www.youtube.com/watch?v=PB_aOAO0c4g (accessed 10 March 2021).

[29] Or, if the pre-1707 Scottish Parliament's legislative power was delegated, it was delegated from the Scottish people.

legislative powers followed a reserved-powers, rather than a conferred-powers, model: the Scottish Parliament is able to legislate on any issue, save for those matters reserved to Westminster.[30] The breadth of these legislative powers is such that they have required little change since 1999, although some modifications have occurred.

The electoral system for the Scottish Parliament is virtually identical to that of Wales, using a version of the additional member system in which constituency representatives chosen on the first past the post system are supplemented with regional representatives drawn from party lists.[31] Like Wales, the Scottish Parliament has reduced the voting age from 18 to 16.[32]

In terms of its tax raising powers, at its inception the Scottish Parliament possessed a limited power to vary income tax.[33] Under the original 1998 scheme, it could raise or lower the basic rate of income tax by up to 3%. This was expanded by the Scotland Act 2012, which conferred the power to vary tax by up to 10%. The Scotland Act 2016 extended these powers still further, giving the Scottish Parliament almost complete control over the amounts of income tax levied and the bands at which different levels of tax are paid. At the end of 2017 the Scottish government announced that it would make use of these powers to vary the levels of tax set in Scotland: higher earners saw their tax bills rise, with the higher rate of tax going from 40% to 41% and the top rate rising from 45% to 46%, but those on lower rates saw their tax bills cut, with a new range of tax bands created for the lower end of earnings, and the lowest tax rate falling from 20% to 19%.[34] Alongside income tax, the Scottish Parliament also exercises control over local taxes and a range of levies and duties. However, calls for full

[30] Wales later shifted to a reserved-powers model: see ch 14.

[31] Chris Himsworth and Christine O'Neill, *Scotland's Constitution: Law and Practice* (3rd edn, Bloomsbury 2015) 98–101.

[32] Scottish Elections (Reduction of Voting Age) Act 2015 (asp 7).

[33] Dominic de Cogan, *Tax Law, State-Building, and the Constitution* (Hart Publishing 2020) 38–45.

[34] 'Scottish Income Tax 2020/21: How It Compares to Rest of UK' *BBC News* (6 February 2020) https://www.bbc.co.uk/news/uk-scotland-51407239 (accessed 10 March 2021). The point at which earners start to pay more in Scotland than England is, for 2020/21, £33,000.

fiscal autonomy, where Scotland would raise and collect all taxes, giving a share of the revenue to the UK, have not been accepted by Westminster. By 2019, a little over half of the Scottish budget of about £32.4 billion was under the control of the Scottish Parliament, but the remainder came in the form of a grant from the national level of government.[35]

In the previous chapter, language rights and the legal order were highlighted as areas in which the Senedd has acted in response to needs and wishes that are specifically Welsh. The measures adopted by the Scottish Parliament have, perhaps, tended to be more ideological than nationalist; rather than the Scottish Parliament adopting policies that have sought to buttress Scottish national identity, its policies have instead sought to place Scotland to the left, politically, of England. The previous paragraph discussed the changes to Scotland's tax system, introduced with the aim of shifting wealth from the rich to the poor. In land reform, the Scottish Parliament has acted to address some of the inequalities brought about by the enclosure of land and clearances in the eighteenth and nineteenth centuries, measures which resulted in a small number of owners controlling large areas of land.[36] In the early years of its existence, the Scottish Parliament abolished the remnants of feudal tenure and created legal structures to help communities acquire the land they live on.[37] More recently, the Scottish Parliament conferred on ministers the power to compel the sale of land to local communities where doing so would contribute to sustainable local development.[38]

As in Wales, language rights have also been an issue addressed by Scotland's devolved legislature but, for various reasons, the salience of language is far less marked in Scotland. Gaelic is spoken in some areas of Scotland and, like Welsh, could not be understood by someone who only spoke English. In 2005, the

[35] Audit Scotland, *Scotland's New Financial Powers: Operation of the Fiscal Framework 2018/19* (October 2019).

[36] Devine (n 11) 134–40, 175–83.

[37] Abolition of Feudal Tenure etc (Scotland) Act 2000 (asp 5); Land Reform (Scotland) Act 2003 (asp 2).

[38] Community Empowerment (Scotland) Act 2015 (asp 6); Land Reform (Scotland) Act 2016 (asp 18).

Scottish Parliament identified Gaelic as an official language of Scotland, but, unlike the parallel legislation in Wales, there is no general duty on public bodies to enable those they engage with to use the language, nor an overarching duty on schools to teach the language.[39] The 2005 Act established the Bòrd na Gàidhlig, a body that requires and supports the production of Gaelic Language Plans. In some areas, where the local situation renders it suitable, these language plans may include the provision of public services in Gaelic. The qualified support given to Gaelic, in contrast to Welsh, turns on the small number of people who speak the language. In the 2011 census, only 87,056 (1.7%) people in Scotland could speak, read, or understand Gaelic (with only 58,000 saying they were able to speak the language).[40] Furthermore, Gaelic speakers are clustered in the Highlands and, at an even higher degree of density, the islands off the northwest coast.[41] In much of Scotland there is little or no demand for the provision of public services in Gaelic. The Scottish government also supports the Scots language, a language which it regards as distinct from English but which, with a little effort, is comprehensible by English speakers. In the 2011 census, 1.5 million people (about 28%) identified as Scots speakers. The support promised by the Scottish government is at the level of encouragement, rather than the imposition of any legal obligations, and includes recognising Scots as a valid means of communication and recognising that education has an important role to play in its promotion.[42]

15.3 LEAVING

Scotland does not have a statutory right to leave the Union, but one strand of the UK's constitutional ideology is the claim that the Union rests on consent rather than coercion. The assertion that the Union is voluntary is, as we have seen, certainly contestable,

[39] Gaelic Language (Scotland) Act 2005 (asp 7).

[40] Scottish Government, *The Scottish Government Gaelic Language Action Plan 2016–2021* (2017) 14.

[41] Scottish Government, *The Scottish Government Action Plan* (n 40) 15.

[42] Scottish Government, *Scots Language Policy* (2015).

but, true or not, subscription to this claim has implications for the capacity of a region to leave: if the Union rests on consent, then when this consent is withdrawn the territory should have the right of exit. The Scottish National Party, as its name suggests, has long campaigned for independence, and when it won a majority of seats in the Scottish Parliament in 2011 this provided a clear mandate to hold an independence referendum.[43] Because matters relating to the Union are reserved to Westminster, the Scottish Parliament lacks the power to take Scotland out of the UK, and could not, of its own initiative, enact legislation that would establish a binding independence referendum. For a time, there was some discussion over the possibility of the Scottish Parliament holding an advisory referendum on independence, one which would not directly alter Scotland's place in the Union but which would provide a mechanism through which the wishes of the people of Scotland could be expressed. The capacity of the Scottish Parliament to hold an advisory referendum was disputed, with some arguing that any referendum would relate to a reserved matter and so fall outside the Parliament's jurisdiction, whilst others argued that as the referendum would only provide a test of the views of the people, leaving the Union untouched, it fell within that body's competence.[44] In the event, this point did not need to be resolved. Under section 30 of the Scotland Act 1998, the jurisdiction of the Scottish Parliament can be altered through an Order in Council. Following the SNP's call for an independence referendum, the Westminster government agreed to issue such an Order, which subsequently was approved

[43] However, as Aileen McHarg notes, many of those who voted SNP were not supporters of independence. See Aileen McHarg, 'The Constitutional Case for Independence' in Aileen McHarg and others (eds), *The Scottish Independence Referendum: Constitutional and Political Implications* (Oxford University Press 2016) 101–102.

[44] Andrew Tickell, 'The Technical Jekyll and the Political Hyde: The Constitutional Law and Politics of Scotland's Independence "Neverendum"' in Aileen McHarg and others (eds), *The Scottish Independence Referendum: Constitutional and Political Implications* (Oxford University Press 2016) 325–28; Adam Tomkins, 'Scotland's Choice, Britain's Future' (2014) 130 Law Quarterly Review 215, 224–30.

by the relevant Scottish and UK bodies.[45] Its jurisdiction having been broadened, the Scottish Parliament then passed the Scottish Independence Referendum Act 2013, which provided the legal basis for the referendum.

As we have seen, in the 2014 referendum a solid majority voted to remain in the Union, with 55.3% of those voting rejecting the proposition that Scotland should become an independent country.[46] After the referendum the Westminster government, having promised to confer more powers on the Scottish Parliament in the course of the referendum campaign, established the Smith Commission to review the devolution settlement. The Smith Commission made a range of proposals which were largely adopted in the Scotland Act 2016, including some, discussed further in Chapters 5 and 18, that related to the continuity of the Scottish Parliament and the capacity of Westminster to legislate in matters devolved to Scotland. The Smith Commission did not, however, consider the regulation of future independence referendums, leaving the question of further referendums open.[47] Westminster's acceptance of the SNP's call for a referendum indicated a broader recognition of Scotland's right to secede, and, having held a referendum once, it might prove hard to resist further demands for independence referendums in the future. The lack of formal constitutional recognition of Scotland's right to secede raises a pair of problems. First, and perhaps most importantly, it is unclear how frequently independence referendums should be permitted: once a year would make secession inevitable, once a millennium would make it effectively impossible.[48] Secondly, it is unclear how a future referendum could be triggered: after a reasonable lapse of time, is Westminster obliged to accept a resolution of the Scottish Parliament for a new referendum—and,

[45] The Scotland Act 1998 (Modification of Schedule 5) Order 2013, SI 2013/242.

[46] For the issues that swayed the vote see Robert Liñeira, Ailsa Henderson, and Liam Delaney, 'Voters' Response to the Campaign: Evidence from the Survey' in Michael Keating (ed), *Debating Scotland: Issues of Independence and Union in the 2014 Referendum* (Oxford University Press 2017).

[47] Tickell (n 44) 328–30.

[48] The Northern Ireland Act 1998 requires seven years between polls: Northern Ireland Act 1998, sch 1.

indeed, to return to the first question, who gets to decide when the lapse of time is sufficient? That these questions have been left unresolved ensures that, sooner or later, another constitutional tussle will arise over the calling of an independence referendum in Scotland.

16
NORTHERN IRELAND

Over the last 900 years, British engagement in Ireland has shifted between exploitation, uninterest, and well-meaning attempts to solve the resulting problems. A number of British constitutional scholars have adopted the second of these three approaches, showing a remarkable willingness to overlook the constitutional issues raised by Ireland. Anthony King, in his otherwise excellent book, *The British Constitution*, wrote that the politics and constitution of Northern Ireland are 'oddly detached' from the rest of the United Kingdom (UK), and that what 'happens in Northern Ireland scarcely affects British constitutional development; constitutional development in Britain scarcely affects what happens in Northern Ireland'.[1] King is partly right. Ireland, and subsequently Northern Ireland, raise difficult constitutional issues that are unlike those faced elsewhere in the UK. The long-standing division between Nationalist, largely Catholic, groups who want the entirety of the island of Ireland to become an independent state, and Unionist, largely Protestant, groups who wish to remain part of the UK, has proved to be a deeper and more destructive constitutional divide than any comparable division elsewhere in the UK. The integrative function of the constitution, its capacity to unite people behind collective decisions, has failed in Ireland for centuries: combining Nationalist and Unionist groups behind collective decision-making has been the core constitutional challenge faced by Ireland for generations. But Ireland's constitutional issues cannot be divorced from Britain's constitutional issues. In part, this is simply because Britain is not a state and, contrary to the title of King's book, does not have a constitution, at least in the sense that King implies. The constitutional structures of Ireland from 1801 to 1922 were constitutional structures of the UK, as are, from this point onwards, are the structures of

[1] Anthony King, *The British Constitution* (Oxford University Press 2007) ix. I am grateful to Colin Murray for bringing this to my attention.

The United Kingdom Constitution. N. W. Barber, Oxford University Press. © Nick Barber 2021.
DOI: 10.1093/oso/9780198852315.003.0016

Northern Ireland; these territories are parts of the UK, and most of those living within them are UK citizens. More worrying still is King's willingness to quarantine the political and constitutional experiences of Ireland from an assessment of the rest of the UK constitutional order. Many of the aspects of the UK constitution, which British constitutional scholars recount with pride, struggled to cross the Irish Sea. Principles such as democracy, the rule of law, basic notions of equality, even parliamentary sovereignty, have all been tested and challenged in the Irish context. By ignoring Ireland, we risk presenting a rose-tinted picture of the UK constitution, one in which many of the most serious failings of that constitutional order are overlooked.

16.1 JOINING

There are two parts to the story of Ireland's membership of the Union. There is the initial union, formally brought about by the Acts of Union 1801, and then the secession of much of Ireland in the early part of the twentieth century, with Northern Ireland remaining as part of the UK. As with Scotland and Wales, an understanding of the context in which these developments occurred requires us to look back to the medieval period, and examine the earlier relationship between Ireland, on the one hand, and England, then Britain, on the other.

As with the other territories of the UK, the kings of England had long asserted overlordship over Ireland, with Geoffrey of Monmouth optimistically grounding the legitimacy of English rule in King Arthur's conquest of the territory.[2] More prosaically, it was the invasion by Henry II in 1169 which marks the beginnings of English control over Irish territory.[3] At this point, Ireland's governing structure, like Wales', consisted of a collection of interconnected kingdoms, and the Normans treated the territory much as they had treated Wales: large areas of land were awarded to Norman lords and thousands of settlers were shipped

[2] RR Davies, *The First English Empire: Power and Identity in the British Isles 1093-1343* (Oxford University Press 2000) 47–48.

[3] James Lydon, 'Ireland and the English Crown 1171-1541' (1995) 29 Irish Historical Studies 281.

in to colonise the country.[4] From this point onwards, Irish society was characterised by a division between the Gaelic Irish and the incoming Anglo-Irish. The Gaelic Irish were a distinct community, who spoke a different language from the Anglo-Irish and possessed their own laws. Maintaining these social and cultural distinctions became a central objective of English policy in Ireland. In the Statutes of Kilkenny (1360) marriage between English settlers and the Irish was proscribed, and the speaking of Irish was forbidden within the English colonies. Many Gaelic Irish were denied access to English law and, in some instances, were treated as falling entirely outside of the protection of English law; effectively becoming outlaws in their own country.[5]

The harshness of these policies was mitigated, to some degree, during the reign of Henry VIII. The Crown of Ireland Act 1542, passed by the Parliament of Ireland, recognised Henry VIII as 'king of Ireland' and annexed Ireland to the English Crown. A consequence of this was that all of those born in Ireland were Henry's subjects and entitled to the protection of the law; the formal exclusion of Gaelic Irish from the protection of the law was ended. Perhaps of even greater significance, however, was Henry VIII's break with Rome, which established England as a Protestant country and created a social distinction in Ireland that persists to this day. The Gaelic Irish, and many of the old Anglo-Irish who arrived in the first wave of colonisation, remained Catholic, whilst their monarch became a Protestant: the equation of Catholicism with disloyalty towards the Crown emerged at this point. The next 150 years saw an influx of Protestant colonisers from England and Scotland, buoyed as much by religious belief as by economic aspiration. The historian Thomas Bartlett reports that by 1690 two-thirds of the territory of Ireland had changed hands, and 100,000 settlers had arrived in Ireland.[6] The vast majority of the population of Ireland remained Catholic, whilst the vast majority of land was held by Protestants. Colonisation was backed by violence, both small- and large-scale. Oliver Cromwell, who is sometimes held up as a hero in British

[4] Thomas Bartlett, *Ireland: A History* (Cambridge University Press 2010) 34–38.

[5] ibid 50–51; Lydon (n 3) 286–88.

[6] Bartlett (n 4) 88.

constitutional scholarship, committed some of the largest massacres of the period. It has been estimated that, as a result of Cromwell's policies in Ireland, between 20 and 40% of the population died between 1641 and 1651.[7]

Until the start of the nineteenth century, Ireland remained a nominally separate state, with its own king, parliament, and system of courts. The practical extent of this constitutional autonomy varied over time and was sometimes more symbolic than real. The most significant instrument of English control was Poynings' Law, also known as the Statute of Drogheda 1494. This was an Act of the Irish Parliament that required bills put before that body to have had received the prior approval of the English Privy Council.[8] Whilst the British Parliament's Declaratory Act 1719 asserted that body's right to legislate over Ireland and stripped the Irish House of Lords of its role as the final court of appeal for Irish cases. Ironically, perhaps, the high point of Irish constitutional autonomy came just prior to the union of Ireland and Britain. Amongst a collection of legislative measures that came to be called the Constitution of 1782, the British Parliament repealed the Declaratory Act 1719 and, in the Irish Appeals Act 1783, declared that British courts would no longer have jurisdiction to hear Irish appeals. The Irish Parliament also modified Poynings' Law, restricting the powers of the English and Irish Privy Councils over Irish legislation. The Irish executive, however, remained under the control of London.

The sudden transformation from a territory that had possessed increasing constitutional autonomy to union with Britain had a number of causes.[9] On the Protestant side, a rebellion in 1798 had proved a reminder that, in a territory in which 80% of the population was Catholic, Protestant power was dependent on British support. In addition, the steadily increasing range of political rights accorded to Catholics in Ireland, which included the right to vote, threatened Protestant hegemony of governing institutions in the longer term: in the UK as a whole Catholics would be

[7] ibid 126. [8] ibid 147–48.

[9] ibid 221–36; Iain McLean and Alastair McMillan, '1707 and 1800: A Treaty (Mostly) Honoured and a Treaty Broken' in Iain McLean (ed), *What's Wrong with the British Constitution?* (Oxford University Press 2010) 175–85.

in a minority, even if elected to Parliament. On the Catholic side, the British Parliament was seen as supportive of measures to reduce discrimination, at least in contrast to the Irish Parliament, and the British indicated that, after Union, Catholic representatives would be permitted to sit in the new UK Parliament—an entitlement that, primarily because of the opposition of King George III, was not realised until 1829.[10] Whilst for the British, union was seen as a means of settling the problems raised by Ireland, in particular, in an echo of the rationale for Scottish Union, the fear that Ireland could be used as a staging point for an invasion of Britain. All sides hoped that the Union would bring economic advantages. As with Scotland, two statutes were passed, by both the British and Irish Parliaments, but unlike Scotland, the Acts of Union of 1800 did not protect the autonomy of the Irish legal system; the relative independence created by the Constitution of 1782 was undone.

The United Kingdom came into existence on 1 January 1801 but, unsurprisingly, this new constitutional structure, with power now explicitly located in London, failed to resolve the underlying tensions in Irish society.[11] These continued to build throughout the nineteenth century, exacerbated by the catastrophic handling of the Irish Famine of the 1840s. Towards the end of the nineteenth century and during the first two decades of the twentieth, opposition to Ireland's membership of the Union became increasingly violent, culminating in the Easter Rising of 1916 and the Anglo-Irish war of 1919–1921 which led to the creation of an independent Irish state. The Anglo-Irish war deserves more attention from constitutional lawyers than it has received.[12] This was, after all, a military engagement fought within UK territory between UK subjects; it might have been thought that it would have been a seminal moment for UK constitutional scholarship, yet it seems to have had relatively little impact on those

[10] Roman Catholic Relief Act 1829. Vernon Bogdanor, *Devolution* (Oxford University Press 1998) 16–17.

[11] For Victorian attempts to accommodate these demands see Bogdanor (n 10) ch 2.

[12] Although see the important discussion in Keith Ewing and Conor Gearty, *The Struggle for Civil Liberties: Political Freedom and the Rule of Law in Britain, 1914–1945* (Oxford University Press 2001) ch 7.

writing about the constitution at the time and in the decades immediately after. During the war, the UK adopted tactics which are hard to reconcile with the usual understanding of the constitution in this period. In an echo of strategies used in the Empire, British troops used reprisal attacks on civilians in order to deter combatants. In 1920, for example, in response to actions by Irish forces, British troops burned and looted the city of Cork and the town of Balbriggan.[13] Whilst the details of these incidents are debated, and the extent to which they were the products of direct policies of the UK state can be questioned, it seems agents of the UK state were free to inflict punishment on UK subjects who had broken no law; the rule of law, as understood and lauded at that period, seems not to have applied to the Irish.

The first step in the creation of Northern Ireland as a constitutional unit was the passing of the Government of Ireland Act 1920. This created two constitutional units in Ireland: with twenty-six southern counties and six north-eastern counties, each given their own parliaments.[14] The twenty-six counties contained a majority Catholic population, whilst the remaining six were largely Protestant. The hope behind the 1920 Act was that each part of Ireland would remain part of the UK, but it quickly became apparent that only independence would satisfy the South. The Anglo-Irish Treaty 1921 committed the UK to creating a new state, the Irish Free State, which would be a self-governing dominion of the British Empire, similar to Canada or Australia. This treaty was given legal force by a UK statute[15] and a second UK statute, the Irish Free State Constitution Act 1922, grounded (so far as the UK constitution was concerned) the new Irish Constitution. A second, parallel, statute was enacted by the Dáil, the Irish legislature, which also purported to legitimate the new Constitution.[16] For the next fifteen years the question of whether the legal source of the Irish Constitution was a UK statute or Irish legislation was debatable, and it could be argued that from 1922 to 1937 Ireland remained within the British Empire, with the UK Parliament retaining a legal capacity to legislate over the

[13] Bartlett (n 4) 401–404. [14] Bogdanor (n 10) 57–66.
[15] Irish Free State (Agreement) Act 1922.
[16] Constitution of the Irish Free State (Saorstát Éireann) Act 1922.

territory.[17] Ireland's 1937 Constitution was adopted in a manner that deliberately broke this constitutional link, and Ireland became an unequivocally autonomous constitutional entity.

The Anglo-Irish Treaty 1921 permitted the Northern Ireland Parliament to apply to the king, requesting that the Government of Ireland Act 1920 continue to apply in that territory, in effect, to remain part of the UK. Such an application was made, and Northern Ireland split from its southern counterpart. From this point until the closure of the Northern Ireland Parliament in 1972, Northern Ireland possessed its own, devolved, legislature with far-reaching law-making powers.

The question of whether Ireland, and then Northern Ireland, consented to join the Union is not easy to answer. Taking the 1801 Union first, this followed a similar model to that set by Scotland a century earlier; there were negotiations between British and Irish representatives, and the agreement was then approved by the legislatures of each territory. But whereas Scotland had developed its own autonomous constitutional, political, and social structures prior to union, those of Ireland had already been radically shaped by its interaction with the English, later British, state. So, whilst there may have been some Irish support for the Union in 1801, this support was largely grounded in hopes that the problems that the British had brought to Ireland would be mitigated or resolved by union; the British had, through settlement, neglect, and oppression, created an environment in which union looked more attractive than the existing constitutional structures. Furthermore, whilst in Scotland independent statehood was, in 1707, an option, in Ireland in 1801 this alternative was not available. The existing Irish political structures could only operate with significant British support, and an alternative (and ultimately more stable) constitutional model in which Catholics were accorded full and effective political rights was not, at that point, a political possibility. The choices facing Ireland were: union, continued tacit domination by Britain, or civil war. However, regardless of the

[17] See the interesting legal disagreement between the Supreme Court of the Irish Free State, sitting in Dublin, in *The State (Ryan) v Lennon* [1935] IR 170 and the Privy Council, sitting in London, in *Moore v The Attorney General for the Irish Free State* [1935] AC 484 (PC).

support that there might have been for union in 1801, this support evaporated throughout the nineteenth century. By the end of the century it was clear that a large majority of the Irish wanted to exit; that it took a civil war for them to do so makes it hard, at that point in history, to claim the Union rested on consent.

The entry of Northern Ireland into the UK might seem simpler; the Northern Ireland Parliament, after all, made an explicit request to remain part of the UK in 1921. This is complicated by at least two issues. First, the 1921 request should be seen in light of the 1801 Union; whilst there is a temptation to date Northern Ireland's membership of the Union from 1921, the constitutional structures that made this request possible predate this moment. The Northern Ireland Parliament was established by the Government of Ireland Act 1920 which, in its turn, depended on the 1801 Union for its constitutional legitimacy. Secondly, and connectedly, Northern Ireland is a democratic unit that was crafted, in part, to guarantee this consent in the event of Irish secession.[18] As we saw in Chapter 13, one of the hardest questions in democratic theory is that of the boundary problem: identifying the group entitled to vote on a given issue. Northern Ireland provides a sharp reminder of this problem; after all, if, in 1921, a vote on the constitutional future of Ireland were taken by all voters on the island of Ireland, there would have been a clear majority for independence. Was the decision of the UK in 1920 to divide Ireland to avoid this outcome defensible? On the one hand, it could be argued that the northern counties, with a strong Protestant majority, had a radically different culture and set of political objectives to the south, and, moreover, were reasonably concerned that a Catholic-dominated polity would not respect their rights and interests. Perhaps the creation of a new democratic unit that recognises and protects these differences was justifiable and the UK was right to recognise Northern Ireland as a constituent territory that was entitled to consent to membership of the Union. On the other hand, it could be argued that the boundaries of Northern Ireland were artificial and were rigged so that London would get the answer it wanted to the question of Union. If so, perhaps

[18] James Mitchell, *Devolution in the UK* (Manchester University Press 2009) 70–73.

the supposed consent given by Northern Ireland to remain part of the UK lacked moral force; the UK was wrong to recognise Northern Ireland as a constituent territory.

16.2 DEVOLUTION

If the aim of creating Northern Ireland was to provide protection for the Protestant majority in the northern counties, the 1921 settlement could be considered a success. Between 1922 and 1972, Unionists controlled the Northern Ireland Parliament, using their position in government to consolidate their power.[19] The voting system was changed from a form of proportional representation to the first past the post system and constituency boundaries were carefully redrawn.[20] This process was undertaken so effectively that Derry, a predominantly Catholic city, was governed by Unionist councillors for decades.[21] Furthermore, rather than giving all adults the vote in local elections, the right to vote was limited to rate-payers (along with their spouses), and Unionist controlled councils were able to exercise control over the allocation of council housing. In additional to control of the constitutional processes, public services in Northern Ireland, including the police, judiciary, and civil service, were also strongly dominated by Protestants, to the extent that Thomas Bartlett describes the police force in this period as a 'Unionist Party militia'.[22] An economic divide also existed; the Catholic population was significantly less wealthy than their Protestant counterparts.

At the end of the 1960s tensions in the community led to protests and then to violence. The UK government sent British troops into the territory and, a few years later, the Northern Ireland Parliament was abolished by a statute of the UK

[19] The UK Parliament invoked devolution as a reason, or excuse, not to intervene in the affairs of Northern Ireland during this period: Bogdanor (n 10) 72–75.

[20] David McKittrick and David McVea, *Making Sense of the Troubles: A History of the Northern Ireland Conflict* (rev. edn, Penguin 2012) 8–11; Mitchell (n 18) 85–86.

[21] Derry is also known as Londonderry, a renaming that marked the role of the London companies in importing Protestant settlers and fortifying their towns: Bartlett (n 4) 100.

[22] ibid 423.

Parliament.[23] From the early 1970s to the signing of the Good Friday Agreement in 1998, Northern Ireland experienced a protracted, if low-scale, civil war, with Republican paramilitaries, Unionist paramilitaries, and the British Army acting as combatants. Around 3,500 people were killed, the majority of whom were civilians. The paramilitary groups showed themselves willing to use extreme and indiscriminate measures, from shootings to leaving bombs in public places. The UK state also resorted to extreme tactics: it introduced internment in the early 1970s, rounding up and detaining those suspected of membership of the IRA (the principal Republican paramilitary group).[24] Over 2,400 people were arrested, although most were released after a short period in detention. Some of those detained were deprived of sleep, food, and drink, and put into stress positions during interrogations, practices the European Court of Human Rights later ruled amounted to inhuman and degrading treatment.[25] As in the 1919–21 war, abuses were also committed by the Army and security services, the most notorious being an incident in January 1972, 'Bloody Sunday', when British troops shot twenty-six unarmed civilians, killing fourteen.[26] Evidence has also been found that British security forces colluded with Unionist paramilitaries in a number of killings.[27] Once again, when investigated, it often proves hard to distinguish between actions that are directly attributable the UK state (that is, acts committed by its agents on its behalf, within the scope of their authority), actions which the UK state facilitated, and actions for which the UK state had created a context in which they were likely to occur (e.g. by sending an Army regiment 'with a reputation for using excessive physical violence' to police a demonstration).[28]

[23] Northern Ireland Constitution Act 1973.

[24] McKittrick and McVea (n 20) 77–86.

[25] *Ireland v UK* [1978] ECHR 1.

[26] Lord Saville, *Report of the Bloody Sunday Inquiry* (2009–10, HC 29-I) https://www.gov.uk/government/publications/report-of-the-bloody-sunday-inquiry (accessed 24 March 2021).

[27] See 'Collusion, Murder, and Cover-up' *The Guardian* (18 April 2003) https://www.theguardian.com/politics/2003/apr/18/uk.northernireland1 (accessed 24 March 2021).

[28] Saville (n 26) para 4.8.

From the early 1970s onwards, the broad outlines of a peace deal were obvious. Disputes between the communities in Northern Ireland, and between these groups and the UK government, needed to be constitutionalised, that is, rather than the participants seeking to achieve their political objectives through violence, these objectives would be pursued peacefully, through constitutional institutions; some sort of power-sharing structure was needed. The 1973 Northern Ireland Assembly, established under the Sunningdale Agreement, was an attempt to create an institution of this type, but the Assembly quickly collapsed and Northern Ireland had to wait until 1998 before a new, and more lasting, power-sharing institution could be established.[29]

The Northern Ireland Act 1998 was the product of many years of negotiation between the UK government, the Irish government, Unionist, and Nationalist parties. The Good Friday Agreement 1998 (also known as the Belfast Agreement) committed the UK and Irish governments to accept that the future of Northern Ireland would be decided by the people of Northern Ireland, and set out a framework for a devolved legislature and executive which would require cross-community cooperation.[30] The Good Friday Agreement also committed the UK and Ireland to recognise the right of the people of Northern Ireland to hold British or Irish citizenship, or both, and that the new constitutional institutions would be bound by the European Convention on Human Rights. It also required the decommissioning of paramilitary weapons, to be verified by an independent commission, and the reform of the police. When the Agreement was put to the

[29] The Sunningdale Agreement may have failed simply because the timing was wrong—many of the relevant parties thought they were more likely to gain their objectives through force rather than through political negotiation at that time—but it may also have failed because it turned on the continued willingness of the parties to share power. The power-sharing structure was not included in the legislation established by the Assembly, as it would be in the later 1998 model. The Northern Ireland Assembly Act 1973 and Northern Ireland Act 1998 provide very different levels of formalisation.

[30] The Northern Ireland Office, *The Belfast Agreement* (Cm 3883, 1998) https://www.gov.uk/government/publications/the-belfast-agreement (accessed 24 March 2021).

voters of Northern Ireland it received strong support, with about 71% in favour of the proposals.

Northern Ireland Assembly elections employ the Single Transferable Vote system. This system allows five representatives to be elected from each constituency. Voters rank their preferred candidates, and, after the number of votes is known, the quota required for election is determined. Candidates who have passed is quota are appointed or, if no candidate passes the quota in a given round, the candidate with the least votes is eliminated. For those who pass the quota, their surplus votes are redistributed, reduced by a fraction calculated by diving the total number of votes the candidate gained above the surplus by the number of second choices on their ballot papers. For eliminated candidates, the second choices are counted as equivalent to first choices, as they have not yet been relied upon to elect a candidate. The system is complex, and only explained in broad outline here, but the results of the system are normally the most proportionate of those used in the UK, with the seats held in the Northern Ireland Assembly more accurately tracking the votes of its electorate than the additional member system used in Wales and Scotland or the first past the post system used in Westminster.[31]

The Northern Ireland Assembly and executive are consociational institutions, structured such that cross-community support is required for decisions to be made.[32] In the Northern Ireland Assembly, members are required to register a designation of identity: Nationalist, Unionist, or other.[33] The default rule of the Northern Ireland Assembly is simple majority, but there are two categories of decisions that depart from this rule—situations in which legal change requires 'cross-community support'. In these instances, the vote must either consist of a majority of those voting in both the Nationalist and Unionist groups, or a supermajority (60%) of those voting, including at least 40%

[31] The Institute for Government, *Electoral Systems Across the UK* https://www.instituteforgovernment.org.uk/explainers/electoral-systems-uk (accessed 24 March 2021).

[32] Arend Lipjhart, *Democracy in Plural Societies* (Yale University Press 1977) ch 2.

[33] Brice Dickson, 'Devolution in Northern Ireland' in Jeffrey Jowell and Colm O'Cinneide (eds), *The Changing Constitution* (9th edn, Oxford University Press 2019) 252–54.

of those voting in both the Nationalist and Unionist groups.[34] First, some of the standing orders that regulate the operation of the Northern Ireland Assembly can only be altered with cross-community consent.[35] These standing orders include rules that govern the election of a Speaker, the process by which representatives are selected to contribute to debate, and the questioning of members of the Northern Ireland executive.[36] Secondly, if thirty representatives (out of a total group of ninety members) sign a 'petition of concern', any piece of proposed legislation will then require cross-community support.[37] The use, or even the threat, of this mechanism compels negotiations between the Unionist and Nationalist groups in the Assembly; before either group can enact a statute it must obtain a measure of support from the other group. Power-sharing within the executive is also required by the consociational settlement, with posts allocated between parties drawn from the two communities.[38] If the First Minister is a Unionist, the Deputy First Minister must be a Nationalist, and this division of posts runs throughout the government.

Perhaps because of the difficulties of decision-making in consociational structures, the Northern Ireland Assembly's powers of taxation are far more limited that those enjoyed by its Scottish and Welsh counterparts. There are no plans to give the Assembly power to vary income tax, although provision is in place to give it power to set corporation tax.[39]

Consociational constitutional structures are almost inevitably problematic, and Northern Ireland's has not proved an exception.[40] First, because these structures require agreement between parties not normally disposed to agree, there are likely to be periods during which an executive cannot be formed. The Northern Ireland Assembly has been suspended on a number of

34 Northern Ireland Act 1998, s 4(5).

35 Northern Ireland Act 1990, s 41.

36 Northern Ireland Act 1998, s 41. 37 ibid s 42.

38 Dickson (n 33) 254–56.

39 Corporation Tax (Northern Ireland) 2015. At the time of writing, the Westminster government has yet to bring these provisions into effect.

40 For a critical appraisal of these criticisms see Chris McCrudden and others, 'Why Northern Ireland's Institutions Need Stability' (2016) 51 Government and Opposition 30.

occasions, the longest of which was between 2002 and 2007.[41] More recently, the Assembly was again suspended from 2017 to 2020. The instability of consociational settlements requires structures that permit government to continue in the event of protracted political deadlock: during the 2002–2007 suspension the UK government resumed direct rule over Northern Ireland, whilst from 2017 until 2020 the primary responsibility for governance fell on the Northern Ireland Civil Service.[42] During these periods of suspension, both the Northern Ireland Civil Service and the UK government were understandably reluctant to take controversial decisions or decisions with long-term policy implications. As a result of this instability, Northern Ireland's voice during the Brexit negotiations was muted.[43] Secondly, because they rest on agreement between opposing parties, consociational structures make it difficult for the electorate to throw parties out of power; the constitution makes coalition between opponents inevitable. Although there has been a shift in the popularity of parties within the two communities, since 2003 the Democratic Unionist Party and Sinn Féin have played leading roles in forming the executive and seem likely to dominate the Assembly for the foreseeable future. Thirdly, whilst consociational structures are normally created to accommodate ethnic division they can also, by accommodating, reinforce these divisions. The structure gives voters an incentive to stay with parties allied to their own ethnic groups; these are the parties, after all, that are most likely to hold power within the consociational arrangements. Consequently, consociational structures can discourage the creation of non-sectarian parties, amounting to a barrier to entry. Of course, all of these criticisms of Northern Ireland's consociational settlement may be valid and yet still fail to show that the settlement is a mistake. The Northern Ireland Act 1998 may be unique in UK constitutional law: it is, in effect, part of a peace treaty, a product of the Good Friday Agreement, agreed between political actors with

[41] McKittrick and McVea (n 20) 273–81.

[42] The Institute for Government, *Governing Without Ministers: Northern Ireland Since the Fall of the Power-Sharing Executive* https://www.instituteforgovernment.org.uk/sites/default/files/publications/governing-without-ministers-northern-ireland.pdf (accessed 24 March 2021).

[43] Alan Greer, 'Brexit and Devolution' (2018) 89 Political Quarterly 134.

connections to groups who had been fighting a low-intensity civil war. The settlement it establishes has, to a significant degree, succeeded in constitutionalising disputes which would otherwise be fought with violence. It is, perhaps, worth emphasising this point: whilst the formal, legal, authority of the Northern Ireland Act 1998 comes, like any other statute, from its enactment by the UK Parliament, its social legitimacy, the reason why it succeeds in guiding conduct, comes from a negotiated agreement between the parties to the conflict in Northern Ireland. In some respects, this statute resembles a contract, a negotiated compromise between parties with conflicting objectives, with the courts acting as guarantor.

In the chapters discussing Wales and Scotland, the issue of language rights was raised. Language rights have also proved controversial in Northern Ireland, with the Nationalist parties pushing for the official recognition of Irish Gaelic, and the Unionists responding with calls for the recognition of Ulster Scots. Irish Gaelic has symbolic importance for the Nationalist movement. It traces its roots back to the earliest days of Irish society and, like Welsh, was marginalised by the British, who prohibited its use in legal proceedings.[44] By the end of the nineteenth century few people could speak the language, but its restoration became one of the objectives of the new Irish state.[45] As part of the resolution of the 2017-2020 suspension of the Assembly, Irish Gaelic is to be given official recognition, and an Irish Language Commissioner appointed to protect and enhance the use of the language. Ulster Scots will receive similar protection, but as, like Scots, it is a language that an English speaker could understand with a little effort, the measures that might be needed to accommodate its use are less demanding than those required by Irish Gaelic.

16.3 LEAVING

Uniquely, Northern Ireland possesses a statutory right to exit the Union. Under the Northern Ireland Act 1998, the future of

[44] Administration of Justice (Language) Act 1737 (Irish Parliament).

[45] Bartlett (n 4) 426–28.

Northern Ireland is recognised as turning on the consent of its people.[46] If the majority of those in Northern Ireland vote for Northern Ireland to become part of the Republic of Ireland, the Secretary of State for Northern Ireland comes under a statutory duty to place proposals before the UK Parliament giving effect to this vote. The statutory right to secession arguably predates the 1998 Act, and may have been implied by the Ireland Act 1949, which required the consent of the Northern Ireland Parliament before Northern Ireland ceased to be part of the UK.[47] The circumstances in which a poll must be held under the 1998 Act are less than clear: the Secretary of State must organise a poll 'if at any time it appears likely to him that a majority of those voting would express a wish that Northern Ireland should cease to be part of the United Kingdom and form part of a united Ireland'.[48] This leaves some discretion to the Minister, but if a majority of representatives in the Northern Ireland Assembly passed a motion calling for a poll, it would be hard to argue this test had not been met.

The chances of such a poll triggering Northern Ireland's exit from the Union have increased in recent years. This is largely due to demographics: the Catholic population in Northern Ireland has grown relative to the Protestant population.[49] The changing population has been reflected in the representatives appointed to the Assembly: in the 2017 election an equal number of seats was won by Unionist and Nationalist parties. Of course, not everyone who is Catholic or who voted for a Nationalist party wants a united Ireland, just as not everyone who is Protestant or who votes Unionist is necessarily opposed to the change. But this broad demographic shift, which is continuing, makes exit more

[46] Northern Ireland Act 1998, s 1.

[47] Vernon Bogdanor, *The New British Constitution* (Hart Publishing 2009) 116.

[48] Northern Ireland Act 1998, sch 1.

[49] '"Catholic Majority Possible" in NI by 2021' *BBC News* (19 April 2018) https://www.bbc.co.uk/news/uk-northern-ireland-43823506 (accessed 24 March 2021).

likely.[50] If that happens, the protections built in to the consociational settlement to protect the Nationalist community may switch round and serve to protect those Unionists who find themselves a minority group within the Republic.

[50] Recent polls seeking to gauge views in Northern Ireland vary wildly, from around a fifth saying they would vote for a United Ireland up to 51% of those with an opinion and saying they would be likely to vote in a 2019 survey: Lord Ashcroft, 'My Northern Ireland Survey Finds the Union on a Knife-Edge' (11 September 2019) https://lordashcroftpolls.com/2019/09/my-northern-ireland-survey-finds-the-union-on-a-knife-edge/ (accessed 24 March 2021).

17

ENGLAND AND ELSEWHERE

The last three chapters have examined the most significant regional constitutional units in the UK: Wales, Scotland, and Northern Ireland. This chapter covers the remainder, the other regionalised elements of the United Kingdom (UK) constitution. The bulk of the chapter will be spent on England, the largest and most populous constitutional unit within the UK, and one which has, largely through its own choice, been overlooked in the regionalisation of power. The second part of the chapter briefly examines other units of constitutional power, local government units and international bodies. There is not space in this book to examine these institutions adequately, but it is important to remember that when powers are regionalised the choice is not just between national institutions and devolved institutions; subsidiarity might also require that powers be pushed down to smaller units, like cities or towns, or up to international bodies.

17.1 ENGLAND

The English have a habit of forgetting that other parts of the UK exist. It is commonplace for the English to refer to the UK, or to the island of Britain, as England, and to talk of the key UK constitutional institutions, such as the Parliament, Crown, or prime minister, as English. The historian Rees Davies argues that this equivocation is not simple linguistic carelessness, but started as one of strategy, tracing the equivocation back to the early expansion of English power over other territories. As English power grew, other territories were reconceptualised as parts of England, and their peoples as English, in order to legitimate their incorporation into what Davies described as the first English Empire.[1] This medieval rebranding has continued into modern times, with

[1] RR Davies, *The First English Empire: Power and Identities in the British Isles 1093–1343* (Oxford University Press 2000) 48–53.

The United Kingdom Constitution. N. W. Barber, Oxford University Press. © Nick Barber 2021.
DOI: 10.1093/oso/9780198852315.003.0017

the imbalance of power continuing to explain English uninterest in devolution: as Vernon Bogdanor argues, it is the contemporary dominance of the English within the UK that explains their indifference towards devolution.[2] And England is indeed dominant: it is by far the largest, most populous, and most economically powerful part of the UK. The Office for National Statistics estimates that in 2019 around 84% of the UK, approximately 56 million people, lived in England. This compares with about 8% living in Scotland, 5% in Wales, and 3% in Northern Ireland.[3] When the Kilbrandon Commission reported on the potential for devolution in 1973, it advised against the creation of an English Parliament for this reason: the size and economic power of the English Parliament would rival any federal parliament, and would dominate the other regions.[4] The 1998 devolution settlement seems to have accepted this point: there was no move to create an English Parliament alongside the other legislatures, and subsequent calls for a parliament from within England have proved muted.[5] The English, it might be speculated, have never felt the need for a distinct set of constitutional institutions because they think they already possess them and, moreover, because through those institutions they not only get to govern England, but have a say in the governance of other regions, too.

To an extent, this complacency is justifiable: English representatives make up the vast majority of Members of Parliament (MPs) in Parliament, and the UK government is almost always reliant on, and controlled by, English MPs. But sometimes the asymmetry of the devolution settlement will put the English at a disadvantage. During the debates over devolution in the 1970s,

[2] Vernon Bogdanor, *The New British Constitution* (Hart Publishing 2009) 107–108.

[3] Office For National Statistics, *Population estimates for the UK, England and Wales, Scotland and Northern Ireland: Mid-2019* (24 June 2020) https://www.ons.gov.uk/peoplepopulationandcommunity/populationandmigration/populationestimates/bulletins/annualmidyearpopulationestimates/mid2019estimates (accessed 22 March 2021).

[4] Bogdanor (n 2) 100, citing the Royal Commission on the Constitution 1969–1973, *Volume I, Report* (Cmnd 5460, 1973) para 531.

[5] Christopher GA Bryant, 'Devolution, Equity, and the English Question' (2008) 14 Nations and Nationalism 664, 670–72; Bogdanor (n 2) 100.

Tam Dalyell, a Labour MP, repeatedly raised what came to be known as the 'West Lothian question'. The West Lothian question turns on the democratic oddities caused by asymmetrical devolution, a situation in which regions such as Scotland have their own legislatures, but England is governed directly from Westminster.[6] The objection has been formulated in various ways, but it can be broken down into three parts. First, there is a concern about the constitutional equality of citizens: on devolved matters, voters in Scotland have two votes, whereas voters in England only have one. Scottish voters elect representatives to the Scottish Parliament who decide devolved matters for Scotland, but they also elect representatives to the UK Parliament, where their representatives play a part in deciding policy for England. Secondly, and relatedly, there is a concern about the constitutional equality of representatives: in the UK Parliament, Scottish representatives vote on English issues but English representatives do not vote on the same issues in Scotland. These two concerns, about the different voting rights given to citizens and the different range of powers accorded to MPs, are, perhaps, less serious than some of the advocates of the West Lothian question thought. Because of the way in which funding for the devolved regions is calculated, decisions about expenditure in England affect the amount of funding given to Scotland, so, it could be argued that just about all decisions of the UK Parliament, even those that are focused on policies applied in England, affect the devolved regions too.[7] Given this, it could be argued that voters and representatives from those regions should participate in them. However, there is a third, and more serious aspect to the West Lothian question. When the Commons votes on policies for England its default rule is one of simple majority: if more MPs vote for a bill than against, the bill is passed. This means it is possible that a piece of legislation passes because of the support of MPs from the devolved regions, even though the majority of English MPs voted to reject it. On a few occasions this has actually happened: the bill establishing tuition

[6] Bogdanor (n 2) 98–110; James Mitchell, *Devolution in the UK* (Manchester University Press 2009) 202–204.

[7] Dominic de Cogan, *Tax Law, State-Building and the Constitution* (Hart Publishing 2020) 42–45.

fees in higher education, the effects of which were almost entirely confined to England, was rejected by a majority of English MPs but passed the Commons because of the support of Scottish MPs.[8] This problem has the potential to become even more serious. Rather than an occasional vote turning on representatives from the devolved regions, the balance of power in the Commons could turn on these representatives: England could elect a majority of, say, Conservative MPs, but Labour could have a majority of UK MPs because of the support of Scottish or Welsh MPs.[9] The UK government and Parliament, both of which spend much of their time governing England, would then be controlled by Labour, whilst the Conservatives would have won a majority in England. It would become common for legislation to be passed by the Commons for England to be passed against the wishes of the majority of English MPs.[10] If this was to occur, as could easily happen, the English would, to their discomfort, realise that the UK Parliament is not an English institution, and the West Lothian question would become hard to ignore.[11]

England was largely overlooked in the 1998 devolution settlement. The initial plan was to enhance local government through the creation of regional assemblies, but, in 2004, a referendum was held on the creation of an assembly in the north-east and the proposal lost badly, with 78% voting against it.[12] Following this referendum, the idea of regional assemblies was quietly dropped. In its place came 'English votes for English laws' (EVEL), a proposal to create a legislative structure within Parliament whereby laws that affected England would be vote on by English MPs. The structure was implemented by a standing order of the House of Commons

[8] Teaching and Higher Education Act 1998; Daniel Gover and Michael Kenny, 'Answering the West Lothian Question? A Critical Assessment of "English Votes for English Laws" in the UK Parliament' (2018) 71 Parliamentary Affairs 760, 762–65.

[9] This is the most likely playing out of this scenario: the Conservative Party tends to gain most of its seats from England.

[10] A position similar to this occurred in 2017, when Theresa May's government relied on the support of the DUP, a party from Northern Ireland, for her majority. However, the Conservative Party had also secured the majority of English seats.

[11] Vernon Bogdanor notes that the Labour governments of 1964 and 1974 relied on the support of Scottish Labour MPs: Bogdanor (n 2) 227.

[12] Bogdanor (n 2) 178; Mitchell (n 6) 210–11.

in 2015. The process is complex but, in short, a new legislative procedure has been created with a double-veto at its core.[13] Once the Speaker has certified that a bill, or provision within a bill, should pass through a special legislative procedure involving English MPs (or English MPs and those of another region), the bill now requires the approval of this subset within the Commons. This group has the power to veto the bill, but not to approve it; the bill must still be approved by the whole of the Commons before it can become a law. Daniel Gover and Michael Kenny report that two of the initial concerns about the process have receded over time: fears that certification decisions made by the Speaker would prove controversial, and concerns over the creation of 'two classes' of MPs, have both been allayed.[14] However, as they note, the process has not answered the West Lothian question; England still lacks a clear voice in legislation. In particular, the structure does not provide a solution to our third set of problems, the difficulties that would be caused if one party had a majority of MPs in England and another had a majority of MPs in the UK as a whole. Because the EVEL structure does not include a parallel executive, the government would continue to be controlled by the UK party, whilst, in the context of English laws, a different party would control the Commons. We could end up, for example, with a Labour Secretary of State for Education, appointed by the UK prime minister, whose responsibilities were almost entirely focused on England, but a Conservative dominated EVEL structure, able to veto any proposed legislation on education put forward by the government. Furthermore, as the EVEL structure is set out in the Commons standing order and not entrenched in any way, it would be legally easy for the larger UK party to remove the English veto: the EVEL structure is constitutionally fragile.

England's position in the Union is anomalous. Lacking its own legislature, it is governed by Westminster, and, as we have seen, this creates the risk of a constitutional crisis: sooner or later, England might find that it has voted for one party, but is being governed by another. It is hard to predict what would happen if this occurred, but one possible outcome has received surprisingly little attention: could England opt to leave the Union? After

[13] Gover and Kenny (n 8). [14] ibid 770–74.

all, Scotland, Northern Ireland, and, probably, Wales, are all recognised as having rights of exit. It seems highly unlikely that England would ever wish to leave, but if it did, it would raise an interesting question. It could be argued that allowing the richest part of the Union to secede, leaving the poorer territories to fend for themselves, would be unjust; perhaps England owes special obligation to these regions, in particular to Wales and Northern Ireland where, it could be argued, some of the problems faced were caused by the actions of the English in the first place.

17.2 ELSEWHERE

The regionalisation of power in the UK constitution is not confined to the devolution settlement. Subsidiarity can require that decisions and powers be passed further down, to cities, counties, or parishes, or, more rarely, passed up, to international bodies. Both the regional bodies within the UK and the structures that recognise and empower international bodies outside of the UK are elements of the UK constitution. Because of their complexity—many books have been written on local government and on the UK's international connections—the following paragraphs stand as mere placeholders for fuller accounts provided elsewhere. These are important constitutional issues, but not ones that can be adequately surveyed within the confines of this book.

Many of the most important decisions that affect people on a day-to-day basis are made by local government. Local government bodies are, very broadly, responsible for planning, some aspects of education, transport, waste disposal, public health, and social care, amongst other tasks. They operate in a complicated, and sometimes tense, relationship with central state institutions, which set the broad direction of policy, control a large portion of their funding, and have the capacity to intervene in some areas. It is sometimes proposed that local government units could be used to mitigate the problems caused by the lack of devolution to England, by empowering local bodies to undertake some of the tasks given to the devolved institutions.[15] To an extent, the rise of

[15] Robert Hazell and Mark Sandford, 'English Question or Union Question? Neither Has Easy Answers' (2015) 86 Political Quarterly 16.

elected mayors could be seen as a development of this type.[16] The elected mayor system comes in a variety of forms, but in a number of areas 'devolution deals' have been struck between groups of local authorities and central government, parts of which involves more powers being passed from the centre to the regions.[17] The most prominent and powerful of these elected mayors is, perhaps, the Mayor of London, who heads the Greater London Authority, a constitutional unit that covers a population roughly equivalent to Scotland's. However, even the GLA's and London Mayor's powers are far less than those given to the devolved assemblies, and local government remains, at present, a poor substitute for the devolution seen elsewhere in the UK.

Until recently, the European Union (EU) would have provided the most prominent example of the UK passing decisions upwards and because the EU is, however imperfectly, a democratic body, with an elected legislature, this could be seen as an application of the principle of subsidiarity: powers and decisions were allocated to the EU because they would be made more effectively by that democratic unit than by a UK constituency. This subsidiarity argument is the inverse of the one that backed the devolution of power to the regions. Whereas some decisions were devolved to, for example, the Scottish Parliament, because decisions in a given area had a greater impact on the people of Scotland than on the people of the UK as a whole, other decisions were remitted up to EU institutions because of the breadth of their impact; these were decisions that would be less effective if taken at the level of the Member States. One aspect of this effectiveness was democratic control: voters in individual Member States, mediated through their national legislatures, exercised only limited control over issues that spanned borders. By combining together at the supranational level, the possibility for effective action was enhanced. After Brexit, the UK remains part of many international bodies,

[16] Mark Sandford, *Directly-Elected Mayors* (CBP 05000, House of Commons Library, 7 May 2019).

[17] Mark Sandford, *Devolution to Local Government in England* (CBP 07029, House of Commons Library, 26 March 2020). For an evaluation of the significance of these 'deals' see Sarah Ayres, Matthew Flinders, and Mark Sandford, 'Territory, Power and Statecraft: Understanding English Devolution' (2018) 52 Regional Studies 853.

such as the North Atlantic Treaty Organization (NATO) and the World Trade Organization, although none of these has the type of democratic mandate possessed by the EU. Nevertheless, even if not required by the principle of subsidiarity, there are still reasons why the UK might entrust decisions to these international bodies. This may facilitate engagement with problems that span states or, perhaps, bring the benefits of supranational review of state action to bear on the UK. Whilst these international structures do not create new democratic units, as those occupying decision-making roles within these bodies are not directly elected, these officeholders may yet be indirectly democratically accountable. Representatives of democratic states who make decisions within these international structures are accountable to their domestic voters, and administrators within international bodies are, in turn, accountable to these representatives.

18

REALISING SUBSIDIARITY

The structures establishing the devolution settlement have at least three objectives: they divide powers between democratic institutions; they protect this allocation from interference by other bodies; and they promote constructive interaction between different levels of the constitution. The achievement of these objectives is made harder by the tensions created by the regionalisation of power. First, regionalisation leads to overlaps of jurisdiction, and, no matter how carefully crafted the empowering rules, there will always be disputes over their interpretation and applicability. Secondly, as the point of devolution is to create multiple sites of democratic power, some degree of friction between these sites is inevitable. One of the reasons for the territorial division of power is to enable different constituencies within the state to formulate their own policies and craft laws that realise these goals; that Westminster and the devolved institutions sometimes disagree is not a constitutional flaw, but a consequence of the successful application of subsidiarity. Although this friction is an inevitable side-effect rather than an objective of subsidiarity, it is a friction which the constitution must then seek to regulate and contain.

There are various, connected, ways in which a constitution can regulate these relationships, protecting the delineation of power and regulating friction between the levels. Perhaps the two most important tools of regulation are the courts and the legislatures themselves. The courts are regularly asked to resolve disagreements over the devolution settlement, with cases turning on the scope of the devolved assemblies' jurisdiction and also, although more rarely, on the obligations of central government towards the devolved regions. Perhaps less obviously, the legislatures themselves also help regulate the relationship, by passing the capacity to legislate up or down the constitutional chain, and, in some instances, by modifying or limiting the legislation enacted by other bodies.

The United Kingdom Constitution. N. W. Barber, Oxford University Press. © Nick Barber 2021.
DOI: 10.1093/oso/9780198852315.003.0018

18.1 THE ROLE OF THE COURTS

There are a number of avenues through which devolution cases come before the courts. Unusually, a challenge to the validity of a statute is possible prior to its enactment: before a bill becomes a law, it is possible for it to be referred to the Supreme Court by one of the law officers.[1] The process is unusual, in that it allows a case to be brought without a substantive dispute arising between parties. It has been used relatively rarely, but has raised some important cases.[2] More commonly, devolution issues arise in the course of ordinary litigation, perhaps when a government body seeks to enforce a statute or when the statute is relied upon in a dispute between private parties. In these cases, mechanisms exist to send the devolution issue directly to the Supreme Court for resolution.[3]

Most devolution cases turn on the jurisdiction of the devolved institutions, asking whether the body had or has the power to enact a given piece of litigation. The primary question is whether the capacity to legislate in the given area was conferred by the devolution legislation, either directly, as in the older cases involving Wales, or by implication, as in the other devolution settlements. Cutting across this are two further jurisdictional limits: even if the legislation falls within the areas conferred by the devolution legislation, the devolved assemblies, like other public bodies, may not legislate contrary to the Human Rights Act 1998 or, prior to Brexit, European law.

It seems reasonable to assume that the courts will adopt a similar approach in each of the devolution statutes, but this is an assumption to be made with caution. The devolution statutes were drafted separately, and do not follow a shared template. Some of these differences are obvious: for instance, as we have seen, until recently the Welsh Assembly could only legislate in areas

[1] Scotland Act 1998, s 33; Northern Ireland Act 1998, s 11; Government of Wales Act 2006, s 112.

[2] Perhaps most notably, *Re UK Withdrawal from the European Union (Legal Continuity) (Scotland) Bill* [2018] UKSC 64, [2019] AC 1022.

[3] Scotland Act 1998, sch 6; Northern Ireland Act 1998, sch 10; Government of Wales Act 2006, sch 9.

expressly conferred by its empowering statute whilst the other devolved legislatures adopted a reserved-powers model, able to legislate in any area save for those reserved to Westminster.[4] Other differences are less immediately obvious, but might still be significant: the different statutes have different structures and sometimes use different forms of words to achieve similar outcomes. The contexts in which the statutes were enacted also differ. The Northern Ireland devolution settlement was the product of a protracted and difficult negotiation between a range of conflicting parties; the Scottish settlement had its origins in extensive, and generally amicable, discussions between civil society institutions; whilst the Welsh scheme was produced in a rush by central government, which may explain why it has had to be modified so frequently. It could be that these different contexts should sometimes lead the judges to interpret the statutes in different ways.

Even though there are profound differences between the devolution statutes, it is still possible to identify some broad principles that guide, or should guide, their interpretation. In the early days of the devolution settlement, the courts were tempted by the view that the devolution statutes were 'constitutional statutes' and that this characterisation, in itself, shaped the correct interpretative approach. Unfortunately, as Tarun Khaitan has shown, this produced radical inconsistencies.[5] Lord Bingham, in *Robinson v Secretary of State for Northern Ireland*, argued that, as a constitutional statute, the Northern Ireland Act 1998 should be read 'generously and purposively',[6] whilst Lord Rodger, in *HM Advocate v R*, wrote that as the Scotland Act was a 'constitutional settlement', judges 'must loyally give effect to the decision of Parliament on

[4] Richard Rawlings, 'Riders on the Storm: Wales, the Union, and Territorial Constitutional Crisis' (2015) 42 Journal of Law and Society 471, 485–87.

[5] Tarun Khaitan, 'How to Interpret Constitutional Statutes?' *UK Constitutional Law Association Blog* (10 January 2012) https://ukconstitutionallaw.org/2012/01/10/tarun-khaitan-how-to-interpret-constitutional-statutes/ (accessed 2 March 2021).

[6] [2002] UKHL 32, [2002] NI 390 [11]. *Robinson* is a good example of a case in which the varying contexts of the devolution statutes might have been significant. The broad interpretation adopted by Lord Bingham which might have been attractive in the context of Scotland or Wales looked to be at odds with the unusual nature of the Northern Ireland Act—it is significant that Lord Hutton, a former Northern Ireland judge, dissented.

this sensitive matter, even if—or perhaps especially if—there are attractions in a different solution'.[7] In short, the claim that constitutional statutes should, because of their constitutional nature, be read generously, is as plausible as the claim that constitutional statutes should, because of their constitutional nature, be read narrowly. Lord Hope, in a comment endorsed by later judges, cut through the dilemma, asserting that the constitutional nature of the devolution statutes could not, in itself, provide a guide to their interpretation.[8]

Even if the constitutional nature of the statutes cannot guide interpretation, it might still be possible to identify broad interpretative principles that can be invoked when reading the devolution statutes; after all, as with other statutes, the general area in which the legislation operates helps determine the goals of the statutes and so helps guide their interpretation. Perhaps the two key principles at play in devolution cases are democracy and subsidiarity. In terms of democracy, the courts look for interpretations of the statute that enable the devolved institutions to legislate effectively, giving voice to the communities they represent.[9] Indeed, it is noticeable that the judges are very slow to invalidate legislation produced by the devolved institutions: these are elected bodies and, as such, judges are reluctant to overturn their decisions.[10] Whilst the principle of democracy is invoked explicitly in devolution cases, the claim that subsidiarity is also an underlying principle is contestable; in many cases, judges have disavowed its significance, asserting that it is not for the courts to determine what powers it is desirable for the devolved institutions to possess.[11] Nevertheless, when there is a dispute over the extent of the jurisdiction of an institution, where the implications of the empowering statute are debatable, the courts tacitly consider subsidiarity. The judges consider whether the capacity is suitable

[7] [2002] UKPC D3, [2004] 1 AC 462 [155].

[8] *Imperial Tobacco Ltd v Lord Advocate* [2012] UKSC 61 [15]. See also *Re Agricultural Sector (Wales) Bill* [2014] UKSC 43, [2014] 1 WLR 2622 [6].

[9] *Imperial Tobacco* (n 8) [15].

[10] *AXA General Insurance Ltd v Lord Advocate* [2011] UKSC 46, [2012] 1 AC 868 [32].

[11] See eg *Attorney General v National Assembly for Wales Commission* [2012] UKSC 53, [2013] 1 AC 792 [79].

for the devolved institution; that is, whether this is an area of public decision-making that should be entrusted to an institution representing a segment of the UK, or whether the breadth of its implications requires it to be exercised at a national level.[12]

Imperial Tobacco Ltd v Lord Advocate provides a good example of the type of questions faced by judges examining the capacity of a devolved institution to legislate in an area.[13] The Scottish Parliament enacted legislation banning the display of tobacco products in shops and prohibiting cigarette vending machines. Imperial Tobacco sued, fearing, no doubt, that these measures would reduce sales of their poisonous and addictive products. The tobacco company argued that the legislation was outside of the powers of the Scottish Parliament. Section 29(2)(b) of the Scotland Act 1998 states that a provision is outside of the competence of the Scottish Parliament so far as it 'relates to' reserved matters. Section 29(3) clarifies this a little, stating that 'the question whether a provision of an Act of the Scottish Parliament relates to a reserved matter is to be determined ... by reference to the purpose of the provision, having regard (among other things) to its effect in all the circumstances'. Reserved matters are set out in Schedule 5 of the Act, and included in that list are product safety and the sale and supply of goods to consumers. Imperial Tobacco argued that the legislation 'relates to' each of these grounds, and fell outside the legislature's jurisdiction.[14] The Scottish government, in contrast, argued that these measures sought to protect public health, and so were within the jurisdiction of the legislature.

When deciding whether a contested piece of legislation 'relates to' a reserved ground, the courts examine two broad groups of arguments: first, the objectives of the legislation, and, secondly,

[12] Many devolution cases show elements of this type of reasoning. See in particular *Martin v HM Advocate* [2010] UKSC 10 [32]–[33]; *Imperial Tobacco* (n 8) [29]; *Christian Institute v Lord Advocate* [2016] UKSC 51 [65]; *Re UK Withdrawal* (n 2) [29].

[13] *Imperial Tobacco* (n 8).

[14] Imperial Tobacco also mounted a third argument, that the legislation altered Scottish criminal law in respect of a reserved matter (the sale and supply of goods). Lord Hope concluded that this argument failed as the new legislation added to, and did not modify, Scottish criminal law in this area: ibid [45] (Lord Hope).

its impact.[15] These two elements are treated as identifying the 'purpose' of the challenged legislation, and are often conflated in judicial reasoning. The predominant reasoning in most devolution cases, including *Imperial Tobacco*, focuses on the first of these, turning on the identification of the legislation's objectives. There are various ways in which judges attempt to pick out these objectives. One strategy is to examine pronouncements made by legislators about the statute, such as the reports issued by ministers before the introduction of the Bill, speeches made in debates, committee reports, explanatory notes attached to the Bill, and so on.[16] A danger with this strategy is that it can shape future debates around legislation, making it defensive (or, indeed, offensive, if the speaker hopes to lay the ground work for future legal challenges) as law-makers strive to avoid giving ammunition to later challengers.[17] Indeed, it would be worrying if the court's decision in *Imperial Tobacco* had turned on a few incautious comments by MSPs. A second, and often complementary, way of assessing the statute's objectives is to ask what ends a reasonable legislature would have been trying to pursue, given the content of the legislation.[18] To identify objectives in this way, the court must make some assumptions about the broad goals that the legislature should be taken to be pursuing—perhaps, in particular, that it is seeking to legislate for socially beneficial ends—and then identify the purpose of the particular statute in this light.[19]

The second approach to assessing whether a piece of legislation 'relates to' a reserved category focuses on its impact, examining the areas of activity that the new legislation will affect. In the case law on devolution, this task is often combined with the identification of objectives, with the suggestion that the objectives of the legislation can be identified by looking at its effects.[20] However,

[15] *Martin* (n 12) [49].

[16] ibid [25]; *Imperial Tobacco* (n 8) [22].

[17] One justification that is commonly given for parliamentary privilege is that fear of litigation might shape parliamentary debates: see Philip A Joseph, 'Parliament's Attenuated Privilege of Freedom of Speech' (2010) 126 Law Quarterly Review 568.

[18] On these two approaches see *Salvesen v Riddell* [2013] UKSC 22 [37]–[40].

[19] Richard Ekins, *The Nature of Legislative Intent* (Oxford University Press 2012) chs 8–9.

[20] See Lord Kerr's dicta in *Martin* (n 12) [161].

these tests must be distinct, as even a measure that is clearly aimed at an objective within jurisdiction may have a significant, even if unwanted, impact on a reserved category.[21] When testing impact on a reserved category, to become problematic the impact must exceed some minimal level; following earlier case law, Lord Hope stated in *Imperial Tobacco* that 'relates to' means something more than a 'loose or consequential connection' to the reserved category.[22] Excluding minimal connections is important, as almost all pieces of devolved legislation impact on reserved matters to some extent; it is hard, for example, to imagine a legislative measure that would not affect the supply of goods to consumers to some degree. Beyond that, the test of impact is left vague, and perhaps understandably so, as it is a hard task for the court to undertake: to do so properly would require the assembling and analysis of a mass of economic and social data, tasks for which the courts' structure and judges' skills are radically ill-suited.

Applying these tests in *Imperial Tobacco*, Lord Hope concluded that the purpose of the legislation was to improve the health of the people of Scotland. Its purpose was not to 'regulate' the sale or supply of goods, as it did not condition the way cigarettes were supplied; instead, the legislation prevented sales occurring from vending machines entirely, and, where sales took place in stores where advertising was banned, the conditions on which cigarettes were supplied would remain unchanged.[23] As to product safety, Lord Hope noted that the new legislation would not make cigarettes any safer; their composition and terms of sale would remain unaffected.[24]

The reasoning used by Lord Hope is characteristic of the style of reasoning used in many devolution cases; it focuses tightly on the words used in the statutes, and looks for ways to explain why, as a linguistic matter, the devolution statute does not cross into reserved areas. It is a type of reasoning the courts are well-equipped to undertake and with which judges are comfortable. Unfortunately, once a dispute gets to the Supreme Court it is rarely convincing. This type of reasoning implicitly draws heavily

21 *Re Agricultural Sector* (n 8) [55]–[56].

22 *Imperial Tobacco* (n 8) [16] (Lord Hope), citing *Martin* (n 12) [49].

23 *Imperial Tobacco* (n 8) [40]–[41].

24 ibid [42].

on our shared linguistic understandings; the judges appeal to our intuitions about the meaning of words. In easy cases, this works well. If the Scottish Parliament tried to pass a statute requiring an extra filter in cigarettes, that would plainly be an attempt to make the product safer and would fall within the category of product safety: only someone who did not understand the term 'product safety' would dispute this. But by the time a dispute has reached the Supreme Court, it is unlikely that this type of simple answer is available; language is often too vague to allow such a resolution. For instance, in *Imperial Tobacco*, the ban on vending machines could plausibly be described as a measure to enhance product safety by making it harder for children to get hold of, and become addicted to, cigarettes.[25] Similarly, our use of language is flexible enough to categorise the banning of vending machines as relating to the 'sale and supply of goods to consumers': the law removes one mode by which cigarettes can be sold and supplied, forcing smokers to buy from shops rather than machines. Using this form of linguistic reasoning, Lord Hope could, if he had wished, have written an equally convincing judgment siding with Imperial Tobacco against the Scottish Parliament.

Nevertheless, the decision in *Imperial Tobacco* was unanimous and predictable; competent lawyers would have been surprised if it had gone the other way. Returning to our earlier discussion, whilst Lord Hope did not explicitly invoke the broader principles underpinning the devolution settlement—democracy and subsidiarity—these strongly supported the outcome of the case. First, the legislation passed by the Scottish Parliament primarily affected the people of Scotland, the group that had elected the legislature that had enacted the legislation, and the broader effects of the measure on the rest of the UK were incidental to these effects. Secondly, this was a measure that went with the grain of the UK approach in the area; the UK as a whole was taking steps to reduce the use of tobacco, and the Scottish Parliament's measures complemented, rather than undermined, UK policy, and did not undermine democratic decisions made at the UK level.[26]

[25] To put it another way, cigarettes are unsafe for children, and the ban reduces the risk of children running the risks of the hazards connected with the product.

[26] Compare *National Assembly for Wales Commission* (n 11) [68].

Given that this was a case in which linguistic argument was not determinative, these may have been the considerations that led the Supreme Court to side with the Scottish government.

The cross-cutting jurisdictional limits on the devolved institutions, from the Human Rights Act 1998 and, before Brexit, European law, can be dealt with more quickly.[27] Rather than these constraints being specific to the devolved institutions, these are restrictions that apply to all public bodies in the UK. Like any other public body, the devolved institutions were, prior to Brexit, subject to European law, and, under the devolution statutes, lacked the capacity to legislate contrary to EU law. Similarly, as with other public bodies, the Human Rights Act binds the devolved institutions, and, indeed, much of the litigation around devolution has turned on human rights issues. The Human Rights Act is discussed in Chapter 21, but it is worth noting that when applying the Act to the devolved institutions, the courts may be more deferential than when applying it to unelected bodies or elected bodies with weaker democratic credentials.[28]

The legal constraints which the devolution settlement places on the national level of government are more limited, and the courts have proved reluctant to intervene here. Whilst the limits on the jurisdiction of the devolved institutions are legal, the corresponding limits on the UK Parliament are matters of convention. The Sewel convention holds that the UK will not 'normally' legislate on devolved matters without the agreement of the devolved legislature.[29] This convention was later incorporated into the Scotland Act and Government of Wales Act 2006, although in terms that made it clear that its conventional status was retained.[30] An attempt was made, in *R (Miller) v Secretary of State for Exiting the European Union* to persuade the Supreme Court to enforce the convention, arguing that legislation bringing about the UK's exit from the European Union would affect devolved matters, and so required the consent of the devolved legislatures.[31] It was unlikely

[27] There is also the suggestion in *AXA* that legislation could be reviewed to assess its compatibility with the rule of law. This has not, so far, lead to any successful challenges: *AXA* (n 10) [51]. See ch 5.

[28] ibid [32].

[29] HL Deb 21 July 1998, vol 592, col 791.

[30] Scotland Act 1998, s 28(8); Government of Wales Act 2006, s 107(6).

[31] [2017] UKSC 5, [2018] AC 61.

this argument would succeed. Applying the principle of subsidiarity, the question of the UK's membership of the EU was one for the UK as a whole; giving a veto to, say, Northern Ireland would allow 3% of the electorate to overturn the decision made by the other 97%. Nevertheless, given the rule was now contained within a statute, the court could have provided an authoritative interpretation of the convention, stating, for instance, whether devolution issues were engaged by Brexit and, perhaps, whether this situation was not 'normal' and so fell into the exception built into the convention.[32] The court firmly declined to undertake this task.

A rare area in which the courts have, effectively, compelled action at the UK level has been over access to abortion in Northern Ireland.[33] Because of the pre-1972 devolution settlement, the statute liberalising access to abortion in the rest of the UK, the Abortion Act 1967, did not apply to Northern Ireland. In 2018, the Supreme Court ruled that abortion law in Northern Ireland was contrary to the Human Rights Act, as it failed to respect pregnant women's right to private life.[34] Whilst no declaration of incompatibility was issued, the Supreme Court was clear that it would have issued such an order, were it not for a technical issue over the standing of the party bringing the case. The Northern Ireland Assembly was suspended at the time, so the immediate response to the ruling came at the UK level. The UK government took the view that abortion was a matter for the Northern Ireland Assembly, and that the UK Parliament should not legislate to liberalise abortion in Northern Ireland. However, the issue arose during the exceptionally weak UK governments of 2019, and the UK Parliament thought differently. The Northern Ireland (Executive Formation etc) Act 2019 liberalised the law on

[32] Aileen McHarg, 'Constitutional Change and Territorial Consent: The *Miller* Case and the Sewel Convention' in Mark Elliott, Jack Williams, and Alison L Young (eds), *The UK Constitution After Miller: Brexit and Beyond* (Hart Publishing 2018).

[33] Sally Sheldon and others, '"Too Much, too Indigestible, too Fast"? The Decades of Struggle for Abortion Law Reform in Northern Ireland' (2020) 83 Modern Law Review 761.

[34] *Re an Application by the Northern Ireland Human Rights Commission for Judicial Review* [2018] UKSC 27, [2019] 1 All ER 173. See also *Ewart's Application* [2019] NIQB 88.

abortion, partly directly, by altering existing criminal law, and partly indirectly, by requiring the Secretary of State to create a scheme of regulation for abortion.[35] For good measure, the statute also gave same-sex couples the right to marry in the territory.[36] Both of these two changes were delayed for a few months, giving the parties in Northern Ireland an opportunity to reconvene the Northern Ireland Assembly to deal with these issues. In the end, despite a last-minute attempt by the Democratic Unionist Party to restart the Northern Ireland Assembly to block the changes, the statute came into effect.

The constitutional story of the liberalisation of abortion in Northern Ireland is complex, but the Supreme Court's decision effectively held that the Human Rights Act required the UK to reform abortion law in Northern Ireland. If it had been in operation, the first response to that ruling would have come from the Northern Ireland Assembly and Executive, as the necessary legal changes fell within their jurisdiction. Given that these bodies were suspended, the situation was similar to that which would have arisen if the Northern Ireland institutions had refused to follow the court's decision: it fell to UK-level institutions to act to protect the rights of people in Northern Ireland. There are, of course, at least two competing conclusions that could be drawn from the episode. Perhaps the abortion example shows the value of devolution over federalism: institutions at the UK level retained the capacity to step in, even in areas within Northern Ireland's jurisdiction, and were able to protect the rights of citizens, effectively compelling Northern Ireland to comply with the Human Rights Act. Alternatively, perhaps the story shows the weakness of devolution, exposing the unwillingness of central institutions, including the Supreme Court, to tolerate different moral choices made by smaller communities: maybe it should have been left to the institutions of Northern Ireland to decide issues like abortion and same-sex marriage within their territory.

[35] All of the Northern Ireland MPs sitting in the Commons who voted on the abortion amendment voted against it: Sheldon and others (n 33) 791.

[36] Conor McCormick and Thomas Stewart, 'The Legalisation of Same-Sex Marriage in Northern Ireland' (2020) 71 Northern Ireland Legal Quarterly 557.

18.2 THE ROLE OF THE LEGISLATURES

As the example of abortion law in Northern Ireland indicates, the courts are not the only constitutional institutions that regulate and shape devolution: the legislatures, both at the devolved and national levels, also play a role. On both sides of the devolution equation, the legislatures have capacity to constrain and empower their counterparts, transferring power to the other institution or altering the laws enacted by that institution.

At the devolved level, the legislatures can empower the UK Parliament through legislative consent motions.[37] When the UK Parliament wishes to legislate in an area within the jurisdiction of a devolved legislature, it applies to that legislature for a such a motion. This process has been widely used and has not, for the most part, caused controversy. The Institute for Government reports that, as of the start of 2020, more than 350 legislative consent motions had been applied for, and the request was refused on only thirteen occasions.[38] Because of the nature of the devolution settlement, the UK Parliament can, if it wishes, legislate without such consent, and legislation around Brexit, such as the European Union (Withdrawal) Act 2018 and European Union (Withdrawal Agreement) Act 2020 were both enacted without consent motions having been secured. Nevertheless, Brexit apart, the system has worked fairly amicably, with the devolved institutions enabling UK-wide legislation where the advantages of broader regulation seem greater than the attractions of regional variation. The devolution legislation contains parallel powers enabling the UK Parliament to transfer legislative capacity to the devolved institutions. Both the Scotland Act and the Government of Wales Act contain provisions that enable Westminster to transfer, temporarily or permanently, powers to the devolved legislatures.[39]

[37] Adam Evans, 'A Tale as Old as (Devolved) Time? Sewel, Stormont and the Legislative Consent Convention' (2020) 91 Political Quarterly 165.

[38] Institute for Government, 'Sewel Convention' (8 December 2020) www.instituteforgovernment.org.uk/explainers/sewel-convention (accessed 4 March 2021).

[39] Scotland Act 1998, s 30; Government of Wales Act 2006, ss 58, 109. See David Torrance, 'Scottish Devolution: Section 30 Orders' (House of Commons Briefing Paper CBP-8738, 16 December 2019).

These transfers of power are undertaken through delegated legislation, an Order in Council, and require affirmative votes by each House of the UK Parliament and by the devolved institution. The Northern Ireland Act 1998 includes a similar, but more limited, power: there remain areas of competency that Westminster cannot transfer to Northern Ireland through delegated legislation.[40] Additionally, of course, Westminster retains the power to alter the devolution statutes through primary legislation and has done so on a number of occasions.

As well as empowering, the legislatures can also constrain the legislative effectiveness of their counterparts by modifying or removing the statutes enacted by that body. The UK Parliament has unlimited power to alter devolved statutes through primary legislation, but the devolved institutions also possess a limited capacity to alter UK statutes. The devolved legislatures have the capacity to alter statutes that fall within their jurisdictions. The Northern Ireland Act 1998 confers this power explicitly in section 5(6), whilst the power is implicit in the Government of Wales Act 2006 and the Scotland Act 1998, which render legislation of those bodies valid so far as they do not engage reserved matters.

When legislation outside of the conferred areas of the devolution settlements is affected, things become a bit trickier; there are some pieces of legislation that cannot be altered, and others that can, in certain contexts, be modified. In Northern Ireland, the Assembly is unable to alter a small range of legislation, such as the Human Rights Act or elements of the Northern Ireland Act.[41] However, UK legislation that falls within the category of 'reserved' matters can be altered if the consent of the Secretary of State is given, and UK legislation that falls within the category of 'excepted' matters can be altered if consent is given by the Secretary of State, and the changes are 'ancillary to' a provision dealing with transferred or reserved matters.[42] Under the Scotland Act, the Scottish Parliament is unable to modify some pieces of legislation, including the Acts of Union, the European Union (Withdrawal) Act 2018, and most of the Scotland Act itself.[43] Paragraph 2 of Schedule 4 of the latter Act limits the

[40] Northern Ireland Act 1998, s 4. [41] ibid s 6(2). [42] ibid s 8.
[43] Scotland Act 1998, sch 4 paras 1, 4.

Parliament's ability to modify legislation on reserved matters more generally: changes can be made, but only if 'incidental to, or consequential on' an enactment that is within jurisdiction and which, moreover, does not have a greater effect on reserved matters than is necessary.[44] The Welsh devolution scheme is now very similar to the Scottish model.[45]

Whilst the question of the ability of the devolved institutions to alter UK statutes is closely related to the broader question of their jurisdictional reach, discussed earlier in this chapter, the two issues are distinct. After all, a piece of devolved legislation may touch on a reserved category without affecting any UK legislation in that area.[46] When a devolved institution enacts legislation that affects UK legislation, the first question is whether that devolved legislation was within jurisdiction; only if the answer to that question is positive can the further question about its impact on UK legislation be raised. The capacity of the devolved legislatures to alter UK statutes gives them a limited power to regulate the devolution settlement. If Westminster legislates in an area given to the devolved institutions, those institutions have the capacity to modify that legislation. Of course, as the Scottish Parliament discovered with the European Union (Withdrawal) Act 2018, in a constitutional dispute Westminster can put the legislation beyond change if it wishes.

18.3 CONCLUSION: DEVOLUTION OR FEDERALISM?

As a number of scholars have argued, seeing the regionalisation of power within the UK as a straight-forward instance of devolution underplays the radicalism of the 1998 settlement.[47] The hallmark of devolution is that power has been handed down by a central legislature and could be taken back by that body; devolved institutions exercise delegated powers. In a federal system, in contrast,

[44] ibid sch 4 para 3(1).

[45] Government of Wales Act 2006, sch 7B.

[46] *Re UK Withdrawal* (n 2) [51].

[47] Stephen Tierney, 'The Territorial Constitution and the Brexit Process' (2019) 72 Current Legal Problems 59, 65–70; Stephen Sedley, *Ashes and Sparks: Essays on Law and Justice* (Cambridge University Press 2011) 178; Andrew Gamble, 'The Constitutional Revolution in the United Kingdom' (2006) 36 Publius 19.

the constitution divides up power and the national legislature's capacity to alter the balance of regionalisation is limited. The UK's system certainly possesses many features that are characteristic of devolution. For instance, the statutes empowering the devolved legislatures are statutes of the UK Parliament and can, and have been, altered by that Parliament. Furthermore, as the Northern Ireland abortion case shows, Westminster can legislate in devolved matters, even without the agreement of the devolved assembly. Nevertheless, there are also many federal features of the settlement. Whilst the Sewel convention can be overridden (or, perhaps, includes an exception broad enough to allow Westminster considerable latitude), in the vast majority of instances it has been honoured; most of the time, Westminster has accepted the limits on its jurisdiction. And it would be a mistake to think that this acceptance is entirely down to the goodwill of national politicians. The creation of the devolved institutions has created new locations of political power within the Union, power potentially backed by rights of exit. A UK Parliament that wanted to abolish the devolution settlement and return to the unitary state of the 1990s might find this politically difficult and costly. In addition, there are now statutory provisions in the Wales and Scotland Acts declaring that a referendum of the Welsh or Scottish people is required before their devolved legislature can be abolished.[48] As with the inclusion of the Sewel convention into the statutes, these statutory provisions were carefully worded to cheer nationalists whilst allowing future incarnations of Westminster to argue that they were not legally binding, if it became convenient to ignore them. However, as was discussed in chapter five, if a UK Parliament were to ignore these provisions and seek to abolish these institutions, it might discover that its supposedly sovereign capacity is more limited than it anticipated; the courts might be less interested in the precise wording of these provisions than their drafters hoped. In short, whilst the UK is clearly not a federal state, it does contain many federal features, and the capacity of Westminster unilaterally to end the devolution settlement is politically and legally equivocal.

[48] Government of Wales Act 2006, s A1; Scotland Act 1998, s 63A.

IV

THE STATE AND ITS PEOPLE

19

INTRODUCTION TO STATES AND PEOPLE

This chapter introduces three concepts that structure the relationship between the individual and the state: liberty, rights, and citizenship. Under the Old Constitution, liberty was at the forefront of this relationship. For A. V. Dicey, the existence of liberty was a key characteristic of the United Kingdom (UK) constitution; the UK's adherence to the rule of law, considered in the next chapter, entailed that its people were subject only to limits imposed by law and were otherwise free to act as they wished. In the New Constitution, liberty has been supplemented by ideas of rights and citizenship. Whereas liberty, as Dicey understood it, turned on the simple absence of legal constraint, rights confer entitlements partnered by duties on other people, obliging them to act or to refrain from acting in certain ways. A connected shift has occurred in the way in which membership of the UK is conceptualised. Under the Old Constitution, state members were mostly subjects; more or less passive recipients of the state's commands. Under the New Constitution, the standard model of state membership has shifted towards citizenship, a form of state membership in which people possess an equal entitlement to participate in the governance of the state.

19.1 LIBERTY

Sir Isaiah Berlin, in his lecture, 'Two Concepts of Liberty', distinguished between negative and positive liberty. Negative liberty is freedom from constraint and exists where a person is free to act without the interference of others.[1] This conception of liberty was championed by J. S. Mill and dominated Victorian political

[1] Isaiah Berlin, 'Two Concepts of Liberty' in Isaiah Berlin (ed), *Four Essays on Liberty* (Oxford University Press 1969) 169–70.

The United Kingdom Constitution. N. W. Barber, Oxford University Press. © Nick Barber 2021.
DOI: 10.1093/oso/9780198852315.003.0019

discourse.[2] For Mill, the preservation of negative liberty was a guiding moral precept: people's liberty should only be interfered with when their actions threatened to cause harm to others.[3] The state's role was, then, to police people's interactions, ensuring that one person's liberty was not encroached upon by the actions of another.[4] Mill's harm principle, the assertion that before conduct is proscribed some sort of harm must be demonstrated to follow from it, is a good rule of thumb for legislators: if it is difficult to specify the harm that a criminal offence seeks to prevent, the law might not be necessary. During the twentieth century, Mill's work was often cited to justify the liberalisation of criminal law, and was frequently invoked during debates over the legalisation of homosexuality in the 1960s.[5] However, whilst the attractions of Mill's account are easy to grasp, there are problems with this simple approach to liberty. Most basically, the core idea of 'harm' is left vague in Mill's work. Whilst Mill stands against paternalism, requiring that the person being 'harmed' identify it as such, what that person can reasonably define as harm is left open. Most actions could be said to 'harm' somebody, even if it is just the distress caused by being aware that the conduct is undertaken by others.[6] More profoundly, Mill's conception of liberty is compatible with people living empty, miserable, lives: it seeks to create space for people to flourish, but does not require that they possess opportunities for flourishing. Someone living with extreme poverty, ill-health, and lacking education may enjoy broad liberty, in that there are no constraints set by others on their actions, but may be unable to make much of their life; the 'liberty' they supposedly enjoy might be worthless.

Berlin's second concept of liberty, positive liberty, focuses on what people are able to do, rather than what they are prevented from doing. There are two strands to the idea of positive liberty, both of which turn on the value of self-authorship, that is, being

[2] Dylan Lino, 'The Rule of Law and the Rule of Empire: A. V. Dicey in Imperial Context' (2018) 81 Modern Law Review 739, 740.

[3] John Stuart Mill, 'On Liberty' in John Stuart Mill, *On Liberty and Other Essays* (John Gray (ed), Oxford University Press 2008) 14.

[4] ibid 83.

[5] HLA Hart, *Law, Liberty, and Morality* (Oxford University Press 1963).

[6] See Mill (n 3) 108–109.

able to decide for yourself how you live your life. The first strand brings forward the importance of opportunity: a person enjoys liberty to the extent that they are able to choose from a valuable range of options.[7] One of the state's tasks is to ensure this range of opportunities exists. Some of these measures relate to the ability to choose itself: poor health, a lack of education, and poverty, are all factors which may prevent people from taking up opportunities which would otherwise be open to them. The state has a responsibility to ensure that people have the capacity to choose, that they are able to understand and reflect upon the options open to them. Other measures relate to the spread of options. For instance, the state might support and encourage the creation of businesses, societies, and families, and might try to ensure that the opportunities for individuals that exist within these social entities are valuable, seeking to prevent abusive relationships. The second strand of positive liberty brings forward the idea of control: a person enjoys liberty to the extent that they are not subject to the domination of others. Republican political theorists, such as Philip Pettit, argue that people are not free when others have the capacity to interfere with their lives on an arbitrary basis.[8] Preventing domination requires the existence of structures through which people can participate in decisions that affect them; rather than being subject to the will of another, these decisions are their decisions, the products of processes in which they were engaged.[9] At this point, constitutional scholars inspired by republican political thought head off in different directions. For some, it is the unelected executive and judges who present a risk of domination, making decisions in which the people, through election, cannot participate. Adam Tomkins, for example, argues that republicanism requires that the legislature

[7] This account of liberty is at the forefront of Joseph Raz's work: Joseph Raz, *The Morality of Freedom* (Clarendon Press 1988).

[8] Philip Pettit, *Republicanism: A Theory of Freedom and Government* (Oxford University Press 1997) ch 2.

[9] Pettit would reject the characterisation of republicanism as a form of positive liberty, presenting it as a political theory that seeks to prevent domination: ibid 27–31. Nevertheless, republicanism can be considered 'positive' in the sense that it requires the creation of institutional structures and the conferral on individuals of rights to participate in decisions.

make decisions about collective action, and he is critical of aspects of the Human Rights Act 1998 that have empowered judges at the expense of parliamentarians.[10] In sharp contrast, other scholars see the legislature as a potential hazard, an institution through which the majority can dominate the minority, and look to the courts to mitigate this risk. For Alon Harel, republicanism requires constitutional entrenchment of rights so that citizens are not at the mercy of their legislatures, with the courts enabling citizens to compel the state to explain and justify its decisions.[11] Whilst the courts are not a democratic forum, they remain, on Harel's account, an institution through which individuals can participate in decisions that affect them.

19.2 RIGHTS

Whilst the idea of liberty provided a lens through which some Victorian scholars analysed the UK constitution, their modern counterparts are more likely to invoke the concept of rights, presenting the relationship between the individual and the state as a set of entitlements and duties. Although rights are a central part of modern constitutional discourse, their nature and institutional implications are often unclear. First, it can be hard to unpick the distinctive nature of a right; that is, what the existence of a right implies for both the right-holder and those around her. Secondly, the basis of rights is unclear. Rights are normally presented as features of the world that are distinct from the rights-holder: in contrast to, say, an individual's wishes or desires, which are grounded in their mental states, rights are external entities that the individual can invoke. Given this, where do these rights come from? Finally, there is a question of enforcement: if a person does possess a right, how, if at all, should the state respond to its existence? The question of enforcement is one which will dominate the remaining three chapters of this book.

[10] Adam Tomkins, 'The Role of the Courts in the Political Constitution' (2010) 60 University of Toronto Law Journal 1, 2–7.

[11] Alon Harel, *Why Law Matters* (Oxford University Press 2015) 150–52, 192–93.

Starting with the nature of rights, the difference between a right and a bare interest is that rights ground duties. Rights are correlative, that is, they go in two directions: a right implies an entitlement possessed by one person tied to a duty owed by another. To say that I have a right not to be tortured is, simultaneously, to say that others are under a duty not to torture me. A further feature of rights is that the duties they impose are distinct from the interests and wishes that the rights-holder has in their fulfilment.[12] So, my right to freedom of expression may impose duties on others even if I have little to say and no wish to say it, whilst my right not to be enslaved applies even if I, bizarrely, want to sell myself into slavery. Conversely, there can be situations in which my interest in you doing something is very strong indeed, but you are under no duty to act, and no right is present. If, for example, you have a rare car part that I need to fix my car, a car I urgently need, I have a strong interest in acquiring the item but no right that you give or sell it to me.

At least two, broad, schools of thought exist as to the source of these moral rights: those theories which are consequentialist, grounded in the outcomes that rights protection brings, and those which are deontological, grounded in some aspect of humanity that generates duties in others. Consequentialist accounts of rights contend that giving individuals rights provides benefits for society as a whole. Even if in a particular instance a right is protected at the expense of the public interest, the public interest, over time, is advanced by the existence of rights: there might, for example, be immediate benefits to be gained from torturing a prisoner, but these benefits would be outweighed by the misery of living in a society in which torture was a possibility. In contrast, deontological accounts of rights, commonly with roots in religion or in the philosophy of Immanuel Kant, identify some feature of what it means to be human, and argue that this feature generates duties on others. So, perhaps, some fundamental sense of moral equality grounds rights: I recognise myself as a moral agent, as an entity whose life matters with the capacity to take decisions and pursue projects, and I should recognise you

[12] Although sometimes rights can be created or waived by choice—as with, for example, rights created by promises and contracts.

as a moral agent, too. Rights are then built out of reflection on this idea of moral equality; there are some actions that run contrary to a person's status as a moral agent, and so should never be undertaken.

Consequentialist and deontological accounts of rights often reach similar conclusions, with theorists disagreeing over the basis of the rights but agreeing on their content. Nevertheless, there are some potential differences between the models of rights generated by these traditions. First, consequentialist models of rights tend to see rights as having weight rather than as being absolutes; the idea the rights can be balanced, or can be balanced with the wider public interest, may be grounded in this tradition. Secondly, it is harder, although far from impossible, for those from the deontic rights tradition to explain positive rights, such as rights to be given a benefit such as education or healthcare. Deontic models of rights tend to present rights as limitations, as constraints on the impositions the community can place on the individual which leave space for individuals to flourish, rather than as things which facilitate this flourishing.

The existence and contents of moral rights may depend on context. There are some rights which may be present whenever two people encounter each other. Even a couple of people, stranded on a desert island, would still possess a basic set of rights: for example, each would possess the right not to be tortured and the right to undertake religious practices without interference. This basic set of rights might be considered *human* rights, in the sense that they are rights that all people, at all times, possess. Other moral rights might be dependent on social context. Rights to healthcare, education, social support, and so on might be viable in some communities but not in others, and the extent of the entitlement might vary. The implications of a right to healthcare, for example, might depend on the resources available to the group. These *social* rights might develop as the community develops. Finally, there might be some moral rights that arise when states come into existence. Once a state is created, those under its authority may be entitled to be treated in a certain way, as citizens, rather than as subjects. The right that states treat their people as citizens may be the primary *civil* right, but it breaks down into a collection of narrower rights relating to creation of the office of citizenship, discussed later in this chapter.

Looking at the legal articulation of rights, a divide can be drawn between those which are presented as absolute and those which are qualified. Article 3 of the European Convention on Human Rights is an example of an absolute right, proscribing the use of torture in all situations. Article 10(1) of the Convention, in contrast, sets out a right to freedom of expression, but this is quickly qualified by Article 10(2), which contains a list of permissible grounds for restricting that right, with the riders that these restrictions must be 'prescribed by law and . . . necessary' for the grounds pursued. Under this formulation, the right must be balanced against other objectives before the permissible scope of state action can be determined.

These legal formulations reflect different scholarly views about the nature of rights. For some, rights and the public interest (and, indeed, rights and other rights) are frequently in conflict, and it falls to legislators and judges to strike balances between these competing claims. On these accounts, the reach of rights can be lavish, encompassing almost all activities, and the hard work is done when the balancing of competing considerations is undertaken.[13] In contrast, others argue that rights are, by their very nature, absolutes; they protect individuals against collective decisions which prioritise the interests of the group. Talk of balancing rights and the public interest consequently misconceives the nature of rights.[14] As Ronald Dworkin put it, rights are 'trumps' that protect the individual from the community.[15] On

[13] Kai Möller, *The Global Model of Constitutional Rights* (Oxford University Press 2012); Mattias Kumm, 'Who Is Afraid of the Total Constitution? Constitutional Rights as Principles and the Constitutionalization of Private Law' (2006) 7 German Law Journal 341.

[14] Grégoire Webber, 'Rights and Persons' in Grégoire Webber and others (eds), *Legislated Rights: Securing Human Rights Through Legislation* (Cambridge University Press 2018) 32–39; Paul Yowell, 'From Universal Rights to Legislated Rights' in Grégoire Webber and others (eds), *Legislated Rights: Securing Human Rights Through Legislation* (Cambridge University Press 2018) 129–33.

[15] Ronald Dworkin, *Taking Rights Seriously* (Harvard University Press 1978) xi, 197–99.

this understanding, rights are much narrower and, when they can be invoked, more potent.

The relationship between legal and moral rights is complex. Legal rights find their source in legal materials, statutes, and case law, and there is an element of artificiality about them; these rights are the creation of law-makers within the constitution, and amount to rules that structure and guide legal reasoning. In contrast, moral rights are commonly presented as existing separate from law and, indeed, separate from the community's understanding of rights. When, for example, a slave argues that their moral right not to be enslaved has been violated, it is no answer to point out that the law enables slavery, or even that slavery is accepted by the community; both the law and the community might be wrong. The gap between moral and legal rights is, in some instances, morally required; whilst the law should strive to be what, morally speaking, it ought to be, it does not follow that legal rights ought always to be identical to their moral counterparts. Legal rights might be more limited or more expansive than moral rights.

In terms of limitation, on the one hand, because legal rights are, normally, intended to be used in court, there will be situations in which it would be a mistake to transpose the moral right directly into law. So, even if there is a moral right to education, we might conclude that putting such a broad right into law would ask too much of the courts, which lack the capacities to specify what should count as 'education' or determine the best way to provide people with this benefit. Legal rights should also be more limited than moral rights when it would be oppressive to marshal the law in the defence of moral rights; so, for instance, adultery might amount to a violation of rights, but it would be excessive to use the law to prevent such breaches. Just because we have identified a moral right, it need not follow that judges should be asked to apply this right in law.

On the other hand, legal rights can be more expansive than their moral counterparts. This might be because the legal right is specifying an element of a broader moral right, and that specification could have been made in a number of different ways. If there is a moral right to education, for instance, even if that right is not transposed into the legal world in its entirety, narrower legal rights may yet need to be created to realise its demands: perhaps parents are given a legal right to a certain number of hours of pre-school care from their local authorities for children under five, or perhaps sixteen year olds are given a legal right requiring their schools to permit them to sit national exams.[16] The moral right to education requires a set of legal rights for its realisation, but there are a variety of legal rights that could play this role and a variety of forms they could take: the legal right to pre-school care could start at the age of three or four, and the age at which people have a right to sit exams could be set at fifteen, sixteen, or seventeen. The law must pick one of these options, and this choice is not determined by the moral right. Legal rights may also be more expansive than moral rights when there is a risk that a narrowly drawn legal right may fail to achieve the ends of the moral right, and over-extension is less morally risky than under-extension. So, for instance, the moral right to freedom of expression might not extend to pornography, but the legal right could be more inclusive, fearing that excluding pornography risks the right failing to protect valid, if controversial, works of art.

19.3 CITIZENSHIP

The relationships that most people have with states can be placed on a spectrum, running from subjecthood, on the one side, to citizenship, on the other.[17] Subjects are state members who are passive recipients of state commands; they are not constitutionally entitled to participate in the production of those commands (although they may sometimes be consulted) and they are unable legally to challenge the commands once produced. The most attractive form of subjecthood is found in benign monarchies or dictatorships, where the ruler seeks to exercise power in the interests of her people; in such a state, the relationship between

[16] Maris Köpcke, 'Why It Takes Law to Realise Human Rights' in Grégoire Webber and others (eds), *Legislated Rights: Securing Human Rights Through Legislation* (Cambridge University Press 2018).

[17] There are also some less common forms, such as monarch, dictator, and tyrant.

state and individual resembles that of a child to her parents. In sharp contrast, citizens share in the government of the state, ruling and being ruled in turn.[18] The commands of the state are their commands, the products of processes in which they participate. Consequently, citizenship brings with it responsibility: as Aristotle put it, the citizen shares in the honours and the dishonours of the state.[19]

Citizenship is partly constructed through law. It is often a legal title conferred by the state, with laws specifying who is and who is not a citizen, but the legal aspect of citizenship is not exhausted by the conferral of this label: citizens also possess a range of legal rights. For instance, they have the right to vote, the right to stand for office, and the right not to be arbitrarily excluded from posts within the executive. Citizens also possess the right to access the court, enabling them to ensure that, when state power is exercised over them, that power has a legal basis. As well as a legal aspect, citizenship has a social dimension.[20] A citizen is treated by her fellow citizens in a distinctive way: they recognise that she is entitled to engage in discussion about state action, and that her interests are ones that the state should protect and advance. There are things that public bodies can do to help foster the social aspect of citizenship, but the moral rights of citizenship are not just directed upwards, towards state institutions, but are also directed horizontally, towards other citizens. That citizenship extends beyond a simple legal title means that people can be subjects who are labelled citizens, or citizens who are labelled subjects. The reality of a person's constitutional relationship with their state may be different from its legal form and, indeed, the basic form of state membership in a country may shift over time, moving along the spectrum between subjecthood and citizenship without any express legal acknowledgment of this change.

[18] Aristotle, *The Politics and The Constitution of Athens* (Stephen Everson (ed), B Jowett (trs), Cambridge University Press 1996) III.IV, 1277b13–22.

[19] ibid III.V, 1278a35–36.

[20] Joseph Carens, *Culture, Citizenship and Community: A Contextual Exploration of Justice as Evenhandedness* (Oxford University Press 2000) ch 7.

19.4 CONCLUSION

The three concepts introduced in this chapter—liberty, rights, and citizenship—all speak to the relationship between the individual and the state. It would be a mistake, however, to think of them as rivals. Many constitutional scholars would regard the three as compatible and, indeed, mutually supportive. Liberty, in all its forms, is protected and fostered by rights, whilst the identification of rights implies that not every interest grounds a duty, and so creates space for liberty. Citizenship is, in part, a creature of rights, created by a mesh of legal and social entitlements and duties between individuals, state institutions, and the community, and is also a key element of the constitutional process through which decisions about rights are made, determining the spread of legal rights that are available to people.

20

THE RULE OF LAW AND LIBERTY

The rule of law requires that the law make the differences it purports to make: legal prohibitions should prevent the conduct they proscribe, and legal rights should be effective, able to be relied upon by those they empower. There are two aspects to the principle. First, the rule of law requires that laws be expressed in a way that enables people to obey the law; its rules must not be hopelessly vague, retrospective, or contaminated by some other flaw that makes them radically difficult to follow. Secondly, the rule of law requires that the social context in which the law operates is such that people are led to obey the law; not only is the law capable of obedience, it must also, in reality, be obeyed. Under the rule of law, people's legal rights are effective, and their lawful activities are not disrupted by unlawful pressure from public or private actors. Where these two aspects are satisfied, the rule of law ties together the formal rules of the legal system and the reality of the rules that structure power within society; this is a society that can truly be said to be 'ruled' by law. Any community that uses law as a tool of governance can be said to be characterised by the rule of law to a degree, but states realise the principle to a greater or lesser extent; no real-world state has managed to ensure the perfect equation of law and power.

This chapter begins by looking at the nature of the rule of law, starting with its seminal formulation in the work of A. V. Dicey. The chapter then examines the operation of the principle within the UK constitution, in particular the emergence of the direct legal recognition of the rule of law within some recent cases. Finally, the chapter concludes by considering whether the rule of law has been supplanted by the Human Rights Act 1998 and whether the positive protection of rights established by that statute has replaced the older protections of liberty brought by the rule of law.

The United Kingdom Constitution. N. W. Barber, Oxford University Press.
DOI: 10.1093/oso/9780198852315.003.0020

20.1 THE NATURE OF THE RULE OF LAW

Although there are many interpretations of the rule of law on offer, amongst the earliest and most influential was provided by A. V. Dicey, in his classic account of the UK constitution.[1] Dicey argued that the rule of law was one of the cornerstones of the UK constitution and, alongside parliamentary sovereignty, that it structured the constitutional order. Dicey divided his account of the rule of law into three parts.[2] The first two parts embodied the demands of the rule of law, whilst the third set out the benefits brought by the principle.

The first part of Dicey's rule of law requires that individuals not be punished unless they have committed a distinct breach of the law.[3] Part of this requirement relates to the form laws should take: laws should be expressed in a manner that enables people to predict the actions that will lead to punishment. Dicey warned against laws that gave people in positions of power 'wide, arbitrary, or discretionary powers of constraint'.[4] Individuals should not be subjected to the caprice of officials, even if that caprice had received legal sanction. But this part of Dicey's rule of law is not merely concerned with the mode of expression of legal rules; it also engaged with the application of those rules within the community. The rule of law does not just require that people can determine when the law permits or requires the infliction of a punishment; it also requires that people only suffer punishment when it has been mandated by the law. So, when Dicey recounted the story of Voltaire being beaten by the servants of the Duc de Rohan—or, as Dicey put it, 'thrashed by lackeys in the presence of their noble master'—he was drawing attention to the failure of French law to constrain de Rohan's capacity to inflict harm.[5] The legal rules did not permit the Duke to punish the author, but the punishment went ahead, all the same; the social context in which the law operated allowed Voltaire to be punished even though

[1] There were many precursors to Dicey's account, and the ideas contained within the principle are as old as political philosophy itself.

[2] AV Dicey, *Introduction to the Study of the Law of the Constitution* (10th edn, MacMillan 1959) ch 4.

[3] ibid 188–93, 202. [4] ibid 188. [5] ibid 190.

the law did not permit this act. There is a pair of intertwined demands in Dicey's first element of the rule of law which combine to render the exercise of force within the state predictable. The rules mandating punishment are expressed in a manner that allow people to predict the infliction of legally sanctioned punishment and, in addition, people can be confident that they will not be exposed to non-legally sanctioned punishment.

The second part of Dicey's rule of law is the mirror image of the first. It requires that everyone, including state officials, be bound by the 'ordinary law of the land and amenable to the jurisdiction of the ordinary tribunals'.[6] Once again, there is a formal aspect to this requirement: the rule of law is set in opposition to the grant of arbitrary legal immunities.[7] This does not mean that the same law applies, or should apply, to everyone: people who occupy specific legal offices have different legal duties and rights. Most obviously, state officials have special legal duties and special legal rights, but these legal offices also exist in the private sphere: company directors, trustees, landlords, spouses—all take on distinct legal duties and rights when they take on their roles. Although Dicey does not make this explicit, it seems that the rule of law requires that these special rights and duties be justified and explained by the legal role occupied by an individual; when they can be so explained, these variations in legal rights and duties are not arbitrary.[8]

As well as not including arbitrary exceptions within the substance of the law, the rule of law further requires that there not be any practical immunities from the ordinary operation of the law; that the law is, in reality, applied to those who break its demands. Once again, there is a social dimension to this aspect of Dicey's rule of law. Returning to Voltaire, the Duke's capacity to inflict punishment stemmed from his practical immunity from the ordinary operation of the law. As Dicey puts it, the rule of law is imperilled where certain people are able to 'defy the law';[9] they

[6] ibid 194. [7] ibid 195, 204.

[8] TRS Allan, *Constitutional Justice: A Liberal Theory of the Rule of Law* (Oxford University Press 2001) 21–25.

[9] Dicey (n 2) 194.

enjoy immunities based on power, even though not recognised by the law.

Dicey's two aspects of the rule of law are complementary, amounting to a broad demand that power be exercised through the law. A strength of Dicey's account is that he does not confine the rule of law to the conduct of state officials; the principle addresses the exercise of power within society more broadly. Whilst the state is one location of power within society, it is far from the only such site, and the rule of law can be imperilled by private actors just as effectively as by state actors. Sometimes, this threat will arise at the national level. Dicey presented trade unions as an example of potentially powerful bodies that can pose a threat to the rule of law, but the list could be widened: privileged individuals, multinational companies, and wealthy pressure groups may also present challenges. On other occasions, threats may arise at a micro-level, within relationships such as between employer and employee, landlord and tenant, or inside family structures. As Jeff King argues, threats to the rule of law are frequently grounded in inequalities of power between actors in society, as the vulnerability of one party to another impedes the capacity of that party to make use of its legal rights.[10] The inequality of power is thus compounded as the initial inequality, grounded in material or physical inequalities, leads to a legal inequality. The weaker party is less able to rely on its legal rights than its stronger counterpart, and the ability of those within the community to rely upon the law is reduced.

Dicey's third element of the rule of law was not a further requirement of the principle, but, instead, a conclusion: the benefits conferred by the rule of law. According to Dicey, the rule of law protected liberty by requiring the state to make explicit the limitations on people's allowed area of action; the legal order was structured such that whatever was not forbidden was permitted. The chapters that followed Dicey's account of the rule of law go on to discuss freedoms of the person, of discussion, and assembly,

[10] Jeff King, *The Social Dimension of the Rule of Law* (forthcoming). See also NW Barber, 'Must Legalistic Conceptions of the Rule of Law Have a Social Dimension?' (2004) 17 Ratio Juris 474.

and, in each case, liberty was presented as the space left to the individual after the encroachments of the law.

Dicey's account of the rule of law is far from the only interpretation of the principle on offer. Alternative accounts of the rule of law depart from Dicey in one or both of two respects: first, there is disagreement over the normative level at which the principle of the rule of law operates; second, there is disagreement over the nature of law, and, as a consequence, over the implications of claiming that a society is governed by law.

As to the first area of disagreement, the principle of the rule of law may operate on at least three levels: as a moral principle, as a convention, or as a legal rule. As a moral principle, the rule of law applies to all states at all times: it is a principle that speaks to how power should be exercised over people within states and which contends that, in some situations, regulating power through law is morally valuable.[11] Approached as a moral principle, the content of the rule of law is whatever, morally speaking, it ought to be. So, in Joseph Raz's account of the principle, the rule of law consists of the features of legal systems which must be present if a society can be said to be governed by law, and, when societies ought to be governed by law, there is a moral reason to create and support these features.[12] In contrast, when taken as a convention, the rule of law is a principle that is recognised by members of the political community and which shapes their conduct. Approached as a convention, the content of the rule of law is rooted in the beliefs of the political community in which the principle operates. Arguably, Dicey presented the rule of law as a convention, as a principle that guided political actors in the UK, but which was not a discrete legal right that litigants could, at that time, plead before the courts. Finally, taken as a legal rule, the rule of law is found within the texts of statutes and the decisions of judges, and is a principle that can be pleaded in cases and which grounds legal claims.[13] For many years, Trevor Allan has argued for a form of

[11] Joseph Raz, 'The Rule of Law and its Virtue' in Joseph Raz (ed), *The Authority of Law: Essays on Law and Morality* (2nd edn, Oxford University Press 2009) 211.

[12] ibid.

[13] Se-shauna Wheatle, *Principled Reasoning in Human Rights Adjudication* (Hart Publishing 2017) ch 3.

the rule of law at this level, and now judges are making similar arguments, presenting the rule of law as a principle that can be invoked to challenge administrative acts and, perhaps, even statutes.[14] Versions of the rule of law could exist at all three of these levels, and the demands of those principles might, justifiably, differ. Some of the apparent disagreements over the principle might, then, not be disagreements at all, as the label 'the rule of law' has been attached to distinct, if related, principles, operating at different constitutional levels.

The second area of disagreement turns on the nature of law. If the rule of law is tied to the application of law in society, its demands will depend on what we understand the application of the law to entail. For some writers, especially those from the positivist tradition, the defining purpose of law is narrow: it is an action-guiding institution. In his early work, Joseph Raz drew attention to the authority claims made by law: law necessarily claims to tell people what they ought to do, but the contents of these commands, whether just or unjust, varies widely.[15] The rule of law, then, exists to the extent that law succeeds in guiding action, and the ends to which law is put, whether to advance justice or to commit injustices, are not directly relevant to the principle because laws can be just or unjust.[16] For others, such as Ronald Dworkin and Trevor Allan, the purpose of law is broader than this: law exists to check the coercive power of the state by requiring the state to justify its decisions before the court.[17] On these accounts, the function of law goes beyond guiding action and includes some of the objectives towards which this guidance should be oriented; the failure of the law to protect rights or to assess the justifiability of state power then amounts to a failure to realise the rule of law. The context in which the rule of law

[14] Allan (n 8). The possibility of the rule of law as a legal rule is discussed later in this chapter.

[15] Joseph Raz, 'Authority, Law and Morality' in Joseph Raz (ed), *Ethics in the Public Domain: Essays in the Morality of Law and Politics* (rev edn, Clarendon Press 1995) 216.

[16] Raz, 'Rule of Law and its Virtue' (n 11) 221–23.

[17] Ronald Dworkin, *Law's Empire* (Hart Publishing 1998) 190; TRS Allan, *The Sovereignty of Law: Freedom, Constitution, and Common Law* (Oxford University Press 2013) 23–24, 119–23.

operates may also help determine the purpose of law that underpins its demands. The rule of law is a principle that applies primarily to constitutional orders, states, and the type of law with which it directly engages is state law. The purpose of state law must then ally with the purpose of the state, existing to advance the well-being of state members. If this broader objective is accepted as the point of state law, state law should no longer be considered merely as an instrument to guide action, but as an instrument that guides action towards a certain end. Dicey, and the early Raz, present liberty as something that is to be found in the spaces left by the restrictions of the law—the 'virtue', as Raz puts it, of the rule of law is that when power is regulated through law people are free to act as they choose outside of the law's constraints—but if the purpose of law is broader than simply guiding action, the virtues of the rule of law may be correspondingly greater. Recalling the discussion of negative and positive liberty in the previous chapter, governing through law helps preserve negative liberty by making the exercise of power predictable, but it also creates the possibility for the state to act, creating institutions and undertaking projects to benefit its people, and so fostering their positive liberty. It is only through law that the state can ensure that the social institutions, like education and healthcare, roads, and market regulation, which its people rely upon, exist and function well.

The distance between these approaches to the rule of law may be less than it first appears. Even narrower approaches to the rule of law have expansive implications once we recognise that poverty, lack of education, and power imbalances all impair the action-guiding capacity of law. Moreover, the presence of unjust laws, an unaccountable executive, or administrative decision-makers who enjoy over-wide discretion, may all reduce people's willingness to comply with the law and reduce its effectiveness. If so, even accounts of the rule of law that start from a limited base may end up making broad claims because the contents of the law and the social context in which it operates affect its capacity to guide action. It is, perhaps, considerations such as these that have led Joseph Raz to revise his views radically, refining his account of the rule of law to the point at which it is similar to that provided by Allan and Dworkin. On Raz's new understanding of the rule of law, the principle requires that the government act with the intention of advancing the interests of the governed; this leads to confidence in the law and in the state, and is, in Raz's words, 'a condition of the government's ability to govern well'.[18]

20.2 THE RULE OF LAW IN THE UK

It is easy to underestimate the extent to which the rule of law is realised within the UK constitution. Examinations of the rule of law tend to dwell on those areas in which the UK has fallen short, or where the implications of the principle are subject to debate. Whilst understandable, this risks obscuring the boring truth that, for the vast majority of time, the rule of law is upheld, and, moreover, is upheld without the intervention of agencies such as the police or the courts. The rule of law flourishes because people, including state officials, by and large accept the law should govern their conduct. This is just as well: like all states, the enforcement mechanisms of the UK constitution would be unable to maintain the operation of the law in the face of widespread lawlessness.

Given that the rule of law speaks to the whole of the legal system, a survey of the operation of the rule of law would require an examination of every area of legal activity within the UK, and an assessment of the extent to which the law in each of these areas achieves its objectives. Such an undertaking is plainly beyond the ambitions of this book, and the sections that follow merely seek to pick out some of the more important judicial decisions relating to the principle, decisions that relate to the structures through which the principle is realised.

20.2.1 State Officials Bound By Law

It is sometimes said, wrongly but temptingly, that the rule of law requires that state officials have legal authority for the actions they undertake.[19] This proposition is commonly tied to the case of

[18] Joseph Raz, 'The Law's Own Virtue' (2019) 39 Oxford Journal of Legal Studies 1, 15.

[19] *R v Somerset County Council, ex p Fewings* [1995] 3 All ER 20, 25 (CA); see further Adam Tomkins, 'The Authority of *Entick v Carrington*' in Adam Tomkins and Paul Scott (eds), *Entick v Carrington: 250 Years of the Rule of Law* (Hart Publishing 2015); Timothy Endicott, 'Was *Entick v Carrington* a Landmark?' in Adam

Entick v Carrington, decided in the eighteenth century.[20] Carrington was one of a group of officials who broke into Entick's house, removed some papers, and caused significant damage in the process. Entick sued Carrington for damages in trespass. Carrington, in his defence, argued that he was acting under a warrant issued by the Secretary of State. The court found that there was no legal basis for the issuing of the warrant, and rejected the Secretary of State's bold claim that, because it was necessary for the state to possess a power of entry, the court should conclude that such a power existed. Lord Camden found that as there was no legal authority for Carrington's actions, his conduct constituted a legal wrong, a tort, and Entick was entitled to damages. The decision in *Entick* is certainly important, and does embody a key aspect of the rule of law: if state officials are to act lawfully in ways that would be unlawful for private citizens (breaking into a house, taking away their property) they must be able to point to a legal rule which empowers them so to act. However, *Entick* does not stand for the wider proposition that all actions of state officials require legal authority. There are at least two groups of situations in which prior legal authority is not necessary.

First, some actions by state officials have no implications for people's legal rights and so need no legal authorisation. State officials can, for instance, make apologies and issue advice, with these capacities empowered by social, rather than legal, rules. For example, when David Cameron apologised for the conduct of the army during the Bloody Sunday shootings in 1972, this was widely recognised as an apology made by the prime minister in his official capacity, speaking on behalf of the state.[21] There are no legal rules conferring this capacity on prime ministers, no legal test that allows us to distinguish between the public and private apologies they make, yet people generally recognise that this power exists, and are able to identify those occasions on which officials speak for the state rather than as private individuals.

Tomkins and Paul Scott (eds), *Entick v Carrington: 250 Years of the Rule of Law* (Hart Publishing 2015).

[20] (1765) 19 How St Tr 1030, 95 ER 807.

[21] HC Deb 15 June 2010, vol 511, cols 739–42.

Secondly, on occasion state officials act contrary to the law, yet their actions continue to be treated as actions of the state. In *Entick*, having concluded that Carrington lacked legal authorisation for his conduct, the court treated him as having acted in a private capacity, but sometimes the law attributes these wrongful actions to the public office held by the individual. Because of this attribution, it is possible for public bodies to act unlawfully. Public bodies can, for example, break contracts, unlawfully detain people,[22] commit manslaughter,[23] and, in *M v Home Office*, the House of Lords found that ministers may be liable for contempt in their official capacity for breach of court orders.[24] Some of these instances of attribution are grounded in statute; perhaps most importantly, the Crown Proceedings Act 1947 allows actions in tort and contract to be brought against the Crown. Outside of the Crown, public bodies are treated, in this respect, like private corporate entities and so are able to commit wrongs.[25] Whilst this all seems obvious and sensible, subjecting public bodies to the same constraints as private ones, it is worth noting that the law's willingness to attribute legal wrongs to state actors should surprise us, at least a little. A closer look at *M v Home Office* helps explain why these attributions are remarkable. In that case, a court had issued an order requiring the Home Office to secure the return of an asylum seeker who had been mistakenly deported to Zaire. The Home Secretary was advised that the judge had made an error, that the order issued was beyond the jurisdiction of the court, and, crucially, that the Home Office did not need to obey the order whilst a challenge to its validity was underway. Consequently, the asylum seeker's return flight to London was cancelled, he remained in Zaire, and subsequently disappeared; the opportunity for his return was lost. It transpired that advisers to the Home Secretary had made a mistake; orders of the High Court are valid until set aside, and so should have been obeyed. The question for the House of Lords was whether the Home Secretary could be

[22] *R (Lumba) v Secretary of State for the Home Department* [2011] UKSC 12, [2012] 1 AC 245.

[23] Corporate Manslaughter and Corporate Homicide Act 2007, s 11(1).

[24] [1994] 1 AC 377.

[25] *Mersey Docks and Harbour Board Trustees v Gibbs* (1866) LR 1 HL 93.

liable for contempt in an *official* rather than a *personal* capacity. Personally, the minister, Kenneth Baker, was probably not guilty of contempt as he had acted on advice he was entitled to accept as correct; however, officially, as minister, he was responsible for the correctness of the advice and so, in his official capacity, was liable.[26]

That the question of whether a minister could be officially liable for contempt was a source of legal dispute might partly be explained by the over-broad statement of the rule of law set out at the start of this section: after all, if state officials always required legal authority for the actions they undertake, they could never, in their official capacities, act contrary to law. Sometimes, as in *Entick*, restricting the power of officials in this way allows the courts to provide redress by finding that the erring official acted in a private capacity; but sometimes, as in *M*, the wrong done can only be identified as a product of the official structures in which the act occurred.[27] When the court concludes that a public body has committed a wrong, it does not retrospectively authorise this act, but the decision of the law to allow the attribution of wrongful acts to public bodies does, nevertheless, empower them to act unlawfully. Is this attribution then contrary to the rule of law? Three factors combine to provide a justification, within the context of the rule of law, for the attribution. First, public bodies possess, for good reasons, a wide range of legal powers, many of which are expressed in very broad terms. Secondly, the demands of the law can be unclear; as the minister discovered in *M*, even competent lawyers can be mistaken about its requirements. These two factors lead to a third: there is often significant uncertainty within public bodies and, even more importantly, in the minds of those members of the public who engage with them, about the scope of the bodies' lawful powers. Consequently, public bodies' actions may be effective, in that private individuals and state officials may accept and comply with them, even if they lack a legal basis. In these situations, it would be unrealistic and dangerous

[26] *M v Home Office* (n 24).

[27] To give another example: only a public body can breach a contract formed by that body; the individuals within that institution cannot, when outside of the institution, breach it.

for the law to expect citizens to resist or ignore the unlawful demands of public bodies. Instead of the rule of law requiring that all actions of state officials be legally authorised, it requires that citizens, and other parts of the executive branch, be able to tackle unauthorised acts through the courts. Here, the rule of law is bolstered rather than undermined by the law's attribution of unlawful actions to officials; not to do so would leave individuals vulnerable to abuses of power committed by state officials outside of their area of legal empowerment.

The discretionary powers of public bodies present a challenge for the rule of law. The rule of law requires that law be expressed in such a way that it is capable of being obeyed; part of that requirement is that the laws be framed with sufficient clarity that those who are affected by them are able to predict how power will be exercised over them. But if people's legal entitlements and obligations are being determined by officials empowered by broad discretionary powers, can either the officials or those subject to them truly be said to be ruled by law? For Lord Hewart, writing at the end of the 1920s, the increase in the executive's discretionary powers spelled the rise of a 'new despotism' and amounted to violation of the rule of law.[28] State officials were being given wide discretionary powers which they could use to govern the lives of citizens. But, contrary to Hewart's view, it is simplistic to imagine the rule of law can be realised solely through precisely drafted laws, and many of the broad discretionary powers he argued against help to foster the rule of law, rather than undermine it. Discretionary powers expanded over the course of the twentieth century as the tasks undertaken by the state grew. The state took on a greater role in people's lives, providing a range of social benefits, such as pensions and unemployment support, and took increasing responsibility for their wellbeing, through education and healthcare provision.[29] Many of these tasks are crucial to the operation of the rule of law. To give just two examples, people who cannot read will struggle to access the law, and a society in which the unemployed are left to

[28] Lord Hewart, *The New Despotism* (Ernst Benn Ltd 1929).

[29] Nicholas Timmins, *The Five Giants: A Biography of the Welfare State* (3rd edn, William Collins 2017).

starve will see vast imbalances of power between employers and employees, deterring employees from asserting their legal rights. Rather than a derogation from the principle of the rule of law, the welfare state is a way of realising some of its demands. In Lord Hewart's day, interactions between the rich, the circle in which he lived, may have been strongly characterised by the rule of law, but for the poor, law played a far less significant role.

Partnering this expansion in activity has been an expansion in judicial regulation, as the scope and role of administrative law has grown steadily over the last 100 years. Administrative law encompasses those rules applied by the courts to state officials, and whilst it is an important element of constitutional law, it is such a big and specialised topic that it can only be touched on in this book. In very brief terms, the courts will review the decisions of state officials and public bodies on three grounds: jurisdiction, procedural fairness, and rationality.[30] Jurisdictional review examines whether the body has a legal basis for its action, an examination that in many cases involves a close reading of the statutes that empower and shape the body's discretion. Procedural fairness requires that the decision has been made in a fair way: those affected by a decision are generally entitled to a hearing before it is made and, after making the decision, the public body must normally explain its reasoning. Finally, the courts will examine the rationality of the decision, scrutinising its substance. Judges will check that decision-makers considered relevant factors, that they were not swayed by irrelevant factors, and will assess whether the balance struck between these factors was reasonable or proportionate. The development of administrative law was largely ignored by Dicey and caused Hewart concern, but, as Jeffrey Jowell has argued, one of the key objectives of administrative law is the working through of the demands of the rule of law in the modern welfare state, responding to the growth of discretionary powers.[31] Administrative law helps ensure that these powers are used in a

[30] What follows is a radically abbreviated account of administrative law. For a fuller account see Paul Craig, *Administrative Law* (8th edn, Sweet & Maxwell 2016).

[31] Jeffrey Jowell, 'The Rule of Law' in Jeffrey Jowell and Colm O'Cinneide (eds), *The Changing Constitution* (9th edn, Oxford University Press 2019). See also Allan, *Sovereignty of Law* (n 17) 105–10, ch 6; Mark Elliott, *The Constitutional Foundations of Judicial Review* (Hart Publishing 2001); Wheatle (n 13).

predictable and non-arbitrary way. The law requires that when public bodies make decisions they base their decisions on reasons appropriate to their role; the decision should not rest on the personal idiosyncrasies of the officials making it, but should, instead, be grounded in the values and objectives of the state, and the policies it has developed to condition this discretion. Consequently, the exercise of public power by the administration is rendered more predictable and is depersonalised: officials possess discretion, but it is legally-bounded and conditioned.

20.2.2 Private Persons Bound By Law

Much writing on the rule of law focuses on the application of the law to state officials, but, as Dicey recognised, the capacity of the law to regulate private power is equally important. The rule of law is undermined where individuals are vulnerable to unlawful pressure from others, pressure that shapes their conduct against their will or which prevents them from asserting their legal rights. These private abuses can be every bit as harmful as abuses of public power. Someone suffering abuse within a family—a child, a spouse, an elderly relative—might find that they are unable to access the law within that relationship, even whilst living within a state that is, generally, strongly characterised by the principle.

Assessing the effectiveness of the law within private relationships would be a huge undertaking. As was discussed earlier, the likelihood is that such a survey would reveal that, in the UK, many areas of law are highly efficacious, and breaches of law are exceptional. Focusing on the courts, judges play a central role in maintaining the effectiveness of law within private relations, a role which is primarily accomplished simply by doing their jobs well: recalling the discussion of the separation of powers earlier in this book, the rule of law makes similar demands to that principle, requiring that the judges apply, and develop, the law in a predictable manner, giving people confidence that the courts will uphold the law. As we saw, however, the courts cannot maintain this confidence without help; the capacity of the courts to vindicate the rule of law is limited by their reliance on the executive branch.[32] It is agencies within the executive that provide

[32] See ch 9.

administrative support for the courts, which investigate possible breaches of the law, and which enforce, where necessary, the decisions of the judges. Whilst the judges have the capacity to review a wide range of executive decision-making, through the process of judicial review discussed in the previous section, they have a particularly strong interest in reviewing decisions of the executive relating to the courts. These decisions directly affect the capacity of the courts to succeed in their constitutional role; without the support of the executive the courts will fail, no matter how skilled and diligent the judges.

If breaches of the law are tolerated by public bodies, and instances of law-breaking are not brought before the courts, the capacity of the courts to uphold the rule of law is reduced. The courts regard public bodies as under a duty to resist unlawful pressure, at least up to a point. The classic example of a judicial demand for executive robustness in the face of illegality is the nineteenth century case of *Beatty v Gillbanks*.[33] In *Beatty*, members of the Salvation Army, a body opposed to gambling and in favour of temperance, were convicted of unlawful assembly and bound over to keep the peace after their march was violently disrupted by the Skeleton Army, a body in favour of gambling and opposed to temperance. The court held that the conviction was a mistake: the violent acts of the Skeleton Army could not justify the punishment of members of the Salvation Army, whose conduct had remained peaceful throughout. Similarly, a century later, in *R v Coventry City Council, ex p Phoenix Aviation*, protests surrounding live animal exports were used as a reason by public bodies to ban such exports from their docks and airports, claiming that the disruption caused by such demonstrations was too great.[34] The court, invoking the principle of the rule of law, held that the public bodies could not ban the lawful transport of live animals because of unlawful pressure brought by protestors. In both *Beatty* and *Phoenix*, the court required public bodies to uphold the rule of law: people who were acting lawfully should not have their liberty restricted by the unlawful acts of others, and it was the responsibility of public bodies to uphold the law and bring potential breaches before the courts.

[33] (1882) 9 QBD 308. [34] [1995] 3 All ER 37.

However, *Beatty* and *Phoenix* are high-water mark cases, at the top end of decisions requiring resistance by public bodies. Weighing against this, and, indeed, weighing against the rule of law, are practical considerations that can make it hard to enforce the law, where the costs of policing or prosecution might be excessive. In *R v Chief Constable of Sussex, ex p International Trader's Ferry Ltd*, in contrast to *Phoenix*, the House of Lords declined to require the police to maintain access to the ports on a daily basis for the exporters of animals: given the limited resources possessed by the police, it was reasonable for them to limit exports to a couple of days each week.[35] And if the Salvation Army were to undertake their march today, they might find that the threat of unlawful violence from the Skeleton Army would be sufficient to empower the police to limit their activities.[36] Perhaps the nadir of judicial reluctance to require public bodies to uphold the law is the recent case of *R (Corner House Research) v Director of the Serious Fraud Office*. This case involved an investigation into alleged bribes paid by a UK company to prominent people in Saudi Arabia. The Saudi government warned the UK that if the investigation continued, they would suspend security cooperation, and the UK government, in turn, encouraged the Director of the Serious Fraud Office to end the investigation, which he then did. Whilst the High Court had delivered a strong judgment, grounded in the rule of law, against the decision, warning that 'the impotence of the law invites at least dismay, if not outrage',[37] the House of Lords managed to swallow its dismay and its outrage, and found for the director.[38] His statutory discretion over the conduct of investigations permitted him to close an investigation on national

35 [1999] 2 AC 418.

36 Public Order Act 1986, ss 11–13. See also *Austin v Commissioner of Police of the Metropolis* [2009] UKHL 5, [2009] AC 564, where the House of Lords held that the police were entitled to confine lawful protesters because others might have been planning to act unlawfully. Ewing and Gearty argue that, even when decided, *Beatty* was exceptional: Keith Ewing and Conor Gearty, *The Struggle for Civil Liberties: Political Freedom and the Rule of Law in Britain, 1914–1945* (Oxford University Press 2001) 30–34.

37 *R (Corner House Research) v Director of the Serious Fraud Office* [2008] EWHC 714 (Admin), [2009] AC 756 [7].

38 *R (Corner House Research) v Director of the Serious Fraud Office* [2008] UKHL 60, [2009] AC 756.

security grounds, in particular where the impact on national security could threaten the lives of UK citizens. *Corner House* sits uncomfortably alongside Dicey's celebration of the rule of law: whilst the criminal law applies equally to the weak and to the powerful, it seems that, sometimes, it does not apply to the *very* powerful.

A further area in which the courts have sought to protect the integrity of the judicial process from executive decisions is that of access to courts. Access to the court (or to a court-like institution) is a crucial part of the rule of law; the contents of the law may be crystal clear, but if individuals are unable to secure redress for its breach, it is virtually worthless. In the case of *R (UNISON) v Lord Chancellor*, the Supreme Court reviewed the fees set by the Lord Chancellor for bringing claims to the Employment Tribunal and to the Employment Appeals Tribunal.[39] The introduction of fees was undertaken through a statutory instrument, a form of delegated legislation, and it was an innovation: access to the tribunals had formerly been free.[40] As this was a decision of a minister, the fees order was susceptible to judicial review. Following the recent trend for Supreme Court decisions to be argued in terms of constitutional principle, the judges identified two that were relevant: the constitutional right of access to courts, and the presumption that rights given by one statute will not be reduced by delegated legislation passed under another statute.[41] These were presented as principles that were implicit within statutes, and which should be used in their interpretation; the statutory power possessed by the Lord Chancellor should be read through their interpretive lens. Having reflected on the financial resources available to those who made use of the tribunals, the Supreme Court concluded that the level of fees set made it unaffordable to bring a case.[42] Indeed, as some of the decisions made by the employment

[39] [2017] UKSC 51, [2020] AC 869; see also *R v Lord Chancellor, ex p Witham* [1998] QB 575.

[40] The purported source of the power to create the statutory instrument was the Tribunals, Courts and Enforcement Act 2007, s 42(1).

[41] Alan Bogg, 'The Common Law Constitution at Work: *R (on the Application of UNISON) v Lord Chancellor*' (2018) 81 Modern Law Review 509.

[42] Perhaps one of the most remarkable things about the *UNISON* case was the Supreme Court's confident engagement with statistical evidence about the impact of the fees order.

tribunal were for small sums or were not awards of money at all, the fees order made it irrational to bring a claim: a successful litigant might end up paying more to get to the court than they would receive at the end of the case. Finding the fees order to be outside of the jurisdiction conferred on the Lord Chancellor by the statute, the Supreme Court struck down the decision: the fees order inhibited access to the tribunals and rendered some of the employee's statutory rights worthless.

20.2.3 A Note on the Rule of Law as a Legal Rule

In *UNISON*, the rule of law was presented as a broad constitutional principle that lay behind the UK constitution. The judges invoked it to help justify the narrower principles identified by the court and to provide an overarching argument for the correctness of the judgment. The rule of law is used in this way in a great many judgments, with the courts presenting it as a principle that shapes the law, and, in judicial review cases, as a principle that should shape the decisions of members of the executive.[43] In some recent cases, however, a more ambitious role has been mooted for the principle: the rule of law has been presented as a legal rule, one that can be pleaded directly. The possibility of the rule of law operating as a discrete rule was discussed in Chapter 5. In a number of cases the courts have indicated that they might, one day, be willing to use the rule of law as a standard against which to assess the contents of statutes.[44] Indeed, it was argued in Chapter 5 that in *R (Privacy International) v Investigatory Powers Tribunal*, a case that fits the trend set by *UNISON*, and was, again, a case concerning access to courts, the best interpretation of the decision would treat it as a direct application of the rule of law, rather than, as the judges somewhat half-heartly claimed, a form of statutory interpretation.[45] Here, the rule of law has shifted from being a consideration invoked in the development of the

[43] A number of whom are under a statutory obligation to uphold the principle: see ch 9.

[44] *R (Jackson) v Attorney General* [2005] UKHL 56, [2006] 1 AC 262; *AXA General Insurance Ltd v Lord Advocate* [2011] UKSC 46, [2012] 1 AC 868; *Moohan v Lord Advocate* [2014] UKSC 67, [2015] AC 901.

[45] [2019] UKSC 22, [2020] AC 491.

law and become a legal rule that a litigant can plead, relying on it to strike down or modify statutory provisions.

If the courts are to embrace the rule of law as a general standard of review, the openness of the principle presents problems.[46] As we have seen, even concepts of the rule of law that start from narrow bases swiftly broaden; as the rule of law requires that the law be effective, it cannot, as a principle, be confined to the clarity of the legal rules or the formal capacity of litigants to access courts; it must also engage with wider issues of social inequality and power imbalances within relationships. The demands of the rule of law are potentially sweeping, raising questions of material inequality, education provision, even healthcare. All of these are factors that can limit a person's capacity to access the law. Whilst this breadth is not a problem, and may be a strength, when the rule of law is treated as a moral principle, it makes it a difficult legal principle for a judge to apply. If it were to be adopted as a general standard of review for statutes, it could require the judges to engage in an extensive and unpredictable review of the merits of their substance. Indeed, the principle is so broad and its application so unpredictable, it is arguable that the adoption of the rule of law as a legal principle would, in itself, run contrary to the rule of law, radically reducing certainty over the content of the law. It might be preferable for the courts to identify those elements within the principle, such as the right of access to the courts, that are suitable for legal enforcement, rather than claiming that the whole of the principle can be applied.[47]

20.3 CONCLUSION: THE RULE OF LAW, LIBERTY, AND RIGHTS

Dicey argued that the rule of law structured the common law and, as a consequence of this, protected liberty within the UK. Under the common law, that which is not forbidden is permitted: in the

[46] Richard Ekins, 'Legislative Freedom in the United Kingdom' (2017) 133 Law Quarterly Review 582, 601–605.

[47] Se-shauna Wheatle, 'Access to Justice: From Judicial Empowerment to Public Empowerment' in Mark Elliott and Kirsty Hughes (eds), *Common Law Constitutional Rights* (Hart Publishing 2020).

application of the law, litigants, including state officials, must point to a pre-existing rule of law if they want legally to compel the conduct of others. Dicey presented this as a special feature of English law, but it is probably a feature of legal orders in general. Because law is an action-guiding institution, because it is an institution that purports to tell people what they ought to do, when it is silent on a matter people are free to decide for themselves how to act: there is a presumption in favour of liberty built into the very nature of law. Dicey was right to claim that this aspect of the rule of law, the presumption of liberty, is the most fundamental protection of freedom within the UK constitution, more important and significant even than the rights discussed in the next chapter. But the rule of law is not, as Dicey sought to argue, in tension with bills of rights; he was wrong to present the rule of law and positive rights as alternatives: a constitution can be characterised by the rule of law and yet also possess a set of positive rights that citizens can invoke against the state. Indeed, these rights can both supplement and support the rule of law. They supplement the rule of law by providing a further level of protection for individuals in the face of the state. If *Entick v Carrington* was argued today, even if Carrington could point to an apparent legal power to enter Entick's house, the court could use the Human Rights Act 1998 to interpret this power restrictively, or could issue a declaration of incompatibility, calling on Parliament to change the law if Carrington's legal powers of entry were not compatible with Entick's rights. Furthermore, some of these positive rights support the rule of law by instantiating its demands. For instance, the right of access to the courts is protected by Article Six of the European Convention on Human Rights, contained within the Human Rights Act, is a right which embodies a key feature of the rule of law. In short, the principle of the rule of law discussed in this chapter and the positive rights discussed in the next should be considered as complementary, rather than competing, protectors of freedom.

21

RIGHTS

Constitutions, like any other human artefact, are subject to fashion. In France and America bills of rights, as instruments individuals can invoke against the state, have a long history dating back to the eighteenth century. The United Kingdom (UK), in contrast, has tended to focus on the democratic process as the means through which people's interests and entitlements are protected. Whilst instruments articulating rights are not unknown within the UK constitution—such as the thirteenth century's Magna Carta, or the Bill of Rights 1689 and the Claim of Right Act 1689—these documents have always been subject to parliamentary revision and could not be relied upon to invalidate legislation. During much of the twentieth century bills of rights that constrained legislatures were viewed with scepticism by those within the UK.[1] On the right, there was an affection for the common law and a scepticism of continental-style bills of rights; the common law grew out of society, whereas bills of rights were imposed upon it.[2] On the left, there was a fear that bills of rights would be used by judges, encouraged by companies and powerful individuals, to stop a socialist Parliament establishing schemes for the nationalisation of industries, the redistribution of wealth, and for the protection of employees. Buttressing each side's concerns was a belief that the rule of law, discussed in the previous chapter, had proved more successful in protecting freedoms in the UK than continental bills of rights had in their territories, a claim that was plausible provided, of course, that the UK's conduct in Ireland and its imperial territories was overlooked.[3] Consequently, whilst UK lawyers and civil servants were closely

[1] AWB Simpson, *Human Rights and the End of Empire: Britain and the Genesis of the European Convention* (Oxford University Press 2004) ch 1.

[2] Martin Loughlin, *The British Constitution: A Very Short Introduction* (Oxford University Press 2013) 8–13.

[3] Dino Lino, 'The Rule of Law and the Rule of Empire: Dicey in Imperial Context' (2018) 81 Modern Law Review 739. See further ch 16.

The United Kingdom Constitution. N. W. Barber, Oxford University Press. © Nick Barber 2021.
DOI: 10.1093/oso/9780198852315.003.0021

involved in the creation of the European Convention on Human Rights (ECHR) in the 1950s, enthusiasm for the document was tepid; a cynic might argue that the UK saw the Convention as a benefit to bestow on other states, rather than as a set of protections required by UK citizens.[4]

During the final quarter of the twentieth century there was a shift in opinion, particularly on the left, as the idea of a bill of rights for the UK gained popularity.[5] A number of factors contributed to this change in attitude. Some were political. The Conservative Party had been in government the UK from 1979 to 1997, during which time the attractions, at least to the Labour Party, of a constitutionally unconstrained Parliament steadily waned, and, as Labour moved towards the centre ground over the course of the 1980s, concerns over the impact of a bill of rights on nationalisation and wealth redistribution became less acute. Other factors were legal. The UK's experience of European law, and the willingness of the courts to use economic rights found in the Treaties to override statutory provisions, demonstrated that the judges could make use of rights instruments—and raised the question of why economic, and not human, rights were accorded this protected status. Finally, however, the change might partly be attributable to a shift in expectations about the role of constitutions: a generation of lawyers, judges, politicians, and scholars who came of age in the 1970s and 1980s had been educated in an academic environment filled with warnings of elective dictatorships[6] and celebrations of the virtues of rights.[7]

Enacted soon after Labour's return to power, the Human Rights Act 1998 is the principal instrument of rights protection in the UK. But the Human Rights Act, and the values that influenced its creation, have had significance beyond the Act. Alongside the Human Rights Act a growing number of statutes have granted

[4] Geoffrey Marston, 'The United Kingdom's Part in the Preparation of the European Convention on Human Rights, 1950' (1993) 34 International and Comparative Law Quarterly 796, 825.

[5] Colm O'Cinneide, 'Human Rights and the UK Constitution' in Jeffrey Jowell and Colm O'Cinneide (eds), *The Changing Constitution* (9th edn, Oxford University Press 2019) 64–67.

[6] Lord Hailsham, *The Dilemma of Democracy* (Collins 1978) ch 20.

[7] Ronald Dworkin, *Taking Rights Seriously* (Duckworth 1977).

citizens various rights they can plead against the state, and, although it would be hard to prove, there seems to have been a rise in rights discourse more generally, as people have begun to couch their political claims in the language of rights.[8] The common law has not been immune from these changes. Around the same time as the enactment of the Human Rights Act, and almost certainly in response to it, the judges began to develop a parallel idea of 'common law rights', rights which supplemented or overlayed those found in the statute. Even if the Human Rights Act were repealed, many of its legal effects would live on through the changes it has inspired in the common law.

21.1 THE HUMAN RIGHTS ACT 1998

Whilst the Human Rights Act brought about significant changes in the law, it would be a mistake to think that before its introduction the UK was an illiberal dystopia. In addition to the implications of the rule of law, discussed in the previous chapter, the political process in the UK brought about many of the liberalising measures that, in other countries, waited for the intervention of judges. It was Parliament that led the decriminalisation of homosexual sex in Britain,[9] ended capital punishment,[10] and introduced measures to combat race discrimination.[11] Furthermore, from 1966, UK citizens were also able to take cases to the European Court of Human Rights, and able to argue that the UK had failed to meet its obligations under the Convention. Whilst adverse rulings by the European Court of Human Rights were, and are, relatively uncommon, the Strasbourg judges had a significant

[8] On the contemporary human rights culture see Joint Committee on Human Rights, *Enforcing Human Rights* (2017–18, HC 669, HL 171) ch 7. On the change in legal culture see Tom Hickman, *Public Law after the Human Rights Act* (Hart Publishing 2010) 12–22.

[9] For England and Wales: Sexual Offences Act 1967; for Scotland: Criminal Justice (Scotland) Act 1980.

[10] For Britain: Murder (Abolition of the Death Penalty) Act 1965; for Northern Ireland: Northern Ireland (Emergency Powers) Act 1973.

[11] Race Relations Act 1965.

impact in some areas of law.[12] It was, for example, rulings of the European Court that lead to the decriminalisation of homosexuality in Northern Ireland,[13] reform of the law of contempt,[14] and the removal of the ban on homosexuals serving in the military.[15] In addition, when interpreting domestic legislation courts presume that Parliament has legislated in conformity with the UK's international law obligations; consequently, even before the Human Rights Act, the courts strove to interpret legislation in line with the European Convention.[16] Nevertheless, the enactment of the Human Rights Act significantly changed the ways in which rights were protected within the UK, giving the courts new powers to protect Convention rights, and placing new duties on the legislative and executive branches.

21.1.1 The Human Rights Act and the Courts

The Human Rights Act incorporated the bulk of the European Convention on Human Rights into the UK's legal orders, and conferred four significant new powers on the courts. Under section 3 of the Act, the courts are required to interpret legislation 'so far as it is possible to do so' in a way which is compatible with Convention rights. Section 4 covers those situations in which such an interpretation is not possible and empowers the court to issue a 'declaration of incompatibility', a declaration which leaves the legal validity of the non-compliant legislation untouched, but which flags to Parliament and the government that the law needs to be changed. Section 6 reinforces section 3 and renders it unlawful for public bodies to act contrary to Convention rights, unless constrained to do so by primary legislation, making it

[12] An overview of the figures can be found in Anthony Bradley, Keith Ewing, and Chris Knight, *Constitutional and Administrative Law* (17th edn, Pearson 2018) 371–72.

[13] *Dudgeon v United Kingdom* (1981) 4 EHRR 149.

[14] *Sunday Times v United Kingdom* (1979) 2 EHRR 245.

[15] *Smith v United Kingdom* (2000) 29 EHRR 493. The Human Rights Act did not come into force until October 2000: Human Rights Act 1998 (Commencement No 2) Order 2000.

[16] *R v Secretary of State for the Home Department ex p Brind* [1991] AC 696 (HL); Murray Hunt, *Using Human Rights Law in English Courts* (Hart Publishing 1997) ch 1.

clear that the courts can strike down acts of public authorities in this situation. Finally, section 8 of the Act empowers the judges to award damages for breaches of Convention rights by public authorities.

Section 3 might be the most important element of the Human Rights Act. When enacted, there was some scepticism about its utility as, after all, the Convention could already be used as an interpretive tool.[17] However, the courts have used section 3 to enable what Aileen Kavanagh has described as 'remedial interpretation'; enabling the courts to depart from the normal meaning they would have ascribed to the statute to make that statute rights-compliant.[18] A pair of cases, *Fitzpatrick v Sterling Housing Association*[19] and *Ghaidan v Godin-Mendoza*,[20] illustrate this. *Fitzpatrick* and *Ghaidan* turned on the same question: whether on the death of one party in a same-sex relationship the surviving partner could become a statutory tenant by succession under the Rent Act 1977. The Rent Act protected statutory tenants from eviction, even after the original lease had expired. Where only one partner of a married couple had signed the lease, the Act enabled the tenancy to pass to the surviving member after the death of the signatory, and, to protect couples who appeared to be married but had never actually taken this legal step, allowed a person living with the original tenant 'as his or her wife or husband' to inherit.[21] In *Fitzpatrick* the House of Lords decided that the surviving partner of a same-sex couple could not be described as having lived 'as his or her wife or husband'. The majority of the Lords took the view that that because, at that time, homosexual couples could not marry, they could not be said to live together as if a married couple; it was for Parliament, not the courts, to change the law if it wished. A few years later the Lords addressed exactly the same legal issue in *Ghaidan* but reached the opposite answer. The Rent Act 1977 now had to be read alongside the Human Rights

[17] Geoffrey Marshall, 'Interpreting Interpretation in the Human Rights Bill' [1998] Public Law 167.

[18] Aileen Kavanagh, *Constitutional Review Under the UK Human Rights Act* (Cambridge University Press 2009) 118–21.

[19] [1999] UKHL 42, [2001] 1 AC 27.

[20] [2004] UKHL 30, [2004] 2 AC 557.

[21] Rent Act 1977, sch 1, para 2(2).

Act 1998. This statute required protection for Godin-Mendoza's Article 8 right to respect for his home, and, moreover, this was coupled with his Article 14 right to have his Convention rights secured in a non-discriminatory fashion. Whilst same-sex marriage was still not yet a legal institution in English law, given that the Rent Act provided protection for unmarried heterosexual couples, the Human Rights Act required that equivalent protection be given to unmarried same-sex couples.[22] Section 3 allowed the court to give a new meaning to the Rent Act, a meaning that the text of the Rent Act, by itself, could not have sustained: the surviving partner of a same-sex couple could now inherit the statutory tenancy. The human rights 'flaw' in the Rent Act could be remedied through the exercise of the interpretative power conferred by the Human Rights Act.

Section 3 has become a powerful remedy, but it cannot be used to cure all statutory ills. The next provision, section 4, enables the courts to issue a declaration of incompatibility when remedial interpretation is not possible, and the existence of this power shows that Parliament did not intend section 3 amount to an unlimited power to rewrite incompatible statutes.[23] The balance between sections 3 and 4, the extent to which the courts are willing to depart from the natural meaning of a statute's language to make it compatible with the Human Rights Act, is central to the operation of the Act. As with the devolution cases, there is a tendency for the courts to focus on the words of the statute when deciding how far they can press section 3. So, in *Ghaidan*, Lord Nicholls tells us that section 3 cannot be used to adopt 'a meaning inconsistent with a fundamental feature of legislation',[24] whilst in *R (Anderson) v Secretary of State for the Home Department*, Lord Steyn warned that the interpretative power cannot be used if the result would be 'contrary to express statutory words or is by

[22] Same-sex marriages marriage were made legally possible by the Marriage (Same Sex Couples) Act 2013.

[23] Although Lord Irvine, then Lord Chancellor, told the House of Lords that, because of s 3 and s 6, in 99% of cases there would be no need for a declaration of incompatibility: HL Deb 5 February 1998, vol 585, col 840.

[24] *Ghaidan* (n 20) [33]; *Re S (Minors) (Care Order: Implementation of Care Plan)* [2002] UKHL 10, [2002] AC 291 [38]–[39].

implication necessarily contradicted by the statute'.[25] But, in another point of comparison with the devolution cases, the textual arguments used by the judges are rarely convincing. Once the obvious cases are removed, those where using section 3 would radically and plainly undermine the purpose of the statute, and there is reasonable disagreement over whether interpretation through section 3 is possible, appeals to the text will not take us very far. A better approach, and one that lies just beneath the surface of the case law on section 3, draws on constitutional principle; in particular, that of the separation of powers.

The separation of powers was discussed in the second part of this book. The principle directs our attention to the structures, skills, and powers within the constitution, and seeks to ensure that these are successfully allied. In the context of section 3, the principle requires that courts compare their institutional strengths and those of the legislature (and sometimes the executive) when deciding whether it is appropriate to use the remedial interpretative power of section 3 to modify a statute, or to issue a declaration of incompatibility under section 4 and send the issue to Parliament for legislative reconsideration. A number of the factors involved in the balance between sections 3 and 4 can be seen as applications of the separation of powers principle.

First, the court is reluctant to use section 3 when bringing a statute into line with the Human Rights Act requires the creation of new institutional structures. In *R (Royal College of Nursing) v Secretary of State for the Home Department* the High Court examined the Safeguarding Vulnerable Groups Act 2006, which established the Independent Safeguarding Authority and which, crucially, required the Authority to create and maintain registers of those barred from working with children or vulnerable adults.[26] The 2006 Act required the Authority to place people on these lists if they had a conviction or caution for a range of offences, some serious, some quite trivial. Those subject to this process could not make representations before being added to the list, although

[25] *R (Anderson) v Secretary of State for the Home Department* [2002] UKHL 46, [2003] 1 AC 837 [59].

[26] *R (Royal College of Nursing) v Secretary of State for the Home Department* [2010] EWHC 2761 (Admin), [2011] PTSR 1193.

they could later contest their inclusion. The High Court concluded that this mechanism ran contrary to Article 6: the decision to place a person on a register affected their civil rights, specifically, their capacity to hold a job, and Article 6 required that they be able to make representations before such decisions were made. Although the possibility of using section 3 was raised, the court instead issued a declaration of incompatibility. Although the reasoning was couched in terms of the language of the statute, the underlying concern was that a new scheme needed to be created, one which distinguished between urgent additions to the registers and those where a delay to permit representations to be made could be justified.[27] This was the type of distinction that needed legislative skills and techniques to draw.[28]

Secondly, the court is slow to use section 3 when a remedial interpretation will have implications that span statutes. In *Bellinger v Bellinger* the applicant was born biologically male but now lived as a woman and had undertaken gender reassignment surgery. She had gone through a marriage ceremony with a man, and, at the time, the legislation specified that marriages required a male and female partner; Bellinger argued that she was, at the time of the marriage, 'female', and so the marriage was valid. The House of Lords agreed with Bellinger that the failure of the law to recognise her as 'female' violated her rights under the Convention and the Human Rights Act, but decided to issue a declaration of incompatibility rather than utilise section 3. One of the reasons given by the court was that classifying Bellinger as 'female' would have broad implications across many areas of law.[29] Where the changes required by the Human Rights Act will have implications across a range of statutes—and, perhaps, where the court will struggle to predict the magnitude of such changes—the court will be reluctant to use section 3 to make the change. It should be left to the legislature, with its superior capacity to investigate and examine the implications of statutory changes, to make the alterations.

[27] ibid [65]–[66].

[28] See also *International Transport Roth v Secretary of State for the Home Department* [2002] EWCA Civ 158, [2003] QB 728 esp [66]; *Bellinger v Bellinger* [2003] UKHL 21, [2003] 2 AC 467 [44]; *R(G) v Chief Constable of Surrey* [2016] EWHC 295 (Admin), [2016] 4 WLR 94.

[29] *Bellinger* (n 28) [45].

Thirdly, the court is reluctant to use section 3 where there is a range of possible ways in which the offending statute could be made Human Rights Act compatible, and the choice between these options is a matter of social controversy.[30] In *R (Steinfeld and Keidan) v Secretary of State for International Development* the Supreme Court considered whether civil partnerships, a legal institution akin to marriage available to same-sex couples, should also be available to heterosexual couples.[31] The court issued a declaration of incompatibility without discussing the relationship between sections 3 and 4, but the reason for not using section 3 was obvious: the legislation could be made Human Rights Act compatible either by abolishing civil unions and reclassifying those in such relationships as married, or by extending the capacity to enter a civil partnership to heterosexual couples. This was a decision for Parliament, not the courts.[32]

A further reason, similar to that discussed in the previous paragraph, sometimes invoked by the court for declining to use section 3 is that the issue is one of social controversy and so should be left to Parliament to resolve.[33] This is harder to defend. Once the court has concluded that the Human Rights Act requires the law to take a position on an issue, that, say, transexuals are entitled to be regarded as women for the purposes of marriage, it would be odd for a judge to decide that the bare fact that this was socially controversial justified referring the matter back to Parliament. In this situation, Parliament, through the Human Rights Act, has already told the judges what they should do: if it is possible to use section 3, they should make use of that provision. A core part of the purpose of the Human Rights Act is to protect those who, justifiably or not, are unpopular in society and we should

[30] ibid [39]–[41].

[31] *R (Steinfeld and Keidan) v Secretary of State for International Development* [2018] UKSC 32, [2020] AC 1. The institution of civil partnership was introduced by the Civil Partnership Act 2004, partly as an attempt to placate advocates of same-sex marriage whilst avoiding opening the institution of marriage to same-sex couples.

[32] *Steinfeld* (n 31) [60]. Parliament decided to open civil unions to heterosexual couples: Civil Partnerships, Marriages and Deaths (Registration etc) Act 2019.

[33] *Bellinger* (n 28) [46]–[48]. See also *R (Nicklinson) v Ministry of Justice* [2014] UKSC 38, [2015] AC 657 [118].

expect that decisions of the court will, on occasion, provoke social controversy.

Countering these reasons against using section 3, the court may be more willing to use its interpretive power when the statute covers matters that relate to the processes of the court. In *R v A (No 2)*, the House of Lords all but reversed a provision in the Youth Justice and Criminal Evidence Act 1999: what had been a statutory bar, with limited exceptions, on the use of the complainant's past sexual behaviour in rape trials was effectively rewritten by the court, using section 3, to allow such material where necessary to enable a fair trial.[34] This substantially weakened the statutory restriction. *R v A* was an early case under the Human Rights Act and might be at the extreme end of what can be accomplished using section 3.[35] But it could be that this radical use of section 3 was regarded as appropriate because the statutory issue raised in the case focused on the trial process. This was an issue that the judges were, rightly or wrongly, confident they understood. It did not raise broader institutional implications and, perhaps most importantly of all, it went to the integrity of the criminal process.

When section 3 cannot be used, a section 4 declaration of incompatibility may be issued. This declaration leaves the statute untouched; the courts lack the power under the Act to strike down incompatible legislation. The constraints of section 4 may have been a consideration in *R v A*: had the court not used section 3 the limitations found in the Youth and Criminal Evidence Act would have continued to apply, risking, in the view of the House of Lords, unreliable convictions. A quick reading of the Human Rights Act could give the impression that there is a straight choice between sections 3 and 4, that the courts either use remedial interpretation to fix an incompatible statute or they issue a declaration of incompatibility. A closer reading of section 4, however, reveals that issuing a declaration is a matter of discretion; a court *may* make a declaration if the statute is incompatible

[34] *R v A (No 2)* [2001] UKHL 25, [2002] 1 AC 45.

[35] Questioning the appropriateness of the decision: Richard Bellamy, 'Political Constitutionalism and the Human Rights Act' (2011) 9 International Journal of Constitutional Law 86, 107–108.

with the Human Rights Act. On a handful of occasions, the court has exercised this discretion and declined to issue a declaration. In *R (Nicklinson) v Ministry of Justice* the majority concluded that the law governing assisted suicide ran contrary to the Human Rights Act, yet the court declined to issue a declaration of incompatibility. Lord Neuberger argued that the issues involved were controversial and sensitive, that in such an area it was appropriate for the legislature to proceed slowly, and noted that Parliament was currently considering the issues it raised.[36] However, as there is no legal duty on Parliament to alter the law after a declaration,[37] Neuberger's fears of over-hasty legislation seem misplaced; Parliament could take as long as it wished to reflect on the declaration. An alternative explanation of the court's reluctance in *Nicklinson* is that it might have been motivated by a concern that Parliament might exercise its entitlement not to act in response to the declaration. To date, declarations of incompatibility have always led to a change in the law, with the exception of a few recent cases where the response is still under consideration or under appeal.[38] If the court in *Nicklinson* had issued a declaration and Parliament, as it is entitled to do, decided not to change the law, the momentum that has built up behind declarations, the pressure that comes from twenty years of parliamentary compliance, might have been weakened.

Whilst sections 3 and 4 are, for the courts, the most important elements of the Human Rights Act, section 6 is also of significance. This section renders it unlawful for a public body to act contrary to a Convention right, unless required to do so by primary legislation and gives the courts a new standard under which to assess the legality of administrative decision-making. In large part, section 6 duplicates section 3 as many of the powers possessed

[36] *Nicklinson* (n 33) [118]. See also Lord Walker in *Re P* [2008] UKHL 38, [2009] 1 AC 173 [83].

[37] A point stressed by the judges: *Nicklinson* (n 33) [343]; *Steinfeld* (n 31) [60].

[38] Jeff King, 'Parliament's Role Following Declarations of Incompatibility under the Human Rights Act' in Murray Hunt, Hayley Hooper, and Paul Yowell, *Parliament and Human Rights* (Hart Publishing 2015). The declaration in the prisoners' voting rights case eventually led to an administrative change enabling a small number of prisoners to vote: Neil Johnson, *Prisoners' Voting Rights: Developments Since 2015* House of Commons Briefing Paper 07461 (19 November 2020).

by the administration are conferred by statutes, which must be interpreted through section 3 in any event. However, where a body possesses a non-statutory power, conferred by the prerogative or common law, section 6 applies Convention rights to its exercise.

21.1.2 The Human Rights Act and Other State Institutions

Whilst the primary focus of the Human Rights Act is the courts, with the statute obliging judges to protect people's Convention rights and giving them a set of legal tools they can use to this end, the Human Rights Act also addresses other constitutional institutions, both indirectly and directly. Indirectly, as after the enactment of the Human Rights Act institutions make decisions in the shadow of that Act; these bodies should be aware that their decisions may be interpreted or challenged by judges, and this awareness may alter the content and processes of their decisions. Directly, as in some areas the Human Rights Act imposes new legal duties on these bodies, duties it is their responsibility to acquit, even without the intervention of judges.

For the most part, the Human Rights Act does not require public bodies to reason in a Human Rights Act compatible way. In Parliament's case, the doctrines of parliamentary privilege precludes scrutiny of its reasoning: the Bill of Rights 1689 prevents the court from assessing the merits of debates in the House.[39] When it comes to administrative bodies, whilst the courts can scrutinise their decision-making process, and do so through judicial review, the judges have treated the Human Rights Act as imposing jurisdictional limits on the range of decisions these administrative bodies can reach, rather than requiring an examination of their reasoning process. So, for example, in *R (Begum) v Denbigh High School*, when the House of Lords examined whether Denbigh's school uniform policy adequately accommodated Begum's right to manifest her religion, the court considered whether the policy violated Begum's Article 9 right, rather than asking if the school governors had properly considered that right

[39] *Wilson v First County Trust Ltd (No 2)* [2003] UKHL 40, [2004] 1 AC 816 [51]–[67]. See ch 4 for a discussion of those cases in which the court has looked at the reasoning process of Parliament, despite the limits of privilege.

in the course of making their decision.[40] However, whilst the court does not require these bodies consider the Human Rights Act in their decision-making, when they have explicitly considered the requirements of Convention rights, or when they have considered factors relevant to those rights, the courts will give weight to these decisions.[41] This has been described, perhaps inaccurately, as the courts giving 'deference' to the original decision-maker, and there are at least three reasons which may lead to deference.[42] First, if the court concludes the original decision-maker possesses superior factual expertise to that of the court, the court should give weight to that expertise. Questions about the balancing of rights and the broader public interest often raise tricky factual questions about the severity of the impact of the measure adopted by the decision-maker or its effectiveness, and the primary decision-maker may be better placed than the courts to gather and analyse relevant evidence.[43] Secondly, if the court concludes that there is a range of acceptable (or, perhaps, a range of correct) answers that could be given to the interpretation of a right and to the balancing of the right and the broader public interest, the court should accept the decision reached by the body empowered by the constitution to make the primary decision.[44] Finally, the court may defer to the decision of an elected body such as Parliament,[45] or to an official accountable to an elected body,[46] because of the value of democracy: the unelected judges defer to the democratically accountable side of the constitution.

[40] *R (Begum) v Denbigh High School* [2006] UKHL 15, [2007] 1 AC 700 esp [29]–[30], [68].

[41] *Belfast City Council v Miss Behavin' Ltd* [2007] UKHL 19, [2007] 1 WLR 1420 [26].

[42] TRS Allan, 'Human Rights and Judicial Review: A Critique of Due Deference' (2006) 65 Cambridge Law Journal 671.

[43] *R (Carlile) v Secretary of State for the Home Department* [2014] UKSC 60, [2015] 1 AC 945 [21]–[22], [32]; *Secretary of State for the Home Department v Rehman* [2001] UKHL 47, [2003] 1 AC 153 [24]; *Bank Mellat v Her Majesty's Treasury (No 2)* [2013] UKSC 39, [2014] 1 AC 700 [21]; *Wilson* (n 39) [63]–[64].

[44] *Roth* (n 28) [84].

[45] *R (Animal Defenders) v Secretary of State for Culture, Media and Sport* [2008] UKHL 15, [2008] 1 AC 1312 [33]; *Huang v Secretary of State for the Home Department* [2007] UKHL 11, [2007] 2 AC 167 [17].

[46] *Carlile* (n 43) [32].

The first two of these arguments for deference rest on the claim that the initial decision-maker is more, or equally, likely to achieve the demands of the Human Rights Act than the courts. The third, the argument from democracy, is more problematic, with the requirements of the Human Rights Act giving way to a distinct constitutional object: the courts defer to the primary decision-maker even if that body is less likely than the courts to have achieved the objectives of the Act.

The willingness of the courts to give weight to these decisions gives public bodies an incentive to consider the Human Rights Act in the course of their decision making. The Human Rights Act also imposes some direct duties on public authorities. Perhaps the most significant of these is found in the combination of section 6 and section 8. Section 6 renders unlawful actions of public authorities that are incompatible with Convention rights, and section 8 enables the courts to award damages for such actions.[47] The Human Rights Act thus creates something resembling a tort: even if public authorities are not bound by a duty to consider the Human Rights Act before acting, they remain constrained by a duty not to undertake actions which violate Convention rights. More broadly still, in certain areas the Human Rights Act imposes positive duties on state bodies. For example, there are positive duties grounded in Article 2 of the Convention to safeguard life and, under Article 3, to prevent inhuman and degrading treatment. In extreme instances the court may award damages if a badly flawed police investigation amounts to a violation of these duties,[48] whilst in *Rabone v Pennine Care NHS Foundation Trust* a hospital breached a patient's rights by allowing her return home in a mentally unstable condition, the patient subsequently committing suicide.[49]

The Human Rights Act places few direct duties on Parliament partly, perhaps, because it is hard to see how the court could enforce them. Section 19, however, requires that the minister in

[47] *R (Greenfield) v Secretary of State for the Home Office* [2005] UKHL 14, [2005] 1 WLR 673.

[48] *Sarjantson v Chief Constable of Humberside* [2013] EWCA Civ 1252, [2014] QB 411; *Re Officer L* [2007] UKHL 36, [2007] 1 WLR 2135; *Commissioner of Police of the Metropolis v DSD* [2018] UKSC 11, [2019] 1 AC 196.

[49] *Rabone v Pennine Care NHS Foundation Trust* [2012] UKSC 2, [2012] 2 AC 72.

charge of a bill make a statement to Parliament about the compatibility of the bill with Convention rights.[50] This serves to remind Parliament of the importance of Convention rights, but also provides an incentive for those drafting the law to make it compatible with the Convention; it is likely to prove easier to get legislation through Parliament if such a statement can be made.[51]

21.1.3 The Human Rights Act and the European Court of Human Rights

One of the arguments for the Human Rights Act was that it 'brought rights home', that is, UK citizens would no longer have to take their cases to the Strasbourg court.[52] Nevertheless, the European Court of Human Rights continues to play a significant role in protecting rights within the UK, both by shaping the interpretation of Convention rights and by continuing to hear cases brought by UK citizens. Section 2 of the Human Rights Act requires UK courts to 'take into account' rulings of the European Court of Human Rights, and some other Strasbourg institutions, where relevant. The courts have generally followed Strasbourg jurisprudence,[53] but are not constrained to do so. They have occasionally departed from the ECHR's interpretation of a right when the judges believe the Strasbourg decision is inappropriate for the legal systems of the UK,[54] or, more bluntly, where they believe Strasbourg got it wrong.[55] On a few occasions, the Strasbourg court appears to have responded to the disquiet of UK judges by shifting its interpretation of the Convention.[56] Rather

[50] Nicholas Bamforth, 'Parliamentary Sovereignty and the Human Rights Act 1998' [1998] Public Law 572, 575–82.

[51] The obligation on ministers not to lie to Parliament is taken exceptionally seriously, and it is unlikely a minister would risk making a statement of compatibility if she had been told by her officials the legislation ran contrary to Convention rights: Adam Tomkins, 'A Right to Mislead Parliament?' (1996) 16 Legal Studies 63.

[52] Home Department, *Human Rights Brought Home: the Human Rights Bill* (White Paper, Cm 3728, 1997).

[53] *R (Ullah) v Special Adjudicator* [2004] UKHL 26, [2004] 2 AC 323 [20].

[54] *R v Horncastle* [2009] UKSC 14, [2010] 2 AC 373.

[55] *R (Haney) v Whatton Prison Governor* [2014] UKSC 66, [2015] 1 AC 1344 [35].

[56] *Al-Khawaja v United Kingdom* (2012) 54 EHRR 23; *Animal Defenders International v UK* (2013) 57 EHRR 21.

than a simple hierarchical relationship, the court systems respond to each other, trying to retain consistency but willing to express disagreement on occasion. National and supranational courts applying different perspectives to legal problems increases the risk of conflict, but also offers potential benefits. The continued capacity of UK citizens to take cases to Strasbourg facilitates this process of dialogue, enabling questions from the UK legal systems to be heard by Strasbourg judges.[57] Particularly after Brexit, which brought to an end the involvement of a second supranational court, the Court of Justice of the European Union, there may be value in maintaining the connection between the UK and the ECHR. Whilst asking judges from outside of the UK to review UK law runs the risk that they will fail to understand the context and implications of the domestic law as well as a domestic judge, it also means that these external judges approach the problems without the assumptions and preconceptions a domestic judge might bring. What may seem reasonable or unavoidable from an insider's perspective, might seem unreasonable and wholly avoidable to those looking in from outside, and, on occasion, the outsiders will be right.

21.2 RIGHTS BEYOND THE HUMAN RIGHTS ACT

Even its most passionate defenders would not claim that the Human Rights Act encompasses the whole spectrum of human rights, or, more broadly still, the whole range of social and civil rights a state should protect. First, the Human Rights Act is limited in terms of its coverage. In part, this is a function of the origins of the Convention which the Human Rights Act incorporates. Drafted in the 1950s, the Convention lacks some of the rights found in contemporary documents. The lack of a general equality right might be the most significant omission,[58] but more recent texts have also included rights undreamed of at the time

[57] Alison L Young, *Democratic Dialogue and the Constitution* (Oxford University Press 2017) ch 8.

[58] But see now Protocol 12 to the Convention, added in 2000 and not incorporated by the Human Rights Act 1998.

the Convention was drafted, such as rights relating to the environment[59] or to healthcare.[60] Moreover, the Human Rights Act focuses on the relationship between individuals and state bodies and does not directly apply to horizontal relationships, interactions between private citizens. Whilst both a state body and a private person can violate your (moral) rights by imprisoning you, the Human Rights Act will only ground an action against the state body. Additionally, whilst the Human Rights Act does sometimes require action by public bodies, as in the *Rabone* case discussed above, it more commonly stops bodies acting in ways which violate rights. It tells public bodies what they must not do, rather than specifying positive actions the body must undertake. This may be partly because of the difficult economic and practical issues such positive demands would raise: if the court was tasked with upholding a general right to healthcare, for example, the judges would struggle to balance the limited budget of the National Health Service with the competing demands of the sick.

None of the limitations outlined in the previous paragraph should be taken as criticisms of the Human Rights Act. Bills of rights can never hope to encompass the full range of moral rights that individuals possess, and, moreover, if bills of rights are to be enforced by the judges, the institutional constraints of the court should shape the rights the document contains. In the UK constitution, the Human Rights Act is far from the only source of rights protection; indeed, much of the legal order could be seen as an attempt to work through and, where appropriate, provide legal protection for, people's moral rights. As Lord Reed argued in *Osborn v Parole Board*, the values of the Convention rights—and, we might add, of other moral rights too—permeate the UK's legal systems.[61] Taking each of the three limitations discussed in the previous paragraph, the protection of rights outside of the Human Rights Act mitigates each of these constraints. First, other areas of law protect rights against public bodies that fall outside

[59] European Charter of Fundamental Rights, art 37; South African Constitution, art 24.

[60] European Charter of Fundamental Rights, art 35; South African Constitution, art 27.

[61] *Osborn v Parole Board* [2013] UKSC 61, [2014] 1 AC 1115 [55].

of the Human Rights Act. So, for example, whilst the Human Rights Act does not include a general equality right or protect rights relating to the environment, these rights are given protection elsewhere. Environmental legislation sets targets that the government is obliged to meet, whilst the Equality Act 2010 imposes anti-discrimination duties on public authorities.[62] Secondly, and relatedly, other areas of law carry the protection of rights into the private sphere. Whilst the rights found in the Human Rights Act cannot be directly pleaded against private bodies, there are many private law rights or criminal law duties which are grounded in the same values. For instance, a person who is wrongfully imprisoned by a private actor will not be able to bring an action through the Human Rights Act, but would be able to bring an action under the common law tort of false imprisonment and could also seek the assistance of the police and the criminal law. Moving beyond Convention rights, much, if not most, of the law aspires to protect or help realise the moral rights and correlative moral duties we owe to each other: contract is ultimately grounded in the voluntary creation of moral obligations between people; tort law rests on notions of the standard of conduct we are entitled to expect from others. Finally, the law, particularly statute law, frequently requires positive action by public bodies. Sometimes the courts play a part in enforcing these duties, with individuals possessing the capacity to sue public bodies for failing to provide them with a specific benefit or, perhaps, able to challenge a body's failure to meet its statutory obligations.[63] On other occasions, however, the role of the courts is marginal, with statutes establishing institutions and structures tasked with achieving the objectives specified by the right. For instance, whilst there may not be a general, justiciable, right to healthcare in the UK that parallels the moral (social) right to it, the state nevertheless spends an enormous amount of money and invests a massive effort in the National Health Service.[64] That there is no legal right

[62] Equality Act 2010, s 149.

[63] As with some environmental targets: *R (Client Earth) v Secretary of State for the Environment, Food and Rural Affairs* [2015] UKSC 28.

[64] *R (Condliff) v North Staffordshire Primary Care Trust* [2011] EWCA Civ 910, [2012] PTSR 460.

to healthcare in the UK does not imply that the state does not recognise and protect this right, even though the courts are not empowered to supervise and enforce its protection.[65]

Given that rights permeate the UK's legal systems in these ways, it is unsurprising that the judges have identified 'common law rights' as a collection of legal entities that exist alongside, and sometimes duplicate, Convention rights. Whilst the recognition of such rights by the common law has a long history, it was the enactment of the Human Rights Act that spurred the judges to develop the concept, with some of the first contemporary cases on common law rights decided in the period between the decision to enact the Human Rights Act and it coming into force, a period during which, perhaps, judges sought to protect the rights of litigants in anticipation of the Act.[66] After the Human Rights Act came into effect judges have continued to use common law rights in their decisions. Common law lawyers played an important role in the drafting of the Convention in the 1950s and the UK courts regard common law rights as closely related to their Convention counterparts; their development of common law rights has been influenced by the case law on the Convention.[67] However, whilst there is a close relationship between these legal entities, common law rights are not limited by their Convention counterparts, and could provide more extensive protections to litigants in some situations.

The courts have made use of common law rights in three areas. First, paralleling section 3 of the Human Rights Act, common law rights, mediated through the principle of legality, have been relied upon by judges to justify adopting interpretations of statutes that protect fundamental rights.[68] As Lord Hoffmann put it

[65] The National Health Service Act 2006, s 1, carefully phrases the duty of the Secretary of State for Health as being to *promote* a comprehensive health service rather than to *provide* such a service.

[66] *R v Secretary of State for the Home Department ex p Simms* [1999] UKHL 33, [2002] 2 AC 115; *Reynolds v Times Newspapers* [2001] AC 127 (HL); *R v Secretary of State for the Home Department ex p Daly* [2001] UKHL 26, [2001] 2 AC 532; Hickman (n 8) 49–56.

[67] *Osborn* (n 61) [57].

[68] Jason Varuhas, 'The Principle of Legality' (2020) 79 Cambridge Law Journal 578.

in *Simms*, a case decided just before the Human Rights Act came into force:

> the principle of legality means that Parliament must squarely confront what it is doing and accept the political cost. Fundamental rights cannot be overridden by general or ambiguous words. This is because there is too great a risk that the full implications of their unqualified meaning may have passed unnoticed in the democratic process. In the absence of express language or necessary implication to the contrary, the courts therefore presume that even the most general words were intended to be subject to the basic rights of the individual. In this way the courts of the United Kingdom, though acknowledging the sovereignty of Parliament, apply principles of constitutionality little different from those which exist in countries where the power of the legislature is expressly limited by a constitutional document.[69]

The power of this interpretative principle was demonstrated by the case of *R (Privacy International) v Investigatory Powers Tribunal*, discussed in Chapter 5, in which it was applied with a vigour that arguably exceeded that seen in cases involving section 3.[70] Secondly, common law rights can also be invoked in actions for judicial review, providing a basis on which executive decisions can be challenged, paralleling section 6 of the Human Rights Act.[71] In *R (UNISON) v Lord Chancellor*, discussed in the previous chapter, it was the common law right of access to court that was relied upon by the Supreme Court rather than the Human Rights Act.[72] Thirdly, common law rights have shaped the development of the common law more broadly, with the judges drawing on these rights to justify the evolution of areas of tort law. For example, in *Campbell v MGM Ltd* the House of Lords crafted a tort of privacy out of the older tort of breach of confidence.[73] In justifying this development, Lord Nicholls argued that it was not

[69] *Simms* (n 66) 131. Hickman (n 8) 105–108.

[70] *R (Privacy International) v Investigatory Powers Tribunal* [2019] UKSC 22, [2019] 2 WLR 1219 [100], [199].

[71] Joanna Bell, 'Common Law Constitutional Rights and Executive Action' in Mark Elliott and Kirsty Hughes, *Common Law Constitutional Rights* (Hart Publishing 2020).

[72] *R (UNISON) v Lord Chancellor* [2017] UKSC 51, [2017] ICR 1037; see also *R v Lord Chancellor ex p Witham* [1998] QB 575 (QB).

[73] *Campbell v MGM Ltd* [2004] UKHL 22, [2004] 2 AC 457.

necessary to examine whether the Human Rights Act required the courts to fashion this new private law obligation, as the values that animated Convention rights also underpinned and animated the common law.[74] But the enactment of the Human Rights Act was far from irrelevant to the case: as Lord Hoffmann noted, the introduction of that Act had shifted the courts' understanding of the values that the common law protected.[75]

21.3 CONCLUSION: RIGHTS AFTER THE HUMAN RIGHTS ACT?

Of the three major constitutional reforms introduced by the Blair government at the start of the millennium, the Human Rights Act is the one which remains most controversial. Whilst there is little demand for the end of devolution or for the return of the hereditary peers to the House of Lords, there have been frequent calls for the repeal of the Human Rights Act.[76] This might reflect the inherently contentious nature of the questions that Parliament, through the Human Rights Act, has asked judges to address. Given the Act was intended to protect the rights of individuals against the encroachment of the state, the decisions of the courts are bound to be unpopular from time to time. It is a mark of success, not failure, that on occasion the judgments of the courts do not align with the wishes of the majority. But a portion of the controversy over the Act might stem from its mode of adoption. Whereas devolution was put to the peoples of Wales, Scotland, and Northern Ireland in referendums, the Human Rights Act was not subject to such a vote.[77] Moreover, the Act was the product of the standard legislative process; there was no attempt to engage the public in a national conversation, no grand constitutional convention or Royal Commission. Whether as a cause or effect

[74] ibid [16]–[19] (Lord Nicholls).

[75] ibid [51]–[52] (Lord Hoffmann).

[76] David Feldman, 'Extending the Role of the Courts: The Human Rights Act 1998' (2011) 30 Parliamentary History 65, 83–84.

[77] Rivka Weill, 'Dicey was not a Diceyean' (2003) 62 Cambridge Law Journal 474; Rivka Weill, 'The New Commonwealth Model of Constitutionalism Notwithstanding: On Judicial Review and Constitution-Making' (2014) 62 American Journal of Comparative Law 127, 133–37

of these decisions, there was, as David Feldman recounts, limited popular support for the Human Rights Bill, and 'it was unpopular from the start with large sections of the population and press'.[78] Given that the Act was passed through the ordinary parliamentary processes, it is hard to argue that, as a matter of constitutional principle, Parliament could not alter the Act through these same mechanisms. Discontent, especially on the right, with the Act has simmered for many years, with conservative scholars and politicians objecting to the way in which the Human Rights Act has limited Parliament and the executive, whilst empowering the courts. At the time of writing this chapter, a review of aspects of the Act has been commissioned by Boris Johnson's government, and it could be that the Human Rights Act will face some significant changes over the next few years.

Parliament can alter or repeal the Human Rights Act if it wishes, but such legislative action faces at least two constitutional hurdles. First, under the Good Friday Agreement the UK is committed to ensure that the European Convention on Human Rights applies to public bodies, to legislation, and to 'key decisions' which affect Northern Ireland, and is committed to incorporating the Convention into Northern Ireland law.[79] The Human Rights Act is not the only way in which these objectives could be achieved but, at present, it forms an important part of the constitutional settlement in Northern Ireland. Secondly, as we have seen in the course of this chapter, the Human Rights Act was the product of a broader shift in legal culture, part of a wider embrace of the idea of human rights as a feature of law and a reassessment of the judges' role within the constitution. Over the last twenty years the values of the Convention and the concept of rights have become imbedded in the common law. If the Human Rights Act were repealed tomorrow, its repeal would certainly alter the way judges approach cases, but perhaps not as much as some advocates of repeal might hope. Common law rights would

[78] Feldman (n 76) 67.

[79] On the Good Friday Agreement see ch 16, and see ch 3 for a discussion of the legal systems of the UK. It is an interesting question whether the Convention could be incorporated into the law of Northern Ireland without also incorporating it into English law.

still be used as interpretive tools, as standards applied in judicial review, and as broad values that guide the evolution of the common law. And unless Parliament prohibited the judges from looking at the jurisprudence of the European Court of Human Rights, it is likely that these decisions would still be cited to and by UK courts, shaping common law rights. Whilst the Human Rights Act is legally easy to change, changing the legal culture of which the Act is an emanation will prove far harder.

22
BECOMING CITIZENS

Everyone within the territory of the United Kingdom (UK), and a large number of people outside its territory, possess UK constitutional identities; that is, they occupy an office of the state, an office identified and constructed by law and bringing with it legal rights and duties. Some of these constitutional identities are foundational, such as citizenship or subjecthood, and are the base-level constitutional relationship that a person has with the state. These base-level constitutional offices can be contrasted with other state offices, such as judge or civil servant, which a person holding a base-level office may subsequently enter. These foundational relationships can be divided into two groups: insiders and outsiders. Insiders are members of the state, people for whose well-being the state exists, and who are morally entitled to share in its governance. Outsiders are non-members, people who may owe obligations towards the state and may possess rights against that institution, but who are not morally entitled to share in its governance and whose well-being is not the state's primary concern. The optimal relationship an insider can possess is citizenship, where a person enjoys the maximum amount of control over the state that is reconcilable with the constitutional equality of other state members. As we shall see, in the UK the constitutional status of both outsiders and insiders is a matter of degree, with each breaking down into a number of different categories and sub-categories, characterised by differing rights and duties. Complicating matters further, as with other state institutions, these foundational offices are only partly the creation of law, they also possess a social dimension and are shaped by the attitudes and beliefs of the political communities in which they exist. A person may be legally identified as a British citizen but if they are not generally recognised as a citizen, the significance of this legal designation is greatly reduced.

The United Kingdom Constitution. N. W. Barber, Oxford University Press. © Nick Barber 2021.
DOI: 10.1093/oso/9780198852315.003.0022

The law governing constitutional identity in the UK is the product of history rather than principle. At the start of the twentieth century, when the British Empire covered a substantial portion of the world, all of those born within its territory were identified as British subjects, entitled to live in the UK and exercise civic rights whilst there.[1] This amounted to around 600 million people but, of course, for most of these travel to the UK was all but impossible, even if they wished to leave their home territories.[2] Over the course of the next 100 years, as the British Empire collapsed and travel became easier, gaining membership of the UK became steadily harder, as various governments sought to restrict the capacity of those outside of the UK to enter or remain in the country. This retrenchment has been spasmodic, and has left nationality law littered with a mess of legal categories and rules most of which were responses to fears, real or imagined, of large-scale migration into the UK. Further complicating the law has been an uncertainty over the nature of UK citizenship, that is, what it means to be a citizen of the UK and, connectedly, what qualities enable a person to flourish in this role. There is, and always has been, a profound uncertainty in the UK over citizenship. As we saw in the chapters on the regionalisation of power, the UK is a combination of constituent regions, and when national identity is invoked it is often identity at the regional, rather than state, level. Examining the laws relating to citizenship gives some insight into how the state conceptualises membership of the UK. Some elements of this conceptualisation are worrying, with nationality rules that have the aim or effect of restricting non-white access to citizenship.[3] Other elements are less offensive but still problematic, with the state seeking to identify a range of values and cultural knowledge that citizens should possess.

[1] Gina Clayton and Georgina Firth, *Immigration and Asylum Law* (8th edn, Oxford University Press 2018) 76.

[2] Randall Hansen, *Citizenship and Immigration in Post-war Britain: The Institutional Origins of a Multicultural Nation* (Oxford University Press 2000) ch 2.

[3] For a rare example of a statute motivated by demonstrably racist concerns see Lord Lester, 'Thirty Years On: The East African Asians Case Revisited' [2002] Public Law 52, discussing the Commonwealth Immigrants Act 1968.

22.1 OUTSIDERS

The creation of a state brings with it the creation of state members, a group of insiders, and a corollary of this is the creation of outsiders, people who are not members of the state. As with insiders, however, the state has a wide range of relationships with outsiders, a spectrum that extends from constitutional offices tantamount to citizenship on one side to the very thinnest of connections on the other.

22.1.1 Outsiders Inside The Territory

The best status accorded by the UK to outsiders gives them indefinite leave to remain in the UK, the right to work and move freely within the country, and access to social benefits, such as the NHS and welfare support. Commonwealth citizens with indefinite leave to remain (and citizens of the Republic of Ireland) are even entitled to vote and stand in elections.[4] Indeed, this set of rights is so close to citizenship that those applying for indefinite leave to remain must, like those applying for citizenship, show a knowledge of the English language and pass the Life in the UK test, discussed further in the next section.[5] However, whilst indefinite leave to remain brings with it rights similar to those possessed by citizens, they are more precarious, with the risk of these rights being lost if the individual becomes liable to be deported.[6] Deportation is most commonly triggered by a conviction for a criminal offence,[7] and the issuance of a deportation order is virtually automatic if the sentence was greater than twelve months.[8] Apart from the precariousness of these rights, in extreme situations a person with indefinite leave to remain may find that the support offered her by the state is less than that given to nationals;

[4] Representation of the People Act 1983, s 4; Electoral Administration Act 2006, s 18.

[5] Clayton and Firth (n 1) 236–39. These requirements do not apply to those applying to remain settled in the UK under the EU Settlement Scheme.

[6] Nationality, Immigration and Asylum Act 2002, s 76.

[7] Clayton and Firth (n 1) 58–62, although the statutory power to deport is wider than this, permitting deportation when the Secretary of State 'deems his deportation to be conducive to the public good': Immigration Act 1971, s 3(5).

[8] UK Borders Act 2007, s 32.

her interests are not accorded the same weight as those of state members. For instance, whilst the UK government intervened to obtain the release of British citizens imprisoned by America in Guantanamo Bay it was not willing to intervene to help non-nationals who had lived in the UK under indefinite leave.[9]

Whilst some outsiders living within the territory of the UK do so under almost the same condition as insiders, many others have limitations placed on the duration of their stay and the activities they can undertake. There is an exceptionally wide range of legal statuses which visitors to the UK can occupy, depending on where they come from, how long they wish to remain, and what they plan to do whilst in the country. An outsider might, for example, enter as a tourist, as a student taking up a place at college, as a skilled worker taking up the offer of a job, or as a family member of someone already living in the country, and their entitlement to do so will vary depending on their country of origin. Once in the UK their range of rights varies depending on their status. Some require a 'sponsor' in the UK, often an employer or college, who will monitor aspects of their conduct on behalf of the state. Some are able to use their period of temporary residence as a stepping-stone to indefinite leave to remain or an application for citizenship, others cannot. And their access to state benefits varies. Everyone in the territory is able to access basic healthcare services for free, but beyond this the availability of welfare services depends on the outsider's status and is subject to wide variations.

Those who come to the UK on a visa or under an agreement the UK has reached with their home state are permitted to enter the territory because the UK has concluded it is in the interests of UK citizens to allow entry. This might be because the immigrants themselves bring benefits—tourists spend money, students pay to study, workers take jobs not filled by UK citizens—or because the agreement with their home state provides reciprocal benefits for UK citizens—perhaps as a consequence of permitting a foreign national to work in the UK, UK citizens are permitted to take jobs in the foreign state. There is, however, another set of

[9] *R (Abbassi) v Secretary of State for Foreign and Commonwealth Affairs* [2002] EWCA Civ 1598; Clayton and Firth (n 1) 76.

classes of outsider staying within the territory who remain at the sufferance of the UK state, people whom the UK permits to stay because it is unable to remove them, rather than because it welcomes their presence. These are people whom the UK has decided it is under a moral obligation to permit to remain within the territory, such as those seeking asylum, refugees, or those subject to a deportation order who cannot be deported because of the dangers they would face in their home state. These categories of persons enjoy the most limited rights of all. Asylum seekers, for instance, are not normally permitted to undertake work during the first year of their application, and when they are permitted to accept work there are limits on the jobs they can take.[10] They are allocated somewhere to live, and, in 2021, given an allowance of £39.63 each week for each family member, along with education and healthcare.[11] However, if the Home Secretary concludes that the application for asylum was not made 'as soon as reasonably practicable' after the applicant reached the UK, even this support may be refused.[12] Thousands of asylum seekers are left virtually destitute by the combination of these rules, unable to work legally and entitled to minimal or no state benefits.

22.1.2 Outsiders Outside of the Territory

Some outsiders are accorded special statuses by the UK, statuses that may affect their capacity either to enter the territory or to make the transition to insiders. These statuses were often accorded to those who saw their entitlements towards the UK reduced as immigration rules became stricter following the UK's retreat from empire, as former imperial subjects lost the broad rights they had enjoyed to enter, live, and work in the UK and got, as partial compensation, new constitutional identities with radically weakened legal rights. As Randall Hansen documents, successive UK governments were divided over the question of

[10] Melanie Gower, *Asylum Seekers: The Permission to Work Policy* CBP 1908, House of Commons Library (21 January 2021).

[11] There are some small supplements for those who are pregnant and young children to help them buy 'healthy food'. See 'Asylum Support: What You'll Get' *Gov.UK* https://www.gov.uk/asylum-support/what-youll-get (accessed 24 March 2021).

[12] Nationality, Immigration and Asylum Act 2002, s 55.

Commonwealth citizens' rights, with many, from all political parties, reluctant to impose limits on immigration which would, in effect, recognise and reinforce the constitutional divisions between the UK and its imperial territories.[13] The most recent example of a special status accorded to those formerly part of the empire can be seen in Hong Kong, many residents of which are able to apply for the status of British Nationals (Overseas) after 1997. This status opens paths to entry and to citizenship that are not available to other outsiders, an acknowledgment that the UK owes a special responsibility to some of those in Hong Kong because of its imperial history.[14]

Those outsiders without special status have the thinnest of all relationships with the UK; so thin, indeed, that it is barely noticeable. Many foreigners who live outside the territory of the UK will, for the most part, never interact with that state, but they are still subject to some legal duties and possess some legal rights by virtue of UK domestic law. In terms of legal duties, as a matter of domestic law the UK can impose obligations on foreigners outside of its territory, but this is a capacity used sparingly, partly because there is often little or no way of rendering these duties effective. For example, some offences relating to terrorism, such as encouraging terrorism or training to commit a terrorist act, are criminal offences in domestic UK law, even if the activity is undertaken abroad by a foreign national,[15] and domestic prosecutions can also be launched against torture[16] and some war crimes[17] committed by foreigners outside of the UK's territory. Such laws stand as a reminder that the sovereignty claims made by states can extend beyond their borders and people. In terms of rights, the UK state allows foreigners to access UK courts to vindicate any legal rights they have which are within the jurisdiction of those courts and permits them to apply for visas to enter the UK and, in many circumstances, to challenge its refusal.

[13] Hansen (n 2) ch 4.

[14] Hong Kong Act 1985; British Nationality Act 1981, s 4.

[15] Terrorism Act 2006, s 17.

[16] Criminal Justice Act 1988, s 134.

[17] Geneva Conventions Act 1957.

22.2 INSIDERS

Insiders are members of the state. As state members, their well-being is the state's objective, and, moreover, insiders are morally entitled to share in the governance of the state, when competent to do so. State membership in the UK comes in two forms, one very extensive, the other exceptionally restrictive. The extensive form of UK state membership is citizenship, with practically all members of the UK, around 66 million people in total, holding this legal office. The second, restrictive, form of state membership is that of monarch, an office which is held by a single individual.

22.2.1 Insiders: Citizens

At first sight, citizenship in the UK appears to be a simple legal status, hard to gain, but straight-forward once secured. On closer inspection, however, UK citizenship is deeply unequal, containing a range of different constitutional statuses of varying levels of attractiveness. This inequality is partly due to law, with the legal rights enjoyed by citizens partially dependent on the mode through which they acquired citizenship, but it is also determined by the state's understanding of citizenship and, indeed, by the broader understanding of citizenship within society as a whole. These conceptions of UK citizenship, although not matters of legal rights or duties, nevertheless shape the way in which citizens are treated and how they understand their own constitutional identity.

There are four processes through which a person can acquire British citizenship: through birth, descent, registration, or naturalisation.[18] Acquisition through birth applies to those born within the territory of the UK one of whose parents is a UK citizen or settled in the UK.[19] Acquisition through descent applies to those born outside of the UK to a British citizen who did not acquire their citizenship through descent; acquisition by descent can,

[18] As a result of the Good Friday Agreement, those born in Northern Ireland can also claim Irish citizenship in many situations. As Irish citizenship brings with it European citizenship accessing this status may become increasingly attractive after Brexit.

[19] British Nationality Act 1981, s 1.

therefore, only span one generation.[20] Acquisition through registration is open to a range of classes of people who have connections with the UK that justify a rapid track to citizenship.[21] For instance, where a child is a British citizen by descent but has a grandparent who was a British citizen otherwise than by descent, and has a parent who lived in the UK for a three year period, they are entitled to be registered as a UK citizen. Registration allows these children to transmit citizenship to their children, a capacity they would lack if they remained citizens by descent and gave birth outside of the territory. Most applications for citizenship by registration are subject to a test of 'good character', which is applied by the Secretary of State to applicants over ten years old, and those adults applying for citizenship through registration must also pass the Life in the UK test.[22] Finally, citizenship may be acquired through the process of naturalisation.[23] Naturalisation is open to those who have lived in the UK lawfully for at least five years, or, if a spouse of a British citizen, for three years, who have sufficient knowledge of one of the UK's languages,[24] have passed the Life in the UK test, and be of good character.[25] Those becoming citizens through naturalisation (or registration, if adults) must also take an oath and swear a pledge.[26] The oath requires the swearing of allegiance to the Queen and her successors, whilst the pledge requires the applicant to state: 'I will give my loyalty to the United Kingdom and respect its rights and freedoms. I will uphold its democratic values. I will observe its laws faithfully and fulfil my duties and obligations as a British citizen.'

The different modes of acquisition create different forms of citizenship. First, as we have seen, the ability to pass on citizenship to your children varies between those who have gained citizenship by descent and those in the other groups—and, indeed, varies amongst those who are citizens by descent with the

[20] ibid s 2. [21] ibid ss 3–5. [22] ibid s 41A.

[23] ibid s 6, sch 1.

[24] These are English, Welsh, Scottish Gaelic: British Nationality Act 1981, sch 1 para 1(1)(c).

[25] On the problems caused by the vagueness of the 'good character' test see Devyani Prabhat, *Britishness, Belonging and Citizenship: Experiencing Nationality Law* (Polity Press 2018) 87–90.

[26] British Nationality Act 1981, sch 5.

additional capacity to register as citizens, and those who lack this capacity. Secondly, the risk of losing citizenship varies across, and within, these groups. Under the British Nationality Act 1981, the Secretary of State is empowered to deprive a person of citizenship in some circumstances. She has a general power to remove citizenship where she concludes it is 'conducive to the public good'.[27] This power cannot be used when its exercise would make someone stateless, unless the person gained citizenship through naturalisation. When citizenship has been gained through naturalisation, the Secretary of State can remove citizenship if she concludes that the deprivation is 'conducive to the public good' because the person has conducted themselves in a manner 'seriously prejudicial to the vital interests of the United Kingdom', and, crucially, that she has reasonable grounds for believing the person is able to become a national of another country.[28] This may require the Secretary of State and, ultimately the UK courts, to take a decision about the nationality laws of other states and the capacity of the person deprived of citizenship to access this alternative constitutional status.[29]

Nationality law is complex, and it is easy to get lost in the maze of rules, but it is worth stepping back and reflecting on the different levels of citizenship created by the statutory rules on acquisition and loss. Most obviously, the rules of acquisition favour those with a UK parent. Less obviously, perhaps, they also favour those with a UK grandparent—those with this connection to the UK have a path they can take to upgrade their status, enabling them to transmit citizenship to their children if their children were born outside of the UK's territory. This nationality rule cuts against first-generation immigrants: if your parents were not UK citizens, it pays to make sure you give birth within the UK. The rules also cut against those who are dual nationals, who run the risk of the Secretary of State removing their citizenship and, even more sharply, cut against those who gained citizenship through

[27] ibid s 40(2). Citizenship can also be removed if gained by fraud or concealment of a material fact: ibid s 40(3).

[28] ibid s 40(4A).

[29] *Pham v Secretary of State for the Home Department* [2015] UKSC 19, [2015] 1 WLR 1591.

naturalisation, who can lose their citizenship even if not a dual national. Even in terms of the legal rights they enjoy, there is not equality between citizens of the UK: this apparently single legal status breaks down into a range of different statuses of differing levels of attractiveness.[30]

The legal rights possessed by UK citizens largely relate to residency, political participation, and access to diplomatic support whilst abroad. As we have seen, some outsiders also enjoy these formal rights, but citizenship is not simply a matter of law, it is also a matter of identity, belonging. A citizen understands herself to be a member of the group that governs the state and in whose interests the state is governed. Moreover, she recognises other members of this group as fellow citizens, sharing this constitutional status, and, in turn, is recognised by them as a citizen. In its fullest form, citizenship rests on mutual recognition within the community.[31] Some of the implications of the social dimension of citizenship push us out of the area of constitutional study and into psychology or political theory: it could be that being treated as a citizen is, in itself, valuable to a person's self-esteem, it could be that citizenship is necessary, in some way, for the legitimation of the authority claims of the state. But the social dimension of citizenship should also be of concern to constitutional scholars. One of the themes that has run throughout this book has been the challenge of integration within the constitution; that is, uniting people behind the decisions of state institutions, even when they disagree with them. When the social aspect of citizenship is lacking, when people do not regard themselves as part of the citizenship group (or are not regarded by others as part of that group), the integrative function of the constitution is likely to be impaired, and the institutions of the state rendered less effective. The social aspect of citizenship is not one that the state can control, but it is one it can shape: the legal rules on citizenship and, more broadly, the ways in which the state conceives citizenship is likely to affect how the community understands this institution.

Given the potential role of the state in shaping the social dimension of citizenship, our earlier discussion of the modes of acquisition and loss requires reconsideration. Most obviously the

[30] Prabhat (n 25) 18. [31] ibid ch 3.

legal rules on citizenship favour those with UK ancestry, who will be predominantly white. It is unsurprising that the UK confers citizenship on those born to British parents, but it is, perhaps, surprising that it provides favourable treatment to those with British grandparents. Similarly, ancestry affects the ease with which the UK can remove citizenship: it is easier to remove citizenship from those who have naturalised as citizens and from those who have dual nationality (which will almost certainly arise because a parent or a grandparent was a foreigner and passed on their nationality to their children). Worryingly, these legal consequences cut against the constitutional equality that should be at the heart of citizenship: there is a core group of citizens who enjoy preferential treatment from the state. Moreover, there may be UK citizens who are, as a matter of law, members of this core group, who have UK grandparents and only possess UK nationality, but who might appear to be part of the less favoured group because their race or cultural identity indicates an ancestry outside of the UK. Nationality laws may, then, have a 'spill-over' effect, unintentionally signalling that some of those in the core group are not, in the fullest sense, citizens.

Concerns about the integration of incoming citizens may also explain the various tests that the state places on those who wish to become citizens. The purpose of some of these is obvious. The requirements that those wishing to naturalise speak a domestic language to a certain level of proficiency, are willing to respect rights and freedoms, and to support democratic values, are clearly linked to citizenship; someone who cannot communicate with their fellow citizens, or who rejects the fundamental principles on which the state rests, will not be able to engage in the discussions and negotiations with their fellow citizens that are central to citizenship. However, elements of the requirements for citizenship go well beyond this minimum. The Life in the UK test was introduced by Tony Blair's government in 2005, and now virtually all adults wishing to become UK citizens or who are applying for indefinite leave to remain are set a short test based on a book about the UK, authored by the Home Office. Thom Brooks notes an interesting shift in emphasis between the second and third editions of the *Life in the United Kingdom* textbook, a shift that tracks the change from a Labour to a Conservative government.[32] Whereas the second edition focused on practical knowledge that new citizen might use—such as how to claim unemployment benefit, details of the state school system, and so on—the third edition puts more emphasis on historical and cultural knowledge. Most UK citizens will never read *Life in the United Kingdom* or take a look at the companion book of practice questions.[33] This is a shame, as they are remarkable documents. The textbook contains a brisk, upbeat, summary of the UK's history, brief facts about notable UK citizens and inventions, chunks of poetry, bits of the constitution, and contains advice to new citizens about their behaviour, including the injunction that they should keep their gardens tidy and only put their bins out on the street when due to be collected.[34] Looking at the practice questions, would-be citizens are set questions on the names of Civil War battles, the titles of Shakespeare's plays, the nature of the Oxford and Cambridge boat race and the Proms, and are expected to know that *The Mousetrap* is a play in the West End.[35] Some of the questions may be trickier than their setters suppose. For example, the test asks whether British values and principles are based on history and traditions, a question that would challenge a philosopher, and whether intolerance and/or inequality are fundamental principles of British life, a proposition that might reasonably be subject to debate.[36]

It is easy to make fun of the Life in the UK test, but it should be taken seriously: it amounts to a statement by the government of the qualities and knowledge it believes UK citizens should possess; an idealised picture of the UK citizen. A related picture of citizenship emerges from education policy. The National Curriculum for England, requires, amongst much else, that

[32] Thom Brooks, 'The *Life in the UK* Citizenship Test and the Urgent Need for Its Reform' in Devyani Prabhat (ed), *Citizenship in Times of Turmoil?: Theory, Practice and Policy* (Edward Elgar Publishing 2019) 41–46.

[33] Home Office, *Life in the United Kingdom: A Guide for New Residents* (3rd edn with amendments, The Stationery Office 2020); Home Office, *Life in the United Kingdom: Official Practice Questions and Answers* (3rd edn, The Stationery Office 2013).

[34] Home Office, *Guide* (n 33) 154.

[35] Home Office, *Practice Questions* (n 33) 16, 34, 36, 56.

[36] ibid 46, 25.

children be educated in the processes of democracy, the ways citizens can contribute to their communities, and be taught about 'the precious liberties' enjoyed by UK citizens.[37] In addition, children are required to have a grounding in a range of English literature, including a number of Shakespeare's plays.[38] Scotland, Wales, and Northern Ireland all have their own versions of the National Curriculum which are less prescriptive than England's, but which also include requirements to teach citizenship.

The emphasis on cultural knowledge in the Life in the UK test may aim to provide a shared cultural base amongst citizens, but if this is its aim it is unlikely to succeed.[39] The cultural knowledge it requires is superficial: whereas the National Curriculum requires children to have read and understood literary texts, those studying for the Life in the UK test are required only to have memorised facts, such as the titles of books and plays. Furthermore, there are large portions of the Life in the UK test that would stump many, probably most, existing UK citizens, who would struggle to recall the achievements of, for example, Sir John Lavery, Richard Arkwright, or Sake Dean Mahomet.[40] It is hard to see how knowing these disconnected facts helps integrate new citizens into the UK's political community or increase their sense of attachment to this group. A more cynical explanation of the point of the Life in the UK test is that it is intended to act as a barrier to citizenship, making it harder to access this status and, moreover, indirectly discriminating against certain groups of applicants. As the test effectively requires the candidates to memorise the handbook, it favours those who speak English as a first language and who have received an education that supports learning of this

[37] Department of Education, *National Curriculum in England: Citizenship Programmes of Study: Key Stages 3 and 4* (11 September 2013) https://www.gov.uk/government/publications/national-curriculum-in-england-citizenship-programmes-of-study/national-curriculum-in-england-citizenship-programmes-of-study-for-key-stages-3-and-4 (accessed 24 March 2021).

[38] Department of Education, *National Curriculum in England: English Programmes of Study* (16 July 2014) https://www.gov.uk/government/publications/national-curriculum-in-england-english-programmes-of-study/national-curriculum-in-england-english-programmes-of-study (accessed 24 March 2021).

[39] Prabhat (n 25) 13–14.

[40] Respectively, a portrait painter, a developer of industrial technology, and the founder of the first curry house in Britain.

type.[41] Thom Brooks reports that about 70% of those taking the test pass, but, of these, Americans and Australians have a pass rate of about 98% whilst Bangladeshis and Turks have a pass rate of about 45%.[42]

22.2.2 Insiders: Monarchs

Walter Bagehot's claim that the UK is a republic in the guise of a monarchy embodies two important truths about the UK constitution: first, that virtually all of the legal powers the monarch possesses by virtue of her office are now exercised by democratically accountable elements of the constitution; and, secondly, that the UK retains the form of a monarchy, even after the monarch's effective legal powers have shifted.[43]

Whilst the monarch possesses extensive and important legal powers, her discretion over their exercise has reduced to the point at which she is now little more than a cipher for her ministers, with the decisions that were once made by kings and queens now being made by democratically accountable office holders. As we have seen, in virtually all areas the powers of the royal prerogative are exercised by ministers, and those constitutional decisions that could be argued to be made by the monarch directly, such as appointing the prime minister, dissolving Parliament, and giving assent to legislation, are so heavily regulated by convention that the monarch normally has no discretion over their exercise.[44] This picture of the monarch as legally inert requires some slight qualification. First, there remain a few legal powers that she continues to exercise. For instance, there are some honours that are conferred on her discretion, such as the Order of Merit, and in a small number of areas Parliament requires her consent before a bill is introduced.[45] More significant, however, is

[41] Prabhat (n 25) 14.

[42] Brooks (n 32) 23, citing 'British Citizenship Test: One in Three Immigrants Fails' *BBC News* (27 May 2010) http://news.bbc.co.uk/1/hi/uk_politics/8707152.stm (accessed 24 March 2021).

[43] Walter Bagehot, *The English Constitution* (Richard Crossman (ed), Watts & Co 1964) 94.

[44] Vernon Bogdanor, *The Monarchy and the Constitution* (Oxford University Press 1997) ch 2.

[45] Thomas Erskine May, *Erskine May's Treatise on the Law, Privileges, Proceedings and Usage of Parliament* (David Natzler and others (eds), 25th edn, LexisNexis 2019)

the monarch's discretion in exceptional cases, situations in which the conventions regulating her conduct are vague or disputed.[46] For example, the conventions that regulate the giving of assent to legislation, the prorogation of Parliament, or the appointment the prime minister, are clear and straight-forward in most cases, but are disputed at the margins.[47] Constitutional scholars disagree about how the monarch should use these powers in exceptional cases, with differing views taken of the proper extent of the monarch's personal involvement in their exercise. Given this disagreement, if these situations arose the monarch would be compelled to choose between different interpretations of the convention; indeed, even rejecting the claim that the convention is unclear would be a choice. Although her legal powers are vastly reduced, the monarch remains a legal actor in the UK constitution, and may be unable to avoid intervening in moments of high constitutional crisis, for good or ill.[48]

In addition to these legal powers the monarch also enjoys influence, although the extent of this influence can only be a matter of speculation. The monarch meets with the prime minister to discuss national affairs on a regular basis, and also has contact,

paras 30.78–30.82. Remarkably, the Prince of Wales' consent may sometimes be required: para 30.81. It seems consent is always given if ministers advise it, but this still amounts to a legal right to see legislation before it is put to Parliament, and appears to enable the monarch to lobby ministers over its content: David Pegg and Rob Evans, 'Revealed: Queen Lobbied for Change in Law to Hide Her Private Wealth' *The Guardian* (7 February 2021) https://www.theguardian.com/uk-news/2021/feb/07/revealed-queen-lobbied-for-change-in-law-to-hide-her-private-wealth (accessed 27 March 2021).

[46] Robert Blackburn, 'Monarchy and the Personal Prerogatives' [2004] Public Law 546. See generally Anne Twomey, *The Veiled Sceptre: Reserve Powers of Heads of State in Westminster Systems* (Cambridge University Press 2018).

[47] See ch 6.

[48] It has been claimed that the security services were told Michael Foot, then Leader of the Opposition, had taken money from the KGB in the 1960s, yet decided not to tell Mrs Thatcher, then prime minister, for fear this information would affect the outcome of the 1983 election. Instead, if Foot won the election the Queen would be informed. What she was supposed to do with this information is anyone's guess. See Ben Macintyre, *The Spy and the Traitor: The Greatest Espionage Story of the Cold War* (Penguin 2018) 141–43. The allegations remain contested, and Foot won a libel case against *The Sunday Times* for printing similar allegations in the late 1990s.

directly or indirectly, with other powerful people from all areas of life.[49] The future monarch, the Prince of Wales, also has a noticeably busy schedule.[50] It is probable that the Royal Family possesses significant 'soft power' within the UK constitution, and that in some policy areas, at some points in time, they have had an impact.

Bagehot's second point about the guise worn by the UK constitution is equally important. The UK retains the form of a monarchy, and this form conditions the constitutional ideology of the state, an ideology that, in turn, affects the relationship between the state and its people. The monarchy is a prominent feature of UK public life. This prominence is not just a matter of coverage—although it is worth remembering that just about every adult in the UK possesses multiple images of the Queen, images often carefully carried about their person—but also the form that coverage takes. The Queen is presented by the state as a special person, a person who deserves to be decked with crowns and jewellery, who is entitled to live in palaces, and who should be treated with exceptional deference. The UK's current monarch, Queen Elizabeth II, has been, as far as these things can be assessed, an exemplary constitutional monarch and may deserve these rewards on her merits, but she was not accorded them through merit, but through right of birth.

There are many constitutional offices that people can enter into—they can become, for example, judges, legislators, or civil servants—but there are only a small number of constitutional offices that can be gained through birth. Monarchy and citizenship are the two most important constitution offices conferred by right of birth in the UK, and they stand in tension. At the heart of citizenship is the idea of constitutional equality: citizens have equal opportunities to participate in the governance of the state, each citizen's well-being is of equal importance within the polity. Of course, some citizens gain constitutional positions or political influence that mean they become more powerful than their fellows, and the state must make decisions about the activities

[49] Asif Hameed, 'The Monarchy and Politics' [2016] Public Law 401.

[50] The public engagements of the Royal Family can be seen in the Court Circular https://www.royal.uk/court-circular (accessed 27 March 2021).

it supports that end up with some citizens benefiting more than others, but, crucially, citizens start from a position of equality, all are equally important; the ideology of citizenship is, ultimately, grounded in the fundamental moral equality of persons. The ideology of monarchy, in contrast, rejects this equality: one state member, and their heirs, are of greater importance than everyone else. They are entitled to a greater say in the governance of the state, and their well-being is of greater importance than other state members. Given that this special concern is accorded as a result of birth, it is hard to see how it could be justified other than in religious or mystical terms. Underpinning monarchy is often the claim that God has picked the monarch, she has been divinely selected for the role, and that the Queen remains head of the Church of England underlines the religious aspect of monarchy. Citizenship and monarchy are animated by sharply contrasting moral claims. Whilst the UK continues to wear the guise of monarchy, citizenship can never be fully realised within our community; the constitutional ideology of the state speaks against it.[51]

Although monarchy is in tension with citizenship, it may yet bring benefits, and these benefits may justify the UK keeping this constitutional form, at least for the present.[52] In the earlier parts of this book the challenges of identification, attachment, were raised: how to persuade state members to accept the institutions of the state even if they continue to disagree with the decisions made by those institutions. Monarchy may provide a basis for this attachment, part of Bagehot's dignified constitution. A constitutional monarch can act as a figurehead for the state, a figurehead gaining lustre from the rites and regalia bestowed on her. A critic might attack this as an exercise in distraction, as a form of constitutional sleight of hand, with the theatre of monarchy diverting attention from the hard realities of political power. But if the distraction works, if it helps maintain the efficacy of the state, it may be valuable none the less. However, monarchy cannot play this role indefinitely, as constitutional monarchy is a time-limited constitutional form which contains the seeds of its own destruction. The ideology of monarchy rests on the claim that the monarch

[51] Adam Tomkins, *Our Republican Constitution* (Hart Publishing 2005) 139–40.

[52] Bogdanor (n 44) 299–302.

should be chosen through birth, it is an inherited position, yet in a constitutional monarchy the monarch must have the capacity to play the role of figurehead successfully—and staying out of politics and avoiding controversy are harder tasks than they might first appear, especially when the institution of monarchy itself rests on highly contestable political claims. The mode of selection of the monarch and the demands of her role are, then, in tension. Sooner or later, a person who is unable or unwilling to meet the demands of the position will become monarch and the UK will face a stark choice, as it has done in the past: find a new person to sit on the throne and admit that the choice of monarch is not divinely determined, or cast off the guise of monarchy and become a republic.[53]

22.3 CONCLUSION

The establishment of citizenship is the most important challenge faced by the UK constitution over the next twenty or thirty years. As we saw in part three of this book, the UK's constitution is subject to centrifugal force, as Scotland, Northern Ireland, and, to a less extent, Wales have gained constitutional autonomy and pressures toward secession have grown. Part of the explanation for these pressures might be found in this chapter, in the struggles of the UK, as a whole, to articulate a sense of UK-wide citizenship. Over the last century, as the British Empire collapsed, one of the projects that had tied the Union together ended, and, moreover, began to be reassessed. What had been a point of national pride, an empire on which the sun never set, became a source of confusion, and then, finally, of shame. In the course of a few decades, a core element of UK national identity has become deeply problematic. Finding a way to rebuild UK citizenship in a form that accommodates and supports regional constitutional identities whilst at the same time creating a stable UK wide constitutional settlement will prove a difficult task.

[53] As Rodney Brazier notes, given the importance of the issue it is surprising how little discussion there is of the creation of a republic in the work of UK constitutional scholars: Rodney Brazier, 'A British Republic' (2002) 61 Cambridge Law Journal 351, 352.

INDEX

For the benefit of digital users, indexed terms that span two pages (e.g., 52–53) may, on occasion, appear on only one of those pages.